Lecture Notes in Computer Science 1648

Edited by G. Goos, J. Hartmanis and J. van Leeuwen

Springer
Berlin
Heidelberg
New York
Barcelona
Hong Kong
London
Milan
Paris
Singapore
Tokyo

Matthew Franklin (Ed.)

Financial Cryptography

Third International Conference, FC'99
Anguilla, British West Indies, February 22-25, 1999
Proceedings

Volume Editor

Matthew Franklin
Xerox PARC
3333 Coyote Hill Road, Palo Alto, CA 94304, USA
E-mail: franklin@parc.xerox.com

Cataloging-in-Publication data applied for

Die Deutsche Bibliothek - CIP-Einheitsaufnahme

Financial cryptography : third international conference ; proceedings / FC '99, Anguilla, British West Indies, February 22 - 25, 1999. Matthew Franklin (ed.). - Berlin ; Heidelberg ; New York ; Barcelona ; Hong Kong ; London ; Milan ; Paris ; Singapore ; Tokyo : Springer, 1999
(Lecture notes in computer science ; Vol. 1648)
ISBN 3-540-66362-2

CR Subject Classification (1998): E.3, D.4.6, K.6.5, C.2, J.1, F.2.1-2

ISSN 0302-9743
ISBN 3-540-66362-2 Springer-Verlag Berlin Heidelberg New York

Printed in Germany

Typesetting: Camera-ready by author
SPIN: 10703870 06/3142 – 5 4 3 2 1 0 Printed on acid-free paper

Preface

The third Financial Cryptography conference was held in February 1999, once again at Anguilla in the British West Indies. The number of attendees continues to increase from year to year, as do the number and quality of the technical submissions.

The Program Committee did a great job selecting the technical program. I thank them for all of their effort's. We were helped by a number of outside reviewers, including Martín Abadi, Gerrit Bleumer, Drew Dean, Anand Desai, Mariusz Jakubowski, Andrew Odlyzko, David Pointcheval, Guillaume Poupard, Zulfikar Ramzan, Aleta Ricciardi, Dan Simon, Jessica Staddon, Venkie Venkatesan, Avishai Wool, and Francis Zane. I apologize for any omissions.

Adi Shamir gave an excellent invited talk that forecast the future of cryptography and electronic commerce. On-line certificate revocation was the subject of a panel led by Michael Myers, following up on the success of his panel on the same topic at last year's conference. Joan Feigenbaum moderated a lively panel on fair use, intellectual property, and the information economy, and I thank her for pulling together from that discussion a paper for these proceedings. A successful Rump Session allowed participants to present new results in an informal setting, superbly chaired by Avi Rubin.

A pre-proceedings, containing earlier versions of the accepted papers, was distributed at the conference. The pre-proceedings were produced on the Xerox DocuPrint 180 NPS printer, at an amazing 180 pages per minute. Special thanks to Russ Atkinson for teaching me its care and feeding. Final versions were prepared by the authors shortly after the conference, and are included in this volume without further review.

I thank everyone who contributed to the successful organization of the conference. In particular, I would like to thank Vince Cate for another outstanding job with the local arrangements, and Ray Hirschfeld for invaluable advice and support. My colleagues at Xerox PARC also helped in many ways. Lastly, I would like to thank all of the authors for making this conference and these proceedings possible.

May 1999

Matt Franklin
FC99 Program Chair

Financial Cryptography '99
Anguilla, BWI
22–25 February 1999

Program Committee

Joan Feigenbaum, AT&T Labs – Research
Yair Frankel, CertCo
Matt Franklin (Chair), Xerox PARC
David Goldschlag, Divx
Markus Jakobsson, Bell Labs
Ari Juels, RSA Labs
Arjen Lenstra, Citibank
Clifford Neuman, University of Southern California
Berry Schoenmakers, Eindhoven University of Technology
Jacques Stern, ENS
Yacov Yacobi, Microsoft
Bennet Yee, U. C. San Diego

General Chair

Rafael Hirschfeld, Unipay Technologies, Amsterdam, The Netherlands

Local Arrangements Chair

Vincent Cate, Offshore Information Services, Anguilla, BWI

Financial Cryptography '99 was organized by the International Financial Cryptography Association (IFCA), and was sponsored by nCipher Corporation, e-gold Transnational, EURO RSCG Interactive, Hansa Bank & Trust Company, and Offshore Information Services.

Table of Contents

Anonymity Mechanisms

Auctions and Markets

Auctions and Markets

Experimenting with Electronic Commerce on the PalmPilot

Neil Daswani[1] and Dan Boneh[2]

[1] Stanford University, Stanford CA 94305, USA,
daswani@cs.stanford.edu,
http://www.stanford.edu/~daswani/
[2] Stanford University, Stanford CA 94305, USA,
dabo@cs.stanford.edu,
http://www.stanford.edu/~dabo/

Abstract. This paper describes our experience with implementing an electronic payment system for the PalmPilot. Although Palm OS lacks support for many desired security features, we are able to build a system suitable for small payments. We discuss the advantages and disadvantages of using a PDA to make secure payments as opposed to using a smartcard or a desktop PC. In addition, we describe the engineering of PDA-PayWord, our implementation of a commerce protocol that takes advantage of both elliptic curve and RSA public key cryptography to support payments efficiently on PDAs with limited processing capability.

Keywords: electronic commerce, personal digital assistants, PalmPilot, digital wallet, electronic payment systems.

1 Introduction

The explosive growth of the market for Personal Digital Assistants (PDA's) has led to a wealth of new applications for them. In this paper, we experiment with electronic commerce for PDA's. Our motivation is clear: since consumers are already carrying digital assistants, why not use them for payments? For example, one could walk up to a vending machine, connect the PDA to the machine via the infrared link and make a purchase. One application of our system does just that (see Section 4.2). One may wonder whether electronic commerce on a PDA is any different than electronic commerce using other digital devices such as smartcards or desktops. The answer is simple – PDA's are a middle ground between smartcards and desktops. They posses advantages and disadvantages over both. As a result, payment schemes and electronic commerce applications need to be fine tuned to properly execute on a PDA.

When compared with smartcards, PDA's appear to be at a disadvantage: (1) they are not *tamper resistant*, (2) unlike many smartcards they are not equipped with cryptographic accelerators, and (3) they do not have limited lifetime as many smartcards do. These features (especially tamper resistance) are helpful

M. Franklin (Ed.): FC'99, LNCS 1648, pp. 1–16, 1999.

in simplifying real world payment schemes. On the other hand, PDA's have several advantages over common smartcards. First and foremost, they have a direct line of communication with the user. Common smartcards can only interact with the user through an *untrusted* reader. In addition, unlike smartcards, PDA's have a reasonable (yet limited) amount of non-volatile memory[1]. Consequently, they can store a longer transaction log. PDA's are also better at general purpose computations; for example, computations that take place during protocol negotiation. We note that when comparing smartcards and PDA's, the issue of unit cost is irrelevant – PDA's may become just as widely deployed as smartcards.

When compared with desktops, PDA's appear to be at a disadvantage once again. Due to their limited memory capacity, they can only store a limited amount of financial instrument data, and a limited number of transaction certificates. Similarly, due to their limited computing power they cannot engage in complicated cryptographic protocols. An intensive protocol such as SET [23] may take too long to execute on a PDA. On the other hand, PDA's are portable and can be used in many environments where a desktop is not available.

The above discussion explains why many existing payment systems cannot simply be ported to a PDA. One must design the system keeping in mind both the limited security features and the limited computation resources. In this paper, we describe our experience with building a payment system for 3Com's popular PalmPilot [1]. Our system is designed to be portable, and the lessons we learned apply to other PDA's, e.g. ones based on Windows CE. Our choice for using the PalmPilot is due its current dominance of the PDA market. We note that existing financial applications [9] for the PalmPilot enable one to keep track of spending, but none provide a payment scheme.

To implement an electronic commerce system one must start with a basic framework for making payments. Our starting point is a generic wallet architecture that we had previously designed [7]. We briefly review the wallet architecture in Section 1.2. We stress that the wallet only provides the skeleton for this work. Our main focus is the design of payment components that can be adequately used on a PDA. We describe these in Section 3. The system implementation details are presented in Section 4, where we also describe our first vendor: the Pony Vending Machine. We begin by describing the (lack of) security features on the PalmPilot.

1.1 Existing PalmPilot Security Features

All data on the PalmPilot is stored in either ROM or RAM. The PalmPilot does not have a disk drive or any other form of persistent memory. The RAM on the PalmPilot is divided into *dynamic* and *storage* memory. Dynamic memory is used as working space. It holds the program stack and other short term data. On the

[1] The PalmPilot IIIx comes with four megabytes of RAM. A Windows CE machine typically has four to eight Megabytes. We note that most memory on a PDA is devoted to applications such as an appointment book. A commerce application can only use a small portion of the memory on the device.

other hand, storage memory is non-volatile and plays the role of a disk drive on desktops. *Databases* in the storage RAM are the equivalent of files on a disk drive. A database on the PalmPilot is made up of a sequence of records. Database access on the PalmPilot is somewhat different than a traditional operating system. In traditional systems, a file is read into memory before data stored in it can be accessed or modified. On the PalmPilot, database records are always in memory. There is no need to move them into dynamic storage to operate on them. They can be *edited in place*.

Unfortunately, Palm OS provides very little support for access control. Although databases have a *creator ID* associated with them, the operating system does not prevent an application from opening a database that does not belong to it. Consequently, malicious applications can easily tamper with sensitive data on the PalmPilot. Individual records in databases have a "secret" attribute associated with them. However, the core OS only views this attribute as a suggestion. There is nothing preventing an application from gaining access to records marked secret. Essentially, the secret attribute tells the application not to display these records unless the user types in a password. The application itself is not prevented from processing records marked secret. It is a bit surprising that although the OS provides a facility for requesting the user to enter a password, it does not provide any support for encrypting data using the password.

The lack of support for access control has prompted a number of developers to attempt to remedy the situation [22]. A number of shareware applications for the PalmPilot enable the user to store data in an encrypted database. This is especially useful when using the PalmPilot to store sensitive information such as PIN's and login passwords. Unfortunately, at the moment these applications use weak encryption. We note that Ian Goldberg [11] ported to the PalmPilot the cryptography-related parts of Eric Yung's SSLeay library. We make use of this port in our protocols.

To summarize, access control on the PalmPilot is poor. The operating system does not enforce access control and there is no support for privacy via encryption. This is very different than a typical smartcard operating system where there is a clear partitioning of memory between applications. We hope future versions of the PalmPilot will pay more attention to security issues. This is likely to be the case as indicated by the recent collaboration between Certicom and 3Com. Certicom is integrating its elliptic curve encryption technology into Palm OS. Finally, we note that things appear to be better on Windows CE, where some support for access control is provided by the operating system.

1.2 A Brief Review of SWAPEROO: The Simple Wallet Architecture for Payments, Exchanges, Refunds, and Other Operations

The starting point for our payment system is a generic wallet architecture that can accommodate multiple payment protocols and multiple financial instruments. The wallet provides the groundwork for us to build on. Since it is not the focus of this paper, we only give a high level overview. Details of the architecture are given in [7]. The overview is necessary to understand how the various payment components described in Section 2 and 3 fit together. The wallet design is based on four principles: (1) *extensible*, it is relatively easy to add new types of financial instruments and payment protocols; (2) *non-web-centric*, does not rely on web based protocols; (3) *symmetric*, we use similar software API's on both the user and vendor sides; (4) *client-driven*, all wallet operations are initiated by the client, not the vendor.

Both the user and vendor make use of the same wallet architecture. The user wallet is part of a larger user application. Similarly, the vendor wallet is part of a larger vendor application. Once the user and vendor applications agree on a certain payment operation (e.g. purchase item #3, or refund 5$) the wallet controllers on both sides take control to execute the transaction. The first thing they do is determine the common financial instruments they support. For example, the user wallet may contain CyberCash coins [6], Millicent scrips [17] and a Visa credit card. The vendor may only accept credit cards and CyberCash coins. The common instruments are the credit card and CyberCash coins, in which case, the user is asked to choose which instrument to use.

Once the financial instrument is chosen, the user and vendor wallet controllers negotiate the payment protocol. Indeed, multiple protocols can be used to make payments with a particular financial instrument. For example, when paying with a credit card one could use SET [23], although other protocols may be used as well. This protocol negotiation is transparent to the user. Once the two agree on a common protocol, the protocol is activated to execute the transaction.

To carry out the above interaction, the wallet architecture provides controllers for manipulating financial instruments and applying protocols to them. The wallet is made up of a Protocol Manager (PM), an Instrument Manager (IM), a Wallet Controller (WC), and a User Profile Manager (UPM). A Communication Manager handles low level communication. Once our wallet architecture was successfully ported to the PDA, we were free to concentrate on the design of financial instruments and payment protocols to be used.

2 Electronic Commerce for a PDA

If PDA's are to be used for digital payments, they will most likely be restricted to small payments (i.e. transactions under 10$). For larger payments one may wish to rely on stronger security properties. Our hope is that PDA's may be used in both local and remote payment transactions. For local transactions, a user may walk into a shop, place the PalmPilot in the vendor's cradle (or use the infrared port) and make a payment. For remote transactions, one may connect the PDA to the Internet (using a PDA modem or by using a desktop as a gateway). The two modes are different: for local transactions there is no need to encrypt communication on the wire. For remote transactions, one must first establish a secure link to the vendor. Throughout the discussion in this section we do not distinguish between the two modes. At the moment, our implementation only supports local transactions that do not require link encryption.

2.1 Performance of Cryptographic Primitives on the PalmPilot

We provide timing measurements for cryptographic primitives running on the PalmPilot[2]. These timing measurements help determine if a payment scheme is feasible for the PalmPilot or if it is too complex. The PalmPilot Professional runs on a Motorola DragonBall chip (68K family) at 16MHz. The figures below are given in milliseconds.

Algorithm	Time	Comment
DES encryption	4.9ms/block	4900ms for 1000 encryptions
SHA-1	2.7ms/block	2780ms for a 1000 long hash chain
512 bit RSA key generation	3.4 minutes	
512 bit RSA sig. generation	7028 ms	
512 bit RSA sig. verify	438 ms	$e = 3$
512 bit RSA sig. verify	1376 ms	$e = 65535$
163 bit ECC-DSA key generation	597 ms	
163 bit ECC-DSA sig. generation	776 ms	
163 bit ECC-DSA sig. verify	2448 ms	

Table 1. Timing measurements for cryptographic primitives on the PalmPilot

We first note that generating RSA key pairs is very expensive on the PalmPilot. To generate a 512-bit RSA key pair, three to four minutes of pure computation time is required of the CPU. In addition to inconveniencing the user at wallet setup time, RSA key pair generation drains the PalmPilot's batteries. One may argue that the key pair could be generated on a desktop and downloaded to the PalmPilot, but this limits mobility since setup must take place on the user's PC. If 1024-bit keys are to be generated on the PalmPilot, approximately 20 minutes of pure computation would be required. On the other hand, elliptic curve key pair generation is about two orders of magnitude faster.

As might be expected, DES encryption and SHA-1 hashing are relatively fast as compared with signatures. This suggests that an efficient implementation of a payment protocol for a PDA-based platform should attempt to take advantage of these operations in favor of signatures as much as possible.

RSA signature generation is somewhat slow, taking approximately seven seconds. Our payment protocols take about 900ms seconds when stripped of the cryptography. Hence, RSA signature generation time is significant in comparison to the entire transaction time.

Our choice of using 512 bits RSA, rather than 1024, is due to the fact that our application is targeted towards small payments. For small payments, 512 bits may provide adequate security.

[2] The performance figures for DES, SHA-1, and RSA operations were obtained using Ian Goldberg's port of SSLeay. The figures for ECC operations were obtained using Certicom's Security Builder SDK Release 2.1

The figures for 163-bit ECC-DSA key generation and signature generation are considerably more efficient than the corresponding 512-bit RSA operations. This suggests that ECC-based key generation and signatures are more feasible for use in commerce protocols on the PalmPilot. ECC-based verification does, however, take about 40 percent longer than RSA-based verification.

To summarize, there exists an asymmetry between the performance of RSA and ECC operations. We would like our payment protocols to be as fast as possible, and both signature generation and verifications may be necessary parts of the protocols. If we need to generate signatures on the PalmPilot, we would like to generate ECC-based signatures, since ECC-based signature generation is faster than RSA signature generation. On the other hand, if we need to verify signatures on the PalmPilot, we would like to use RSA since RSA signature verification is faster than ECC-based signature verification. We discuss how our payment protocols take advantage of this asymmetry in Section 3.2.

2.2 Authentication

Common smart cards do not have any means of directly communicating with their owner. They must do so through an untrusted card reader. As a result, it is difficult for the owner to authenticate herself to the card. Often, smartcards require the owner to enter a password. However, there is nothing preventing the machine operating the card reader from recording and replaying the password [10]. The smartcard cannot use challenge-response authentication since humans are incapable of participating in such protocols.

On the other hand, a PDA has *a direct line of communication* with its owner. Before executing a transaction, the wallet controller prompts the user for a password. This password is used for two purposes: first, it authenticates the owner to the PDA. Second, as we shall see in the next section, we use the password to decrypt specific instrument data. Note that the user is prompted for a password only once a transaction is about to take place. Prior to this, the PDA may freely communicate with the vendor.

Unfortunately, entering a password on the PalmPilot is somewhat painful. Clearly, it is desirable to enter the password in no-echo mode. However, since characters are entered using error prone Graffiti, no-echo makes it hard to correctly enter the password. We note that the standard security utility on the PalmPilot prompts the user to enter a password in full echo mode!

2.3 Memory Management and Backups

Since Palm OS provides very limited access control, one must ensure that malicious applications do not have access to private financial information. They must also be prevented from tampering with such data. Our solution is to store all instrument data in encrypted form. This is automatically done by the Instrument Manager [7]. Encryption is done using the user's password which must be entered in order to initiate a transaction. We also append a cryptographic checksum to ensure data integrity.

Nevertheless, malicious applications can delete encrypted instrument data blocks due to the lack of access control in PalmOS. There is no way to prevent this other than to rely on a backup copy stored on a desktop PC. The HotSync Manager application distributed with the PalmPilot automatically backs-up these databases. In the case that the wallet application discovers corrupted data, it may ask the user to perform a HotSync with the desktop. Of course, care must be taken to ensure that already spent digital cash is not doubly spent after the backup process.

3 PDA-PayWord: A Payment Scheme Optimized for a PDA

The lack of tamper resistance on a PDA is unfortunate, although not fatal. Tamper resistance on smartcards can simplify payment protocols such as those used in stored value techniques (see e.g. Mondex [18]). However, one must keep in mind that tamper resistance is not impenetrable (see [3]). As a result, payment schemes on smartcards must also have some mechanisms in place to discourage tampering. Here, a PDA has an advantage over a smartcard: it has more memory and processing power, and can incorporate stronger mechanisms to discourage tampering. We chose to avoid stored value techniques and instead focused on a hash-chain-based digital cash scheme based on PayWord [21]. PDA-PayWord is our implementation of PayWord.

Hash-chain-based micropayment schemes have been studied extensively. The idea of using hash chains to reduce the number of signature generations was independently discovered by a number of groups. These include PayWord [21], Pederson's tick payments [19], micro-iKP [12] and NetCard [2]. Jutla and Yung [14] study a variation where hash trees are used rather than chains. Hash chains are based on a technique due to Lamport [15].

Since we wish to focus on the PalmPilot (user) to vendor interaction (rather than vendor to bank), we allow the bank and vendor to reside on the same machine. This tight coupling between the vendor and bank can be broken at any point in the future.

3.1 Overview of PDA-PayWord

This section contains a high-level overview of PDA-PayWord. A discussion of the design trade-offs involved in PDA-PayWord is given in the next section, and a detailed discussion of our PalmPilot implementation can be found in Section 4.3.

PDA-PayWord is a pre-pay, vendor-specific variant of a hash chain system. To setup a chain of coins the PalmPilot generates $Y_k = h^{(k)}(Y_0)$ where $h^{(i)}$ denotes a repeated iteration of a hash function (we use SHA-1). Y_0 is kept on the PalmPilot as part of a *hash chain instrument.* The PalmPilot sends Y_k, k, d to the bank. The bank returns a *hash chain certificate* containing Y_k, k, d, a vendor-id, an expiration date, and a signature of the certificate using the bank's private key. k is the pre-paid height of the hash chain and d is the denomination of each

Y_i. To spend the ith coin when Y_{k-j} was the last coin spent, the PalmPilot sends $Y_{k-j-i} = h^{(k-j-i)}(Y_0)$, i, and the hash chain certificate to the vendor. Initially $j = 0$, and $i = 1$. Recall, these are vendor specific chains and the vendor can verify that the PalmPilot is not double-spending or over-spending.

3.2 Discussion of PDA-PayWord Design Choices

As described in [21], PayWord was designed to amortize the cost of signatures across multiple purchases and minimize on-line communication. In addition to these goals, PDA-PayWord: 1) minimizes the number of and time spent executing cryptographic operations on the user's wallet, and 2) minimizes storage requirements for the hash chain instrument on the user's wallet.

In PDA-Payword, the user's wallet must first generate a hash chain instrument and obtain a hash chain certificate from the bank that binds the "coins" in the hash chain to real value. In this withdrawal phase of the protocol, the user's wallet sends Y_k, k and d to the bank to request a withdrawal of $k * d$ dollars. The bank needs to ensure that the request is being made by the user herself, and therefore PDA-Payword requires that this widthdrawal request be signed. Since this signature needs to take place on the PalmPilot, the withdrawal request is signed using an ECC-DSA signature (as opposed to an RSA signature) to minimize the signature generation time. (Recall that from Table 1, ECC-DSA signature generation takes 776ms on average, while RSA signature generation takes over 7000ms.)

After the bank receives the withdrawal request and verifies the user's signature, the bank then generates a hash chain certificate, signs it, and sends it to the user's wallet. The user's wallet then needs to verify that the bank's signature on the certificate is authentic. This verification takes place on the PalmPilot, and we would like the verification to be as efficient as possible. As such, in PDA-PayWord, the bank signs the hash chain certificate using a RSA signature (as opposed to an ECC signature) since RSA verification is more efficient on the PalmPilot than ECC-DSA signature verification. By taking advantage of the asymmetery between the performance of RSA and ECC signature and verification times, we are able to minimize the amount of time spent on the PalmPilot executing cryptographic operations.

To achieve our second goal of minimizing storage requirements, PDA-PayWord only stores Y_0 as part of the instrument data in the user's wallet, rather than the entire hash chain. The chain is recomputed for every purchase transaction. This is done to save storage space on the PalmPilot, and incurs minimal cost since hashing on the PalmPilot is sufficiently fast. On a smartcard, one might have to store every ith payword along the hash chain since hashing may not be as quick. Of course, a PalmPilot could also take advantage of this technique to reduce the time spent hashing if the user decides to give the wallet more memory in which to run. In our implementation, we conservatively assumed the user would not want the wallet to use more than the minimal amount of storage necessary. Also, thanks to its speed, the PalmPilot can manage longer hash chains than a smartcard.

4 System Design

We briefly summarize some of our design choices. We demonstrate the user interface as well as explain the internal implementation of the various protocols involved. In Section 4.2, we describe our first vendor, a vending machine in our building.

4.1 Wallet Design & Implementation

Our SWAPEROO-based implementation consisted of a digital wallet application written in C++ for the PalmPilot, and a Java implementation of the vendor application. Timing measurements were obtained by running the user's wallet on a PalmPilot III with 2MB of RAM. The PalmPilot III runs on a Motorola DragonBall chip at 16MHz. The bank/vendor application runs on a 300 MHz Pentium PC with 64MB of RAM.

Communication between the PalmPilot and the PC was conducted using TCP/IP over a serial RS232 communications channel.

User Interface The user interface is a collection of forms running on the PalmPilot. When interacting with the vendor, they guide the user through the choice of available items for sale. The user chooses an item and is then asked to choose the payment method, i.e. the payment instrument to be used for the purchase. Once the instrument is selected, the appropriate purchase protocol is activated. As a first step, the user is asked to enter a password to decrypt the instrument data.

A subset of the forms guiding to the user through its interaction with the vendor are presented in Figure 1[3].

Product negotiation We implemented a simple protocol enabling a vendor to download a set of items along with their prices onto the PalmPilot. This protocol is used to convey the customer's choice back to the vendor. Once the required item is agreed upon by both parties the wallet controllers on both the vendor and client take control and execute the transaction.

Instrument and Protocol Negotiation Instrument negotiation is done by computing the intersection of available instrument types on the vendor and the customer wallets. The set of instruments in the intersection is presented to the user who chooses one of them. We hope the list of available instruments will increase over time. Once the transaction is initiated, the two parties negotiate which protocol is to be used to carry out the transaction (for a given payment instrument there may be multiple protocols offering different levels of efficiency and security). Protocol negotiation is done via a Protocol Negotiation Protocol (PNP) as explained in [7].

[3] These figures were produced by taking a snapshot of our wallet application running under the copilot emulator.

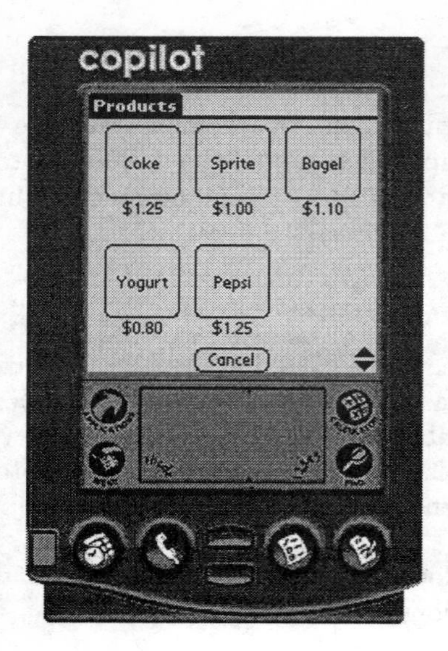

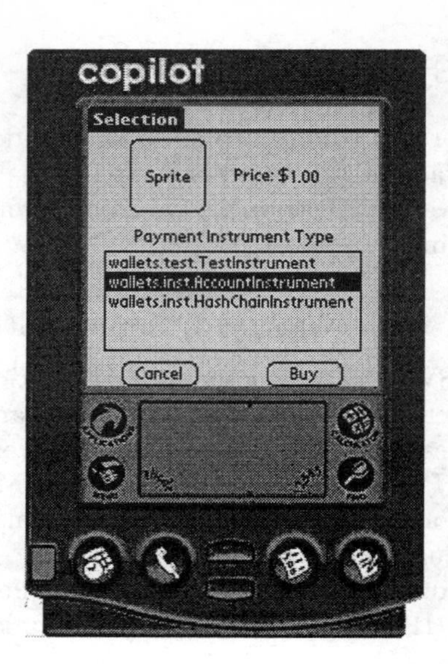

Fig. 1. Example interaction with the vendor. The left form displays available items for sale. The right displays the user's choice and the list of available payment instruments. The textual description of items will eventually be replaced by icons.

Instrument Storage on the PalmPilot Instruments carry some financial information with them. For example, in the case of a PDA-PayWord instrument, the data includes the bottom end of the hash chain, the current position on the hash chain to be spent, and other parameters as well. Each of our instruments is implemented as an encrypted database on the PalmPilot. This data resides in non-volatile memory and is backed up to the desktop during a HotSync.

Link Encryption At the moment the implementation assumes all transactions are local, i.e. the PalmPilot is placed into the vendor's cradle. The PalmPilot does not establish a secure link to the vendor since there is little concern that a direct line between the PalmPilot and vendor can be tapped.

4.2 The Pony Vending Machine

The Pony vending machine[4] supports an interface through a proprietary connection. We were able to interface with it and send it commands through a

[4] The Pony (short for Prancing Pony) is a vending machine on the fourth floor of the Gates Computer Science Building on the Stanford campus. Similar to the Prancing Pony in J.R.R. Tolkien's "The Fellowship of the Rings," the Pony vending machine is a common place which those in need of nourishment may go to.

laptop-PC which serves as a proxy to it. The laptop-PC runs the vendor application, and may issue commands to the Pony vending machine through its proprietary interface. The digital wallet application running on the PalmPilot connects to the vendor application running on the laptop-PC.

When the PalmPilot connects to the Pony-Vendor (the laptop-PC), the user can choose from a list of available products. The set of available products is downloaded onto the PalmPilot as soon as the connection is set up. The user then tells the PalmPilot directly which item to purchase and which instrument to use for payment. The PalmPilot then initiates a purchase protocol with the Pony-Vendor. Once the appropriate funds are transfered to the Pony-Vendor it instructs the Pony-vending machine to dispense the required item. The connection is then closed and the Pony-Vendor is ready to service the next customer.

4.3 PDA-PayWord Implementation Details

Withdrawal Protocol Before being able to make purchases from the vendor, the user must first make a "withdrawal" from the bank. In our current system, the user takes her PalmPilot to a bank teller and inserts it into a cradle attached to the bank teller's computer. The user authenticates herself by entering her password. The user then enters the withdrawal amount on the PalmPilot, and the PalmPilot generates a *hash chain instrument.* It then executes the withdrawal protocol. Since our implementation uses 5-cent denominations ($d = 5$), the wallet divides the withdrawal amount by 5, yielding the hash chain size, k. The wallet then constructs a hash chain instrument by generating $Y_0 \dots Y_k$. Average hash chain generation times for various dollar amounts using our 5-cent denomination hash chain instrument are shown in Table 2.

Amount ($)	Hash Chain Size (words)	Average time (ms)
5	100	504
10	200	896
20	400	1667
50	1000	3970

Table 2. Average Hash Chain Generation Timing Results

For amounts up to $10, a single 5-cent denomination hash chain instrument might provide acceptable performance on the PalmPilot; for larger amounts, using multiple hash-chains with larger denominations might be necessary to achieve acceptable performance.

The user's wallet then kicks off the withdrawal protocol by sending a signed *withdrawal request* to the bank. The user's password is used to decrypt her private key, and the private key is used to sign the withdrawal request. For efficiency, an ECC-DSA signature is used to sign the withdrawal request. The withdrawal request is shown in Table 3.

field:	Y_k	k	d
byte-length:	20	2	2

Table 3. Withdrawal Request Message Format

The bank receives the withdrawal request, and verifies the signature on the request. The bank then either deducts the withdrawal amount ($k * d$) from the user's "bank account," or the user gives the bank teller the amount in physical currency. If the user has the appropriate funds in her account, or gives the bank teller the appropriate amount in non-counterfeit currency, the bank teller approves the transaction. Upon approval, a *hash chain certificate* is sent to the user's wallet and stored in the user's hash chain instrument. Note that the user's hash chain instrument has no value without a signed hash chain certificate. The hash chain certificate is also stored on the vendor's wallet in a vendor-side hash chain instrument that can be quickly looked up during execution of the purchase protocol. The vendor-side hash chain instrument also stores the last Y_i spent by the user. (In the case that the bank teller does not approve the transaction, an error message is sent to the user's wallet.)

Generation of the hash chain certificate requires the bank to generate a signature, and an RSA signature is used to sign the hash chain certificate in PDA-Payword (as explained in Section 3.2); note that this task takes place on the bank-PC. The PalmPilot verifies the bank's signature, but does not need to generate a signature itself. The signature generation time for our 300 MHz Pentium bank-PC was 170ms on average. The total time for the PalmPilot to generate and sign the withdrawal request, send it to the bank, and receive a hash chain certificate in response was 1874ms on the average.

field:	d	k	*vid*	Y_k	*sno*	*sublen*	*subject*	*elen*	*expdate*	*siglen*	*sig*
byte-length:	1	2	1	20	4	2	variable	2	variable	2	variable

Table 4. Hash Chain Certificate Format

A hash chain certificate is shown in Table 4. Many of the fields in the hash chain certificate have already been described, but a brief explanation of all of them can be found in Table 5.

Using 512-bit RSA signatures on a 20-byte message digest of the certificate, the average length of the entire hash chain certificate is 358 bytes. (The length of a 512-bit RSA hash chain certificate can vary because of the variable subject and expiration date fields.) The bulk of the certificate is made up of the signature field, which is 302 bytes. Although a 512-bit RSA signature on a 20 byte message digest is only 64 bytes, the signature field also contains the bank's public key which can be used to verify the signature (81 bytes), and a public key certificate (151 bytes) signed by the certificate authority that can be used to verify the bank's public key. The CA's public key is hard coded in the wallet application.

d	denomination
k	hash chain size
vid	unique vendor identification number
Y_k	top word of hash chain
sno	unique serial number of this certificate
$sublen$	length of variable subject field
$subject$	"subject" of this certificate. currently used to store a comment.
$elen$	length of variable expiration date field
$expdate$	text representation of expiration date in "UNIX" format
$siglen$	length of variable signature field
sig	RSA signature of SHA-1 message digest of this certificate

Table 5. Description of Hash Chain Certificate Fields

Once the hash chain certificate is received by the user's wallet, the wallet verifies the hash chain certificate. Verification of the hash chain certificate took approximately 1008ms in our implementation. Note that two RSA verifications are necessary to check that a hash chain certificate is authentic: one verification using the bank's public key to check the signature on the certificate, and one verification using the CA's public key to check the signature on the bank's public key certificate. The RSA verifications take about 438ms each (for e=3), and hence a total hash chain certificate verification time of 1008ms is reasonable.

If verification of the hash chain certificate is successful, the certificate becomes part of the user's hash chain instrument. (If the hash chain certificate does not verify, an error message is displayed, and the user should demand her money back!)

To summarize, the key components contributing to the total transaction time of the withdrawal protocol are 1) hashing required to construct the instrument, 2) ECC-DSA signature of the withdrawal request, 3) communication overhead between the PalmPilot and the bank, and 4) verification of the hash chain certificate. The time reqiured for (1) is shown in Table 2, and is dependent upon the amount and denomination being withdrawn. The time required for (2) and (3) combined is approximately 1874ms, and the time required for (4) is approximately 1008ms.

Hence, withdrawal times range from just under 3.5 seconds to just under 7 seconds for instrument amounts from 5$ to 50$. From a usability standpoint, these withdrawal times would seem to be acceptable for most users. [5]

Purchase Protocol Once the hash chain instrument's construction is complete by adding the hash chain certificate to it, a purchase may be accomplished by

[5] Indeed, for larger amounts, the instrument creation time becomes the dominating factor and can be reduced by using larger denomination coins (choosing a larger value for d). Using multiple hash chains, each with a different d, can also be employed to reduce the amount of hashing necessary, but would necessitate the verification of multiple hash chain certificates.

having the user's wallet send a *purchase request* to the vendor application. If the user has already spent j hash words, then to spend the next i words, the user's wallet sends the purchase request message shown in Table 6 to the vendor application.

field:	Y_{k-j-i}	i	*hash-chain-certificate*
byte-length:	20	2	variable

Table 6. Purchase Request Message Format

The number of hash words to spend, $i = price/d$, is determined based on the price of the product the user wishes to buy and the denomination of the hash chain instrument. Since the hash chain instrument on the user's wallet only stores Y_0, the user's wallet needs to compute $k - j - i$ hashes to construct the purchase request message.

instrument amount($)	*hash iterations required* (words)	*transaction time*(ms)
5	70	1090
10	170	1467
20	370	2267
50	970	4580

Table 7. Purchase Transaction Times

After the vendor wallet receives the purchase request, it retrieves the corresponding vendor hash chain instrument from its Instrument Manager and checks that $h^{(i)}(Y_{k-j-i})$ is equal to the Y_{k-j} that it had stored after the instrument's last use. Note that the first time the instrument is used, $j = 0$ and the vendor wallet checks that $h^{(i)}(Y_{k-i}) = Y_k$. The vendor wallet also checks the validity of the hash chain certificate that is presented in the purchase request, and if the certificate is valid, the vendor wallet stores Y_{k-j-i} in its vendor-side hash chain instrument and sends back "OK" as the *purchase response*. If any of the above checks fail, an "ERROR" purchase response is sent back to the user wallet.

Purchase protocol timing measurements to do a first-time $1.50 buy with 5-cent denomination hash chain instruments of varying initial sizes are presented in Table 7.

5 Summary and Conclusions

Our experiments show that a PDA may be viewed as a *portable commerce device without tamper resistance* that is suitable for small payments. PDAs are computationally more powerful than smartcards. However, since they do not contain cryptographic accelerators certain operations take longer, and the performance of cryptographic primitives need to be taken into account when designing commerce protocols for PDA's. For instance, RSA signature generation is slow, while RSA verification is fast. On the other hand, ECC-based signature generation is fast while verification is slow.

In conclusion, commerce protocols can be implemented to perform transactions efficiently on a PDA platform. PDA-PayWord is an example of an implementation of a commerce protocol that is designed to achieve acceptable performance on a PDA by taking advantage of the performance characteristics of both RSA and elliptic curve cryptograpy on the PalmPilot.

Acknowledgments

Special thanks to Andrew Toy for revitalizing the PC interface to the Pony vending machine.

References

1. 3Com Corporation, `http://www.3com.com`
2. R. Anderson, C. Manifavas, C. Sutherland, "Netcard – a practical electronic cash system", in Fourth Cambridge Workshop on Security Protocols.
3. R. Anderson, M. Kuhn, "Tamper resistance – a cautionary note", In 2nd USENIX Workshop on electronic commerce, 1996, pp. 1–11.
4. Certicom Co., `http://www.certicom.com`
5. B. Cox, D. Tygar, M. Sirbu, "NetBill security and transaction protocol", `http://www.ini.cmu.edu/netbill/home.html`.
6. CyberCash, `http://www.cybercash.com`
7. N. Daswani, D. Boneh, H. Garcia-Molina, S. Ketchpel, A. Paepcke "SWAPEROO: A Simple Wallet Architecture for Payments, Exchanges, Refunds, and Other Operations", Proceedings of the Third USENIX Workshop on Electronic Commerce, 1998.
8. DigiCash, `http://www.digicash.com`
9. Financial applications for the PalmPilot, `http://www.pilotzone.com/prod_business.html`
10. A. Glass, "Could the smartcard be dumb", Proceedings of Eurocrypt '86, 1986.
11. I. Goldberg, pilotSSLeay-2.01, `http://www.isaac.cs.berkeley.edu/pilot/`
12. R. Hauser, M. Steiner, M. Waidner, "Micro-payments based on iKP", In 14th Wolrd-wide congress on computer and communication security protection, 1996.
13. S. Jarecki, A. Odlyzko, "An efficient micropayment system based on probabilistic polling", Proc. Financial Cryptography '97.
14. C. Jutla, M. Yung, "Paytree: amortized signature for flexible micropayments", In 2nd USENIX Workshop on electronic commerce, 1996, pp. 213–221.
15. L. Lamport, "Password authentication with insecure communication", Communications of the ACM, vol. 24 (11), 1981, pp. 770-771.
16. R. Lipton, R. Ostrovsky, "Micro-Payments via efficient coin flipping", Proc. Financial Cryptography '98.
17. M. Manasse, "The Millicent protocols for electronic commerce", Proc. of the 1st USENIX workshop on Electronic Commerce.

18. Mondex International, `http://www.mondex.com`
19. T. Pederson, "Electronic payments of small amounts", Tech. Report, DAIMI PB-495, Aarhus University, Computer Science Dept., Aug. 1995.
20. R. Rivest, "Lottery tickets as Micro-Cash", Financial Cryptography '97.
21. R. Rivest, A. Shamir, "PayWord and MicroMint", CryptoBytes, Vol. 2, No. 1, pp. 7–11. Available from `http://www.rsa.com`
22. Security applications for the PalmPilot, `http://www.pilotzone.com/util_security.html`
23. Secure Electronic Transactions. `http://www.setco.org`
24. Y. Yacobi, "On the continuum between on-line and off-line e-cash systems – I", Proc. Financial Cryptography '97.
25. Windows CE 2.0, `http://www.microsoft.com/windowsce/`

Blinding of Credit Card Numbers in the SET Protocol

Hugo Krawczyk[1,2]

[1] Department of Electrical Engineering,
Technion, Haifa, Israel,
hugo@ee.technion.ac.il
[2] IBM T.J. Watson Research Center, New York, USA.

Abstract. We present and analyze the cryptographic techniques used in the SET protocol to implement the blinding of credit card numbers in SET certificates. This blinding is essential to protect credit card numbers from eavesdroppers in the network, and even from some merchants, as required by SET. Without these measures, bulk credit card information could be easily collected thus significantly increasing the risk and amount of credit card fraud.
We first present the security requirements from this blinding operation, which include aspects of secrecy and fraud protection, then show a solution to the problem (implemented in SET) and analyze its security based on well-defined cryptographic assumptions. Interestingly, we show that the requirements for blinding in SET are equivalent to the requirements of non-interactive commitment schemes in cryptography. Thus, our solution for SET represents an efficient implementation of a commitment function and as such may be suitable for use in other practical contexts as well.

1 Introduction

The Secure Electronic Transactions (SET) protocol has been defined by MasterCard and VISA, in joint work with other companies, to serve as the international standard for credit card transactions over the Internet [1].

SET relies heavily on cryptography to mimic in the electronic world much of the traditional (paper and phone based) credit card practices. In SET the traditional plastic card is replaced by a digital version in the form of a certificate, while the cardholder's hand-signature is replaced by a cryptographic digital signature. The digital certificate is a binding (signed by a banking institution or some other form of certification authority) between a credit card number and a public key. The private key corresponding to this public key is kept secret by the cardholder and used to sign payment requests (these electronic requests are digital versions of today's credit card paper slips). Thus SET includes two main cryptographic components: certification management and payment protocol. The techniques involved in this paper touch both aspects of SET.

M. Franklin (Ed.): FC'99, LNCS 1648, pp. 17–28, 1999.

1.1 Overview of SET

Here we provide a minimal overview of these components of SET as needed to motivate the particular problem we solve, to establish the security requirements for a solution, and to justify the soundness of the proposed solution. This description over-simplifies many of the details and system aspects of the protocol. For a complete and accurate description of SET see [1].

Certification in SET involves the participation of the cardholder and an issuing bank (the latter can be thought of as the banking institution where the cardholder maintains his account). Using special software, the cardholder[1] generates a pair of RSA private and public keys in her own computer (SET currently supports RSA only). She then communicates with the bank to register this public key and to receive a certificate signed by the bank and which includes the cardholder's account identifier (see below for more discussion about this account identifier) and the registered public key.[2]

SET's payment protocol is a three-party protocol designed to convey all the payment and authorization information between customer, merchant and the banking network. The 'banking network' is an existing (pre-Internet) infrastructure through which payment requests and authorizations are processed between banking entities. A main requirement of SET is to leave this infrastructure unchanged. Therefore, the "banking party" in SET is a *payment gateway* that translates the electronic requests coming through the Internet (from merchants and cardholders) into their traditional and existing format for processing by the banks that manage cardholder accounts. In particular, the verification of certificates, digital signatures, etc. are performed by this gateway and not at the bank where the actual cardholder's account is held.

A basic run of SET's payment protocol is initiated when a cardholder decides to pay for a purchase using her credit card. (The "shopping session" preceding this payment is out of the scope of SET; this shopping session can be carried in a variety of ways such as over the Web, using an electronic catalog, by e-mail, etc.) The cardholder then prepares a payment request to be sent to the payment gateway which includes cardholder's information as well as purchase information such as time, merchant identity, amount of transaction, and a cryptographic digest of the order details. This information, which can be thought of as a "digital payment slip", is encrypted under the payment gateway's public key and signed with the cardholder's private signature key. The cardholder's certificate is appended. The composed data is then sent to the merchant who, after performing his own verification steps and adding other information, transmits all the data to the payment gateway. The latter decrypts the cardholder's slip, verifies certificates and signatures, and creates a payment authorization request that is sent to the cardholder's bank for authorization (as said before, this later

[1] In our description, we usually do not explicitly distinguish between the human actions and computer actions related to the cardholder steps in the protocol.

[2] We omit here any aspects of how this communication between bank and cardholder is carried out as well as issues of global SET certification authorities that provide certificates for issuing banks and merchants.

part of the authorization process is identical to today's credit card procedures). When the bank returns a response to the payment gateway, the latter sends the response (authorization or failure) to the merchant. This ends the core part of the payment protocol.

For a more detailed, yet concise, presentation of the cryptographic design principles underlying SET's payment protocol see the *i*KP protocol [4], a precursor of SET.

1.2 Blinding of credit card numbers

A main aspect of the security of SET, and the main motivation for the techniques presented in this paper, is the following. Cardholder certificates are sent in the clear over the Internet during purchase and payment sessions. They are to be seen by merchants and can be eavesdropped by anyone watching the network. These certificates include as an essential part the cardholder's account information in the form of an "account identifier". The natural value for this identifier would have been the credit card number (which identifies the cardholder's banking institution and specific account). However, it is a main requirement of SET that credit card numbers are not exposed over the Internet and that they do not even reach merchants in general[3]. Indeed, sending this information in the clear is unacceptable in today's credit card world. Collecting credit card numbers (possibly together with additional information about the cardholder) is a main goal for attackers interested in committing credit card fraud. Assuming huge volumes of SET transactions this risk would endanger the whole credit card business. In particular, note that the protection of credit card account information from merchants is one of the main differentiations of SET from current solutions, e.g based on SSL, that only protect the customer-merchant link.

It is clear, therefore, that the account identifier in the certificate cannot be the credit card number itself. On the other hand, it is a must that this identifier will be bound to the cardholder's credit card number in order to identify the right account to charge. To bridge over these conflicting requirements, SET uses a "blinding" technique to produce a cardholder identity derived from the credit card number and included in SET certificates. This identity, called "unique cardholder identity" in SET, and denoted here by CID, uniquely identifies a cardholder account to the payment gateway, but makes it impossible for any other parties to relate it to (or derive from it) the actual credit card number. This identity can be seen as an alias or pseudonym for the credit card number. At time of payment the actual credit card number and information for binding it to the CID are sent secretly (i.e., encrypted) by the cardholder to the payment gateway.

This paper is mainly devoted to present the security requirements for this blinding operation, and to present and analyze the specific solution developed

[3] The protocol does allow for designated and specially authorized merchants to receive this information from the payment gateway, but it discourages the dissemination of this information for small or not well-established merchants in the net. Such merchants could be created for the sole purpose of collecting credit card information.

for SET. While the secrecy protection of credit card numbers via blinding is an obvious requirement here, the relation of this technique to fraud protection is less apparent. We expand on these requirements in Section 2.

1.3 Commitment schemes

One of the (somewhat surprising) conclusions from analyzing the requirements for account blinding in SET is that this operation posses essentially the same cryptographic requirements as commitment schemes do. Commitment schemes are well known and widely used in many cryptographic protocols, especially zero-knowledge protocols. In our case the need for such schemes is not obvious a-priori but it will become clear from our analysis in Sections 2 and 5. A vast literature exists on the subject of commitment schemes. We refer to [9] for a relatively recent work with pointers to further papers in the area.

Informally, a commitment scheme is a protocol for "committing" to a value in such a way that the committer cannot later change his mind about the committed value, while the recipient of the commitment cannot learn anything about the committed value from seeing the commitment (the reader unfamiliar with this notion can easily imagine the usefulness of such a scheme in electronic bids). One interesting problem in cryptography is how to build such a scheme from very simple primitives, in particular, from one-way functions only. Naor [11] has provided an *interactive* scheme based on pseudorandom generators (and then on any one-way function) already in 1989. However, it remains open since then the question of whether the same can be achieved non-interactively. The weakest assumption known to suffice for this task is the existence of collision-resistant hash functions. Combining these with a universal hash function one can build a non-interactive commitment scheme [6,9].

In this paper we present a solution that assumes a function which is simultaneously collision-resistant and pseudorandom. See Section 4 for the details. Fortunately, this combined assumption is natural and generally accepted for cryptographic hash functions such as SHA-1. In our solution we use a keyed version of these functions based on the HMAC algorithm [2,10]. Under this combined assumption our techniques can be proven to achieve the requirements of the SET protocol or, equivalently, the requirements of a (non-interactive) commitment scheme. Since this solution is highly efficient (computationally and communication-wise) and cryptographically sound, it is a good candidate for consideration when such a commitment scheme is required in practical scenarios. In particular, it achieves the efficiency of solutions based on the random oracle model [5] but under much weaker, well-formulated and realistic, cryptographic assumptions. We expand on this subject in Section 5.

2 Blinding Requirements

Let CCN be the credit card number of cardholder C. (In SET CCN is called Primary Account Number (PAN).) Let G and M denote the payment gateway and merchant, respectively. Our goal is to design a suitable blinding function B that when applied to CCN will produce a certificate identifier CID, i.e. CID $=$ B(CCN). The latter is used as follows: cardholder C is issued a certificate that binds the value of CID together with C's public key under the signature of a banking institution (or other certification authority CA). Whenever C activates the SET payment protocol, C sends the certificate to M as well as an encrypted slip (under G's public key) containing, among other information, the actual credit card number CCN of C. After merchant M checks some information related to C's certificate (the details here do not concern us) it sends to G the certificate of C as well as the information encrypted and signed by C. Gateway G decrypts the value of CCN and checks that the value of CID as it appears in the certificate is indeed a blinding of CCN (i.e., G checks that CID $= B$(CCN)). If so, it verifies the signature of C on the payment request (the slip) using the public key appearing in C's certificate. After all these validations succeed (including the verification of the CA's signature on the certificate), G sends a request for authorization (for the amount in the transaction) to the bank identified by CCN. The bank will check the status of account CCN (e.g., credit limit and balance) but will not perform any further checks on C's signatures or other information already verified by G. (Remember that the bank's part in this process is identical to the processing of nowadays paper/phone requests and independent of the details of SET.) This scenario imposes two requirements on the function B:

1. Secrecy: no information on CCN should leak from seeing CID $= B$(CCN);
2. Fraud prevention: it should be infeasible to find CCN, CCN$'$ such that B(CCN) $= B$(CCN$'$).

The first requirement is obvious as it constitutes the motivation for introducing the blinded identity, namely, protecting the value of CCN from eavesdroppers and even merchants. Moreover, note that we need secrecy protection in a strong sense: credit card numbers belong to a relatively small range of values (they are short and structured) thus it should be infeasible to mount dictionary attacks on the encryption. What is required is the full secrecy protection as captured by the notion of *semantic security* [8], namely, no partial information on the plaintext should be derivable from the ciphertext by a (computationally-bounded) attacker. In particular, this implies that the function B must be probabilistic. (If B is deterministic then the attacker can, for example, test different candidate values of CCN to determine which one corresponds to a given CID.) We show below how to deal with the randomization of this function.

The necessity of the second requirement is less obvious. It does not directly follow from the need to hide the credit card number, but it is needed to prevent fraud opportunities that the blinding technique introduces. Here we give a brief argument to motivate this and expand on it later. Assume that an attacker A has a certificate issued for account CCN' and for which A holds the corresponding private key. Assume also that CID $= B$(CCN$'$) $= B$(CCN) where CCN is some other cardholder's credit card number. In this case, A can pay for any purchase using account CCN rather than A's account CCN'. This is done as follows: A sends to G

his own certificate containing CID and signs using his own private key; however, instead of encrypting CCN' in the slip he encrypts CCN. Now all verification steps of G succeed but the account being charged is CCN' not CCN ![4]

Since we saw that B must be a probabilistic (or randomized) function, we will consider it as a deterministic two-argument function β. The first argument is a random quantity, while the second is a credit card number. This random quantity is generated as follows. At certification time, cardholder C chooses a random value k that she sends to the certification authority CA[5]. The value CID for C will be fixed to $\text{CID} = \beta(k, \text{CCN})$ where CCN is the credit card number of C. After computing CID, CA does not need to keep the value of k, but C does keep it secretly for later use. Each time that C will be sending a payment request to G (via M), cardholder C will encrypt both values k and CCN under G's public key. After decryption G will check that $\text{CID} = \beta(k, \text{CCN})$ where CID is the blinded ID that appears in C's certificate.

With respect to β we can restate the second (fraud prevention) requirement above as the infeasibility to find, for given CCN and CCN', values k and k' such that $\beta(k, \text{CCN}) = \beta(k', \text{CCN}')$. If this was possible, then an attacker A that holds account CCN' can charge another account CCN as follows. Attacker A finds k, k' as above, and uses k' at registration time to obtain a certificate identifier $\text{CID} = \beta(k', \text{CCN}')$. When coming to pay, A sends to the gateway G the values CCN and k which G verifies as correct since $\text{CID} = \beta(k, \text{CCN})$. Thus, account CCN is charged and not CCN'. (It is important to note that in this attack A does not need to know the values of CID or k used by the legitimate owner of CCN.) In another attack variant, the attacker A (possibly using an accomplice) certifies two accounts CCN and CCN' under two different names and using blinding values k and k', respectively, such that $\beta(k, \text{CCN}) = \beta(k', \text{CCN}')$. Now A can charge CCN using the certificate (and signature) issued for CCN', and then dispute the charge to CCN alleging a wrong signature on the slip.

Note: An even stronger requirement is the infeasibility of finding a quadruple $k, k', \text{CCN}, \text{CCN}'$ such that $\beta(k, \text{CCN}) = \beta(k', \text{CCN}')$. However this seems to be more than needed in SET since it is hard to see how an attacker could use these values to mount a real attack: in particular, the values of CCN, CCN' he may find will probably not be legal credit card numbers and even if so these will probably be credit card numbers for which A does not hold the private key, or cannot get them certified with a public key of his choice. In any case, our solution achieves this stronger requirement as well under standard assumptions.

[4] Note that A could be possibly traced after fraud was committed; however, by then A can be safely resting in Anguilla or could have just used somebody else's stolen certificate and private key as the CCN' account. In the later case A could have just impersonated the broken cardholder and pay using CCN' directly; still targeting a better protected and higher-value CCN account could prove a more rewarding strategy for A.

[5] This value k is called PANSecret in SET and its generation involves a random nonce provided by the CA to increase the amount of randomness in k

We stress that it is *not* a requirement of SET to disallow linkability of payments. Indeed, different purchases by the same cardholder can be linked via the public value of CID, the public key, etc.

3 Sufficient Conditions on the Blinding Function β

In this section we prove a theorem that establishes a set of sufficient conditions for a function β to satisfy the requirements stated in the previous section. In the next section we present a particular implementation of β, as adopted by SET, for which it is believed that these sufficient conditions do hold. The conditions in the next theorem involve the notion of collision-resistance and pseudorandom functions. The latter were introduced in [7] and are widely used in multiple applications of cryptography such as key generation, message authentication codes, encryption and more. Keyed hash functions and block ciphers are typical realizations of pseudorandom functions whose basic property is that the output of the function on a given point is unpredictable even after seeing the value of the function in a number of other points.

Theorem 1. *Let $\beta(k, x)$ be a deterministic function for which the following two conditions hold:*

1. *the function $\beta(k, x)$ is collision resistant, namely, it is hard to find k, x, k', x' such that $\beta(k, x) = \beta(k', x')$;*
2. *the family of keyed functions $\{f_k(x)\}_k$, where $f_k(x) = \beta(k, x)$, is pseudorandom.*

Then $\beta(k, x)$ satisfies the blinding requirements of SET (see Section 2).

Proof. Finding two values CCN and CCN' that map to the same value under β with (possible) different values of k and k' would clearly contradict the collision-resistance condition imposed on β by the first assumption in the theorem. Thus the second requirement of the blinding operator is satisfied by β.

As for the first requirement of Section 2 the assumption that $f_k(x) = \beta(k, x)$ behaves as a family of pseudorandom functions guarantees that nothing is learned about CCN from seeing $f_k(\text{CCN})$. Indeed, it takes a standard argument to show that any algorithm that can extract any partial information, not known a-priori, on CCN given $f_k(\text{CCN})$, can also be used to create a predictor (or distinguishing test) for the family $\{f_k(x)\}_k$. This guarantees the semantic security of CCN; in particular, even an attacker that has only two candidate values for CCN cannot decide on the correct value with probability essentially better than 1/2. □

4 HMAC-Based Solution

The solution adopted by SET for implementing the function β uses the function HMAC-SHA1. HMAC is described in the SET specifications as well as in RFC 2104 [10]. It is also the subject of the paper [2]. However, the latter deals with the use of HMAC for the purpose for which it was originally designed, namely, as a secure MAC (message authentication code). In SET the use of HMAC and the requirements from this function are very different. In particular, the sole assumption that HMAC is a secure MAC does not suffice to guarantee that its use for our purposes is secure. Indeed, one can show examples of (other) functions that are secure for message authentication but totally insecure as blinding functions for SET. Here we analyze the use of HMAC for the specific purposes of blinding in the SET protocol.

We first recall the definition of HMAC which uses a key K and applies to a value x. H represents an iterative cryptographic hash function (i.e. one that iterates a compression function over blocks of data) such as SHA-1, RIPEMD, etc. In the specific implementation of SET the function H is SHA-1. HMAC is defined as

$$\mathrm{HMAC}_K(x) = H\big(K \oplus \mathsf{opad} \cdot H(K \oplus \mathsf{ipad} \cdot x)\big)$$

where $\cdot$ is the concatenation operator, K is typically of the length of the hash output (20 bytes for SHA-1) and is padded with 0's to the hash block boundary (64 bytes). The pads opad and ipad are fixed 64-byte strings, and their values are the byte 0x36 repeated 64 times and the byte 0x5C repeated 64 times, respectively.
In SET, we define

$$\beta(k, \textsc{ccn}) = \text{HMAC-SHA1}_k(\textsc{ccn})$$

where k is a string of length 160 bits.

We now argue that the conditions of Theorem 1 are likely to be satisfied by this function (when implemented with SHA-1 or similar functions).

COLLISION-RESISTANCE. Collision resistance is the main design principle behind the definition of SHA-1 and then a reasonable assumption to make. Finding collisions for SHA-1 is indeed believed to be a very hard task. Finding collisions in the case of HMAC seems even harder as this requires a very particular structure for the colliding values. Indeed, note that finding k, x, k', x' for which $\mathrm{HMAC}_k(x) = \mathrm{HMAC}_{k'}(x')$ would mean finding collisions for the external application of H (or SHA-1) where the colliding values have the special format dictated by the use of the constants opad and ipad and by the internal application of H. Such a break to the collision resistance of SHA-1 seems highly improbable given current knowledge.

PSEUDORANDOMNESS. The second requirement from Theorem 1 asks for the family HMAC_k, where k ranges over random 160-bit quantities, to be pseudorandom. Justifying such a property of HMAC_k requires some assumption about the pseudorandomness of the underlying hash function; i.e., SHA-1 in the case of SET. This property of SHA-1 has been less investigated than collision-resistance. However, we note that similar, and actually stronger, random-like properties are usually assumed on SHA-1. In particular, the designers of SHA-1 proposed the use of this function as the basis to a pseudorandom generator for DSS [12]. Moreover, keyed cryptographic hash functions based on SHA-1 are widely used for applications such as key derivation in key exchange protocols (in reality, people often refer to these functions, even in the unkeyed version, as as a source for "ideal randomness" as assumed in applications of the random oracle model).

Here we show that for our purposes a weaker assumption about the pseudorandomness of the function H suffices. The arguments below follow the approach and results of [2,3]. Let h denote the "compression function" underlying the construction of iterative hash function like H (e.g. SHA-1). Consider this compression function as a family of functions keyed via the initial variable (IV) of h, namely, let h_k represent the function h with its IV set to k. We claim that the second requirement from Theorem 1 holds with respect to $\beta(k, \text{CCN}) = \text{HMAC}_k(\text{CCN})$ if the family $\{h_k\}_k$ is pseudorandom. Indeed, one can see that our application of HMAC translates into the nested application of two functions from the family h_k with different keys k_1 and k_2 (this has been called NMAC in [2]). Namely, $\text{HMAC}_k(\text{CCN}) = h_{k_1}(h_{k_2}(\text{CCN}))$ where $k_1 = H(k \oplus \mathsf{opad})$ and $k_2 = H(k \oplus \mathsf{ipad})$ (here we use the fact that ipad and opad are *different* strings). It is important to note that the input CCN to h_{k_2} is shorter than a full block of h (64-byte for SHA-1) and then a single application of the compression function is used in this computation. Now if the family $\{h_k\}_k$ is pseudorandom then certainly the composition of two elements from this family is pseudorandom too (actually, this is a strengthening relative to a single application of the function, similarly to the case of "double-encryption").

A further strengthening of the security of our scheme comes from the fact that the pseudorandom function cannot be attacked via probes to the values of the function on different inputs. There is no way for an attacker that tries to learn the value of CCN from CID to query the function HMAC_k in any value other than CID.

In conclusion, based on Theorem 1 and the above discussion we see that if H is collision-resistant and the family of keyed compression functions $\{h_k\}$ is pseudorandom then $\beta(k, x) = \text{HMAC}_k(x)$ constitutes a secure blinding function for SET. In particular, these assumptions are natural and reasonable for the function H when implemented via SHA-1.

5 Non-interactive Commitment Schemes

As discussed in the introduction, the requirements for the blinding operation of SET coincide with the requirements for commitment schemes and therefore our solution to the blinding problem provides also a practical implementation of a commitment scheme. Here we extend on this subject.

A *commitment scheme* is a protocol involving two parties, S (the sender or committer) and R (the recipient or committee), and it is composed of two phases. Here we concentrate on protocols where both phases are non-interactive. Thus, we define two functions commit and verify. In the first phase, called the *commitment phase*, the committer S computes $c = \mathsf{commit}(v)$, where v is a value (a string, in general) to which S wants to commit. S then sends c to R. In the second stage, the *opening phase*, S sends to R the value v and auxiliary verification information a, and R verifies that $\mathsf{verify}(c, v, a)$ is satisfied.

A *secure* commitment scheme is one for which: (i) R does not learn anything from c about the value of v, except for what he knew about v before seeing c (namely, the function commit protects v with semantic security); (ii) it is infeasible for S to find values v', a' such that $v \neq v'$ and $\mathsf{verify}(c, v', a')$ is satisfied. These properties guarantee that R does not learn anything about the value v committed by S until the latter opens (or reveals) the committed value. On the other hand, after having sent c, the committer S cannot change her mind about the committed value, i.e., S can open c to a unique value v.

We note that the above description is a simplification of the more general notion of commitment schemes which allows for both phases, commitment and opening, to be fully-interactive protocols. On the other hand, in many practical applications (blinding of credit card numbers in SET being one example) interaction can be costly or even prohibitive.

Let us now consider the blinding requirements from Section 2. Note that the requirements on the function B established there are essentially the same requirements stated above for a (non-interactive) commitment scheme. Therefore, we can see the function B as the commit function, while verification by R involves re-computing B on the opened value v. More precisely, when considering the function β (instead of B), we can define $c = \mathsf{commit}(v) = \beta(k, v)$ (for $v = \textsc{ccn}$ and randomly chosen k, and thus $c = \textsc{cid}$), and opening is done by sending v together with k. The verification $\mathsf{verify}(c, v, k)$ is performed by testing whether $c = \beta(k, v)$ (for c, v, k as received from S).

As shown in Section 4, the function $\mathrm{HMAC}_k(v)$ is a secure implementation of the function β, and then also a suitable implementation of the function commit for a secure commitment scheme. This solution to non-interactive commitment schemes compares favorably in performance relative to other solutions such as those based on public key encryption (see below) or universal hashing [6,9]. On the other hand, the latter uses weaker cryptographic assumptions (it requires collision-resistance as in our case, but gets rid of the pseudorandomness requirement via the use of universal hashing). However, the performance advantages of HMAC are significant here. They involve both computation time as well as the size of the information sent from S to R (or from C to G in the case of SET). The latter is important since $c = \textsc{cid}$ goes into the digital certificate (which one wants to keep as short as possible), and $v = \textsc{ccn}$ and k need to fit in a single public key encryption (under G's public key).

Another suggestion considered at the time of SET design was to use a public key RSA operation for the commitment function. This can be implemented using a public key for which the private key is not known to anyone (say, it is destroyed immediately after generation). The commit function is then implemented as a randomized encryption of v under this public key. Opening is done by sending v together with the random value k used to compute the randomized encryption. This results in a long (1024 bit) value for $\textsc{cid}$, however this can be shorten by applying a collision-resistant hash function to this value. It is not hard to see (and the techniques are well known) that this provides a secure commitment scheme if the encryption is secure. Eventually, the HMAC-based solution was selected as being faster and simpler (e.g., it does not require the complexities of generating a public key, destroying the private key, and keeping this key as a static – very long-lived – key in the protocol).

It is also interesting to compare the HMAC-based solution with heuristic constructions of commitment schemes based on the random oracle model [5]. If one is willing to assume that SHA-1 is such a "random oracle" then one can use SHA-1(k, v), for random k, as the commit function. However, the random-oracle assumption here is clearly an idealized notion, that cannot be implemented via a single fixed function. The cost of the HMAC-based solution is slightly higher in computation but it is founded on well-defined and realistic assumptions.

6 Concluding Remarks

We have shown the motivation and rationale for introducing the blinding of credit card numbers in SET certificates. We presented the security requirements for this operation which include aspects of secrecy and fraud prevention. We presented sufficient cryptographic conditions for a function to constitute a secure blinding operator, and showed that the specific HMAC-based solution adopted in SET is likely to satisfy these conditions. Finally, we argued that such a solution represents a practical and sound candidate for the implementation of cryptographic commitment schemes.

It is interesting to note that, in principle, all the blinding issue could have been avoided in SET by issuing special credit card numbers for use with SET certificates which are different than the regular numbers used by cardholders for traditional shopping. Indeed, if one makes sure that these new credit card numbers are used only in conjunction with a digital signature from the cardholder then the sole knowledge of CCN does not help an attacker. This possibility was discussed by the SET designers. However, it was strongly discouraged by the credit card organizations as they considered it impractical (given current banking practices) to require banks to issue alternative account numbers linked to existing cardholder accounts. Besides this business consideration, it is not clear how well one can guarantee that these new credit card numbers will never be used without an accompanying digital signature. SET itself defines a "cert-less" option (this is similar to 2KP from [4]) where the user does not carry (or does not use) any certificate and, in particular, does not apply a digital signature. In this case the credit card number becomes, again, a valuable information.

Acknowledgment

This paper is based on work carried out by the author in IBM during the design of the SET protocol in 1995. I thank Bob Jueneman and Mark Linehan for helpful discussions during the design of the techniques presented here. Additional thanks to Mark for his useful comments on an early draft of this paper.

References

1. http://www.setco.org/set.html
2. Bellare, M., Canetti, R., and Krawczyk, H., "Keying Hash Functions for Message Authentication", *Advances in Cryptology – CRYPTO 96 Proceedings*, Lecture Notes in Computer Science, Springer-Verlag Vol. 1109, N. Koblitz, ed, 1996, pp. 1–15.
3. Bellare, M., Canetti, R., and Krawczyk, H., "Pseudorandom Functions Revisited: The Cascade Construction". *Proc. of the 37th IEEE Symp. on Foundation of Computer Science*, 1996, pp. 514–523.
4. M. Bellare, J. Garay, R. Hauser, A. Herzberg, H. Krawczyk, M. Steiner, G. Tsudik, and M. Waidner, "iKP – A Family of Secure Electronic Payment Protocols", Proceedings of the *First USENIX Workshop on Electronic Commerce*, NY, July 1995, pp. 89–106.
5. Bellare, M., and Rogaway N., "Random Oracles are Practical: A Paradigm for Defining Efficient Protocols", *Proc. of the First ACM Conference on Computer and Communications Security*, 1993, pp.62-73.
6. I. B. Damgard, T. P. Pedersen and B. Pfitzmann, "On the Existence of Statistically Hiding Bit Commitment Schemes and Fail-Stop Signatures", Advances in Cryptology: CRYPTO '93, Lecture Notes in Computer Science, volume 773, Springer, New York, 1994. Pages 250–265.
7. O. Goldreich, S. Goldwasser and S. Micali, "How to construct random functions," *Journal of the ACM,* Vol. 33, No. 4, 210–217, (1986).
8. Goldwasser, S., and S. Micali, "Probabilistic Encryption", *JCSS*, Vol. 28, No. 2, 1984.
9. Halevi, S. and Micali, S., "Practical and Provably-Secure Commitment Schemes from Collision-Free Hashing", in Advances in Cryptography - CRYPTO '96, pages 201-215, 1996. Springer-Verlag.
10. Krawczyk, H., Bellare, M., and Canetti, R., "HMAC: Keyed-Hashing for Message Authentication", RFC 2104, February 1997.
11. Naor, M., "Bit Commitment Using Randomness", *Journal of Cryptology,* Vol. 2, pp. 151-158, 1991. (Preliminary version in Crypto'89.)
12. National Institute for Standards and Technology, "Digital Signature Standard (DSS)", Technical Report 169, August 30 1991.

Trustee Tokens: Simple and Practical Anonymous Digital Coin Tracing

Ari Juels

RSA Laboratories
Bedford, MA 01730, USA
ari@rsa.com

Abstract. We introduce a trustee-based tracing mechanism for anonymous digital cash that is simple, efficient, and provably secure relative to its underlying cryptographic primitives. In contrast to previous schemes, ours may be built on top of a real-world anonymous cash system, such as the DigiCash™ system, with minimal modification to the underlying protocols. In addition, our scheme involves no change to the structure of the coins. On the other hand, our scheme requires user interaction with a trustee, while many other such systems do not. This interaction occurs infrequently, however, and is efficient both in terms of computation and storage requirements. Our scheme also achieves more limited security guarantees in the presence of malicious trustees than many other systems do. While this is a disadvantage, it represents a tradeoff enabling us to achieve the high level of practicality of our system.

Keywords: anonymity, blind digital signatures, coin tracing, digital cash, e-cash, trustee-based coin tracing

1 Introduction

Anonymous digital cash, known informally as *e-cash*, is a form of digital currency that provides anonymity to users with respect to both merchants and banking institutions, thereby affording a heightened assurance of consumer privacy. Since David Chaum first proposed the idea in 1982 [2], it has been a major focal point of academic research in electronic commerce. Researchers observed early on, however, that if anonymity in payment systems is unconditional, it may be exploited to facilitate crimes like blackmail and money laundering [13]. This observation spurred research into the idea of making anonymity in payment systems conditional, and, in particular, revocable by a third party or *trustee* under court order. This notion, known as *trustee-based coin tracing*, was developed by Brickell, Gemmell, and Kravitz [21] and independently by Stadler, Piveteau, and Camenisch [10]. A National Security Agency report has since declared the availability of such tracing in e-cash systems vital to the security interests of the United States [22]. The importance of traceability in e-cash systems has

M. Franklin (Ed.): FC'99, LNCS 1648, pp. 29–45, 1999.

motivated the proposal of many new trustee-based coin tracing schemes, among them [23,24,17,19,25,3,6,26,12,27].

Several trustee-based coin tracing schemes have offered notable innnovations in functionality and flexibility. In general, however, these improvements are achieved at the cost of diminished simplicity and practicality. In this paper, we introduce a simple and highly efficient trustee-based tracing mechanism that may be added on top of anonymous cash schemes based on blind RSA signatures. Rather than seeking to offer new functionality with respect to other tracing schemes, our scheme does the opposite: it trades off some functionality against a higher degree of simplicity and practicality. Thus, while our scheme has limitations with respect to some previous ones, it also has several important advantages:

- **Practicality** Unlike previous schemes, ours can be incorporated straightforwardly on top of a commercially implemented on-line anonymous e-cash scheme, namely the DigiCash™ scheme [1,15] (also referred to as Chaumian e-cash [2]). Our scheme involves no change to the structure of the coins or the spending or deposit protocols, and can be easily applied to off-line e-cash variants as well.
- **Efficiency** Our scheme imposes minimal computational overhead on the underlying withdrawal scheme for the user – essentially just several modular multiplications and a MAC. Most other tracing schemes carry overhead for the user amounting to several modular *exponentiations* per transaction.
- **Provability** In contrast to other schemes in the literature, our system is provably secure with respect to underlying cryptographic primitives. We state theorems treating both the anonymity and non-forgeability properties of our scheme in Section 4.
- **Simplicity** Our scheme is conceptually very simple.

Like most other schemes, ours can support both tracing of the identity of a user from a coin, known as *coin tracing*, and generation of a list of all coins belonging to a given user, known as *owner tracing*. Both of these operations require very little computation and database access.

The tracing mechanism we propose in this paper has two shortcomings with respect to other schemes. First, our scheme requires user registration with a trustee upon set up of the user's account (and possibly again later, if the user spends a large number of coins). While some systems, such as, e.g., [6], require on-line participation of trustees, others, like [19], do not. As a result of this interaction between user and trustee, our system requires storage of a small amount of authorization data for withdrawals, which many other systems do not. A second drawback to our scheme is its limited privacy guarantees when multiple trustees are used. We require the use of what amounts to a *trusted dealer* (see, e.g., [11]) upon user registration. This is discussed in Section 5.2.

The idea behind our scheme is quite simple. Before making a withdrawal at a bank, a user contacts a trustee. The user shares with the trustee secrets used to generate a coin x and a blinding factor r. The user receives from the trustee what is called a *trustee token*. A trustee token is a piece of information entitling the user to withdraw an anonymous coin generated using r and x. It is essentially a short (say, 10-50 bit) proof to the coin issuer, i.e., bank, that the coin in question can be traced by the trustee. By requesting many trustee tokens in advance of coin withdrawals, and batching trustee tokens so that they apply to multiple coins, the user can achieve a very low frequency of interaction with the trustee.

1.1 Previous Work

As mentioned above, trustee-based tracing schemes were first elaborated independently by Brickell et al [21] and Stadler et al [10]. Brickell et al describe two schemes. The first is based on a blind Schnorr-like signature scheme and requires interactive proofs between trustees and the bank. The second is based on blind RSA signatures and makes use of a cut-and-choose protocol, resulting in a scheme that is flexible, but has large coin sizes and computational requirements.[1] Stadler et al introduce several schemes, the most practical of which makes use of a blind signature scheme based on that of Chaum and Pedersen [4]. In their scheme, the user requests a pseudonym and registration information from a trustee. The user presents this registration information to the bank, and also incorporates it into the coins she withdraws. Although use of a pseudonym for multiple withdrawals can lead to linkage of user identity across coins, this problem can be addressed in part by having the user register multiple pseudonyms.

Jakobsson and Yung [3] introduce the notion of "challenge semantics", enabling flexible determination of coin value, so that coins can be invalidated in case of, e.g., a bank robbery. Their scheme is capable of addressing stronger attack models than many others and a wider range of commercial settings. It is also adaptable to use with any underlying digital signature scheme. On the other hand, their scheme requires on-line participation of a trustee in both coin withdrawal and coin spending. The "Magic Ink" construction of the same authors makes use of blind DSS signatures [6]. In this scheme, signing and anonymity revocation can be conducted by differing quorums of trustees. Trustees are again, however, fully on-line, and the scheme is also rather computationally intensive for most operations. In [26], Jakobsson and Yung show how to combine the benefits of Magic Ink signatures with those of challenge semantics.

Camenisch, Piveteau, and Stadler [17] introduce a slightly different approach to trustee-based tracing. They propose a system, based on blind Schnorr signatures, in which a user transfers funds from a non-anonymous to an anonymous account, and a trustee is capable of linking the two accounts. The chief disadvantage of this approach is that once the two accounts are linked, anonymity is eliminated.

Camenisch, Maurer, and Stadler [23] demonstrate a system, based on blind Schnorr signatures, in which the trustee is wholly off-line. Their system is quite

[1] Often overlooked in the literature is the fact that the RSA-based system of Brickell et al is very likely the first with fully off-line trustees.

complex, and involves well over a dozen modular exponentiations by the user at each coin withdrawal. A system with very similar properties was introduced independently by Frankel et al [25]. Davida et al [19] improve on the system in [25], reducing the computation required in the withdrawal protocol, as well as the database search requirements in owner tracing. Their withdrawal protocol, however, still requires over a dozen modular exponentiations by the user.

Most of the above schemes rely on discrete-log based blind signature schemes. The exceptions are those in [21] and [3], which can make use of blind RSA signatures. Both schemes, however, involve changes or additions to the underlying structure of the coins, and have the inefficiencies mentioned above. In contrast, our scheme may also be used in conjunction with blind RSA signatures, but does not require any modification to the underlying coin structure. This is the reason why our scheme may be quite practically adopted in conjunction with DigiCash™ and like e-cash systems.

Trustee participation in our scheme is minimal, limited to interaction between the user and trustee upon account set-up and perhaps on an infrequent basis afterward. Our scheme does not suffer the communications and computational overhead of a scheme like that in [6], but, on the other hand, has a small amount of overhead not present in, e.g., [19]. Additionally, our scheme requires storage of trustee information, but this information is not sizeable, particularly with respect to the large coin sizes of many trustee-based tracing schemes.

The chief advantage of our scheme is its overall efficiency. The user requires minimal computation on coin withdrawal – as much as one hundred times less than in schemes like [23,19]. Computational and storage requirements for the bank are also comparable to or smaller than in most other schemes. Tracing is also highly efficient in our scheme, more so than in most others. In the case of coin tracing, for instance, our scheme requires no database lookups, which most other schemes do.

Although papers describing schemes with off-line trustees do not discuss the issue at any length, many such trustee-based tracing schemes allow for multiple trustees or a distributed trustee in a strong privacy model. A notable exception is that of Stadler et al [10]; our scheme is similar in this regard. When deployed with multiple trustees, our scheme essentially requires distribution of owner tracing information through a trusted dealer, as discussed in Section 5.2.

The basis of our scheme is in fact quite similar in flavor to that of Stadler et al [10]. The key idea behind both schemes is to use trustee registration prior to coin withdrawal. While the Stadler et al scheme makes use of a digital signature where ours uses a MAC, ours can, of course, be adapted to use a digital signature, as discussed in Section 4.1. The Stadler et al scheme differs crucially from ours in that the trustee registration is part of the coin structure. Hence their scheme is bound to, rather than added on top of the underlying signature scheme. It may be used with a special-purpose discrete-log based blind signature scheme, but not straightforwardly with blind RSA signatures.

We stress in general, however, that our scheme does not really bear direct comparison to most previous trustee-based tracing schemes. Rather, it seeks to strike a different balance, sacrificing some flexibility and privacy guarantees in favor of heightened efficiency and practicality.

1.2 Organization

The remainder of this paper is organized as follows. Section 2 gives notation and definitions. We describe the details of our trustee-based tracing scheme in Section 3, and discuss security issues in Section 4. In Section 5, we discuss the efficiency of our system and also describe a means of incorporating multiple trustees.

2 Background

2.1 Notation

An anonymous digital cash scheme involves the following participants. The first three - namely the Bank, the Trustee, and the User - will be central to the description of our scheme in this paper.

- The *Bank* is a financial institution that issues anonymous digital coins and manages accounts. The Bank publishes an RSA modulus $N = pq$, whose factorization it alone knows.
- The *Trustee* (which we denote by T) is a trustworthy device or agency responsible for tracing coins on presentation of a valid court order. In our scheme, the Trustee holds a secret key SK_T for some public key encryption algorithm; it publishes the corresponding public key PK_T. The Trustee also holds a symmetric key w, which it shares with the Bank.
- The *User* (whom we denote by U) is any entity that withdraws money from the Bank. In our scheme, the User possesses a unique identifier or account number denoted by ID_U, and also a secret s_U associated with ID_U and used to prove the User's identity. The Trustee knows a binding of ID_U to the User's real-world identity, although the Bank may transact with the User on an entirely anonymous basis using only account information.
- The *Government* is any law enforcement body that is authorized to request the tracing of coins on presenting a valid court order to T.
- The *Merchant* is any party with whom the User spends money. Our trustee-based tracing scheme does not involve any modification to the underlying digital cash protocols involving the Merchant, i.e., the spending and deposit protocols. We therefore do not have cause to discuss the role of the Merchant at any length in this paper.

We use f to denote a secure one-way or hash function, and $MAC_w(m)$ to denote a MAC (Message Authentication Code) computed using a symmetric key w. (See [18] for definitions and a discussion of MACs.) $E_{PK_X}(m)$ will indicate the encryption (under some appropriate asymmetric cipher) of the message m using the public key PK_X. We let PS denote an indexed pseudo-random generator (although a chained generator can easily be adapted to our schemes as well), and $PS_A(i)$ stand for the output of this generator with secret seed A on index i. We write $\{X_i\}$ to mean the set of values X_i over all appropriate values of i. The symbol $\|$ will denote concatenation of strings, $\oplus$, the XOR operation, and $\in_R$, uniform random selection from a set.

There are three security parameters in our scheme, denoted by k_1, k_2, and k_3. The parameter k_1 is the length of the seed to the pseudo-random number generator PS, and thus, as we shall show, specifies the level of security on the User's anonymity. The parameter k_2 specifies the length of the digital signature modulus N used by the Bank for signing coins, and thus the hardness of existential forgery in our scheme. The parameter k_3 specifies the length of the trustee tokens or MACs used in our scheme. This is essentially equivalent to the level of security on the Trustee's ability to trace the User's coins.

We write $1/2 + 1/poly$ to denote a probability greater than or equal to $1/2 + 1/k^c$, where c is some constant and k is the pertinent security parameter. For example, in the proof of Theorem 1, the security parameter in question is k_1, the pseudo-random seed length. Using somewhat rough notation, we write $< 1/2 + 1/poly$ to indicate a probability which is asymptotically less than $1/2 + 1/k^c$ for any constant c.

2.2 Definition of Blindness

Informally, a digital cash scheme is *blind* or *anonymous* if the Bank is unable to determine, either at the time of withdrawal of a coin, or later, upon examining circulating or deposited coins, which coin was withdrawn by which user. Chaum [2] first put forth the notion of blind signatures in connection with payment schemes, demonstrating an RSA-based signature scheme, described in Section 2.3 of this paper, that is unconditionally blind. A number of papers, e.g., [14], have described a weaker notion of blindness informally in terms of a lack of statistical correlation between the view of the signer at the time of signing and the set of produced signatures. A more formal definition of computational blindness, proposed in [16], may be described in terms of the following experiment. The User produces two messages m_0 and m_1 of length polynomial in k_1. The User sets a bit b uniformly at random. In two arbitrarily interleaved (and presumed blind) digital signature protocols, she presents the documents m_0 and m_1 to the Bank in an order specified by b, i.e., in the order $\{m_b, m_{1-b}\}$. In this interaction, she obtains from the Bank signatures $s(m_0)$ and $s(m_1)$ on the two messages. The User presents the message/signature pairs $(m_0, s(m_0))$ and $(m_1, s(m_1))$ to the Bank. The Bank then attempts to guess the bit b. If no polynomial-time algorithm exists which enables the Bank do so with probability $1/2 + 1/poly$ (over its own coin-flips and those of the User), then we say that the digital signature scheme is blind (or secure with respect to anonymity).[2]

[2] As noted in [16], by standard hybridization arguments this definition is as general as one involving polynomially many withdrawals by polynomially many users.

2.3 Blind RSA Signatures

Blind digital signatures were introduced by Chaum [2] as a means of implementing anonymous digital cash. As explained above, the anonymous digital cash schemes of Chaum et al, as in [2] and [8], make use of blind RSA signatures. In these schemes, the Bank publishes a public modulus $N = pq$, for which it alone knows the factorization; it creates RSA signatures in this modulus. Depicted in Figure 1 is Chaum's protocol enabling the User to obtain a blind RSA signature (or coin) with public exponent 3 from the Bank. This coin takes the form $(x, f^{1/3}(x))$. All computations here are mod$N$.

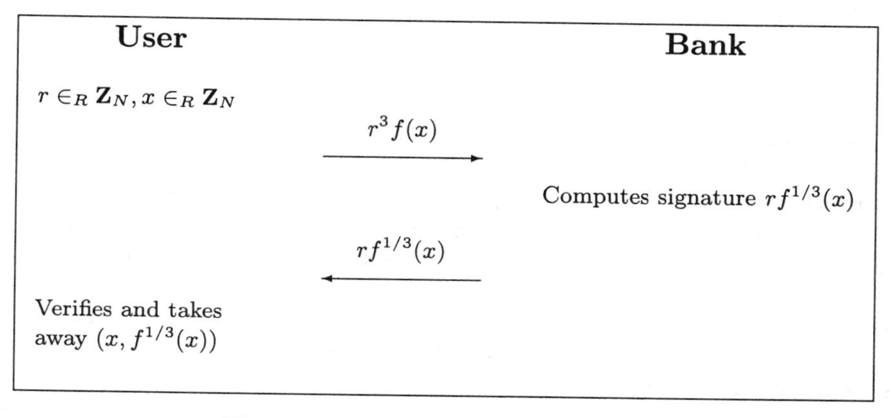

Figure 1. Blind RSA Signature Protocol.

Note that this protocol is unconditionally blind, i.e., the blindness does not rely on computational assumptions or statistical arguments.

2.4 DigiCash™

There are several DigiCash™ variants, not all of which have been implemented commercially. In this paper, we describe trustee-based tracing as it applies to a commercially implemented, on-line version of DigiCash™.

In the version of DigiCash™ (Chaumian e-cash) we consider in this paper [1,15], a coin consists of an RSA signature by the Bank on the hash of a message x. If, for instance, the Bank uses a public (encryption) exponent of 3, then a valid coin would assume the form $(x, f^{1/3}(x) \bmod N)$. To distinguish among different denominations in this scheme, the Bank uses different public exponents, e.g., $(x, f^{1/3}(x) \bmod N)$ might indicate a \$.50 coin, while $(x, f^{1/17}(x) \bmod N)$ indicates a \$1 coin. The full system works as follows. The User with identifier ID_U authenticates herself in a secure manner to the Bank. She then withdraws coins using the blind RSA signature protocol described above, the Bank deducting the corresponding funds from her account. To spend a coin with the Merchant, the User simply transmits it to the Merchant. To prevent double spending of a coin, the Merchant verifies on-line with the Bank that the coin is still valid. While this description overlooks some details, the reader may find a complete explanation of the DigiCash™ protocols in [15]. As explained there, newer variants of the DigiCash™ system have begun to make use of a redundancy function f with message recovery. This coin structure can be accommodated with only minor modifications to the scheme we present here.

Note that there are digital cash systems other than DigiCash™ that rely on the use of RSA signatures, e.g., the "X-cash" scheme described in [5]. Our trustee token scheme may be applied equally well to the anonymous variants of such systems.

3 Our Scheme

3.1 Key Ideas

Before interacting with the Bank in our system, the User obtains from the Trustee a set of trustee tokens $\{M_i\}$. Recall from Section 1 that a trustee token is essentially a short (say, 10-50 bit) proof that the blinded information the User is presenting to the Bank has been seen and its correctness verified by the Trustee. This proof is presented to the Bank when the User withdraws a coin. It reveals no information to the Bank about the coin the User obtains. Note that for the sake of simplicity, we assume in our presentation that one trustee token is used for each coin withdrawal. As we show later, however, a single token can in fact be used for multiple coins.

Our scheme makes use of an enhancement to improve communications and storage efficiency. On performing a withdrawal from the Bank, the User generates her coin and blinding data pseudo-randomly from random seeds R and S. In her interaction with the Trustee, it therefore suffices for the User just to transmit R and S: the Trustee is then able to generate all of the desired trustee tokens. The seeds R and S constitute all of the data required by the Trustee to perform owner tracing against the User. Note that R and S are given as separate seeds for notational convenience. In practice, they may be combined into a single seed.

Recall that in the anonymous withdrawal protocol described above, to obtain a coin $(x_i, f^{1/3}(x_i) \bmod N)$, the User sends to the Bank the blinded quantity $r_i^3 f(x_i) \bmod N$. In our protocols, the quantity x_i will contain the User's identifier ID_U encrypted under the public key of the Trustee. This will facilitate coin tracing by the Trustee. We let $x_i = E_{PK_T}(ID_U \parallel s_i)$, where $s_i = PS_S(i)$. Hence x_i may be computed using S and ID_U. The integer r_i is generated from the random seed R. In particular, $r_i = PS_R(i)$.

We are now ready to present the trustee token and coin withdrawal protocols. Note that all computations are performed $\bmod\ N$. To simplify notation, we omit explicit indication of this fact.

3.2 Protocols

Trustee token withdrawal In the trustee token withdrawal protocol, the User proves her identity to the Trustee. She then reveals the secret seeds R and S used to generate the pseudo-random data for withdrawals, and indicates the number j of tokens she wants. The Trustee computes a set of trustee tokens $\{M_i\}_1^j$ on these seeds for $1 \leq i \leq j$. He sends these tokens to the User. The protocol should take place over an authenticated and encrypted channel to prevent compromise of R and S. Figure 2 depicts the trustee token withdrawal protocol.

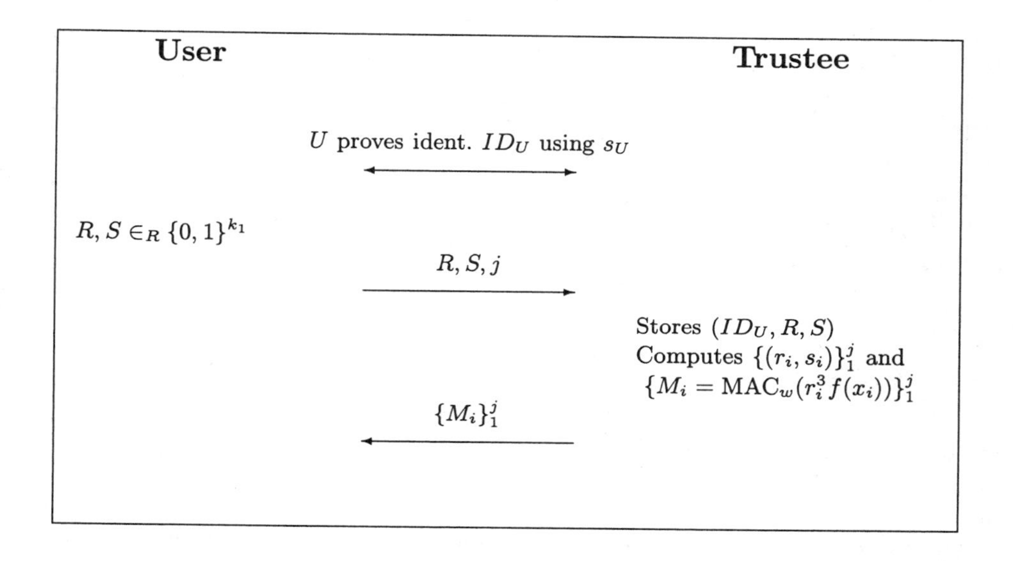

Figure 2. Trustee Token Withdrawal.

Observe that the User can request and store a large number of tokens, since tokens are small (again, say, 10-50 bits apiece). These tokens may be used for future withdrawals without the need for additional contact with the Trustee until the User exhausts her supply. Note also that although we present the token withdrawal protocol as an interaction with an on-line trustee, this need not be the case. For example, trustee tokens can be requested using a secure store-and-forward system, or, alternatively, loaded on a smart card by the Trustee.

Coin withdrawal protocol The coin withdrawal protocol in our scheme is essentially the same as in the underlying Chaumian e-cash protocol. The only difference is that the Bank verifies, by means of a valid trustee token, that the User's withdrawal request has been authorized by the Trustee. To prevent theft of the User's coins, the coin withdrawal protocol should take place over an authenticated and encrypted channel (on which even the Trustee cannot eavesdrop). Figure 3 depicts the coin withdrawal protocol.

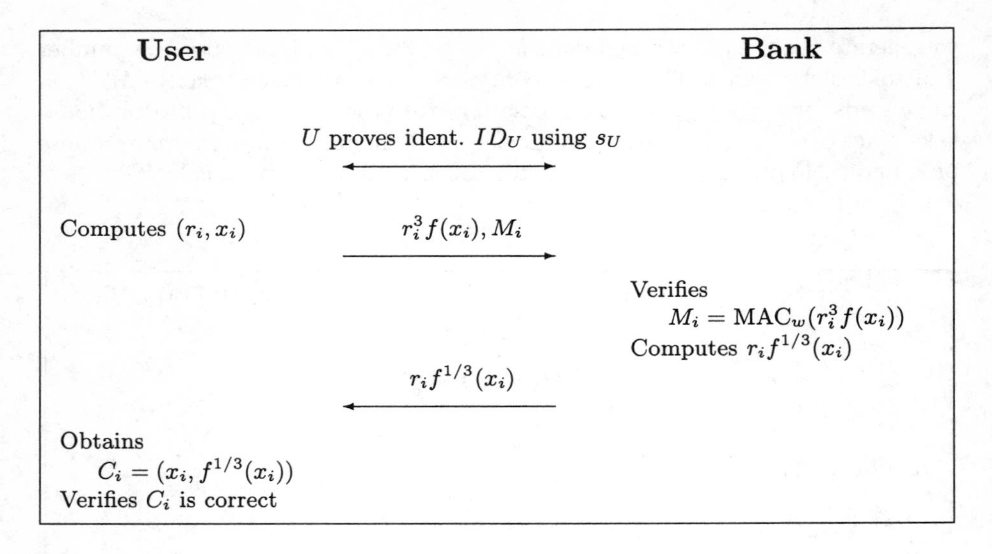

Figure 3. Coin Withdrawal Protocol.

We do not present coin spending and deposit protocols for our scheme, since these are exactly as in the underlying scheme.

Off-line e-cash As mentioned above, our scheme can be applied fairly straightforwardly to off-line variants of Chaumian e-cash, such as [8]. Off-line schemes involve the User's embedding tracing information in coins that gets revealed when a coin is double-spent. To employ trustee tokens, then, in an off-line scheme, it suffices for the User to generate this tracing information from the seed S. Note that our tracing scheme presents the possibility of making off-line systems more efficient by allowing the Trustee to verify coin information incorporated to prevent double-spending. We leave further details to the reader.

Tracing Both coin and owner tracing are straightforward in our system. To trace a coin C_i, the Government presents it (along with a valid court order) to the Trustee. Since $x_i = E_{PK_T}(ID_U \parallel s_i)$, the Trustee may extract ID_U from a coin C_i simply by performing a decryption with its secret key SK_T. To perform owner tracing, the Government presents ID_U (along with a court order) to the Trustee. The Trustee then uses S to compute all $\{x_i\}$. This is sufficient to identify all coins withdrawn by the User ID_U.

Observe that owner tracing in our scheme has an interesting property. In contrast to many other schemes, it is possible for the Trustee to identify not only all coins withdrawn by the User and subsequently deposited, but also all coins in current circulation, and even some coins to be withdrawn by the User in future transactions.

4 Security

We discuss four aspects of the security of our scheme. These are:

1. **User anonymity** The Bank should not be able to extract any information from its interactions with users that reveals which coins have been withdrawn by whom. This property was described more formally above in terms of the definition of blindness given above from [16]. As we shall show, the security of user anonymity in our system is dependent on k_1, the security parameter, i.e., seed length in bits, of the pseudo-random number generator. (An acceptable level of security may be achieved by letting k_1 be about 80.)
2. **Non-forgeability of coins** The users of the system and the Trustee, even in collaboration, should not be able to mint coins without express participation of the Bank. The hardness of forgery in our system is determined by security parameter k_2, equal to the length of the modulus N. (The security parameter k_2 may safely be set at 1024.)
3. **Traceability** The Trustee should be able to perform both coin tracing and owner tracing with high probability. The security of tracing in our system is determined by security parameter k_3, equal to the length of the trustee tokens in bits, and by security parameter k_2. (For most purposes, it would be acceptable to let k_3 be 10-50 bits.)
4. **Inability of Trustee to steal User's cash** Although the Trustee should be able to link the User to her coins, he should not be able to steal her coins or make withdrawals from her account. It is common practice in the literature not consider efforts by the Bank to steal the User's money: it is assumed that the Bank, which has control of the User's account in any case, must be trusted in this respect.

We are able to prove that our system is secure in all four of the above senses, relative to underlying cryptographic primitives. Due to constraints of space, we provide only proof sketches.

In the underlying blind RSA signature scheme, anonymity is unconditional, i.e., information theoretically secure. In particular, use of the blinding factor r ensures that the Bank receives no information about withdrawals. In our system, however, we introduce a pseudo-random number generator PS to enhance efficiency. We can prove the security of anonymity relative to that of PS.

First some definitions. Let PS_S denote the output (of an appropriate length) of PS given seed S. Let A be a polynomial time algorithm that outputs a 0 or a 1. Let $\mathrm{EX}_Z[A(M)]$ denote the expected output of algorithm A given input M over uniform random choices of Z, i.e., the probability that $A(M) = 1$. By a definition equivalent to those in [7], the pseudo-random generator PS may be said to be broken if a polynomial time algorithm A may be found such that $\mid \mathrm{EX}_S[A(PS_S)] - \mathrm{EX}_R[A(R)] \mid = 1/poly$. This notion may be used in a formal proof of the following theorem.

Theorem 1. *If the Bank is able to break the anonymity in our scheme, then it can break the pseudo-random generator PS.*

Proof (sketch): User anonymity is information theoretically when the User employs purely random inputs. If user anonymity can be broken when the User employs a pseudo-random number generator, then it is possible to use the trustee token scheme to distinguish between random and pseudo-random inputs. This is equivalent to breaking the pseudo-random number generator PS. □

We address the issue of forgeability in the following theorem.

Theorem 2. *It is as hard in our scheme for the User and Trustee to forge coins collaboratively as it is for the User to do so herself in the underlying blind digital signature scheme.*

Proof (sketch): Formal proof of this theorem depends upon the fact that the User can simulate the establishment of a secret key between Trustee and Bank. In carrying out the withdrawal protocol in the underlying scheme, the User can then simulate both the role of the Trustee and the role of the Bank in processing trustee tokens. Thus, in our scheme, the Trustee can provide no additional information useful to the User in committing forgery. □

Our next theorem regards the assurance of the Trustee that the User cannot cheat and evade tracing of her coins.

Theorem 3. *Suppose that the User is able to produce a coin which cannot be traced by the Trustee. Then the User was successful at either forging a coin or forging a MAC.*

Proof (sketch): If the User is able to produce an untraceable coin C, then either the User forged C, or the User withdrew C from the Bank. If the User withdrew C, and C is untraceable, then the User must have provided the Bank with an invalid MAC. □

By Theorem 2, it is presumed that the User cannot forge a coin in polynomial time with more than a negligible probability. Therefore the probability that a given coin C held by a cheating User is untraceable is roughly equal to the User's ability to forge a MAC. Under reasonable assumptions (see, e.g., [20,28]) this is about 2^{k_3}, where k_3 is the length of the trustee tokens in our scheme. Thus, a 10-bit trustee token should yield a probability of less than 1/1000 of the User being able to evade tracing for a given coin. For most law-enforcement purposes, this should be adequate, particularly as law enforcement officers are likely to have multiple coins available for tracing in most scenarios. Moreover, the User can only verify the correctness of a MAC by interacting with the Bank. Her efforts at cheating are thus likely to be detected by the Bank before she obtains an untraceable coin. For very high security applications, it may be desirable, however, to use MACs of up to, say, 50 bits. (Note that while MACs of 32 or even 64 bits are typical in most financial transactions, the risks in such cases are much greater, involving the potential for many millions of dollars to be misdirected.)

Finally, we consider the ability of the Trustee to steal the User's money. Although the Trustee has access to the secrets of the User employed to generate coin data, the Trustee does not have access to the User secret s_U. Therefore, the Trustee cannot impersonate the User and withdraw money from the User's account without the Bank's collusion. This yields the following theorem.

Theorem 4. *It is infeasible for the Trustee to steal money from the User's account without the collusion of the Bank or the User.*

Proof (sketch): The Bank only withdraws money from the User's account if authorized to do so through a channel authenticated by means of the User's secret s_U. This channel is authenticated so that no eavesdropper, even the Trustee, can steal the User's coins. □

4.1 Untrustworthy Trustee

In our exposition above, we assume the trustworthiness of Trustee, and that the MAC held jointly by the Trustee and Bank is well protected. In some scenarios, it may be desirable to make weaker security assumptions. We can achieve this – at the cost of computational and storage efficiency – with more extensive record keeping and use of digital signatures by the Trustee.

Compromised MAC If an attacker manages to seize the MAC shared by the Bank and the Trustee, and the theft goes undetected, he can present false Trustee authorization to the Bank. This would enable him to withdraw untraceable coins. There are many possible defences against this attack, representing a spectrum of tradeoffs between efficiency and security. One possible countermeasure would be to refresh the shared MAC on a frequent basis. Another option would be to have the Trustee digitally sign tokens using a public key signature algorithm, rather than MACing them. While this variant on our scheme provides stronger security guarantees, is rather less efficient in terms of the computation required to produce a token.

Failed tracing In the above variants of our scheme, if the Government presents a coin C to the Trustee and the coin cannot be traced, it is unclear whether the Trustee or the Bank permitted withdrawal of an untraceable coin. This can be remedied by having the Trustee digitally sign all tokens, and requiring the Bank to keep track of all coin withdrawal transcripts for each User and the Trustee to keep track of the number of token withdrawals. If untraceable coins surface, then the Bank and Trustee records can be compared, and a determination made as to whether the cheating party is the Bank or the Trustee.

Framing by Trustee In our scheme as described above, the Trustee can frame the User. In particular, the Trustee can generate a value x based on a pair of values (r_i, s_i) not yet employed by the User (or based on false seed pair (R', S')), withdraw from the Bank a coin C_i based on x_i, spend the coin on some illicit purchase, and then claim that the User was responsible, adducing the registered seed pair (R, S) as evidence.

It is possible to prevent attacks of this nature as follows. We have the User digitally sign (R, S). We then have the Bank record all blinded values presented for signing, as well as the number of withdrawals by the User. The Bank rejects any withdrawal request based on a previously presented blinded value. Now if Trustee attempts, under a false identity, to withdraw a coin C_i (based on a User's seed pair (R, S)) when C_i has already been withdrawn, he will be stopped. If he withdraws a coin C_i not already withdrawn by the User, then the User is able to prove, on revealing (R, S) and adducing the Bank's counter as evidence, that she was not responsible for the initial withdrawal of C_i. Hence, framing of the User would require collusion between both the Bank and the Trustee.

Note that framing of the User by the Bank is infeasible, as the Bank has no knowledge of S.

5 Efficiency and Extensions

As explained above, our trustee-based tracing scheme adds very little computational overhead to the underlying coin withdrawal protocol. The Bank must compute a MAC which it would not otherwise compute, but this requires negligible effort in comparison with generation of the signature on the coin. The User must compute the values r_i and x_i from a pseudo-random generator, but these values would likely be computed in some pseudo-random fashion in any case. In fact, if the Bank uses a signature exponent of 3, the User need only compute two pseudo-random values, a hash, six modular multiplications, and a modular inversion per withdrawal (including verification that it has a valid coin). In contrast, the scheme in [19], for example, requires fifteen (160 bit) modular *exponentiations* on the part of the User at the time of withdrawal - and even more if the scheme is to permit owner tracing.

The token withdrawal process requires no computationally intensive cryptographic operations - just a few hashes and computations of MACs. The storage requirements for trustee tokens are also minimal. The Trustee must store a pseudo-random seed for each User (perhaps 80 bits). In the scheme described above, the User must store perhaps 10 bits for each trustee token. A coin in Chaum's scheme consists of roughly 1000 bits [15]. Hence, the storage of a collection of trustee tokens will not be difficult on a device capable of storing anonymous digital cash. In fact, at 10 bits per token, 1K bytes of memory is enough to store more than 800 trustee tokens.

5.1 Improving Efficiency

For the sake of simplicity, we have assumed in the above description of our scheme that one trustee token is used for every withdrawal. It is possible to improve the storage efficiency of trustee tokens substantially by making a single trustee token good for multiple withdrawals, at the cost of some linkage of User identity across coin. Suppose, for instance, that the User always withdraws coins in multiples of ten. We let $M_j = MAC_w(r_{10j}^3, f(x_{10j}), r_{10j+1}^3 f(x_{10j+1}), \ldots, r_{10j+9}^3 f(x_{10j+9}))$.

The token M_0 is good for the first ten withdrawals, M_1 for the next ten withdrawals, etc. In fact, it is not even necessary for the User to withdraw coins in groups of ten. If she wishes to use a trustee token to withdraw fewer than ten coins, shbibliographystylee need only send an appropriate number of blank withdrawal requests, i.e., a sequence of $r_i^3 f(x_i)$ for which she does not wish to receive the corresponding coins. If enough batching is performed, it may be efficient to use digital signatures instead of MACs, eliminating the need for secret key establishment between the Trustee and Bank.

5.2 Multiple Trustees

Our scheme as described has only a single trustee. It is possible, however, to achieve k-out-of-n tracing with any number n of trustees by sharing the secret SK_T among the n trustees in an initialization phase. It is also necessary, however, to share R, S, and ID_U for each user after the corresponding trustee tokens have been distributed. Sharing may be performed using any of a number of threshold and/or proactive secret-sharing techniques, such as, e.g., [9].

While flexible, this method of incorporating multiple trustees into our scheme achieves weaker security guarantees than in many other systems, such as [19]. In [19] and related schemes, secrets enabling compromise of the User's identity are never revealed to the trustees, except during tracing. In the scheme we describe above, the secrets R and S are revealed by the user, and must then be shared among trustees. These secrets, which enable owner tracing (but not coin tracing), are thus vulnerable to attack during the token withdrawal protocol. Hence the entity handling the user secrets acts essentially like a trusted dealer. This is generally acceptable if sufficient controls on handling of user secrets are set in place. A more elegant and robust approach to incorporation of multiple trustees into the proposed scheme would nonetheless represent a desirable advance.

Acknowledgements

The author wishes to express thanks to Markus Jakobsson, Burt Kaliski, and Berry Schoenmakers for their helpful comments and suggestions.

References

1. Digicash, Inc. Web site. http://www.DigiCash.com, 1998.
2. D. Chaum. Blind signatures for untraceable payments. In David Chaum, Ronald L. Rivest, and Alan T. Sherman, editors, *Advances in Cryptology - CRYPTO '82*, pages 199–203. Plemum, 1982.
3. M. Jakobsson and M. Yung. Revocable and versatile e-money. In *3rd ACM Conference on Computer Communications Security*. ACM Press, 1996.
4. D. Chaum and T. Pedersen. Wallet databases with observers. In Ernest F. Brickell, editor, *Advances in Cryptology - CRYPTO '92*, pages 89–105. Springer-Verlag, 1992. LNCS No. 740.

5. M. Jakobsson and A. Juels. X-cash: Executable digital cash. In Rafael Hirschfeld, editor, *Financial Cryptography '98*. Springer-Verlag, 1998. To appear.
6. M. Jakobsson and M. Yung. Distributed Magic-Ink signatures. In Walter Fumy, editor, *Advances in Cryptology - EUROCRYPT '97*, pages 450–464. Springer-Verlag, 1997. LNCS No. 1233.
7. M. Luby. *Pseudorandomness and Cryptographic Applications*. Princeton University Press, 1996.
8. D. Chaum, A. Fiat, and M. Naor. Untraceable electronic cash. In Shafi Goldwasser, editor, *Advances in Cryptology - CRYPTO '88*, pages 319–327. Springer-Verlag, 1988. LNCS No. 403.
9. T. Rabin. A simplified approach to threshold and proactive RSA. In Hugo Krawczyk, editor, *Advances in Cryptology - CRYPTO '98*, pages 89–104. Springer-Verlag, 1998. LNCS No. 1462.
10. M. Stadler, J.M. Piveteau, and J. Camenisch. Fair blind signatures. In Louis C. Guillou and Jean-Jacques Quisquater, editors, *Advances in Cryptology - EUROCRYPT '95*, pages 209–219. Springer-Verlag, 1995. LNCS No. 921.
11. D. Boneh and M. Franklin. Efficient generation of shared RSA keys. In Burton S. Kaliski, Jr., editor, *Advances in Cryptology - CRYPTO '97*, pages 425–439. Springer-Verlag, 1997. LNCS No. 1294.
12. D. M'Raïhi. Cost-effective payment schemes with privacy regulation. In M. Y. Rhee and K. Kim, editors, *Advances in Cryptology – Proceedings of ASIACRYPT '96*, pages 266–275. Springer-Verlag, 1996. LNCS No. 1163.
13. B. von Solms and D. Naccache. On blind signatures and perfect crimes. *Computers and Security*, 11(6):581–583, 1992.
14. D. Pointcheval and J. Stern. Provably secure blind signature schemes. In M. Y. Rhee and K. Kim, editors, *Advances in Cryptology – Proceedings of ASIACRYPT '96*, pages 252–265. Springer-Verlag, 1996. LNCS No. 1163.
15. B. Schoenmakers. Basic security of the ecash™ payment system. In Bart Preenel et al., editors, *Computer Security and Industrial Cryptography: State of the Art and Evolution, ESAT Course*, pages 338 – 352, 1998. LNCS No. 1528. Corrected version available on-line at http://www.win.tue.nl/ berry/papers/cosic.ps.gz.
16. A. Juels, M. Luby, and R. Ostrovsky. Security of blind digital signatures. In Burton S. Kaliski, Jr., editor, *Advances in Cryptology - CRYPTO '97*, pages 150–164. Springer-Verlag, 1997. LNCS No. 1294.
17. J. Camenisch, J.-M. Piveteau, and M. Stadler. An efficient fair payment system. In *3rd ACM Conference on Computer Communications Security*, pages 88–94. ACM Press, 1996.
18. A.J. Menezes, P.C. van Oorschot, and S.A. Vanstone. *Handbook of Applied Cryptography*. CRC Press, 1996.
19. G. Davida, Y. Frankel, Y. Tsiounis, and M. Yung. Anonymity control in e-cash systems. In Rafael Hirschfeld, editor, *Financial Cryptography '97*, pages 1–16. Springer-Verlag, 1997. LNCS No. 1318.
20. M. Bellare, R. Canetti, and H. Krawczyk. Keying hash functions for message authentication. In Neal Koblitz, editor, *Advances in Cryptology - CRYPTO '96*, pages 1–16. Springer-Verlag, 1996. LNCS No. 1109.
21. E.F. Brickell, P. Gemmell, and D. Kravitz. Trustee-based tracing extensions to anonymous cash and the making of anonymous change. In *Proceedings of the Sixth Annual ACM-SIAM Symposium on Discrete Algorithms*, pages 457–466, 1995.
22. L. Law, S. Sabett, and J. Solinas. How to make a mint: the cryptography of anonymous digital cash. Technical Report 96-10-17, National Security Agency, 1996. Available at http://www.ffhsj.com/bancmail/bancpage.html.

23. J. Camenisch, U. Maurer, and M. Stadler. Digital payment systems with passive anonymity-revoking trustees. In *Computer Security - ESORICS '96*, pages 31–43. Springer-Verlag, 1996. LNCS No. 1146.
24. J. Camenisch, U. Maurer, and M. Stadler. Digital payment systems with passive anonymity-revoking trustees. *Journal of Computer Security*, 5(1):254–265, 1997.
25. Y. Frankel, Y. Tsiounis, and M. Yung. Indirect discourse proofs: Achieving fair off-line e-cash. In M. Y. Rhee and K. Kim, editors, *Advances in Cryptology – Proceedings of ASIACRYPT '96*, pages 286–300. Springer-Verlag, 1996. LNCS No. 1163.
26. M. Jakobsson and M. Yung. Applying anti-trust policies to increase trust in a versatile e-money system. In Rafael Hirschfeld, editor, *Financial Cryptography '97*, pages 217–238. Springer-Verlag, 1997. LNCS No. 1318.
27. D. M'Raïhi and D. Pointcheval. Distributed trustees and revokability: A framework for internet payment. In Rafael Hirschfeld, editor, *Financial Cryptography '98*. Springer-Verlag, 1998. To appear.
28. M. Bellare, R. Guerin, and P. Rogaway. XOR MACs: New methods for message authentication using finite pseudo-random functions. In Don Coppersmith, editor, *Advances in Cryptology - CRYPTO '95*, pages 15–28. Springer-Verlag, 1995. LNCS No. 963.

Flow Control: A New Approach for Anonymity Control in Electronic Cash Systems

Tomas Sander and Amnon Ta–Shma

International Computer Science Institute
1947 Center Street, Berkeley, CA 94704, USA
{sander,amnon}@icsi.berkeley.edu

Abstract. Anonymity features of electronic payment systems are important for protecting privacy in an electronic world. However, complete anonymity prevents monitoring financial transactions and following the money trail, which are important tools for fighting serious crimes. To solve these type of problems several "escrowed cash" systems, that allow a "Trustee" to trace electronic money, were suggested. In this paper we suggest a completely different approach to anonymity control based on the fact that law enforcement is mainly concerned with large anonymous electronic payments. We describe a payment system that effectively limits the amount of money a user can spend anonymously in a given time frame. To achieve this we describe a technique to make electronic money strongly non-transferable. Our payment system protects the privacy of the honest user who plays by the rules, while introducing significant hurdles for several criminal abuses of the system.

1 Introduction

Anonymous electronic payment systems are regarded as essential for the protection of the privacy of consumers participating in electronic transactions. On the other hand anonymity features have the potential of being abused for criminal activities. These include tax evasion, money laundering and blackmailing scenarios. To address these concerns several "escrowed cash" systems that allow to revoke the anonymity have been proposed, cf. [8,3,4,13,17]. Although these schemes differ in their individual features, they share the common characteristic of the existence of Trustees, i.e., escrow agents that are able to revoke the anonymity of each individual payment (cf. [8] for an overview and further references). The supported revocation features are usually coin tracing (the ability to associate a deposited coin with a withdrawal) and owner tracing which allows to identify the owner of a spent coin.

In this paper we describe a different approach to help to prevent criminals from abusing electronic cash systems which avoid the necessity to make each individual payment potentially traceable. It is based on the observation that honest users and abusive users of electronic cash usually have different interests in using anonymous money. Criminals are usually interested in huge anonymous transactions (e.g., laundering one million dollars that stem from drug deals)

M. Franklin (Ed.): FC'99, LNCS 1648, pp. 46–61, 1999.

while the common user usually does not even have these amounts of money, and is usually interested in small anonymous transactions (e.g. buying a political magazine or an adult video dealing with a certain fetish he does not want to be revealed - neither to his wife nor to the government). For high value transactions like buying a new car or a house, anonymity is not really an issue for most honest users.

This discrepancy is also reflected in U.S. policy: The Bank Secrecy Act, passed in 1970, instructs banks to report any cash transactions exceeding $10,000 to the IRS. These regulations practically eliminate the anonymity of huge cash transactions. Stanley E. Morris, at that time director of the U.S. Department of Treasury's Financial Crime Investigation Network stated that his organization is mainly interested in *large* payments [16]. Furthermore Morris suggests in [16] to solve some of the problems associated with electronic cash transactions by putting limits on the amounts people can spend with cyber payment and smart card based systems.

Thus in contrast to electronic cash systems with revokable anonymity that limit the overall privacy users of electronic payment systems enjoy, by making each individual transaction potentially traceable, we limit the privacy of users by allowing them to have unconditionally anonymous transactions *up to a certain amount*, i.e., we limit the money flow each user can create in a certain time frame. Via regulations one may enforce that to obtain anonymous electronic cash a user needs to open an electronic cash account, and when doing so he has to identify himself (with a photo-id, say). Furthermore, the bank checks that each person holds only one such account, and each month each person has the opportunity to buy at most, say, $ 10,000 in anonymous electronic cash from the bank.

However, there are at least two problems with this naive approach. First a user may accumulate large amounts of electronic cash throughout time. Second, and more serious, electronic money can be traded. Because the money is absolutely anonymous it can change hands without leaving any traces and anonymous money could be accumulated in large sums.

To avoid money–trading we introduce in Section 2 the requirement of *non–transferability* for a payment system and argue that it is an important feature to have for electronic cash system to limit criminal abuses. In Section 4 we describe an on–line system that is non–transferable, amount–limited and guarantees unconditional payer anonymity. It builds upon the provable secure system presented by Damgard [6] (and later corrected in [20]). This basic system has the disadvantage of forcing users to exchange their unused expired coins every month. This gives the bank a good estimate of the amount a user has spent per month and may be regarded as a privacy violation. In Section 5 we describe a coupon based variant of this protocol that achieves accumulation control and does not have this disadvantage. Both systems are described in the general computation model and make use of secure multi party computations, so they are polynomial–time, but not efficient in a practical sense. In Section 6 we sketch how an efficient, off-line, amount-limited payment system can be constructed from Brands' scheme [2,1].Finally in Section 7 we argue how this helps to defend against common attacks and abuses of electronic payment systems.

2 Non–transferability and Amount–Limitedness

2.1 On the importance of non–transferability

A considerable amount of work has been done to design payment systems that are transferable (i.e. where a coin received during a payment can be further spent by the receiver without intermediation of a bank, cf e.g. [18,19,5,7]), so that electronic cash enjoys some of the conveniences of physical cash. However physical cash is only conveniently transferable in small amounts (e.g. also by mail) or in large amounts between users that are physically close to each other. It was stated in a recent report on research performed by RAND for FinCEN [15] that “the physical movement of large quantities of cash is the money launderer's biggest problem”. This hurdle to criminal abuse is potentially removed by cyberpayment systems ([15]): “The international dimension of these systems, and the fact that value transfers may take place with rapidity and with a degree of anonymity that impedes oversight by governmental authorities, is clearly a serious concern.” Thus transferable electronic money seems not to be a good idea from the perspective of crime prevention.

Developers of (anonymity controlled) electronic payment systems have not yet paid explicit attention to the problems transferability presents. To illustrate this problem consider a non-anonymous system that is also fully transferable (each coin carries a serial number that is recorded during withdrawal and deposit). At first sight the authorities can have full information about the system, but is it really so?

In a fully-transferable system, after a few hand changes of the cash token among different users and shops it is likely to be *practically* anonymous, and the information of who withdrew the coin in the first place is probably going to be irrelevant as the transaction chain of the token during its life span will be almost impossible to reconstruct. Money changing organizations may exploit transferability intentionally to create huge amounts of anonymous money that then can be used for anonymous (criminal) transactions. Thus, a revokable but also easily transferable escrowed cash system might turn out to be too weak. Recall that the off–line electronic cash systems that had been suggested so far are only non–transferable up to the degree that payers and receivers are not willing to take double spending related risks.

2.2 How to build a non-transferable system

A coin usually passes three stages in its life: a user (whose identity is known to the bank) withdraws a coin. We call him the *owner* of the coin. In the payment phase a merchant is *paid* with a coin. In the deposit phase a merchant deposits a coin into the bank. We say a payment scheme is *non-transferable* if only the person who withdrew a coin is able to use it for payment. Thus, dollar bills are clearly transferable, checks are usually transferable but can also be made non-transferable, and credit card payments are normally non–transferable.

Can a non–transferable system be built? Suppose Alice withdraws a coin c. If Alice gives the coin c to Bob, along with all the information needed for paying with it, then Bob can use the coin c himself, and the money is made transferable. In general, as coins are bit strings that can be easily copied and transmitted it seems impossible to achieve non-transferability by purely technical means, unless tamper–resistant hardware is used. Thus instead of making it technically impossible for a user to copy and transfer coins we want to design a system in which a (rational) user does *not want* to transfer his coins.

We suggest the following ways of achieving that: we assume each user holds *one* secret that he does not want to (or can not) give away. We call this a "non–transferability secret". When a user withdraws electronic money his non–transferability secret is imprinted in the coin, and the payment protocol assures that only a person knowing this secret is able to *pay* with the coin. Thus, giving away the knowledge how to spend the coin gives away the non–transferability secret which he does not want.

One way to provide users with secrets they do not want to give away is to have a public key infrastructure in place such that liabilities are assigned to the secret key of a digital signature scheme. For example if a receiver of the secret key could completely impersonate the owner in a digital world, e.g. for receiving loans, signing contracts, etc. This secret key seems to be well suited to serve as a non–transferability secret which its owner may not *want* to give away. Examples for physical protection measures are: the secret is generated and stored on a tamper–resistant device (like a smart card) in a way that the secret is kept hidden from its owner. Even more, the usage of the device could require a biometric authentication of the holder as comparing the fingerprint of the card holder to the registered fingerprint.

It is clear that no system is absolutely non-transferable. E.g., a criminal can kidnap his victim, "cut off his finger" and use the stolen smart card to make a transaction. However, as each user is limited in the amount of coins he can spend, to get a significant amount of money a criminal will have to do that procedure for many persons. While everything is theoretically possible, we consider it unlikely.

A similar idea using non-transferability secrets has been suggested by Dwork, Lotspiech and Naor in their construction of "digital signets" [9] in the context of copyright protection for digital goods. The concept of non–transferable secrets is probably useful in many other situations where one does not want the user "to give something away", and for anonymity controlled payment systems in particular. It may be desirable to add this feature to other existing payment systems to make their anonymity control features stronger. We expect that many existing payment schemes can be technically modified to achieve non–transferability. In this paper we show how to add these features to Damgard's on-line cash system, and to Brands' efficient off-line system.

Jakobsson and M'Raihi recently described an on-line payment system which is account based [12]: users initiate fund transfers from their bank account to another user's bank account. Anonymity is achieved by a mix–network involving banks and an Ombudsman by which fund transfers are processed. By its account based nature, no "value" that could be transferred ever leaves the bank. Thus, although the system was not designed to be non-transferable, the system has strong non–transferability features by its very nature. Amount–limitedness can be added easily to the system by restricting the amount of funds a user is allowed to transfer per time frame. However the anonymity of transactions is revokable by a quorum of banks (and Ombudsman), and the system is on-line.

2.3 Technical requirements

From now on we assume that the infrastructure provides each user with a non–transferability secret and formalize the technical requirements that a payment systems needs to have to make use of it:

Non–transferability :

- If a coin c was withdrawn by A and c is spend by C, then C knows the non–transferability secret S_A of A.
- Under no scenario of system events any coalition of polynomial time players can learn any information about a non–transferability secret S_A of a user not within that coalition.

Amount limitedness : During each time frame T_i each user U can spend at most b electronic coins that were withdrawn by him.

We first note that amount–limitedness is very easy to achieve by restricting the amount of coins a user can withdraw within a time frame. To avoid that users spend coins that have been withdrawn during earlier time frames coins may carry e.g. an expiration date and it could be enforced that coins are only used during the time frame in which they were withdrawn. Yet, as argued, this property is not of much use unless it is combined with the non–transferability property.

We now concentrate on the non–transferability definition. The first part of the definition requires that a person who spends a coin knows the non–transferability secret of the person who withdrew that coin. Thus, the non–transferability property is useful in the real-world only when users are unwilling (or unable or both) to surrender their non–transferability secrets.

The second part of the non–transferability definition requires that under no chain of system events a non–transferability key is revealed. This definition is more delicate than it first seems. Brands' off-line system, e.g., is a system where each user has a secret that normally remains statistically secure, and is only revealed when a user double spends. Brands' system does not achieve, as it is, the non–transferability requirement as double spending is a possible chain of events that results in the revelation of a non–transferability secret. This is clearly not appropriate as a disclosure of the non–transferable secret may cause serious damage for the user. Our off-line system achieves the above strict requirement. In particular, each user in our system has two secrets: one is the non–transferability secret (that never gets revealed) while the other is revealed whenever a user double spends.

3 System

The participants: users, merchants, a bank, a CA and the government.

Infrastructure: We assume there is a public-key infrastructure (PKI) in place s.t. each participant holds a public/private key pair (P_U, S_U), there is a reliable way to authenticate a user's public key P_U via a CA. We make the central:

NTA (Non-transferability Assumption) - We assume each user U has a *non-transferability* secret S_U s.t. most users U will not do any action that will reveal their non-transferability secret S_U to any other group of players.

Finally we assume that the bank's and CA's public keys are known to everybody.

Time: We assume that there are consecutive time frames denoted $T_1, T_2, \ldots$. (in our earlier examples the T_i's were consecutive months)

Amount–limit: We assume that there is a limit b, s.t. that each user is allowed to spend b electronic coins anonymously during a time frame T_i.

Computing Power: All participants are probabilistic polynomial time players.

Trust Model: Users and merchants trust the bank not to steal their money. The government (i.e. the party who is interested in controlling anonymity) trusts the CA to reliably identify persons, and the bank to perform the necessary checks (as described in the protocol) reliably during all transactions. The network is reliable and communication over it is anonymous.

System Events: We focus on the following system events: Opening an account, withdrawing money, paying money to a merchant and depositing money (or expired coins) at the bank.

We have the following requirements for our system:

Unforgeability: It is infeasible for any coalition of participants in the system excluding the bank to create an amount of payments accepted by the bank that exceeds the amount of withdrawn coins.

Non–transferability: is defined as in Subsection 2.3.

Amount limitedness: is defined as in Subsection 2.3.

Unconditional Payer Anonymity: A payer has unconditional anonymity, i.e. transcripts of withdrawals are statistically uncorrelated to transcripts of payments and deposits.

4 A Protocol for an On–Line Amount Limited Cash System

Our protocol is based on the system suggested by Damgard [6] with the correction suggested by [20]. At withdrawal time Alice receives a signature from the bank for a coin M by employing a secure computation protocol that encodes the non–transferable secret of Alice in M, and at spending time Alice presents M along with a proof that she knows a signature for it. We start with some necessary background:

Digital Signatures: A digital signature scheme for signing messages M by B consists of a (possibly randomized) polynomial time signature algorithm $\sigma(M, S_B)$ which produces a signature of M using the secret key S_B of B and a polynomial time verification algorithm $V(\sigma, M, P_B)$ which returns "true" iff σ is a valid signature for the message M w.r.t the public key P_B. For formal definitions see, e.g., [11]. A signature scheme is history independent if an honest signer can sign a message without knowing his previous signatures. Signature schemes that are existentially unforgeable (cf. [11]) and simultaneously history–independent exist under the random oracle hypothesis (cf. e.g. [21]), and under the general assumption that one–way permutations exist [14]. [1]

Secure computation: Two players, Alice and Bob, hold private inputs x and y respectively. If one way trapdoor permutations exist [26,10] then for any functionality (f_A, f_B) there is a multi-round two party protocol s.t. Alice learns $f_A(x, y)$ and Bob learns $f_B(x, y)$ with the following properties: Both players have computational confidence in the result , Alice has *perfect* privacy and Bob has *conditional* privacy . Furthermore the value $f_A(x, y)$ can be learned by Alice only as the last message of the protocol. There is an efficient simulator which can simulate the view of each of the players (cf. [10]), even in the presence of early abortions and malicious faults.

4.1 The protocol

Opening an account: During account opening a user Alice identifies herself to the bank (e.g. by a driver's license or with a certificate issued by a CA). The bank checks the authenticity of the user's public key. The bank checks that Alice does not have another electronic cash account by querying its database of registered users. The bank registers the user's identity together with the user's public key.

Withdrawal: Alice identifies herself to the bank. The bank checks that the amount of electronic coins withdrawn by Alice in the time frame T_i is smaller then the maximal amount b. Alice chooses a random string R. Alice and the bank engage themselves in a secure computation with perfect privacy for Alice. The public data are $P_A, P_B, Time$, Alice's private input is S_A, R and the Bank's private input is S_B. The outputs are obtained in the following way. First it is verified that S_A is a secret key matching P_A and if not the output FAILED is given to Alice and the bank, otherwise the bank gets COIN ISSUED and Alice's output is the bank's signature $\sigma\ (S_A \circ Time \circ R\ ,\ S_B)$.

After receiving the output Alice checks that this is indeed a valid signature for $M = S_A \circ Time \circ R$. The bank deducts the value of the electronic coin from her account and increases the number of coins withdrawn by Alice during the time frame T_i by 1.

[1] In [14] even a computationally *blind* secure signature scheme is described. However we do not need the blindness property for our protocol to work.

Spending: Alice wants to spend a coin $M = S_A \circ Time \circ R$ to a merchant C. Alice sends R to the merchant. Alice sends R and the merchant's identity P_C to the bank. Alice and the bank again engage themselves in a secure computation with perfect privacy for Alice. This time the public data are $P_C, R, Time$ and Alice's private input is $S_A, \sigma = \sigma(S_A \circ Time \circ R)$. If $V(\sigma, S_A \circ Time \circ R, P_B) = True$, i.e. if σ is a valid signature of $S_A \circ Time \circ R$ the Bank's output is VALID, otherwise NOT VALID. If the output is VALID, the bank checks that R has not been spent before, and records it in its database of spent coins. The bank credits C's account and sends C a notice that a payment for transaction R has occurred to his account.

Depositing expired coins: Alice wants to deposit her unused expired coins to her account. This is implemented in an analogous, obvious way. Alice identifies herself to the bank. It is checked, via a secure computation, that Alice knows the secret encrypted in the coin and that this secret matches the public key registered with her account.

Notice that the bank does not know what signatures were produced and therefore the t'th signature can not depend on the previous $t-1$ signatures, which forces us to use history-independent signature schemes.

Theorem 1. *The payment system described above achieves non-forgeability, unconditional payer anonymity, non-transferability and is amount limited.*

Proof. The proof for non–forgeability is standard and follows the arguments in [6,20]. We omit it here. Amount–limitedness is immediate.

Non-Transferability: Suppose Charlie is spending a coin. Then Charlie convinces the bank with a secure computation that he knows some M along with its signature σ. It is easy to see that the coin must have been withdrawn before. Let us assume it was obtained by Alice. At withdrawal time Alice had to posses $S_A, Time$ and R_A s.t. $M = S_A \circ Time \circ R_A$, and S_A matches Alice's public key P_A. Hence, in particular, Charlie who knows M also knows S_A the secret key of Alice.

Anonymity: We need to show that the distribution the bank sees at deposit time π_D is statistically independent of the distribution at withdrawal time π_W. What does the bank get at deposit time? By the privacy property of secure computation the bank only gets to know a VALID/NOT VALID answer (so all valid coins generate a VALID answer) and a value R which is statistically independent of π_W and all previous values seen by the bank. Thus π_D is statistically independent of π_W. The situation does not change even if some of the other players collaborate with the bank.

□

In the next section we describe a refinement of this basic protocol for non–transferable, amount–limited, electronic cash which allows for greater flexibility in the use of the system.

5 Anonymity Coupons

There are two disadvantages of the on–line amount limited cash system described in the last paragraph. First a user has to deposit and exchange his expired coins that he did not use during a time frame T_i. This gives the bank a good estimate of the amount a user has spent during T_i and may be regarded as a privacy violation. Second the amount limitedness property of this payment system limits its use as a universal payment system, as a user's total transactions using these electronic coins can not exceed the limit b during T_i.

Both disadvantages can be solved with the following variant of the described payment system that we sketch here briefly. To do this we introduce "anonymity coupons"[2]. Coupons look like coins: they are of the form $(S_A \circ Time \circ R)$, i.e., they encode Alice's non-transferability secret and the time frame $Time$, together with a signature T from the bank created with the bank's coupon signature scheme. However coupons do not carry any monetary value and a user Alice obtains $b = 10.000$ of them at the beginning of each month *for free.* Their sole function is to limit the amount a user can spend anonymously. Electronic coins (that do carry monetary value) can be withdrawn *without amount restrictions* for the user. Coins may carry an expiration date much longer then T_i. Coins, too, contain Alice's non–transferability secret. The spending protocol is modified as follows: During payment Alice has the choice to make an anonymous or a non–anonymous payment. In anonymous payments Alice pays both with a valid coin and a valid coupon (and for that she needs, as before, to know the common non–transferability secret imprinted in them). In non–anonymous payments Alice reveals her public identity, pays with a coin only and proves that the non–transferability secret imprinted in the coin matches her public key.

After having demonstrated the ideas and concepts of non–transferable, amount–limited electronic cash in the framework of general computation based payment systems we now turn to the description of a practical system.

6 An Efficient Off–Line System

We now modify Brands' system s.t. double-spending does not reveal the non-transferability secret of the user. In our system each user has one fixed identity (P_A, S_A) where S_A serves as the non-transferability secret and remains private even in the case of double spending, and one per transaction secret (u_1, u_2, s) that gets revealed in case of his double spending. This results in some changes to Brands' system which we now describe. We mention that our modification also makes the system overspending robust, i.e. even if a user double spent he can not be framed for double spendings he has not done.

Let m', g_1, d_1, d_2, d_3 be elements of a prime order subgroup of Z_p^*. We say that a value m' has a representation (a_1, a_2, a_3, a_4) with respect to a set of generators (g_1, d_1, d_2, d_3) if $m' = g_1^{a_1} d_1^{a_2} d_2^{a_3} d_4^{a_4}$. Brands suggested a *restrictive*

[2] see also [24], where unlinkable serial transactions were studied for some other possible applications of our techniques.

blind signature scheme such that after withdrawal Alice (and also any other participant) can know only one representation of m' and this representation has to take a specific form. In our case it takes the form (sS_A, su_1, su_2, s) where S_A is Alice's non–transferability secret, and u_1, u_2, s are random numbers of her choice. The blinded signature is received for $m' = m^s$ where m is the message sent to the bank. At spending time the payer has to reveal $a_3 + ca_4$ for a random challenge c, and to prove knowledge of $a_1 = sS_A$ and $a_4 = s$. ¿From this we can deduce non-transferability, anonymity and more.

In our system S_A always remains private, even in the case of double spending. The per transaction secret (u_1, u_2, s) gets revealed in case of double spending. Using s the bank can associate the double spent coin with the user who withdrew it. We use a variant of Brands' system that was suggested by Brands ([1] , pages 31-32, Method 1) and has the feature that double-spending reveals some parts of the information the user has about the representation of the coin, while keeping other parts secret. This results in a minor inefficiency by increasing the number of rounds at withdrawal and payment time.

6.1 The protocol

Bank's setup: p, q long enough primes. $p = cq + 1$ for some integer c. G_q is the subgroup of order q of Z_p^*. The bank picks random elements $g, g_1, d_1, d_2, d_3 \in G_q$, a secret $x \in G_q$ and computes $h = g^x$. The bank uniformly selects hash functions $\mathcal{H}, \mathcal{H}_0$ from a collection of collision intractable hash functions. The bank makes $p, q, g, g_1, d_1, d_2, d_3$ and its public key h public and keeps x secret. By convention $a \cdot b$ is computed modulo p, except for exponents where $g^l = g^{l \bmod q}$ that are computed modulo q as g will always be taken from G_q.

Account opening: Alice identifies herself along with a number $P_A (= g_1^{S_A})$, and proves to the bank that S_A is Alice's non–transferability secret. The bank records Alice's identity together with P_A.

Withdrawal: Alice identifies herself to the bank. Then she picks $u_1, u_2 \in_R Z_q$ and computes $T = d_1^{u_1} d_2^{u_2}$. She sends T to the Bank along with a proof of knowledge of a representation of T according to the generators (d_1, d_2) (Proofs of knowledge of a representation are performed as described in [1]). Then Alice obtains a "restrictively blind" signature [1] of $m = T \cdot P_A \cdot d_3$. Alice will end up with a Schnorr-type [23] signature on $m' = m^s$ where s is a secret random number chosen by Alice. We also require that $m' \neq 1$. The signature is $sig(m') = (z', a', b', r')$ s.t. $g^{r'} = h^{H(m', z', a', b')}$ and $(m')^{r'} = (z')^{H(m', z', a', b')} b'$. See Figure 1 . We note that Alice knows a representation of m' according to the generators g_1, d_1, d_2, d_3, namely $(sS_A, u_1 s, u_2 s, s)$. The bank records that user P_A obtained a blind signature on m and deducts the corresponding amount from her account.

Payment: During payment Alice supplies the merchant with the coin $(m', sig(m'))$. She receives a challenge $c \in Z_q$ and answers with $a_3 + ca_4$, where (a_1, a_2, a_3, a_4) is her representation of m' according to the generator–base (g_1, d_1, d_2, d_3). The protocol for this is identical to ([1] , pages 31-2, method 1). See Figure 2.

Fig. 1. Withdrawal

Alice		Bank
$u_1, u_2 \in_R Z_q$, $T \leftarrow d_1^{u_1} \cdot d_2^{u_2}$	$\xrightarrow{T}$	
	Alice proves knowledge of representation of T with respect to (d_1, d_2) $\leftrightarrow$	
		$m = T \cdot P_A \cdot d_3$ $z \leftarrow m^x$, $w \in_R Z_Q$ $a \leftarrow g^w$, $b \leftarrow m^w$
$s, u, v \in_R Z_Q$	$\xleftarrow{z,a,b}$	
$z' \leftarrow z^s$, $m' \leftarrow m^s$, $m' \neq 1$ $a' \leftarrow a^u g^v$, $b' \leftarrow b^{us}(m')^v$ $c' \leftarrow \mathcal{H}(m', z', a', b')$ $c \leftarrow \frac{c'}{u}$ *mod* q	$\xrightarrow{c}$	
$h^c a \stackrel{?}{=} g^r$, $z^c b \stackrel{?}{=} m^r$	$\xleftarrow{r}$	$r \leftarrow w + cx$ *mod* q
$r' \leftarrow ur + v$ *mod* q		

Deposit: The merchant sends the transcript of the payment protocol execution to the bank and the bank checks its correctness. The bank checks that m' has not been spent before and then credits the merchant's account. If the same payment transcript is deposited twice the bank knows that the merchant tries to deposit the same coin twice. Otherwise if there are two different transcripts for the same money, they reveal two different linear equations $r = a_3 + ca_4$ and $r' = a_3 + c'a_4$. ¿From these two linear equations the bank computes $a_4 = s$. Recall that $m' = m^s \neq 1$, thus $q \not| s$, and as q is prime it follows that $(s, q) = 1$. Therefore, using the extended gcd algorithm, the bank can compute a number l s.t. $s \cdot l = 1(\ mod\ q)$. Now, $(m')^l = m^{ls\ mod\ q} = m$. The bank then searches its database to find the transaction in which m was withdrawn, revealing the identity of the double spender.

6.2 Security of the off–line system

For the security proofs we make the following (reasonable) assumptions, that have been commonly used in security proofs for (variants of) Brands' system. We assume *DLOG* is hard and make the

Random oracle assumption : $\mathcal{H}, \mathcal{H}_0$ behave like random functions.

Withdrawal protocol assumption : The withdrawal protocol is a restrictive blind signature protocol, i.e. for the message $m = g_1^{a_1} d_1^{a_2} d_2^{a_3} d_3$ the receiver obtains a signed message of the form $g_1^{sa_1} d_1^{sa_2} d_2^{sa_3} d_3^s$ for a number s.

Theorem 2. *Under the above assumptions, the system is non–transferable, unforgeable and allows to detect double–spenders. Single–spenders have uncondi-*

Fig. 2. Payment

Alice		Merchant
$m' = g_1^{a_1} d_1^{a_2} d_2^{a_3} d_3^{a_4}$	$\overset{m', sig(m')}{\longrightarrow}$	Verify signature , $m' \neq 1$
		$TD \leftarrow$ Time/Date
		$ID \leftarrow$ Merchant-ID
	$\overset{c}{\longleftarrow}$	$c = \mathcal{H}_0(TD, ID, m')$
	$\overset{r = a_3 + c a_4}{\longrightarrow}$	
	Alice proves knowledge of representation of $\frac{m'}{d_2^r}$ w.r.t. $(g_1, d_1, \frac{d_3}{d_2^c})$ $\leftrightarrow$	

tional anonymity. If a user double spends his identity is revealed, but no knowledge is gained about his non-transferability secret key. If, in addition, Alice is required to sign each interaction during withdrawal, then no polynomial time bank can falsely accuse her of double spending she has not done.

Proof.
Unforgeability: Schnorr-type signatures are unforgeable under the random oracle assumption [21]. Brands showed that this implies that it is infeasible to existentially forge a coin [1].

Anonymity: If a user spends each coin once, then the information that the bank gets to learn includes: T and c at withdrawal time, m' and $sig(m')$ along with r on spending time and proofs of knowledge of a representation. Proofs of knowledge of a representation do not reveal, in an information theoretical sense, any information about the representation the user has. We next observe that until r is revealed the bank gets to see only T and has no clue as to the actual representation $T = d_1^{u_1} d_2^{u_2}$ the user has for it. Thus, from the bank's point of view, u_2 and hence $r = su_2 + cs$ (for a known c) is uniform and independent of all other values. We are left with T, c, m' and $sig(m')$ that participated in the signature generation. However as the signature scheme is unconditionally blind we have that c and T are independent of m' and $sig(m')$ as required. Thus the withdrawal and spending transcripts are statistically independent.

The non-transferability secret is protected: The non-transferability secret is protected even when a user double spends. To see that notice that the only place a user Alice uses her knowledge of S_A is in the payment protocol where she gives a proof of knowledge of a representation. However, this proof of knowledge, provably does not reveal any information about the actual representation Alice knows. All the rest can be simulated with the knowledge of P_A alone, and the bank can simulate it itself. Thus the bank does not get any information that he could not have obtained from P_A itself.

Double spending: First, because of the unforgeability property, when a user Alice double spends she uses a coin m' that has been withdrawn before, let us say w.l.o.g. again by Alice. As all players (including the bank) are polynomial time players they can not find two different representations for any number in G_q (unless with negligible probability) and in particular, Alice knows at payment time at most one representation (a_1, a_2, a_3, a_4) of m' with respect to the generators (g_1, d_1, d_2, d_3). As the signature scheme is restrictive the representation Alice knows of m' has the form (sb_1, sb_2, sb_3, sb_4) where (b_1, b_2, b_3, b_4) is the representation of $m = TP_A d_3$. Now we note that Alice knows a representation of T with respect to (d_1, d_2), let's say this representation is (u_1, u_2). Hence Alice knows a representation $(S_A, u_1, u_2, 1)$ of m, and as we noted before, this is the only representation *Alice* knows for m. We conclude that $b_4 = 1$ and $a_4 = s$.

If Alice convinces the merchant at payment time, then (except for negligible probability) she has to reveal $a_3 + ca_4$ by the the soundness property of the proof of knowledge protocol. Now, if Alice double spends the same coin appears in two payment transcripts with two different linear equations, and a_3 and $a_4 = s$ are revealed. In particular s is revealed and the bank can find m from m' as described in the protocol. Finally, the bank has full knowledge as to who withdrew m.

Non–transferability: If a user Charlie spends a coin m' this coin must have been withdrawn before. Let us say Alice withdrew the coin. As before, Alice knows a representation (sS_A, su_1, su_2, s) of m' with respect to the generators (g_1, d_1, d_2, d_3). By the properties of the proof of knowledge of a representation r must be $a_3 + ca_4$. We further notice that Alice knows a representation (a_1, a_2, a_4) of $\frac{m'}{d_2^r}$ with respect to the generators $(g_1, d_1, \frac{d_3}{d_2^c})$. Charlie also proves he knows a representation of $\frac{m'}{d_2^r}$ with respect to $(g_1, d_1, \frac{d_3}{d_2^c})$. As all the players are polynomial Charlie (in coalition with other players including Alice) can only know one representation (a_1, a_2, a_4), as polynomial players can know at most one solution to the representation problem. Hence, he knows $a_4 = s$ and $a_1 = sS_A$, and Charlie knows S_A.

Framing–freeness: If the bank claims Alice double spent $m' = m^s$ it has to present the signature Alice gave for m. Therefore, if the bank claims Alice double spent $m' = m^s$, then indeed Alice withdrew m and Alice knows a representation $(b_1 = sS_A, su_1, su_2, b_4 = s)$ of m'. As we assume the bank is also polynomial time the bank can not know any other representation for m'.

Now to prove double spending the bank also has to show two different transcripts for the deposit of the same coin m'. However, to show a valid transcript the bank has to answer a random challenge it has no control of (because of the random oracle assumption). We already showed that for a polynomial time bounded machine this amounts to the knowledge of b_1 and b_4 and hence of S_A. Thus, a polynomial time bank can not falsely accuse a user of double spending.

Finally, the bank can implement time frames by using different generator tuples for different time frames.

7 Defenses against Attacks and System Abuses

In this section we discuss how amount–limited and non-transferable payment systems help to defend against several attacks and abuses of payment systems.

Anonymous blackmailing : The anonymous blackmailing attack was introduced by van Solms and Naccache in [25]. The major benefit of amount limited non–transferable electronic cash is that *private* person to person blackmailing involving large sums of electronic cash is now impossible as a blackmail victim can withdraw at most 10. 000 $ per month. The cooperation of the powerful player of the bank is needed. The bank has its own interests and is unlikely to surrender. We do not claim blackmailing for electronic money becomes impossible. We do claim, however, that it becomes extremely more complicated and that it can be handled and controlled by policy decisions of bank and government.

Money laundering : The non–transferability and the amount limitedness feature of the system assure that the overall amount of tradable electronic money in the payment system is small. A consequence of this is that in order to move large funds anonymously around (e.g. from one country to another), the cooperation of many users is necessary who withdraw the needed amounts of electronic cash from their account and is thus probably impractical. Important traditional money laundering detection techniques like the observation of bank accounts that have a transaction activity bigger then the business of the account holder would justify may help to detect these type of suspicious activities.

Bribery : Suppose Alice wants to bribe Bob. As our system is non–transferable coins that have been withdrawn from Alice's account can only be spent by a user who knows Alice's non–transferability secret. Unless Alice is willing to reveal her non–transferability secret to Bob coins withdrawn from her account can not be used by Bob. Our system can not easily be made payee anonymous.

Purchase of illegal goods : As the system is amount–limited consumers may buy their weekend dose of cocaine with the system anonymously, however it is not possible to buy a pound of cocaine with it. A society might tolerate these "minor" abuses of electronic payment systems as it already does today with physical cash.

Bank robbery attack : This very strong attack where the secret key used by the bank to sign coins is compromised was introduced and defended against in [13]. The system that we describe in this paper does not defend against this attack.

It has been pointed out before in [12] that the vulnerabilities of several electronic payment systems to the bank robbery and the blackmailing attack have been a consequence of their usage of (blind) digital signature techniques. In [22] the authors describe an amount–limited and non–transferable payment system that does not rely on blind digital signature techniques and strongly defends against the blackmailing and the bank robbery attack. This shows that the vulnerabilities to these strong attacks are not a consequence of the anonymity features of electronic cash systems but rather of the technologies that have been used to implement them.

8 Acknowledgments

We would like to thank Andres Albanese, Oded Goldreich and Omer Reingold for interesting conversations. We are very thankful to Birgit Pfitzmann and the anonymous referees for their most valuable comments on an earlier version of this paper. Special thanks go to Markus Jakobsson for his many helpful comments that greatly improved the presentation of this paper.

References

1. S. Brands. An efficient off-line electronic cash system based on the representation problem. In 246. Centrum voor Wiskunde en Informatica (CWI), ISSN 0169-118X, December 31 1993. AA (Department of Algorithmics and Architecture), CS-R9323, URL=ftp://ftp.cwi.nl/pub/CWIreports/AA/CS-R9323.ps.Z.
2. S. Brands. Untraceable off-line cash in wallet with observers. In Douglas R. Stinson, editor, Crypto 93, volume 773 of LNCS, pages 302–318. SV, 1993.
3. Ernie Brickell, Peter Gemmell, and David Kravitz. Trustee-based tracing extensions to anonymous cash and the making of anonymous change. In Proceedings of the Sixth Annual ACM-SIAM Symposium on Discrete Algorithms (SODA'95), pages 457–466. Sandia National Labs, January 1995.
4. J. Camenisch, U. Maurer, and M. Stadler. Digital payment systems with passive anonymity-revoking trustees. Lecture Notes in Computer Science, 1146:33–, 1996.
5. D. Chaum and T. Pedersen. Transferred cash grows in size. In R. A. Rueppel, editor, Advances in Cryptology—EUROCRYPT 92, volume 658 of Lecture Notes in Computer Science, pages 390–407. Springer-Verlag, 24–28 May 1992.
6. I. Damgard. Payment systems and credential mechanisms with provable security against abuse by individuals. In S. Goldwasser, editor, Crypto 88, LNCS, pages 328–335, Santa Barbara, CA, USA, August 1990. SV.
7. S. D'Amiano and G. Di Crescenzo. Methodology for digital money based on general cryptographic tools. In Alfredo De Santis, editor, Advances in Cryptology—EUROCRYPT 94, volume 950 of Lecture Notes in Computer Science, pages 156–170. Springer-Verlag, 1995, 9–12 May 1994.
8. G. Davida, Y. Frankel, Y. Tsiounis, and Moti Yung. Anonymity control in E-cash systems. In Rafael Hirschfeld, editor, Financial Cryptography: First International Conference, FC '97, volume 1318 of Lecture Notes in Computer Science, pages 1–16, Anguilla, British West Indies, 24–28 February 1997. Springer-Verlag.
9. C. Dwork, J. Lotspiech, and M. Naor. Digitalsignets: Self-enforcing protection of digital information. In Proceedings of The Twenty-Eighth Annual ACM Symposium On The Theory Of Computing (STOC '96), pages 489–498, New York, USA, May 1996. ACM Press.
10. O. Goldreich, S. Micali, and A. Wigderson. How to play ANY mental game. In Alfred Aho, editor, Proceedings of the 19th Annual ACM Symposium on Theory of Computing, pages 218–229, New York City, NY, May 1987. ACM Press.
11. S. Goldwasser, S. Micali, and R. Rivest. A digital signature scheme secure against adaptive chosen-message attacks. SIAM Journal on Computing, 17(2):281–308, 1988. Special issue on cryptography.
12. M. Jakobsson and D. M'Raihi. Mix-based electronic payments. In Fifth Annual Workshop on Selected Areas in Cryptography, 1998.

13. M. Jakobsson and M. Yung. Revokable and versatile electronic mony. In Clifford Neuman, editor, 3rd ACM Conference on Computer and Communications Security, pages 76–87, New Delhi, India, March 1996. ACM Press.
14. A. Juels, M. Luby, and R. Ostrovsky. Security of blind digital signatures. In CRYPTO: Proceedings of Crypto, 1997.
15. R.C. Molander, D.A. Mussington, and P. Wilson. Cyberpayments and money laundering. RAND, 1998. http://www.rand.org/publications/MR/MR965/MR965.pdf/.
16. S. Morris. Contribution to the panel "a session on electronic money: Threat to law enforcement, privacy, freedom, or all three?" at the sixth conference on computers, freedom, and privacy (cfp96), cambridge, ma. available as RealAudio document at http://swissnet.ai.mit.edu/ switz/cfp96/plenary-money.html, 1996.
17. D. M'Raihi. Cost-effective payment schemes with privacy regulation. In Kwangjo Kim and Tsutomu Matsumoto, editors, Advances in Cryptology— ASIACRYPT '96, volume 1163 of Lecture Notes in Computer Science, pages 266– 275, Kyongju, Korea, 3–7 November 1996. Springer-Verlag.
18. T. Okamoto and K. Ohta. Disposable zero-knowledge authentications and their applications to untraceable electronic cash. In Advances in Cryptology: CRYPTO '89, pages 481–497, Berlin, August 1990. Springer.
19. T. Okamoto and K. Ohta. Universal electronic cash. In Joan Feigenbaum, editor, Proceedings of Advances in Cryptology (CRYPTO '91), volume 576 of LNCS, pages 324–337, Berlin, Germany, August 1992. Springer.
20. B. Pfitzmann and M. Waidner. How to break and repair a "provably secure" untraceable payment system. In Joan Feigenbaum, editor, Proceedings of Advances in Cryptology (CRYPTO '91), volume 576 of LNCS, pages 338–350, Berlin, Germany, August 1992. Springer.
21. D. Pointcheval and J. Stern. Security proofs for signature schemes. In Ueli Maurer, editor, Advances in Cryptology—EUROCRYPT 96, volume 1070 of Lecture Notes in Computer Science, pages 387–398. Springer-Verlag, 12–16 May 1996.
22. T. Sander and A. Ta–Shma. Auditable, counterfeiting resistant electronic cash. In preparation.
23. C. Schnorr. Efficient signature generation by smart cards. Journal of Cryptology, 4(3):161–174, 1991.
24. Paul F. Syverson, Stuart G. Stubblebine, and David M. Goldschlag. Unlinkable serial transactions. In Rafael Hirschfeld, editor, Financial Cryptography: First International Conference, FC '97, volume 1318 of Lecture Notes in Computer Science, pages 39–55, Anguilla, British West Indies, 24–28 February 1997. Springer-Verlag.
25. S. von Solms and D. Naccache. On bline signatures and perfect crimes. Computers and Security, 11(6):581–583, October 1992.
26. A. Yao. How to generate and exchange secrets. In 27th Annual Symposium on Foundations of Computer Science, pages 162–167, Los Angeles, Ca., USA, October 1986. IEEE Computer Society Press.

Risk Management for E-Cash Systems with Partial Real-Time Audit

Yacov Yacobi

Microsoft Research, One Microsoft Way, Redmond, WA 98052,
yacov@microsoft.com

Abstract. We analyze "coin-wallet" and "balance-wallet" under *partial* real-time audit, and compute upper bounds on theft due to the fact that not all the transactions are audited in real time, assuming that everything else is perfect. In particular, we assume that the audit regime holds for innocent players. Let v be the maximum allowed balance in a wallet, $0 \leq \mu \leq 1$ be the fraction of transactions that are audited in real time in an audit round that includes overall n transactions. Assume one unit transactions. We show that for $\mu << 1$ the upper bound on expected theft for coin-wallet is $\frac{v}{e^{\mu^2 v}-1}$ (which if $v << \mu^{-2}$ becomes $(e^{\mu^2} - 1)^{-1}$), while for plausible parameter choice the bound for a balance-wallet is $O(exp(v^2/n))$. This last bound can become huge in some cases, implying that partial audit, while suitable for coin-wallets with low denomination coins, may be too risky for balance-wallet. Some implications to the design of anonymous and non-anonymous systems are discussed.

Keywords: Cryptography; e-cash, randomized-audit, risk-management, economy.

1 Introduction

1.1 Background

We use the term "coin-wallet" (in short c-wallet) for a device in which individual fixed value coins are maintained, and "balance-wallet" (b-wallet) for a device in which only the total value available is maintained. We analyze those systems separately, even though real devices can (and probably should) support both.

Processing cost of a transaction must be very small compared to transaction value. For micropayments this may become a challenge. One way to save on transaction processing costs is to use off-line systems, where the bank is involved only in large batch processing during withdrawal and deposit, but is not a party in ordinary payment transactions. This approach requires HW wallets that are very hard to break. Reasonably priced consumer electronics devices (e.g. smart cards) are not very hard to break. Alternatively, a payment system can be fully on-line, where the bank is involved in every transaction. On-line systems have a much higher processing cost per transaction. On-line and off-line e-cash systems are at the ends of a spectrum characterized by audit sampling rate, $0 \leq \mu \leq 1$.

M. Franklin (Ed.): FC99, LNCS 1648, pp. 62–71, 1999.

A system is *sound* if its breaking cost exceeds the expected theft (theft is due to the fact that possibly not all transactions are audited). On the plane *audit rate Vs. breaking cost* we want to explore the continuum along which soundness is maintained. The hope is that for some realistic breaking cost we can find the required sampling rate to assure soundness, and that this sampling rate is small enough so that the system is much cheaper to operate compared with a fully on-line system.

We show that under the assumption that a constant audit sampling rate μ is enforced (along with some other common assumptions about trust and cryptography, and some reasonable assumptions on parameters sizes) the tight upper bound on the value of theft, T, from one broken coin-wallet is $E(\mu) \approx (e^{\mu^2} - 1)^{-1}$, measured in the units of coins. This approximation agrees with our intuition. For example, for $\mu = 0$ there is no audit at all, hence theft can go to infinity ($E(\mu)$ is not defined), while when all the transactions are audited in real time ($\mu = 1$) theft goes to zero, and in this approximation we get $1/(e-1) \approx 0.58$ coin, which is close enough.

For "Balance-wallet" with similar parameters the upper bound on expected theft, $E(\mu)$, can be $O(exp(v^2/n))$ which in some cases can become huge. Implying that when partial audit is desired, Coin wallets are much safer.

The meaning of $0 < \mu < 1$: Every wallet has its source of randomness that dictates audit with probability μ. When the current transaction is audited the payee must connect to the auditor and the transaction is processed in real time. Other transactions are batch-processed when a wallet reaches its maximum allowed capacity at which point it must deposit. The system is designed so that the cost of subverting the audit process of honest payee exceeds its maximum allowed balance, thus we can rule out this case. If a crooked payer colludes with a crooked payee we lump them together into one *crooked node* (for the sake of gain – loss considerations).

We use C_B to denote the overall cost of subverting a wallet. C_B may be composed of several components, such as a damage-deposit, the cost of breaking the hardware of a wallet, the cost of a false identity, etc. *A pure software e-cash system may be sound, even if not fully audited.* As mentioned before, an e-cash system is *sound* if $C_B \geq E(\mu)$. On the sampling rate Vs. breaking cost (μ, C_B) plane there is a continuum connecting the points (1,0) and (0,∞) along which soundness is maintained. This property is independent of other characteristics, such as anonymity.

Consider the economies of the thief, and of the bank. We assume that the players behave rationally, so in a sound system we have zero theft. If operations costs of a fully audited wallet through its lifetime is C_p, then we estimate that when only a fraction μ of the transactions is audited in real time, the operating costs become roughly μC_p. The cost of fortifying the wallets (to achieve a large enough C_B) should be smaller than the reduction in operating costs, $C_p(1 - \mu)$.

Example: Suppose a smart card that costs \$1 to manufacture, creates a breaking cost of over \$100. Then for 1 cent coins a sampling rate of $\mu = 0.01$ is sufficient to create an upper bound on theft of $E(0.01) \approx \$100$, and the system is sound.

Suppose the life span of a wallet is 2 years, and a user does 100 transactions per day (say 1 cent per article on the web). That's about 10^5 transactions throughout the life of the wallet. The break-even condition for the bank is $C_p \approx \$1$. So, if overall processing cost of a transaction (including communications, DB processing, signature verifications, etc.) is $\leq \$10^{-5}$ (i.e. a millicent) then the move to partial audit doesn't make sense. If the overall handling cost per transaction is higher than a millicent or if the market adopts smart cards for other reasons, then partial audit makes economic sense.

Implications to the design of anonymous e-cash systems: Anonymous e-cash systems are usually c-wallet systems, with the property that the identity of the user remains hidden on the *condition* that he spends each of his coins at most once.[1] This is the intent of the design, but, of course, a malicious user can subvert the system and open her account under a false identity. If false identities are not too expensive to acquire (as indeed is the case) then in fact we should expect a rational thief to do just this. Then the total effect that we achieve with those systems is an increase in the overall breaking cost, C_B, by the cost of a false identity[2]. This is a positive effect in the fight against crime. However, soundness ($E(\mu) < C_B$) can be achieved easier by increasing the audit sampling rate, μ. For example, for c-wallet, $E(0.01) \approx 10,000$, while $E(0.02) \approx 2,500$.

We do not have to expose a true identity in order to revoke a misbehaving wallet. Also, we do not have to design total unlinkability among transactions coming from any single wallet. Controlled linkability, where a user can cut linkability at his discretion is sufficient (and is much cheaper). With these guidelines it is possible to design a coin-wallet system in which each of *payment, withdrawal,* and *deposit* costs just one signature, where in the cases of withdrawal and deposit this is amortized over a whole batch (of any size). This is true for anonymous and non-anonymous systems.

In the case of a pure software anonymous system, which is not fully audited, some form of conditional anonymity may make sense since the added component to C_B may be important. Pure SW e-wallets cannot have a large breaking cost, therefore, to assure soundness, coin value must be small.

Related work on e-cash (with emphasis on randomized audit): The first balance-wallet is described in [4]. Paper [6] is the first known to me that proposes the use of randomized audit with e-cash systems. Papers [7] and [16] started the analysis of risk-management aspects of randomized audit on e-cash systems. The first analyzes balance-wallets, while the second discusses coin-wallets, and finds the probability of failure to detect fraud for a burst attack (the optimal attack,

---

[1] So, we call this *conditional anonymity*. In the literature it is usually called "unconditional anonymity."

[2] In the case of wallet revocation, the cost of the wallet itself is also added to C_B. This is true for non-anonymous systems as well.

as shown here, is a “trickle” attack). [12] proposed a payment system based on lottery tickets. In [14] another randomized system is presented, where the payees do not always pay (in [12] they always pay, but the payee does not always deposit). Papers [2], [3] pioneered the research on conditional anonymity. Later papers along these lines include [5], [9], [10],[11], [15].

1.2 Assumptions

1. Banks, auditors, and certification authorities are honest, and cryptographic signatures are unbreakable.[3]
2. The First Depositor of a coin Wins (FDW),
3. Audits happen in rounds. If a payer is detected as misbehaving, and is revoked before or during the current round then all of his transactions in the current round are invalidated.
4. A uniform distribution of randomized audit is enforced on all the honest players.

The last item is difficult to approximate. We hint at a possible approach in the appendix. The idea is to design the system such that the cost of subverting the audit process of honest payee exceeds the maximum allowed balance in a wallet. Since this cannot violate soundness this subversion can be excluded from consideration.

1.3 Glossary

- ADW: All Depositors Win reimbursement policy,
- Alarm threshold: A real value $x > 1$, such that a B-wallet is signaled as a potential violator if the total value of audited transactions exceeds $v\mu x$,
- $a = n\mu$: The total number of audited transactions out of n (see n below),
- B-wallet, c-wallet: balance-wallet, coin-wallet, respectively,
- C_B: Total breaking cost of a wallet,
- ΔCRL: Update to Certificate Revocation List,
- $E\{T\}$: Expected theft,
- FDW: First Depositor Wins reimbursement policy,
- $h : \{0,1\}^\infty \to \{0,1\}^n$: Hash function (assumed to behave like a random function),

[3] These assumptions may seem too strong, but if we want users to be able to withdraw money from their bank accounts, and vendors to be able to deposit into their bank accounts, then we must trust that banks do not steal from those accounts. Likewise, we must trust that CA is honest, so that user A cannot impersonate user B, when talking to the bank. If risk management relies on some audit process, as advocated here (and as done in any quality control) then the auditor must be trusted. Finally, it is convenient to assume that cryptographic signatures are unbreakable, since currently, to the best of our knowledge they are by far the most reliable element in any protection system.

- k-off C-wallet: A C-wallet in which a coin may change k hands before it must be deposited,
- μ: Audit (constant) sampling rate,
- m: Multispending factor, a wallet with initial balance v, which spends s, has a multispending factor of $m = s/v$,
- m_b, m_c: The value of the optimal (for the adversary) multispending factor for B-wallet and C-wallet, respectively,
- n The total number of transactions in the sample space,
- $q_b(m), q_c(m)$: Failure to alarm probability for B-wallet and C-wallet, respectively, for multispending factor m,
- q_{b1} : False alarm probability for B-wallet,
- v: The maximum balance in a wallet,

1.4 Structure of the rest of the paper

The analysis in 2 is done under the assumption (among others) that the audit regime is enforced on all unbroken payees. In 2.1 we tightly upper bound the expected theft. In 2.2 we analyze balance-wallet under similar conditions, and find both the false alarm and the failure to alarm probabilities. We argue that in a b-wallet the false alarm probability must be extremely small, and show that under these assumptions expected theft may be in some cases a few orders of magnitude higher than for a c-wallet system. Finally in the appendix we give an example of a system that approximates the theoretical model. In this example all the transactions have to wait the same time, however, the infrastructure is cheaper, since it has to accommodate only the audited transactions in real time.

2 Analysis

2.1 Coin-wallet

A thief spends v original coins, where coin i is multispent $m_i > 1$ times, $i = 0, 1, ...v-1$. in one audit-interval, after which the auditor takes a fraction μ of samples for an audit, out of a total of n transactions. Let $a = n\mu$.

Failure to alarm probability for a given wallet, W:
q_c=Pr[none of the (multispent) coins is audited more than once].

$$q_c \approx \prod_{i=0}^{v-1}[\sum_{j=0}^{1} \binom{m_i}{j} \mu^j (1-\mu)^{m_i - j}] = \prod_{i=0}^{v-1}[(1-\mu)^{m_i} + m_i\mu(1-\mu)^{m_i-1}]$$
$$= \prod_{i=0}^{v-1}[(1-\mu)^{m_i-1} \cdot (1 + \mu(m_i - 1))]$$

Lemma 21 *For a fixed fraud volume (i.e. fixed value of $\sum_{i=0}^{v-1} m_i$), the choice of a uniform value for m for all coins maximizes q_c. In that case we denote it $q_c(m)$*

Proof:

Consider the case $v = 2$ (i.e, just two original coins). Let $m_0 \neq m_1$. We compare $\prod_{i=0}^{1}(1-\mu)^{m_i-1} \cdot (1 + \mu(m_i - 1))$ to $[(1-\mu)^{m-1} \cdot (1 + \mu(m-1))]^2$, where $m = (m_0 + m_1)/2$. One can easily see that if $m_0 \geq 1$ and $m_1 \geq 1$ then $(1-\mu)^{m_0-1} \cdot (1-\mu)^{m_1-1} = [(1-\mu)^{m-1}]^2$, and that if $m_0 \neq m_1$ then $(1+\mu(m_0-1)) \cdot (1+\mu(m_1-1)) < (1+\mu(m-1))^2$. This implies that the adversary is better off replacing m_0 and m_1 with m.

The case $v > 1$ follows likewise. If any two coins, i, j with $m_i \neq m_j$ are replaced with two coins with the same $m = (m_i + m_j)/2$ then we know that q_c increases. We can repeat this process until all coins have the same m, changing one pair at a time.

This technique could also be used to show that Information-Theoretic entropy is maximized for a uniform density. □

For $m << \mu^{-1}$ $q_c(m) \approx [(1-(\mu(m-1))^2]^v$, which for $v << (\mu(m-1))^{-2}$ is $q_c(m) \approx e^{-(\mu(m-1))^2 v}$.

Lemma 22 *For $v << (\mu(m-1))^{-2}$, $q_c(m)$ is maximized for $m = 2$.*

Proof: $q_c(m) \approx e^{-(\mu(m-1))^2 v}$. $\frac{d}{dm}(q_c(m)) = -2\mu^2(m-1)v \cdot e^{-(\mu(m-1))^2 v}$. For $m > 1$ the above is negative. Hence the smallest $m > 1$ maximizes $q_c(m)$. The discrete case behaves similarly. For a c-wallet m must be an integer, hence $m = 2$ maximizes $q_c(m)$. □

Let $E\{T\}$ denote the expected theft in the following experiment:

Experiment 21 *In each audit round, as long as he is not revoked, the thief withdraws v fresh coins, and multispends each m times.*

$$E\{T\} = (m-1)v \sum_{i=1}^{\infty} q_c(m)^i = (m-1)v \frac{q_c(m)}{1-q_c(m)}$$

Lemma 23 *For $m > 1$, if $v << (\mu(m-1))^{-2}$ then $\frac{d}{dm}(E\{T\}) < 0$.*

Proof: Plug $q_c(m) \approx e^{-(\mu(m-1))^2 v}$ into $E\{T\} = (m-1)v\frac{q_c(m)}{1-q_c(m)} = \frac{(m-1)v}{e^{+(\mu(m-1))^2 v}-1}$. Clearly the m in the exponent of the denominator dominates the m in the nominator, so that $E\{T\}$ is maximized for the smallest $m > 1$. □

Conclusion: Homogeneous $m = 2$ maximizes $E\{T\}$. In this case $q_c(2) \approx [1-\mu^2]^v$. If $\mu << 1$ then $q_c(2) \approx e^{-\mu^2 v}$ and $E\{T\} = v\frac{e^{-\mu^2 v}}{1-e^{-\mu^2 v}} = \frac{v}{e^{\mu^2 v}-1}$

Let $\epsilon = e^{\mu^2} - 1$. If $\mu << 1$ then $\epsilon << 1$. In addition, note that our assumption that $v << (\mu(m-1))^{-2}$ becomes $v << \mu^{-2}$ when $m = 2$, and it implies also $v << \epsilon$, which in turn implies $(1+\epsilon)^v \approx 1 + \epsilon v$. Under these conditions $E\{T\} = \frac{v}{e^{\mu^2 v}-1} = \frac{v}{(1+\epsilon)^v - 1} \approx \epsilon^{-1}$. We proved:

Theorem 21 *The upper bound on theft for audit rate $\mu << 1$ is $E\{T\} = \frac{v}{e^{\mu^2 v}-1}$. If in addition the maximum allowed balance in a wallet $v << \mu^{-2}$ then $E\{T\} = (e^{\mu^2} - 1)^{-1}$.*

2.2 Balance-wallet

Let W be a wallet under consideration, with maximum balance v, and overspending factor m. Suppose that in a given audit interval there are overall n transactions, and the uniform audit rate is μ. Transactions have uniform value of one unit.

Alarm policy: *Declare wallet W guilty if in an audit interval the number of samples coming from W (denoted S) exceeds $v\mu x$, where $x > 1$ is real.* The assumption here is that within an audit interval a wallet cannot both spend and withdraw (to replenish its balance).

Define $a = n\mu$ and let $X_i, \quad i = 1, 2, 3...a$ denote mutually independent 0-1 random variables. $X_i = 1$ iff audit i came from W. $Pr[X_i = 1] = p(m) = mv/n$ and $Pr[X_i = 0] = 1 - p(m)$. $S = \sum_{i=1}^{a} X_i$. We define:
False alarms probability: $q_{b1} = Pr[S \geq v\mu x \mid m = 1]$, and
Failure to alarm probability: $q_b(m) = Pr[S < v\mu x \mid m > 1]$.

False alarms: Define $\delta_1 = v\mu(x-1)$. Then from Chernoff bound ([1] Th. A4)

$$q_{b1} = Pr[S > v\mu x] < e^{-2\delta_1^2/a}.$$

So, x must be somewhere in the range $2 < x < 15$, where the lower bound on x corresponds to roughly 4% annual revocation rate, and the upper bound corresponds to practically zero false alarms. The upper bound is needed if we want to actually accuse someone of theft. The lower bound is sufficient if a bank revokes a wallet that seems to misbehave, without making any accusations. In this case the bank provides a free new wallet, and "eats the losses."

Failure to alarm: For $1 < m < x$ define $\delta_2 = v\mu(x-m)$. $q_b(m) = 1 - Pr[S > v\mu x]$, $Pr[S > v\mu x] < e^{-2\delta_2^2/a}$. So, $q_b(m) > 1 - e^{-2\delta_2^2/a}$. As before, in the case of c-wallet, $E\{T\} = (m-1)v\frac{q_b(m)}{1-q_b(m)}$, so

$$E\{T\} > (m-1)v\frac{1 - e^{-2\delta_2^2/a}}{e^{-2\delta_2^2/a}} = (m-1)v(e^{2\delta_2^2/a} - 1).$$

In some circumstances $2\delta_2^2/a = v^2(x-m)^2\mu/n$ can be $>> 1$. For example, it is plausible to have $(x-m)^2\mu \approx 1$. In that case $E\{T\} = O(exp(v^2/n))$ can become huge (in contrast, for c-wallet we have $E\{T\} = \frac{v}{e^{\mu^2 v}-1}$, which goes down as v goes up).

The audit anomaly of B-wallets: The expression

$$E\{T\} = (m-1)v(e^{2(v\mu(x-m))^2/a} - 1) = (m-1)v(e^{2\frac{v^2}{n}\mu(x-m)^2} - 1)$$

is troublesome. Theft is monotonically increasing in the audit rate μ and in v, which seems crazy, but is true. Once $m < x$ an increase in μ reduces the right tails, but increases its complement, which is the failure to alarm for $m < x$.

If we compensate with x (the alarm-threshold) for the increase in μ so as to keep false alarm fixed, then as μ goes up, x decreases. Once $x < m$ everything at once goes back to normal (the failure to alarm probability becomes a small left tail as we'd like it to be).

3 Practical Considerations

3.1 Example attacks

Attacker monitor payees interaction with auditor. He multispends a coin (not to the same payee) until it is sent for audit. Then he goes on to next coin.

Solutions:

1. Engineer the system so that monitoring cost per payee > max allowed balance, v (payee must deposit when v is exceeded), or
2. Payee delays all transactions by the same amount[4].

3.2 Anonymity

Conditional anonymity (user-ID $\in$ coin) Conditional anonymity increases the overall "breaking cost" C_b by the cost of a *false identity.* If we want $C_b > E\{T\}$ for c-wallet it is easier to achieve by reducing $E\{T\}$ via a tiny increase in μ.

Conditional anonymity (Machine-ID $\in$ coin) If user cannot change machine ID (and still have it certified) then the above argument doesn't hold. However, a simpler system is using machine-pseudonym changeable by the user at will[5].

Attack: Multispend then quickly change pseudonym.

Solution: Pseudonyms are changed in one time interval (say around midnight GMT). CA and auditor compare notes, and allow the change if machine in good standing. Audit is slowed in that time interval. Only Auditors and CA need be synchronized.

Acknowledgment

I thank Brian Beckman, Josh Benaloh, Wei Dai, Paul England, Dan Simon, Matt Thomlinson, and Gideon Yuval, for many helpful discussions.

References

1. N. Alon, J.H. Spencer, and P. Erdos *The Probabilistic Method,* Wiley Interscience, ISBN 0-471-53588-5
2. D. Chaum *Achieving Electronic Privacy* Scientific American, August 1992, pp. 96-101.
3. Chaum Fiat and Naor: *Untraceable Electronic Cash,* Proc. Crypto 1988.

[4] In this case the saving is the reduced load on the infrastructure: especially number of DB accesses at the banks, and hangups when communication with banks fail.

[5] Requires CA intervention: User starts a session with CA under old pseudonym, and submits a new blinded candidate certificate. CA signs it only if old certificate is in good standing. Old cert is revoked.

4. S. Even, O. Goldreich, Y. Yacobi: *Electronic Wallet*, Crypto'83 (See also the Zurich'94 Seminar.)
5. M Franklin and M. Yung *Secure and efficient off-line digital money*, Proc. 20th ICALP 1993,
6. E. Gabber and A. Silberschatz: *Agora: A Minimal Distributed Protocol for Electronic Commerce*, USENIX Workshop on E-Commerce, Oakland CA, Nov. 1996.
7. S. Jarecki and A. M. Odlyzko:*An efficient micropayment system based on probabilistic polling*, Proc. Financial Cryptography – 97.
8. R.C. Merkle: *Protocols for Public Key Cryptosystems*, Proc. of 1980 Symp. on Security and Privacy, IEEE Computer Society, pp. 122-133 (April 1980).
9. T. Okamoto:'*An Efficient Divisible Electronic Cash Scheme*, Proc. Crypto'95, Springer Verlag LNCS 963, pp. 438-451.
10. T. Okamoto and K. Ohta: *Disposable Zero-Knowledge Authentications and Their Applications to Untraceable Electronic Cash*, Proc. Crypto'89, Springer-Verlag LNCS 435, pp. 481-496,
11. T. Okamoto and K. Ohta: *Universal Electronic Cash*, Proc. Crypto'90, Springer-Verlag LNCS 576, pp. 324-337,
12. R. L. Rivest: *Electronic Lottery Tickets as Micropayments* Financial Cryptography 97, Springer Verlag LNCS 1318, pp. 306-314, Rafael Hirschfeld (Ed.)
13. D.R. Simon: *Anonymous Communication and Anonymous Cash*, Proc. Crypto'96, Springer Verlag LNCS 1109, pp 61-73.
14. D. Wheeler: *Transactions Using Bets*, Proc. ARE, 1997, LNCS 1189, pp. 89-92,
15. Y. Yacobi: *Efficient E-money*, in Proc. Asiacrypt'94, Springer Verlag LNCS 917 , pp. 153-163.
16. Y. Yacobi: *On the Continuum Between On-line and Off-line E-cash Systems – I*, Proc. Financial Cryptography – 97.

4 Appendix A: An Approximation of the Theoretical Model

One of our basic assumptions in the body of this paper was that the audit regime is correctly enforced on all players. The auditor is a new player in cryptographic games, and we need to consider attacks against it. In this appendix we briefly outline provisions needed in the system which enforce a reasonable approximation of this assumption. Clearly, we cannot force a bunch of broken wallets to comply. However, we can design a system, where we can eliminate attacks on the audit process of non-colluding payees, and then eliminate patterns of misbehavior of the colluding payees. In our case all the eliminations are grounded on economic considerations. A behavior which doesn't make economic sense from the attackers point of view is eliminated. Thus we ignore vandalism. This justifies the assumption that the audit regime is enforced.

Let ΔCRL denote updates to Certificate Revocation Lists (with a proper design a CRL for the whole USA may be on the order of 1 MByte; so many hand held devices can store it). $\Longrightarrow$ denotes broadcast, $\leftarrow$ denotes transmissions.

$x_i, x_{i+1}, ..$ denote audit instructions. We assume they are randomly generated in each wallet. T_i^+, T_i^- denote signed hash trees ([8]) for "good" and "bad" transactions that were audited in round i; $trans$ = transaction. Recall that we assume that all communications are cryptographically protected for secrecy and integrity (and omit the mechanisms from this description).

A typical audit round may look like this:

Auditor		*Payee*
$(\Delta CRL_{i-1}, T_{i-1}^+, T_{i-1}^-)$	$\Longrightarrow$	
		If $h(trans) = x_{i-1}$ then
	$\longleftarrow$	(trans)
$(\Delta CRL_i, T_i^+, T_i^-)$	$\Longrightarrow$	
		Conclude current *trans* if payer not revoked, and for audited *trans*, $trans \in T_i^+$.

Table: *Round i of the audit protocol*

Note that in this approximation both audited and non audited transactions have the same one round delay before completion (we still benefit from randomized audit in terms of load on the infrastructure; there are other approximations which allow non-audited transactions to conclude immediately, but they are riskier). As before, we assume that the First Depositor Wins (FDW).

This approximation requires some more assumptions about the system. One major assumption is that the amortized cost of subverting the audit process of a non-colluding payee (denoted c) exceeds the maximum allowed balance in a wallet, v. This leads to the convenient conclusion that for economically motivated adversaries, non-colluding payees are within the audit regime.

It should be noted that the cost of subverting the audit distribution of non-colluding payees may vary among different systems. At the lowest end, for ordinary Internet connections, it may go as low as \$10.-. For other systems it can become practically impossible to subvert non-colluding payees.

The Simple Attack Observation for non-transferable coins:
It is sufficient to consider a simple attack in which one broken payer pays out to (unlimited) number of $non - colluding$ payees.

Reason: We only care about the total adversarial revenues of any colluding set, i.e. about how much they can gain when paying out to non-colluding payees. Since coins are not transferable, each broken payer must independently pay out.

Recall that the payees dictate audit distribution, and payers cannot influence it (thus we do not need to ask that bad payers comply with audit distribution).

A similar observation holds for systems with transferability (and even with All-Depositors-Win policy), however, the arguments become more complex, and this is beyond the scope of this paper.

Assessment of Effectiveness of Counterfeit Transaction Detection Systems for Smart Card Based Electronic Cash

Kazuo J. Ezawa, Gregory Napiorkowski, and Mariusz Kossarski

Mondex International Limited, Atlantic Technology Center
Suite 109, 100 Campus Drive, P.O. Box 972
Florham Park, New Jersey, 07932-0972, USA

Abstract. In this paper, we discuss a process to evaluate the effectiveness of counterfeit detection systems for an electronic cash scheme which is not fully accounted (i.e., off line, peer to peer transactions are allowed, and no shadow accounting for each purse). The process includes a use of a micro dynamic simulator to simulate various counterfeit scenarios (in addition to testing on the actual non-counterfeit transaction data sets from the real deployment) and generate transaction data sets for detection systems to use for the counterfeit detection systems training and testing. A case study of preliminary test results related to the effectiveness of the detection systems in a simulated counterfeit scenario is also provided.

1 Introduction

Effectiveness of various counterfeit detection systems is one of the most critical concerns for smart card based electronic cash community. As discussed in the assessment of overall threats for smart card based electronic cash [Ezawa & Napiorkowski, 1998][1], it is an enormous challenge for the counterfeiter's inject sufficient amount of counterfeit values to obtain economic benefit due to organizational, human behavioral, and technological barriers. None-the-less, prudent risk management requires installation of various risk management systems and a sound scheme governance structure in the event of counterfeit activity in the future.

In this paper, we discuss a process to evaluate the effectiveness of counterfeit detection systems for an electronic cash scheme which is not fully accounted

[1] It found that counterfeiter's challenges are both strictly technical as well as of organizational and behavioral nature, and go well beyond the security break, a formidable barrier itself, but only the first barrier to be broken. It discussed how a global smart card based electronic cash product (such as Mondex electronic cash) using various security, risk management capability, and taking advantages of other natural human and organizational behaviors prevents the counterfeiter from achieving its ultimate goal.

M. Franklin (Ed.): FC´99, LNCS 1648, pp.72 -85, 1999.

(i.e., off line, peer to peer transactions are allowed, and no shadow accounting for each purse).

The process includes a use of a micro dynamic simulator to simulate various counterfeit scenarios (in addition to testing on the actual non-counterfeit transaction data sets from the real deployment) and generate transaction data sets for detection systems to use for the counterfeit detection systems training and testing. A case study of preliminary test results related to the effectiveness of the detection systems in a simulated counterfeit scenario is also provided.

The paper describes the effectiveness of detection systems based on the simulated counterfeit attack scenarios. The use of simulation is an absolute necessity due to that fact that actual counterfeit transaction has not been encountered, and at the same time, the detection systems have to be developed, deployed, and tested their performance in the event of counterfeit attack. Simulation allows us to evaluate the effectiveness of the detection systems quantitatively, and validate the system performance.

The paper is organized as follows. Section 1 describes the evaluation process. Two counterfeit detection systems, the currency monitoring system and the merchant monitoring system are selected for the demonstration of this process. It discusses overall integrated approach to evaluate these two systems performance. Section 2 discusses the case study of a simulated counterfeit scenario. Section 3 summarizes the discussion.

2 Evaluation Process and Two Counterfeit Detection Systems

First, we briefly discuss the characteristics of electronic cash based on smart card. There are many different variety of such products, and we discuss only a special variety which allows off-line transactions without central clearance.

2.1 Global Smart Card Based Electronic Cash Product

The global smart card based electronic cash product such as Mondex electronic cash is designed for the efficient electronic cash payment transactions. It performs purse (chip) to purse (chip) transactions without central authorization. It has strong security and risk management to prevent, detect, contain, and recover from potential counterfeit activities. It has many on-chip capability and features such as physical security, cryptographical security, purse class structure, purse limit, on-chip risk management capability (e.g., credit turnover limit), and migration[2]. Security issues related to Mondex electronic cash application are discussed in [Maher, 1997].

Ideally, a smart card based electronic cash scheme, a substitute for "real" money, should parallel the existing money supply and banking system. Therefore such a scheme would include a currency "originator" (equivalent of central bank), and "members" (commercial banks and other financial institutions with

---

[2] It involves switching of one public key scheme to the other.

their branches). There are merchants who transact with consumers and members, and consumers transacting with other consumers, merchants, and members.

Figure 1 shows a high level representation of layers of risk management capability and a scheme governance structure. It provides multiple level of monitoring capability. It starts with on-chip (on the smart card) risk management capability on the consumers and merchants cards. At the member (financial institution) level, its issued cards (i.e., consumer and merchant) transactions to the financial institution are fully accounted and monitored. We show one of the risk management monitoring system, the merchant monitoring system's performance in the section 2. Above the financial institutions, there is a currency originator. One of the risk management monitoring system for the originator is the currency monitoring system. We demonstrate its performance in the section 2. At the top of currency originators resides a global risk management that monitors the activities of various currency originators.

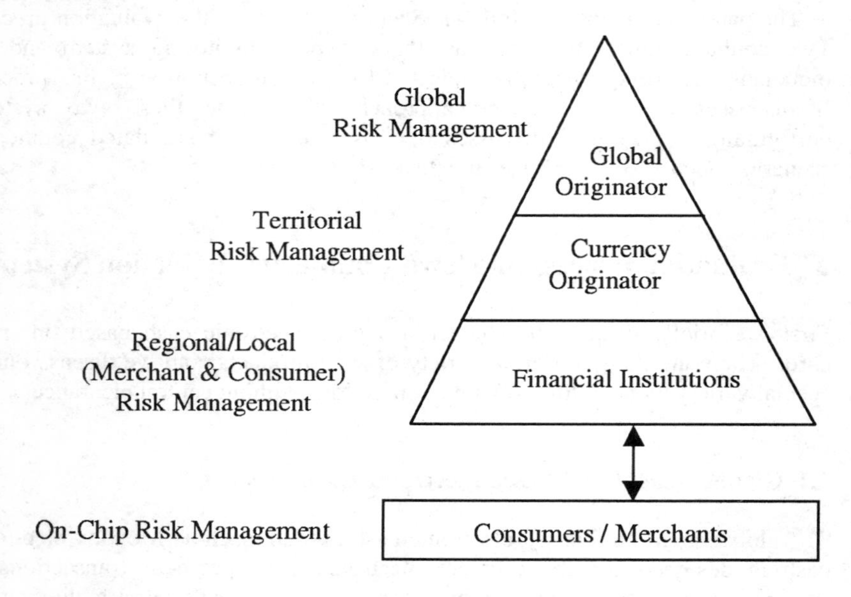

Fig. 1: Multiple Levels of Scheme Governance and Risk Management

2.2 The Risk Management Challenge.

The risk management challenge is to provide a methodology that allows maximization of the net income earned from the float of the electronic cash. This goal can be reached by providing a method to select the best risk management tools from a pool of existing systems and determine values for all available parameters for those tools and other scheme variables.

2.3 The Evaluation Process:

The risk management systems are evaluated using two-stage process. The first stage is the optimization process with given counterfeit attack scenario, time period and risk management tools being evaluated. The best possible behavior of the system is determined.

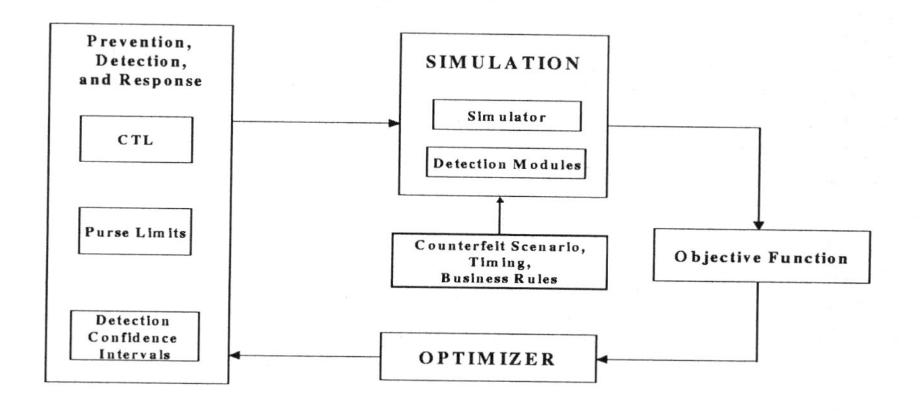

Fig. 2: Optimization Stage of the Evaluation process.

The optimization process utilizes Mondex Micro Dynamic Simulator described later in the paper. The objective function maximizes net income defined as

Net income *(T,FS)* = Float income*(x | T, FS)* - Redeemed counterfeit value*(x | T, FS)* *(1)*

Where FS – given counterfeit scenario
T – given time period.

The Optimizer software is not available at this time. Series of simulations are run and the set of variables yielding the best value of the objective function is selected as an estimation of the optimal solution.

The second stage of the evaluation process contains two steps. The risk management system under the normal environment (i.e., no counterfeit activities) is evaluated in the first step. It uses actual electronic cash transaction data sets from various territories of the world to test the effectiveness of the risk management system. Standard statistical estimates and performance measures are collected (e.g., goodness of fit, etc.) The risk management systems were initially designed and developed using the experience of actual electronic cash behaviors and transactions. Hence it is natural to expect the systems to perform well in the normal environment, and they actually do.

The second step is the evaluation of risk management system under various simulated counterfeit attack scenarios – not necessary close to the one used during the optimization stage. This paper focuses on this part of the process. As we discussed, the actual counterfeit attack has not been taken place, and no actual counterfeit attack transaction record is available. One of the ways to test the risk management system is based on the use of the simulator. Note that for the risk management system to be effective, it has to demonstrate it functions well under the normal as well as the counterfeit attack environment.

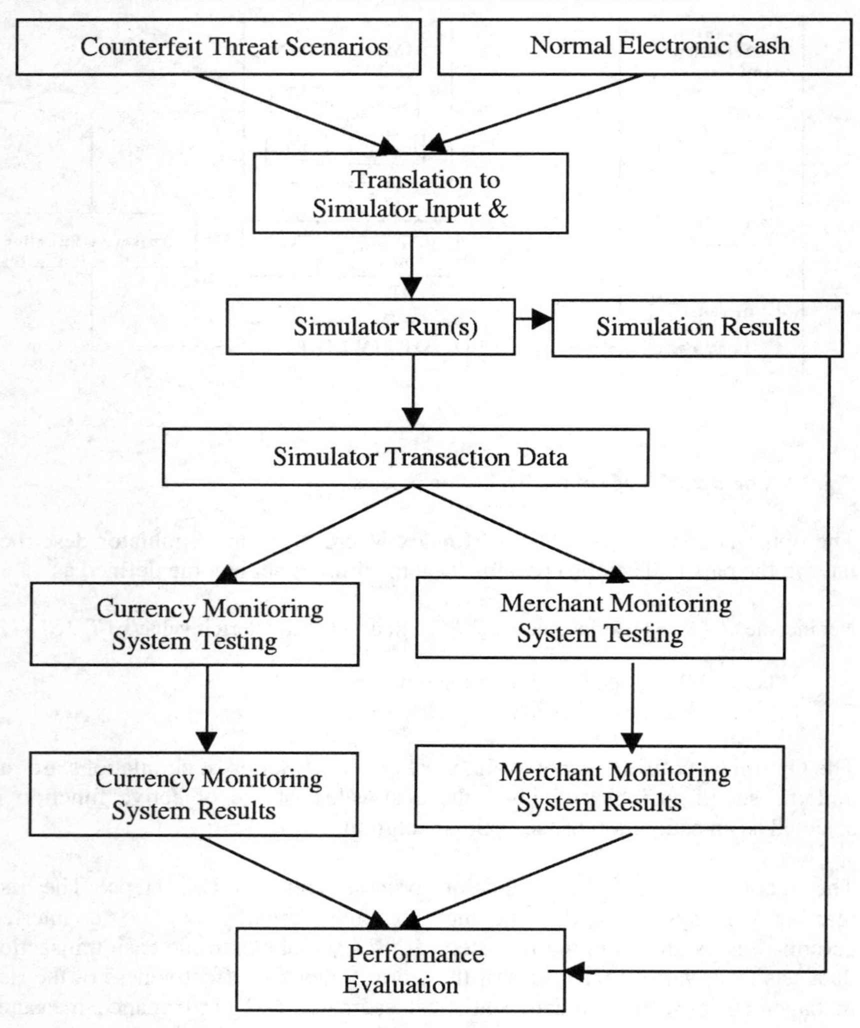

Fig. 3: The Evaluation Process in the Simulated Counterfeit Attack Environment

Figure 3 shows the evaluation process in the simulated counterfeit attack environment.

First, the normal electronic cash economy related parameters (which are estimated from the actual transaction characteristic information from various territories of the world and/or surrogate/substitute transactions characteristic information) are used to set up the normal simulated environment. At the same time, a specific counterfeit attack scenario is provided to the simulator.

The simulation run generates the transaction records for a counterfeit attack scenario. The simulated transaction records are preprocessed to feed the detection systems. The detection systems identify abnormal behaviors and inform an existence of potential counterfeit attack.

Various statistics are collected to evaluate the effectiveness of the detection systems. Some of the information are, amount of counterfeit value injected by the simulator, amount of counterfeit value detected by the detection systems, the speed of the identification of counterfeit attack incident, etc.

2.4 Micro Dynamic Simulator

As we discussed, at the moment, no actual data on the counterfeit activities exist in the new electronic cash economy. Moreover, it is extremely unlikely that any actual observations regarding counterfeit value will be available in the foreseeable future. Therefore a quantification of a given threat scenario has to be based on the observations generated in a laboratory-like environment. Simulation modeling offers such an environment. It allows, through setting distributions of various parameters, to control and observe the behavior of all phases of a threat scenario.

In general, the micro dynamic simulator (e.g., developed by Mondex) is a computer model that imitates the dynamics of the electronic cash scheme. It mimics the expected long term evolution of the electronic cash scheme, and reflects, through respective model parameters, short term behavioral patterns, e.g. seasonal fluctuations. It follows the transaction behavior of individual purses, e.g. a number and frequency of transactions, and keeps a complete record of all individual transactions.

The essence of every experiment is to design a threat scenario and inject the related counterfeit value into the system, and build in and invoke during the simulation the on-chip (on the smart card) and off-chip based responses.

The simulated diffusion of the counterfeit value and an effectiveness with which it can be detected and contained provide the critical information that allows us to quantify a threat scenario in question.

An ability to produce and analyze multiple runs of the simulator model under different scenarios allows the user to experience the management of the electronic cash economy before the scheme is actually rolled out.

In addition to being a tool to evaluate the impact of counterfeit scenarios, the simulator model also generates transactions that can be used to train off-chip detection model(s). The simulator model is to be calibrated for every respective currency originator (i.e. country) to reflect the particular behavior of its purse users and their transaction patterns of their territories.

2.5 Currency Monitoring System

The objective of currency monitoring system is to detect the presence of potential counterfeit value in (almost) real time for the three types of attacks; rapid (i.e. a sudden redemption of counterfeit value), moderate, and long term (skimming). And to provide recommendations as to what steps should be taken to identify sources for the potential counterfeit value, once detected.

The methodology of detecting the potential counterfeit value rests on the fact that any injection of counterfeit value into the Mondex economy will be eventually deposited with the originator and redeemed for "regular" money. Consequently, an unusual surge in the redeemed electronic cash value should be carefully scrutinized.

The procedure to identify surges in value redemption consists of following two distinctive steps:

- Describe the **normal** pattern for redemption flows.
  Depending on the type of attack, it tracks the currency redemption, at the originator level, for three time periods: Day, Week (rolling week) and Month (rolling 35 day periods). The respective statistical models of redemption flows are, in general, a function of present and past electronic cash value issuance, reflecting the seasonal pattern (e.g. day of the week). The models are estimated and executed using a commercially available statistical software that allows for an efficient data processing and analysis as well as for applications of the state of art modeling techniques.
- Set the rules that identify the **abnormal** redemption flows.
  The statistical models predict the normal or expected redemption of the electronic cash value to the originator. It is a standard statistical procedure to define the range of normal redemption by its confidence interval, given the level of significance. Since we are concerned about the unusually high redemption, we will pay a special attention to the upper boundary of the confidence interval.

2.6 Merchant Monitoring System

The objective of the Merchant Monitoring System is to detect the presence of the counterfeit value in a timely fashion and provide decision support when the potential incursion of the counterfeit value is detected.

To accomplish these tasks, two complementary methods will be employed, namely, counterfeit detection based on statistical models, and counterfeit detection based on machine learning method [Ezawa, *et al*, 1995 & 1996]. In this paper, we discuss the models based on the statistical methods.

Merchant Monitoring System primarily tracks the electronic cash value transactions between individual merchant and its acquiring member. These transactions, i.e., value transfer from a merchant to a member are fully accounted. One can also conclude that the merchant transaction values should be transformed in order to properly apply various statistical tests and model estimation methods. The preliminary evidence suggests, for instance, that the nominal transaction values are approximately log-normally distributed.

Similarly to currency monitoring system, separate models are build to detect the three different types of attacks, rapid, moderate, and long term ("skimming") attacks that would be carried out via merchant purses while taking into account the length of a given merchant history.

Accordingly, the statistical procedures and criteria used to identify the unusual merchant deposits are separately applied to the following time periods: day, week (rolling seven day period) and month (rolling 35 day period). The advantage of such five weeks "months" is that they all have the same number of days and do not break up natural weekly spending cycles.

Analysis is performed on a daily basis (even if weekly or monthly totals are used) at the ***individual merchant*** level. On every day, all the merchant deposit time series are classified into two sub-series: the *samples* (as a rule, large) containing only previously validated deposits and the *forecasts* (as a rule, small – frequently just one day) to be verified. This naming convention corresponds to the type of data used by time series models, where sample is used for model estimation and forecast data are used for model verification.

Three time series models are estimated using *sample* daily, weekly and monthly observations provided the series contains at least 35 observations. These models provide the ***core criteria*** to identify the individual merchant's deposit pattern that is unusually high compared to the expected level, considering trend and seasonal (day of the week, calendar month) effects. The corresponding models for the merchant segments are also estimated to provide the above mentioned benchmark behavior for every merchant (including local promotion effects).

3. Case Study

We evaluated the above mentioned detection systems in the "Street Corner Counterfeit Value Distribution Threat Scenario" that is discussed in [Ezawa & Napiorkowski, 1998].

This counterfeit threat scenario assumes that the counterfeiters will sell, at a discount, counterfeit electronic cash to a fraudulent population, in exchange for "real" local currency. The fraudulent population is defined as the one that would engage in such transactions knowingly and willingly.

The fraudulent population is not necessarily as loyal as agents of counterfeit organization and the "secret" is bound to be leaked to the law enforcement institutions or electronic cash issuing institution.

In the paper [Ezawa & Napiorkowski, 1998][3] showed that this is quite a difficult task to carry out flawlessly. For the sake of the evaluation of counterfeit detection systems, we assumed the following:

- Counterfeit organization has a well financed, well-established worldwide network, and a large number of dedicated agents in place.
- It successfully broke the security of the chip / purse application on the smart card that required a complete secrecy over an extended period of time while various tasks are performed to break security.
- It created a counterfeit electronic cash application -- "shrink wrap" product of "golden goose" that can generate counterfeit electronic cash with flawless imitation of electronic cash application (e.g., Mondex purse) functionality.
- It established counterfeit value distribution channels with no "informants".
- Counterfeiter/agents can correctly identify "fraudulent" population who is willing to buy counterfeit values with discount. They never make mistakes. If they approach a normal/honest person, he or she might inform the financial institution or authority.
- No on-chip risk management (detection) capability on the electronic cash (purse) application to monitor on the smart card itself.

Simulation model was set to run 230 days and the counterfeit attack starts at the last 6 days. The length of the run is set so that simulation transaction data will provide significant amount of normal transactions. One the first day of the attack, April 1, 2000, the counterfeiters inject a very small amount of counterfeit value to the electronic cash economy to test the system. On the second day, April 2, 2000, they inject amount they desire. On the third day, April 3, they stop their activities completely to observe and evaluate their performance of the previous day. They resume the counterfeit value distribution for the rest of the three days. Note that the calendar days are important, since the simulator simulates the day of the week, the seasonality and holiday impacts to the behaviors of various consumer and merchant segments.

In the simulation model, there are 5 member bank segments (four bank segments and one counterfeit bank segment). There are four consumer segments (normal consumer, high-end consumer, unregistered card holder, and fraudulent consumers). There are three merchant segments.

---

[3] As the counterfeiter's value chain shows, due to the product features (as described in the next section), it requires some formidable organization and resources, up front capital investment, and flawless executions of technical as well as operational tasks against determined foes (various authorities and electronic cash organizations such as Mondex) to make a financial gain. Another prerequisite for a business success is a well financed, functioning, controlled, and coordinated organization with extremely loyal followers. Moreover, it needs people with a variety of technical and operational skills. Some of them have to be world class experts in various fields (e.g. cryptography). Finally, one has to establish a country wide or even world wide network to be able to "cash in" large amounts of counterfeit values in a very short time before the incidence responses are triggered by the electronic cash operators.

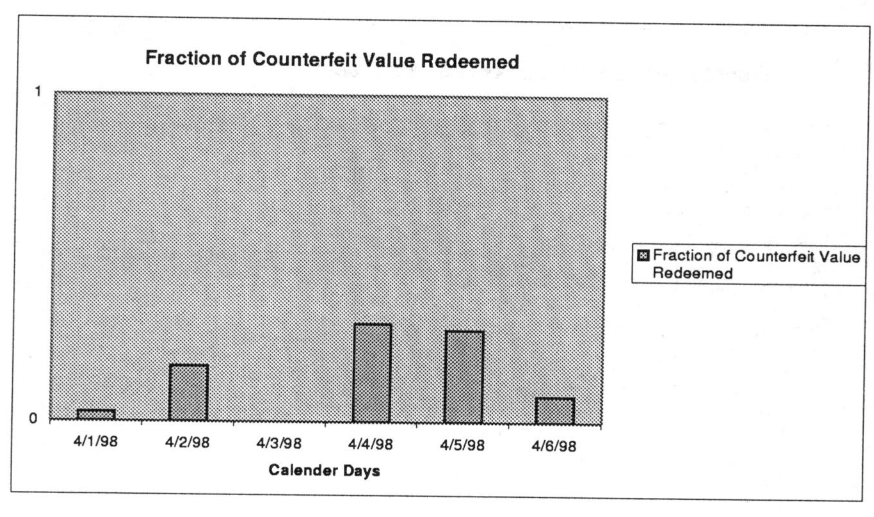

Fig. 4: Fraction of Counterfeit Value Redeemed (against Total Value Redeemed) through the Members during the Counterfeit Attack Period

3.1 Results from the Currency Monitoring System

As discussed, the currency monitoring system resides with the territory originator, and monitors the value issuance and redemption of the members. It monitors the electronic cash flow at the aggregate level, thus by design, its performance is relative to the total size of the electronic cash economy of the territory.

Figure 4 shows the fraction of counterfeit value redeemed by the members (against the total value redeemed by the members) during the counterfeit attack period. Please note that due to business sensitivity, actual scale of counterfeit value redemption is removed. As discussed, there was a small redemption of counterfeit value through members on April 1, no redemption of counterfeit value on April 3, but larger amount of counterfeit value redeemed on April 2, 4, and 5.

Figure 5 shows the ratio of estimated loss and actual loss due to the counterfeit value redeemed through members during the counterfeit attack period. As it indicates that the system didn't recognize the counterfeit incursion on April 1, but it detected the attack on April 2, 4, and 5, and correctly predicted that there was not attack on April 3.

During normal period, there was no false positive or negative identification by the system. Although the results are still preliminary, as shown, overall the system works well for this counterfeit scenario.

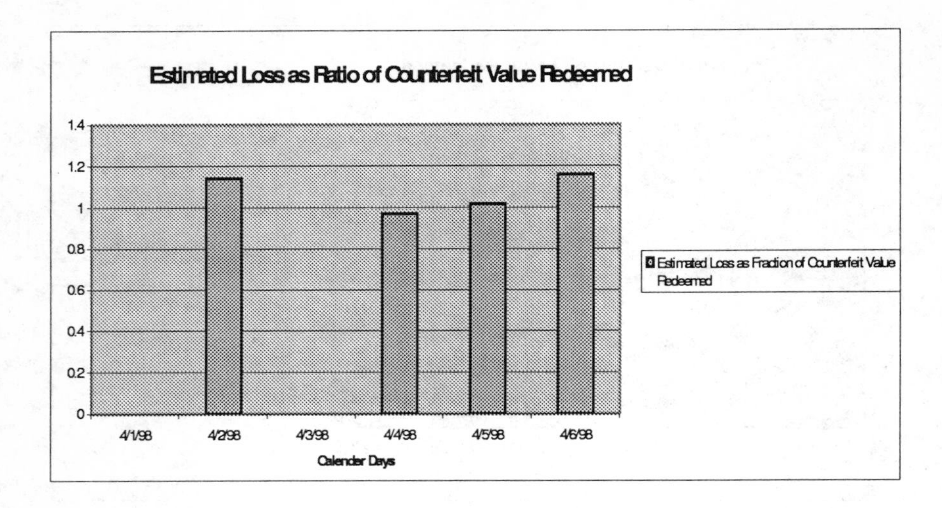

Fig. 5: Ratio of Estimated Loss and Actual Loss due to the Counterfeit Value Redeemed through Members during the Counterfeit Attack Period

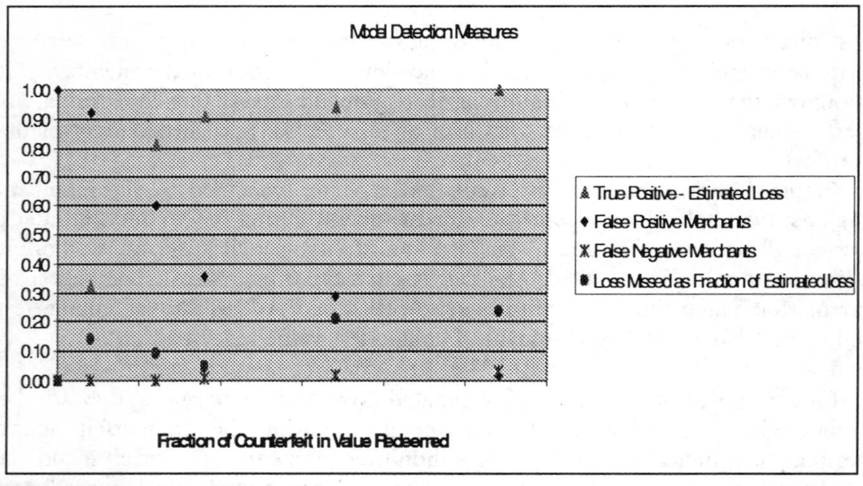

Fig. 6: Performance Measures

3.2 Results from the Merchant Monitoring System

As discussed, the merchant monitoring system resides with the member financial institution and monitors electronic value redemption by its merchants. Since it monitors the redemption patterns against its merchant's historical patterns as well as its peer group (i.e., their merchant segment), the model is independent of the size of the electronic cash economy (in comparison with the currency monitoring system.)

Figure 7 shows some of the performance measures for the system. Please note again that due to business sensitivity, actual scale of counterfeit value redemption is removed.

As shown, all 5 days of attack were recognized by the system as well as no attack day. True positive indicates the correct identification of counterfeit value redemption (whole or partial) by merchants measured as a fraction of estimated loss shown in Figure 7. True positive rate improves rapidly as the fraction of counterfeit value redemption against the total value redemption increases. And consequently, false positive identification of merchants declines (measured in number of merchants). Note that these two measures have different units, one is by the estimated loss, and the other, number of merchants.

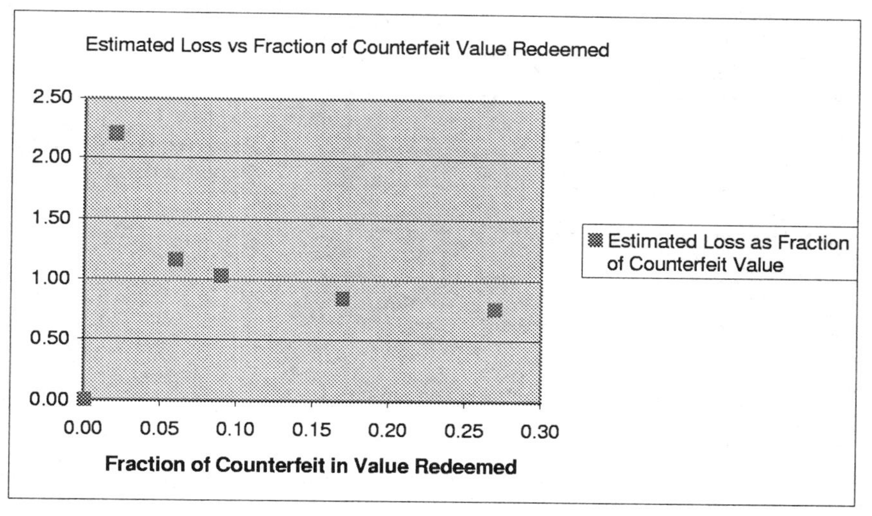

Fig. 7: Estimated Loss over Fraction of Counterfeit Value Redeemed

Figure 7 shows the estimated loss over the fraction of counterfeit value redeemed against the total value redeemed by the merchants. It shows that when the counterfeit value redemption is small, there's over estimation of counterfeit value redemption (due to false positive identification of counterfeit merchant redemption.) As the injection of counterfeit value increases, the estimate becomes more accurate and stabilizes.

Figure 8 shows the relationship between the fraction of merchants with counterfeit value redemption and fraction of counterfeit value redeemed. Naturally, the more counterfeit value injected, the more merchants are involved in the counterfeit value redemption.

The measures defined above are used to compare available systems, understand how they behave under different types of attacks and make recommendations in specific economic environment about choice and setup of the individual systems.

The characteristics of the electronic cash counterfeit problem are very different from other industries such as telecommunications or credit card industries. But in terms of purely technical measures such as:

- true positive rate
- detected fraction of counterfeit value redeemed

the performance of the tested merchant monitoring system (only one available for this study) is equivalent to, if not superior to systems described in studies by [Ezawa, *et al*, 1995 & 1996] in the telecommunications industry.

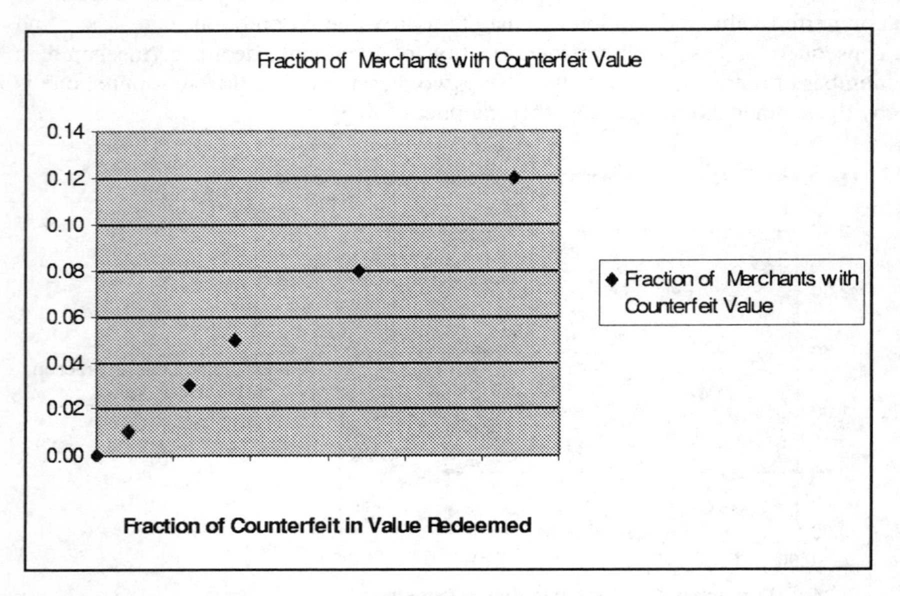

Fig. 8: Fraction of Merchants with Counterfeit Value over Fraction of Counterfeit Value Redeemed

4. Summary

In this paper, we discussed the process to evaluate the effectiveness of counterfeit detection systems for the electronic cash scheme that is not fully accounted. The process includes the use of micro dynamic simulator to simulate various counterfeit scenarios (in addition to testing in the actual non-counterfeit transaction data sets from the territories) and generate transaction data sets. The use of simulation is an absolute necessity due to that fact that actual counterfeit transaction has not been encountered, and at the same time, the detection systems have to be developed, deployed, and tested their performance in the event of counterfeit attack. Simulation allows us to evaluate the effectiveness of the detection systems quantitatively, and validate the system performance. Two selected detection systems at the different level of hierarchy, the currency monitoring and the merchant monitoring system for the counterfeit detection were used for the evaluation. A case study of preliminary test results of the performance of these systems in a simulated street corner counterfeit value distribution scenario was described and demonstrated their effectiveness.

References

1. Ezawa, K.J., and Napiorkowski, G., 1998, "Assessment of Threats for Smart Card based Electronic Cash," *Financial Cryptography '98.*
2. Ezawa, K.J. and Schuermann, T., 1995, "Fraud/Uncollectible Debt Detection Using a Bayesian Network Based Learning System: A Rare Binary Outcome with Mixed Data Structures," *Proeedings of the 11th Conference Uncertainty in Artificial Intelligence*, Morgan Kaufmann, pp. 157-166.
3. Ezawa, K.J., Singh, M., and Norton, S.W., 1996, "Learning Goal Oriented Bayesian Networks for Telecommunications Risk Management", *Proceedings of the 13th International Conference on Machine Learning*, Morgan Kaufmann.
4. Ezawa, K.J., and Norton S., 1996, "Constructing Bayesian Networks to Predict Uncollectible Telecommunications Accounts," *IEEE EXPERT*, Vol. 11, No. 5, pp. 45-51.
5. Maher, D.P., 1997, "Fault Induction Attacks, Tamper Resistance, and Hostile Reverse Engineering in Perspective," *Financial Cryptography '97 – First International Conference*, Springer Verlag.

Reasoning about Public-Key Certification: On Bindings between Entities and Public Keys

Reto Kohlas and Ueli Maurer

Department of Computer Science
Swiss Federal Institute of Technology (ETH)
CH-8092 Zürich, Switzerland
{kohlas,maurer}@inf.ethz.ch

Abstract. Public-key certification is of crucial importance for advancing the global information infrastructure, yet it suffers from certain ambiguities and lack of understanding and precision. This paper suggests a few steps towards basing public-key certification and public-key infrastructures on firmer theoretical grounds. In particular, we investigate the notion of binding a public to an entity.
We propose a calculus for deriving conclusions from a given entity Alice's (for instance a judge's) view consisting of evidence and inference rules valid in Alice's world. The evidence consists of statements made by public keys (e.g., certificates, authorizations, or recommendations), statements made physically towards Alice by other entities, and trust assumptions. Conclusions are about who says a statement, who owns or is committed to a public key, and who transfers a right or authorization to another entity, and are derived by applying the inference rules.

1 Introduction

1.1 Motivation

In recent years, cryptography has become a key technology for digitizing business processes, and this development is going to continue both with increased intensity and with global impact. While technical aspects of cryptographic mechanisms (security and efficiency of cryptographic algorithms, standardization of APIs and platforms, etc.) have received substantial attention in the past years, a precise understanding of their role in business processes is still in development.

A key aspect that is not precisely understood is the notion of *binding* a public key to an entity in order to achieve authenticity and/or non-repudiation. This paper's contribution is to propose some initial steps in the direction of a formal understanding of the role of such bindings and of digital signatures in a global public-key infrastructure (PKI).

1.2 Previous Work

There exists a large body of literature on formal methods related to information security (e.g. [12,23,24,25,18,26,10,27]). Much of this research is aimed at

M. Franklin (Ed.): FC'99, LNCS 1648, pp. 86–103, 1999.

analyzing and designing protocols or security mechanisms, most importantly bilateral authentication protocols. In contrast, the goal of the formal approach taken in this paper is to illustrate a number of important points in the context of public-key certification that have previously not been made precise. Our calculus models desirable conclusions when using digital signatures and public-key certificates as evidence and hence contributes to a more precise understanding of what one tries to achieve with a PKI.

Previous Work on PKIs. From a high-level point of view, a possible classification of problem areas and research contributions related to PKIs is as follows:

- *Certificate format and content.* It has been recognized that PGP- and X.509-certificates are not well-suited for electronic commerce, and several research efforts have been made to define new certificate formats and semantics [15,8,2,21,28].
- *Revocation.* One particular area of interest is to design efficient mechanisms for withdrawing public keys or certificates that have become invalid for a certain reason [11,16,4,9,27,13,5].
- *Name spaces.* It is non-trivial to establish and implement a global, context- and application-independent naming scheme as in the X.500 recommendation. To avoid this problem, SDSI proposes the linking of local name spaces [29,6].
- *Trust models and uncertainty management.* Most evidence in real life is to some degree uncertain. It can therefore be desirable to model uncertainty by assigning confidence values to evidence and conclusions, in particular regarding the trustworthiness of entities.[1] Similarly, the reliability of the identification underlying certification can depend on the procedure that is used. The term trust model is often used to refer to models and techniques for dealing with uncertainty in these contexts [22,3,14,17,19,30,7,20,31].
- *Information systems aspects.* A global PKI will be a complex distributed information system whose design and implementation are a research area of independent interest.

Notions of Bindings Between Entities and Public Keys. This paper's contributions should be seen as an extension of the work in the first of the above research areas.

In the literature on public-key certification, "binding" is a term that is often used to indicate that a public key represents an entity. A digitally signed statement that asserts a binding between an entity and a public key is sometimes called an "identity-based certificate" [2], but the exact nature of the binding is often unclear. We summarize different notions of bindings in the literature.

In X.509 [32], a public key is bound to the entity if the entity "possesses" (or controls or owns in our terminology) the public key. It is expected explicitly that

[1] In PGP for instance, trustworthiness can be estimated by five different values: (unknown, no trust, marginally trusted, fully trusted, ultimate trust)

the key owner keeps the secret key confidential. It is unclear whether a X.509 certificate should be interpreted as an assertion by the certificate issuer that the entity controls the contained public key or simply claimed that it controls the key. It is further unclear to what extent the key owner was instructed by the certification authority to assure that the secret key remains confidential and to what extent he or she will be liable for messages (or statements according to our terminology) signed by the secret key.

"A PGP public-key certificate is, in essence, a public key together with a user ID testifying that the user ID associated with this public key is valid" [1]. It is not specified in the documentation when a public key is valid for an entity, and the notion of binding is left unspecified. Common practice of PGP users is to issue a certificate when another user claims ownership of a key.[2]

SDSI [29,2] explicitly assumes that every key is controlled by at most one entity; hence the binding of SDSI certificates is similar to that of X.509 certificates. SPKI certificates are sometimes called *authorization-based* certificates [8,2]. SPKI also explicitly assumes exclusive ownership of the keys. A prominent example in SPKI is that an issuer (i.e., a public key) delegates an authorization to another key. The entity controlling the key can obtain the authorization by digitally signing the requests. SPKI naming is based on SDSI.

Lampson, Abadi, Burrows, and Wobber [24] model, among other things, the role of public-key certificates and certification authorities (possibly organized hierarchically) in the context of access control. Because the focus is on access control, where the access control mechanism is trusted by default, trust is in this paper not a resource explicitly expressed. The only type of binding between public keys and an entities is the "speaks for" relation, meaning that if a statement s is digitally signed with a key speaking for the entity, then the entity says s. It is not considered that different entities might have different views; in particular, certification authorities are always universally trusted. Thus, all entities will draw the same conclusions.

1.3 Contributions of this Paper

We illustrate a number of points that have previously not been made explicit:

- Because sole ownership can inherently not be verified (except in a context where a physical device internally generates and uniquely controls a secret key), one should not rely on such a claim or assumption. While in certain contexts exclusive ownership is not needed and a claim of ownership suffices, in other contexts the liability of a claimed key owner must be made explicit, making it the owner's interest to be and remain the sole owner, i.e. to protect the secret key.

  For instance, in the case of encryption and signature keys, an entity (say Alice) can be trusted by default to be the exclusive owner of a particular

[2] In general, the user presents a hash value (the "fingerprint") of the public key to the introducer.

key. Alice has no interest in claiming false ownership, since otherwise another entity could sign in Alice's name or decrypt messages sent to Alice, which, if it were desirable for Alice for some reason, Alice could also achieve by performing herself the operations requiring the secret key on behalf of another entity.
In contrast, in a legal context a claim by Alice to be the exclusive key owner of a signature key is not sufficient evidence; the key could have been intended for other applications (e.g. PGP), and it would be inappropriate to silently let the entity be legally bound to statements signed by the key. Rather, Alice must declare explicitly her intention to use the key in a legal context. We call such a statement to accept the legal consequences of using a signature key a *commitment* of an entity to a key. A commitment to a key can be seen as a special kind of ownership claim.
- The main role of a certification authority is to make statements, through its own public key, about statements (claim of ownership or commitment) made by other entities.
- The role of self-certificates. If a right or privilege is transferred to a key owner of the signature public key, then Alice's mere claim of ownership of the key or the commitment of Alice to the key cannot be used to conclude that Alice is authorized to receive the right. Rather, Alice must prove ownership of the key, for instance by digitally signing the statement that Alice is a owner of the key with the same key. This is a self-certificate. On the other hand, in contrast to the recommendations made in PGP (e.g. see [1] (p. 97)), self-certificates do not contribute to drawing conclusions when exchanging signature or encryption keys.

1.4 Outline

In Section 2 we informally introduce the basic concepts of the calculus, and in Section 3 we state basic definitions. The inference rules are discussed in Section 4. The purpose of Section 5 is to illustrate the use of the calculus in a few typical scenarios. Some open problems and directions for future research are mentioned in Section 6.

2 Concepts

2.1 Principals: Entities and Public Keys

The two types of principals[3] in our model are *public-key pairs* and *entities*. A public-key pair consists of two parts. The public part is used to verify signatures or to encrypt data. The private part allows to generate digital signatures or

[3] The term "principal" is sometimes used differently in the cryptographic literature. While in SPKI/SDSI public keys are called principals, in the calculus of Lampson et al. [24] and [23] all "sources for request" (users, machines, cryptographic keys) are called principals.

to decrypt data; it must therefore be protected from unauthorized access. For simplicity, we will refer to public-key pairs by "public keys" or "keys".

Entities are human beings or legal entities. An entity *controls* (or *owns*) the public key if it can use the public key to decrypt or sign data. In practice, a public key is controlled through knowledge (e.g. of the secret key or a pass phrase protecting the secret key), or through possession of a physical token (e.g. a smart card).

2.2 Statements

In any formal system one defines the basic units of concern, often called formulas, which can take on different truth values, most often the values true and false. In our calculus, these basic units are called *statements*, and the truth values are *valid* and *not valid* rather than true and false, for reasons explained in Section 2.3. The term statement refers (1) to what principals "say", (2) to the pieces of evidence, and (3) to what is concluded in the calculus.

One kind of statements that one may wish to conclude is that an entity Alice made a certain statement s (i.e. Alice said s), in particular in a case where s is signed by a certain signature public key. This process of deriving the statement that Alice said s is traditionally known as *authentication* in the case where an entity draws this conclusion in her own view. It is also known as *non-repudiation* in the case where a legal system (e.g. a court) draws this conclusion or, more precisely, where an entity takes the court's view and convinces herself that the statement Alice said s would be derived by the court from the given evidence.

Note that in the case of non-repudiation, the final goal is often not to conclude that an entity said something, but rather that a certain privilege, value, or right (e.g. a payment agreement) has been transferred to another entity. We capture all of them in concept of a *right.* Transferring a right is a basic statement.

2.3 Views

The basic idea behind our calculus is that an entity (say Bob) draws conclusions from his evidence, consisting of statements, by applying certain inference rules. We call the collected evidence and the inference rules of a given entity his *view.*[4] The view reflects Bob's initial belief from which further believed statements can be derived. The fact that a statement s is in Bob's view does not imply that it is true in an absolute sense, only that in Bob's context it is reasonable to make this assumption. Similarly, the fact that s is not in Bob's view does not mean that s is false; it could be that Bob simply does not pay attention to s. Statements in an entity's view or derived from it according to the inference rules are therefore called *valid* rather than true. All statements that cannot be derived

[4] The concept of a view was introduced in [7], and four different statements have been defined. In contrast, we recursively define a set of statements. Moreover, because different entities might interpret the evidence in different ways, also inference rules are part of a view.

could be called "not valid" to define the second truth value, but this term will not be used.

The views (beliefs) of different entities are generally different. Trust relations in particular can be subject to an entity's experience, context, or policy. For instance, one can think of the legal system as consisting of a certain agreed-upon and published set of rules and statements (when neglecting many aspects related to the fact that not everything can be formalized and that human beings (e.g. judges) play an important role.) In a dispute, these statements and rules can be taken into a judge's view. Such statements could for instance be about the trustworthiness of certain legally or otherwise appointed certification authorities. An entity must therefore adopt a different view depending on whether the conclusions should be convincing only for herself or for a legal entity, say a judge.

3 Definitions

We clearly distinguish between the syntactic definitions of our calculus (which can be glanced through in a first reading) and the meaning of the statements.

3.1 Syntactic Definitions

Let $\mathcal{K}^e$ and $\mathcal{K}^s$ denote the (not necessarily distinct) sets of encryption public keys and signature public keys, respectively, and let $\mathcal{K}$ denote denote the set of all keys: $\mathcal{K} = \mathcal{K}^e \cup \mathcal{K}^s$. Let $\mathcal{E}$ be the set of entities. The set of principals consists of the public keys and entities and is denoted by $\mathcal{P}$: $\mathcal{P} = \mathcal{E} \cup \mathcal{K}$. By $\mathcal{R}$ we denote the set of rights. Elements of a set are written in small letters and variables in capital letters. Key variables and values carrying as subscript the name of an entity stand for the key allegedly belonging to the entity.

For describing the syntax of the statements and the rules, we use the Extended Backus-Naur Formalism (EBNF).[5] Each statement consists of a predefined name , together with a list of arguments in parenthesis. Each argument is a term of a certain type. All statements are in prefix notation, with exception of the st atement says.

Definition 1.

$$
\begin{array}{lcl}
\mathit{term}(\mathcal{T}) & = & \mathit{element}(\mathcal{T}) \mid \mathit{variable}(\mathcal{T}) \\
\mathit{statement} & = & \mathsf{own}(\mathit{term}(\mathcal{E}), \mathit{term}(\mathcal{K})) \mid \\
 & & \mathsf{transfer}(\mathit{term}(\mathcal{E}), \mathit{term}(\mathcal{E} \cup \mathcal{K}^s), \mathit{term}(\mathcal{R})) \mid \\
 & & \mathit{term}(\mathcal{E} \cup \mathcal{K}^s)\ \mathsf{says}\ \mathit{statement} \mid \\
 & & \mathsf{commit}(\mathit{term}(\mathcal{E}), \mathit{term}(\mathcal{K}^s), \mathit{statement}) \mid \\
 & & \mathsf{trust}(\mathit{term}(\mathcal{E}), \mathit{statement}) \\
\mathit{inference\text{-}rule} & = & \text{“}\langle\text{”}\ \mathit{statement}\{\text{“,”}\ \mathit{statement}\}\ \text{“}\vdash\text{”}\ \mathit{statement}\ \text{“}\rangle\text{”}
\end{array}
$$

[5] AB stands for the concatenation of the expressions A and B, $A|B$ for the the alternative between A and B, and $\{A\}$ for the repeated concatenation of A (including the empty word). Let *element*($\mathcal{T}$) stand for an element of a set $\mathcal{T}$ and *variable*($\mathcal{T}$) for a variable of type $\mathcal{T}$ (a type is a set).

For convenience, we allow an equivalent notation for rules:

$$\textit{inference-rule} \;=\; \frac{\textit{statement}\{\text{“,”}\,\textit{statement}\}}{\textit{statement}}$$

Extending the above definition (this can be seen as syntactic sugar), we interpret a statement in which a set of values of the corresponding type (rather than a single term) is used as an argument, to be the set of statements resulting from plugging in, one by one, every element of the set.

Definition 2. The *view* of an entity a, denoted by View_a, is a set consisting of statements and inference rules. ○

The following definitions describe the mechanism of deriving a statement from a view.

Definition 3. Let V be a variable of type $\mathcal{T}$ occurring in the statement s and let v be an element in $\mathcal{T}$. Let W be a variable of the same type as V. Then $s[V = v]$ denotes the statement that is obtained by replacing all occurrences of V in s by v (instantiation of V). Similarly, if s is a statement in which W does not occur, then $s[V = W]$ is the statement where V is renamed to W (variable substitution). ○

Definition 4. Let $s_1, \ldots, s_i$ be statements. A *variable assignment* $\mathcal{I}$ for an inference rule $\langle s_1,\ s_2,\ \ldots,\ s_{i-1} \vdash\ s_i\rangle$ maps each variable occurring in the inference rule to an element of the corresponding type. $s_j^{\mathcal{I}}$ is the statement that is obtained by replacing all occurrences of the variables in s_j by the values specified in $\mathcal{I}$. ○

Definition 5. A statement is *valid* in View_a if it is either contained in View_a or if it can be derived from View_a by repeated application of the inference rules in View_a. More precisely,

- All statements in View_a are valid.
- Let V be a variable of type $\mathcal{T}$ occurring in s, let W be a variable of the same type not occurring in s, and let v be any element of $\mathcal{T}$. If s is valid, then the statements $s[V = v]$ and $s[V = W]$ are also valid.[6]
- Let $s_1, \ldots, s_i$ be statements. If for a rule of the form $\langle s_1, \ldots, s_{i-1} \vdash s_i\rangle$ in View_a there is a variable assignment $\mathcal{I}$ such that $s_j^{\mathcal{I}}$ is valid for $j = 1, \ldots, i-1$, then $s_i^{\mathcal{I}}$ is also valid. ○

Example. We illustrate the mechanisms of variable instantiation and variable substitution in a simple example. Note that in the examples of Section 5, these formal steps are not shown explicitly. Consider the following view:

$$\begin{aligned}\mathsf{View}_A = \{\ & \langle X \text{ says } S,\ \mathsf{trust}(X, S) \vdash S\rangle,\\ & \mathsf{trust}(b, \mathsf{trust}(Y, X \text{ says } \mathsf{own}(X, K))),\\ & b \text{ says } \mathsf{trust}(c, Y \text{ says } \mathsf{own}(Y, K))\ \}\end{aligned}$$

[6] Hence if an argument is a variable, all the occurrences of the variable are universally quantified ($\forall$).

One can derive $\text{trust}(c, X \text{ says own}(X, K))$ by the following sequence of application of Definition 5.

- $\text{trust}(b, \text{trust}(Y, X \text{ says own}(X, K)))$ is valid, because it is in the view.
- $\text{trust}(b, \text{trust}(Y, X \text{ says own}(X, K)))[Y{=}c] =$
  $\text{trust}(b, \text{trust}(c, X \text{ says own}(X, K)))$ is valid.
- $\text{trust}(b, \text{trust}(c, X \text{ says own}(X, K)))[X{=}Y] =$
  $\text{trust}(b, \text{trust}(c, Y \text{ says own}(Y, K)))$ is valid.
- The inference rule $\langle X \text{ says } S, \text{trust}(X, S) \vdash S\rangle$ can now be applied. Let $X = b$ and $S = Y \text{ says own}(Y, K)$ be a variable assignment of the rule. The statements $\text{trust}(b, \text{trust}(c, Y \text{ says own}(Y, K)))$ and b says $\text{trust}(c, Y \text{ says own}(Y, K))$ are valid and therefore $\text{trust}(c, X \text{ says own}(X, K))$ is also valid.

3.2 Meaning of Statements

We now discuss the meaning of the statements. We only describe the case where all arguments are elements of a set ($x \in \mathcal{E}$, $k \in \mathcal{K}$, $k^s \in \mathcal{K}^s$, $e \in \mathcal{E} \cup \mathcal{K}^s$, $r \in \mathcal{R}$), rather than variables. The symbol s stands for a specific statement. If a statement contains variables as arguments, the meaning is implied by the meaning for specific values through the above definition of validity. Variable substitutions do not change the meaning of a statement.

$\text{trust}(x, s)$ Entity x is trustworthy with respect to the statement s. The statement $\text{trust}(x)$ means that x is trustworthy with respect to all statements.

k^s says s The statement s is digitally signed with the signature key k^s. We assume that every entity has a trusted computing base for checking digital signatures, i.e., every entity can verify whether k^s says s is valid.

x says s An entity x can say s by a variety of mechanisms. Saying s can mean to pronounce s, to write s on a piece of paper, to type s into a computer, to initiate a process that generates a string corresponding to s, or to create any other unique representation of s. Note that the act of signing s is not an act of saying s but rather of creating evidence for other entities to conclude that x says s.
Note that for instance in authentication protocols (e.g., for access control), it is important to know that a statement is fresh. In contrast to the BAN logic, it is not the goal of this paper to model authentication protocols, and hence freshness is not modeled. However, it is a possible extension of this work to include time aspects like freshness.

$\text{own}(x, k)$ Entity x is an exclusive owner of the public key k or, equivalently, x solely controls the public key k in the sense that he can perform any operation requiring access to the secret key.

$\mathsf{commit}(x, k^s, s)$ Entity x is committed to the signature public key k^s with respect to statement s. A commitment of x to k^s with respect to s means that x agrees to be liable in a legal sense to have said s, provided s is digitally signed with k^s. $\mathsf{commit}(x, k^s)$ stands for the statement that x is committed to k^s with respect to all statements.

$\mathsf{transfer}(x, e, r)$ Entity x delegates a right r to e (or owes a right to e). If e is a signature public key k^s, then $\mathsf{transfer}(x, k^s, r)$ means that the right is delegated to an entity owning the public key k^s.[7]

4 Inference Rules

Throughout the paper, $K \in \mathcal{K}^e \cup \mathcal{K}^s$, $K^s \in \mathcal{K}^s$ and $K^e \in \mathcal{K}^e$ are variables standing for any public key, for a signature public key and for an encryption public key, respectively. Similarly, X, $Y \in \mathcal{E}$, $E \in \mathcal{E} \cup \mathcal{K}^s$, and $R \in \mathcal{R}$ are variables for an entity, for an entity or a signature public key, and for a right, respectively. Furthermore, S is a variable of type $\mathcal{S}$, where $\mathcal{S}$ is the set of all syntactically correct statements.
We introduce inference rules that illustrate the conclusions that a can draw from the statements contained in her view View_a. We discuss rules for using trust and rules applicable in the two settings of bilateral communications and legally binding statements. We do not claim in any sense that the rules proposed here are the only reasonable way for an entity to interpret the evidence. The rules might for instance differ from one legal environment to another; as explained in the previous section, we therefore allow the rules to be part of an entity's view.

4.1 Trust

Trust can be seen as a basic mechanism which allows one entity to believe a statement made by another. If one trusts X on S, and if X says S, then one has reason to believe S. Note that the statement X says S makes no sense because it means that every entity says every statement. However, it makes sense to use it within a rule because S will always be instantiated to a concrete statement or a set of statements.

Rule 1a.

$$\frac{\mathsf{trust}(X, S),\ X \ \mathsf{says}\ S}{S}$$

One can have a more detailed understanding of trust. In the BAN logic for instance, a server cannot only be trusted to provide the correct keys, but also to generate good keys.

[7] In fact, a right could also be delegated to an encryption key: an entity can prove ownership by challenge-response protocol.

Trust is a fundamental and rare resource. Many of the trust relations used in real life are not based on personal experience but rather on explicit or implicit recommendations, a concept first formalized in [17]. A recommendation is a statement of an entity about the trustworthiness of another entity. a could for instance recommend b for making statements about the ownership of keys: a says trust$(b, \mathsf{own}(Z, K^s))$. An entity must explicitly be trusted to issue recommendations, otherwise the recommendation cannot be used as evidence to draw further conclusions.

4.2 Bilateral Communication

Assume that one wants to encrypt a message for X or verify whether a digitally signed message has been sent by X. In both cases, one needs to establish that X eexclusively owns a certain key. We argue that ownership need not be proven (in fact sole ownership cannot be proven), but what is needed is a statement by X that he solely owns the key. By making a false claim of ownership (either for a key not controlled or not exclusively controlled), X cannot achieve more than what he could achieve by other means. Namely, instead of violating secrecy by making a false claim of ownership for an encryption public key, X could achieve the same goal by revealing the contents of an encrypted (for X) message to another entity. Similarly, X could sign a message provided by another entity, thus violating authenticity. Hence, if X says that he solely controls K, one can derive that K is exclusively owned by X.

Rule 2a.

$$\frac{X \text{ says } \mathsf{own}(X, K)}{\mathsf{own}(X, K)}$$

Note that this rule could be replaced by the statement $\mathsf{trust}(X, \mathsf{own}(X, K))$. If one believes that X solely owns the signature key K^s, and if there is a statement S digitally signed with K^s, then one has reason to believe that X says S:

Rule 2b.

$$\frac{\mathsf{own}(X, K^s),\ \ K^s \text{ says } S}{X \text{ says } S}$$

Similarly, if one believes that X solely owns the encryption key K^e, then one can use K^e to encrypt a message for X. However, secrecy is not captured as a concept in this first version of our calculus, and hence there is no rule corresponding to Rule 2b.

4.3 Commitments and Non-repudiation

As has been recognized by the legislative bodies issuing digital signature legislation, one has to be very cautious when taking digital signatures as evidence in a legal sense. For one thing, there are various technical risks (key compromise or system misuse due to flaws and bugs), cryptographic risks (e.g. the discovery of a fast factoring algorithm), and risks due to incompetence and negligence by the users.

On the other hand, there is also the problem that ownership statements are strongly context-dependent, and that this is not reflected in previous technical proposals for public-key certification. For instance, the statement by X that he controls a certain PGP public key K^s cannot be used as evidence that X agrees in a legal sense to be liable for statements signed by K^s. Rather, X must declare explicitly his intention to use the key in a legal context and, furthermore, for which kinds of statements (e.g. for any statements implying liability up to $1000). We call such a statement to accept liability for statements made by a signature key a *commitment* of an entity to the key. A commitment by X to a signature key K^s with respect to the statement S can be seen as a special kind of ownership claim.[8]

Rule 3a.

$$\frac{X \text{ says } \mathsf{commit}(X, K^s, S)}{\mathsf{commit}(X, K^s, S)}$$

Rule 3b.

$$\frac{\mathsf{commit}(X, K^s, S),\ K^s \text{ says } S}{X \text{ says } S}$$

Note that in a legal context there will be a restriction of what constitutes "saying" in our sense. In particular, the statement of being committed must be made in a specific way (e.g. by an ordinary signature on a paper contract).

4.4 Transfer of Rights

In many legal scenarios, the statement of interest is not whether an entity X said something, but whether X delegated a right to another entity Y. A right is transferred from X to E if X says so.

Rule 4a.

$$\frac{X \text{ says } \mathsf{transfer}(X, E, R)}{\mathsf{transfer}(X, E, R)}$$

Privacy and anonymity are increasingly important issues in electronic commerce. It will become more and more common to transfer privileges to a key or pseudonym, without knowing the identity of the person controlling the key except in case of a dispute (for an example, see Section 5). Therefore one needs a mechanism for a key owner to claim the right transferred to a public key. Note that if a right is reproducible (e.g., access to a database), then several entities could control the public key. For rights that must inherently be restricted to one receiving entity (e.g., a payment), it must be assured in the first place by the receiving entity that the rights are transferred to a key it solely owns.

Rule 4b.

[8] Note that by replacing $\mathsf{commit}(X, K^s, S)$ with $\mathsf{own}(X, K^s)$, Rules 3a and 3b exactly correspond to Rules 2b and 2a.

$$\frac{\mathsf{transfer}(X, K^s, R),\ \mathsf{own}(Y, K^s)}{\mathsf{transfer}(X, Y, R)}$$

One possibility to prove ownership for redeeming a right is a self-certificate, i.e., a statement that is digitally signed with K^s and asserts who the key owner of K^s is. Only a key owner of K^s can issue a self-certificate. One can postulate the rule that a self-certificate proves ownership of a key, i.e. the rule

Rule 4c.

$$\frac{K^s \text{ says } \mathsf{own}(Y, K^s)}{\mathsf{own}(Y, K^s)}$$

However, this rule makes sense only in the context of redeeming a right transferred to K^s, but of course not in the context of bilateral communication. An attacker could attach, by a self-certificate, an arbitrary identity to a public key it generated, and hence this statement should not be applicable in that context. In the sequel, we denote by

$$\mathsf{IR_P} = \{1\text{a}, 1\text{b}, 2\text{b}, 2\text{a}\}$$

the set of inference rules applicable in a private or bilateral scenario and by

$$\mathsf{IR_L} = \{1\text{a}, 1\text{b}, 3\text{a}, 3\text{b}, 4\text{a}, 4\text{b}, 4\text{c}\}$$

the rules that can be applied in a legal context.

5 Scenarios

We illustrate our rules on some concrete scenarios. The first example shows various ways in which an entity can derive that a certain public key is owned by a certain entity. The purpose of the second example is to give a simplistic and idealized framework for concluding digital contracts (e.g., for electronic commerce). In the third scenario an entity delegates a right to a key owner, without knowing the identity of the key owner.
In order to keep the examples readable, we will not explicitly show the variable instantiations and substitutions made in the derivations. Instead, we only show, for every application of an inference rule, the instantiated preconditions and the consequence of the rule, separated by the symbol $\Rightarrow$ to indicate that the latter follows from the former.

5.1 Exchange of Public Keys for Authenticating and Encrypting Mail

Alice (denoted by a) wants to check whether a digitally signed e-mail message (which contains the message s) has been sent by Bob (denoted by b). Since the mails are for private use only, a will not require b to commit to the key k_b^s. In order to apply Rule 2a, a must somehow derive the statement b says $\mathsf{own}(b, k_b^s)$. This can happen in various ways.

Exchange of Public Keys by Non-Digital Means. a could directly obtain b's public key k_b^s from b. a could meet b in person, or b could provide his key during a telephone call; in this case a can verify that b says $\mathsf{own}(b, k_b^s)$ is valid. Assume that a later gets the digitally signed message s. Thus, her view contains the following two statements.

$$\mathsf{View}_a = \{\ k_b^s \text{ says } s,\ b \text{ says } \mathsf{own}(b, k_b^s)\ \} \cup \mathsf{IR_P}$$

a can apply the following two rules to derive b says s.

$$b \text{ says } \mathsf{own}(b, k_b^s) \Rightarrow \mathsf{own}(b, k_b^s) \qquad (2a)$$
$$\mathsf{own}(b, k_b^s),\ k_b^s \text{ says } s \Rightarrow b \text{ says } s \qquad (2b)$$

a could also rely on the statements of entities she trusts in order to derive b says $\mathsf{own}(b, k_b^s)$. In the following, let

$$s_1 = X \text{ says } \mathsf{own}(X, K^s)$$

If her friend Carol (c) says that b says $\mathsf{own}(b, k_b^s)$, and if a trusts c to provide the keys of other entities (i.e., c is trusted on s_1), a can authenticate b's key.

$$\mathsf{View}_a = \{\ k_b^s \text{ says } s,\ c \text{ says } b \text{ says } \mathsf{own}(b, k_b^s),\ \mathsf{trust}(c, s_1)\ \} \cup \mathsf{IR_P}$$

The statement $\mathsf{trust}(c, s_1)$ means that c is trusted on the statements that some entity X has claimed exclusive ownership of some key K^s. Thus c is trusted on b says $\mathsf{own}(b, k_b^s)$ (variable instantiation), and because c says b says $\mathsf{own}(b, k_b^s)$ is valid in a's view, a can apply Rule 1a to derive the statement b says $\mathsf{own}(b, k_b^s)$. From this, a can apply the same two rules as above to conclude that b says s.

Certificates and Certificate Chains. Instead of making the statement c says b says $\mathsf{own}(b, k_b^s)$ directly towards a, this is achieved, in a typical scenario, with a certificate containing this statement. Of course, we also need the statement c says $\mathsf{own}(c, k_c^s)$.

$$\mathsf{View}_a = \{\ k_b^s \text{ says } s,\ k_c^s \text{ says } b \text{ says } \mathsf{own}(b, k_b^s),\ c \text{ says } \mathsf{own}(c, k_c^s),\ \mathsf{trust}(c, s_1)\ \} \cup \mathsf{IR_P}$$

Since c is trusted to provide her own signature key, a concludes $\mathsf{own}(c, k_c^s)$ by Rule 2a. Thus, by Rule 2b, a can derive c says b says $\mathsf{own}(b, k_b^s)$. Finally, a can again apply the same rules as in the previous view to derive b says s.
Perhaps another friend of Alice, Dave (d), knows that c says $\mathsf{own}(c, k_c^s)$. If a trusts him to provide the keys of other entities, and if a has d's signature key (d says $\mathsf{own}(d, k_d^s)$), a can obtain c's key.

$$\mathsf{View}_a = \{\ k_b^s \text{ says } s,\ k_c^s \text{ says } b \text{ says } \mathsf{own}(b, k_b^s),\ d \text{ says } \mathsf{own}(d, k_d^s),\ k_d^s \text{ says } c \text{ says } \mathsf{own}(c, k_c^s),\ \mathsf{trust}(c, s_1),\ \mathsf{trust}(d, s_1)\ \} \cup \mathsf{IR_P}$$

Here d issues a certificate for c (digitally signed with k_d^s) and c for b (with k_c^s). Since a trusts both c and d to provide the keys of other entities, a can retrieve the signature key of b. The following sequence of rules is applied:

$$
\begin{array}{rcll}
d \text{ says own}(d, k_d^s) & \Rightarrow & \text{own}(d, k_d^s) & (2a)\\
\text{own}(d, k_d^s),\ k_d^s \text{ says } c \text{ says own}(c, k_c^s) & \Rightarrow & d \text{ says } c \text{ says own}(c, k_c^s) & (2b)\\
d \text{ says } c \text{ says own}(c, k_c^s),\ \text{trust}(d, s_1) & \Rightarrow & c \text{ says own}(c, k_c^s) & (1a)\\
c \text{ says own}(c, k_c^s) & \Rightarrow & \text{own}(c, k_c^s) & (2a)\\
\text{own}(c, k_c^s),\ k_c^s \text{ says } b \text{ says own}(b, k_b^s) & \Rightarrow & c \text{ says } b \text{ says own}(b, k_b^s) & (2b)\\
c \text{ says } b \text{ says own}(b, k_b^s),\ \text{trust}(c, s_1) & \Rightarrow & b \text{ says own}(b, k_b^s) & (1a)\\
b \text{ says own}(b, k_b^s) & \Rightarrow & \text{own}(b, k_b^s) & (2a)\\
\text{own}(b, k_b^s),\ k_b^s \text{ says s} & \Rightarrow & b \text{ says s} & (2b)
\end{array}
$$

Such a scheme where one entity certifies the key of another entity is often referred to as a certificate chain.

Trust in c could also be established by a recommendation of d for c. d could for instance recommend c for certifying ownership of keys. In this case, a must explicitly trust d for recommending other entities.

$$
\begin{aligned}
\text{View}_a = \{\ & k_b^s \text{ says } s,\ k_c^s \text{ says } b \text{ says own}(b, k_b^s),\ \text{trust}(d, s_1),\ \text{trust}(d, s_2)\\
& k_d^s \text{ says } c \text{ says own}(c, k_c^s),\ d \text{ says trust}(c, s_1),\ d \text{ says own}(d, k_d^s)\ \} \cup \text{IR}_\text{P}
\end{aligned}
$$

where

$$
s_2 = \text{trust}(X, Y \text{ says own}(Y, K^s))
$$

The statement $\text{trust}(d, s_2)$ stands for a's trust in d to issue recommendations for other entities.

Exchanging an Encryption Key. While in some systems (for instance PGP), the same key is used for signing and encrypting messages, it makes sense to separate these two functions. The authentication of an encryption key is identical to the authentication of a signature key, i.e., the statement $b \text{ says own}(b, k_b^e)$ must be derived.

Self-Certificates. The main purpose of PGP is to encrypt and authenticate mail messages. There seems to be a misconception about the role of self-certificates. For instance, [1] suggests to append self-certificates to a public key. However, as illustrated by the rules, self-certificates do not occur as a precondition of a rule and are not needed for exchanging encryption and signature keys on a bilateral basis. Hence they can at most mislead an entity a to believe that a key is b's, if a draws incorrect conclusions. More precisely, neither the statement $b \text{ says own}(b, k_b^s)$ nor the statement $\text{own}(b, k_b^s)$ can be derived from the following view

$$
\text{View}_a = \{\ k_b^s \text{ says own}(b, k_b^s)\ \} \cup \text{IR}_\text{P}
$$

because an impostor e could of course generate a public key k_e^s and sign with it the self-certificate: $k_e^s \text{ says own}(b, k_e^s)$.

5.2 A Simple Legal Framework

In the following example we describe an infrastructure allowing two entities to conclude a contract with digital signatures. A contract can be seen as a transfer of a right r_1 from a to b ($\mathsf{transfer}(a, b, r_1)$), and possibly also a right r_2 from b to a ($\mathsf{transfer}(b, a, r_2)$). In order to achieve non-repudiation, each entity's goal is to be able to derive in the legal system's view that the other party has transferred the corresponding right.
Unlike in the scenarios described in Section 5.1, it does not matter for a whether she believes that a certification authority is trustworthy, but rather whether the legal system does. It can be assumed that the legal system's policy and trust relations, i.e. its view, is clearly specified and publicly known, and that also the public keys root CAs are publicly known in an authenticated manner.
In the sequel, we adopt the legal system's (e.g., a judge's) view who wants to verify (i.e. derive) the statement $\mathsf{transfer}(a, b, r_1)$.
It is conceivable that the legislator defining the legal system appoints a set of distinguished authorities that are trusted by default (i.e. in the legal system's view): certification authorities, naming authorities registration authorities, key revocation authorities (if not part of the CA), etc., subsumed below under the term CA. In the sequel, let

$$s_1 = \mathsf{transfer}(Y, Z, \{R | R \text{ stands for a cash value up to \$1000}\})$$
$$s_2 = Y \ \mathsf{says}\ \mathsf{commit}(Y, K^s, s_1)$$
$$s_3 = \mathsf{trust}(X, s_2).$$

Note that from a syntactical point of view, s_1 is not a statement but stands for a set of statements. In our scenario, b tries to collect evidence that a owes him \$500. The judge trusts one root certification authority ca_1 to license other certification authorities (this corresponds to the statement $\mathsf{trust}(ca_1, s_3)$ in the view shown below). Furthermore, he trusts ca_1 to correctly certify the keys of other entities ($\mathsf{trust}(ca_1, s_2)$). Additionally, the judge believes that ca_1 uses k_1^s as its signature key.
Assuming that ca_1 has licensed ca_2 (ca_1 says $\mathsf{trust}(ca_2, s_2)$), b can retrieve a digitally signed statement of ca_2 asserting that a is committed to k_a^s with respect to s_1 (ca_2 says a says $\mathsf{commit}(a, k_a^s, s_1)$ The statement k_a^s says $\mathsf{transfer}(a, b, r_1)$ is in the judge's view because a signed the contract and b produced the fact as evidence in the dispute. Thus, the judge's view is:

$$\begin{aligned} \mathsf{View}_{judge} = \{ & ca_1 \ \mathsf{says}\ \mathsf{commit}(ca_1, k_1^s),\ k_1^s \ \mathsf{says}\ \mathsf{trust}(ca_2, s_2), \\ & k_1^s \ \mathsf{says}\ ca_2 \ \mathsf{says}\ \mathsf{commit}(ca_2, k_2^s),\ k_2^s \ \mathsf{says}\ a \ \mathsf{says}\ \mathsf{commit}(a, k_a^s, s_1), \\ & k_a^s \ \mathsf{says}\ \mathsf{transfer}(a, b, r_1), \mathsf{trust}(ca_1, s_2), \mathsf{trust}(ca_1, s_3)\ \} \cup \mathsf{IR_L} \end{aligned}$$

The following table summarizes the complete sequence of applications of inference rules for deriving $\mathsf{transfer}(a, b, r_1)$ in the judge's view. Note again that it is irrelevant in this context whether an actual dispute is being resolved by the judge or whether b convinces himself that in case of a dispute, he would be able to produce a convincing collection of evidence for $\mathsf{transfer}(a, b, r_1)$.

$$\begin{aligned}
ca_1 \text{ says commit}(ca_1, k_1^s) &\Rightarrow \text{commit}(ca_1, k_1^s)\\
\text{commit}(ca_1, k_1^s),\ k_1^s \text{ says trust}(ca_2, s_2) &\Rightarrow ca_1 \text{ says trust}(ca_2, s_2)\\
ca_1 \text{ says trust}(ca_2, s_2),\ \text{trust}(ca_1, s_3) &\Rightarrow \text{trust}(ca_2, s_2)\\
\text{commit}(ca_1, k_1^s),\ k_1^s \text{ says } ca_2 \text{ says commit}(ca_2, k_2^s) &\Rightarrow ca_1 \text{ says } ca_2 \text{ says commit}(ca_2, k_2^s)\\
ca_1 \text{ says } ca_2 \text{ says commit}(ca_2, k_2^s),\ \text{trust}(ca_1, s_2) &\Rightarrow ca_2 \text{ says commit}(ca_2, k_2^s)\\
ca_2 \text{ says commit}(ca_2, k_2^s) &\Rightarrow \text{commit}(ca_2, k_2^s)\\
\text{commit}(ca_2, k_2^s),\ k_2^s \text{ says } a \text{ says commit}(a, k_a^s, s_1) &\Rightarrow ca_2 \text{ says } a \text{ says commit}(a, k_a^s, s_1)\\
ca_2 \text{ says } a \text{ says commit}(a, k_a^s, s_1),\ \text{trust}(ca_2, s_2) &\Rightarrow a \text{ says commit}(a, k_a^s, s_1)\\
a \text{ says commit}(a, k_a^s, s_1) &\Rightarrow \text{commit}(a, k_a^s, s_1)\\
\text{commit}(a, k_a^s),\ k_a^s \text{ says transfer}(a, b, r_1) &\Rightarrow a \text{ says transfer}(a, b, r_1)\\
a \text{ says transfer}(a, b, r_1) &\Rightarrow \text{transfer}(a, b, r_1)
\end{aligned}$$

5.3 Transferring a Right to a Key Owner

We sketch a scenario where a delegates a right to a key owner, without knowing who the key owner is.[9] It is likely that a marketplace on the Internet for certain services involving digital information (e.g. designing clip art, programming a shell script, etc.) will emerge in the near future. In this context, it may be quite possible that some of the service providers are known only by a pseudonym which could typically be the public key itself. The following example illustrates how a right (e.g. a payment obligation) can be transferred to a public key.
Assume that b, known by the public key k_b^s has done a job for a and that a has written a digital cheque (called r) payable to k_b^s. Adopting the judge's view as in the previous example, b collects the following evidence:

$$\begin{aligned}
\text{View}_{judge} = \{\ & ca \text{ says commit}(ca, k_1^s),\ \text{trust}(ca),\ k_1^s \text{ says } a \text{ says commit}(a, k_a^s),\\
& k_a^s \text{ says } a \text{ transfer}(a, k_b^s, r)\ k_b^s \text{ says own}(b, k_b^s)\ \} \cup \text{IR}_\text{L}
\end{aligned}$$

The following sequence of derivations convinces b that the evidence is sufficient.

$$\begin{aligned}
ca \text{ says commit}(ca, k_1^s) &\Rightarrow \text{commit}(ca, k_1^s) && \text{(3a)}\\
\text{commit}(ca, k_1^s),\ k_1^s \text{ says } a \text{ says commit}(a, k_a^s) &\Rightarrow ca \text{ says } a \text{ says commit}(a, k_a^s) && \text{(3b)}\\
ca \text{ says } a \text{ says commit}(a, k_a^s),\ \text{trust}(ca) &\Rightarrow a \text{ says commit}(a, k_a^s) && \text{(1a)}\\
a \text{ says commit}(a, k_a^s) &\Rightarrow \text{commit}(a, k_a^s) && \text{(3a)}\\
\text{commit}(a, k_a^s),\ k_a^s \text{ says } a \text{ transfer}(a, k_b^s, r) &\Rightarrow a \text{ says transfer}(a, k_b^s, r) && \text{(3b)}\\
a \text{ says transfer}(a, k_b^s, r) &\Rightarrow \text{transfer}(a, k_b^s, r) && \text{(4a)}\\
k_b^s \text{ says own}(b, k_b^s) &\Rightarrow \text{own}(b, k_b^s) && \text{(4b)}\\
\text{transfer}(a, k_b^s, r),\ \text{own}(b, k_b^s) &\Rightarrow \text{transfer}(a, b, r) && \text{(4c)}
\end{aligned}$$

6 Concluding Remarks and Open Problems

The proposed calculus captures a number of important aspects of public-key certification, but it is by no means a formalism that could directly be used in a concrete legal system. However, we hope that it is a possible starting point for research into formalizing and reasoning about processes in the digital economy.

[9] This example was first given by C.Ellison in similar form.

Many issues remain open including time aspects (e.g. the concept of freshness, time stamping, etc.), modeling certificate and public-key revocation (more generally the revocation of any statement), and extending the model to capture degrees of belief and contradicting evidence.

Acknowledgments

We wish to thank Christian Cachin and Thomas Kühne for interesting discussions and comments, and the anonymous referees for helpful suggestions.

References

1. W. Stallings. *Protect your privacy.* Prentice Hall, 1996.
2. I. Lehti and P. Nikander. Certifying trust. In H. Imai and Y. Theng, editors, *Proceedings of the first international workshop on Practice and Theory in Public Key Cryptography, PKC'98*, pages 83–98, 1998.
3. P. R. Zimmermann. *The Official PGP User's Guide.* MIT Press, Cambridge, MA, USA, 1995.
4. M. Myers. Revocation: Options and challenges. In R. Hirschfeld, editor, *Financial Cryptography*, volume 1465 of *Lecture Notes in Computer Science*, pages 165–172. Springer Verlag, Berlin, 1998.
5. S. Micali. Efficient certificate revocation. Technical report, Technical Memo MIT/LCS/TM-542b, 1996.
6. M. Abadi. On SDSI's linked local name spaces. In *Proceedings of the 10th IEEE Computer Security Foundations Workshop*, pages 98–108. IEEE Computer Society, 1997.
7. U. Maurer. Modelling a public-key infrastructure. In E. Bertino, H. Kurth, G. Martella, and E. Montolivo, editors, *Proceedings 1996 European Symposium on Research in Computer Security (ESORICS' 96), Lecture Notes in Computer Science, Springer*, LNCS, pages 325–350, 1996.
8. C. E. et al. SPKI http://www.clark.net/pub/cme/html/spki.html. Internet Draft, 1998. Expires: 16 September 1998.
9. P. Kocher. On certificate revocation and validation. In R. Hirschfeld, editor, *Financial Cryptography*, volume 1465 of *Lecture Notes in Computer Science*, pages 172–177. Springer Verlag, Berlin, 1998.
10. C. Boyd. Security architectures using formal methods. *IEEE Journal on Selected Areas in Communications*, 11(5):694–701, 1993.
11. R. Rivest. Can we eliminate certificate revocation lists? In R. Hirschfeld, editor, *Proceedings of Financial Cryptography 1998*, pages 178–183, 1998.
12. M. Burrows, M. Abadi, and R. Needham. A logic of authentication. *ACM Transactions on Computer Systems*, 8(1):18–36, 1990.
13. M. Naor and K. Nissim. Certificate revocation and certificate update. *Proceedings of Usenix '98*, pages 217–228, January 1998.
14. M. Blaze, J. Feigenbaum, and J. Lacy. Decentralized trust management. In *Proceedings of the Symposium on Security and Privacy*, pages 164–173. IEEE Computer Society Press, 1996.
15. C. Ellison. Establishing identity without certification authorities. In USENIX Association, editor, *6th USENIX Security Symposium, July 22–25, 1996. San Jose, CA*, pages 67–76. USENIX, July 1996.

16. B. Fox and B. LaMaccia. Certificate revocation: Mechanisms and meaning. In R. Hirschfeld, editor, *Financial Cryptography*, volume 1465 of *Lecture Notes in Computer Science*, pages 158–164. Springer Verlag, Berlin, 1998.
17. T. Beth, M. Borcherding, and B. Klein. Valuation of trust in open systems. In D. Gollmann, editor, *Computer Security - Esorics '94*, volume 875 of *Lecture Notes in Computer Science*, pages 3–18. Springer Verlag, Berlin, 1994.
18. J. Glasgow, G. MacEwen, and P. Panagaden. A logic for reasoning about security. *ACM transactions on Computer Systems*, 10(3):226–264, 1992.
19. D. Chadwick and A. Young. Merging and extending the PGP and PEM trust models. *IEEE Network Magazine*, May 1997.
20. U. Maurer and P. Schmid. A calculus for secure channel establishment in open networks. In D. Gollmann, editor, *Proc. 1994 European Symposium on Research in Computer Security (ESORICS' 94)*, volume 875, pages 175–192. Lecture Notes in Computer Science, 1994.
21. T. M. C. Group. MCG - internet open group on certification and security, http://mcg.org.br/, 1998.
22. M. Reiter and S. Stubblebine. Path independence for authentication in large-scale systems. *Proceedings of the 4th ACM Conference on Computer and Communications Security*, pages 57–66, 1997.
23. M. Abadi, M. Burrows, B. Lampson, and G. Plotkin. A calculus for access control in distributed systems. *ACM Transactions on Programming Languages and Systems*, 15(4):706–734, September 1993.
24. B. Lampson, M. Abadi, M. Burrows, and E. Wobber. Authentication in distributed systems: Theory and practice. *ACM Transactions on Computer Systems*, 10(4):265–310, November 1992.
25. P. Syverson and C. Meadows. A logical language for specifying cryptographic protocols requirements. In *IEEE Conferences on Research in Security and Privacy*, pages 165–180, 1993.
26. E. Campbell, R. Safavi-Naini, and P. Pleasants. Partial belief and probabilistic reasoning in the analysis of secure protocols. In *The computer Security Foundations Workshop V*, pages 84–91, 1992.
27. S. Stubblebine and R. Wright. An authentication logic supporting synchronization, revocation, and recency. In *SIGSAC: 3rd ACM Conference on Computer and Communications Security*. ACM SIGSAC, 1996.
28. S. Consortium. Basic services, architecture and design, available at http://www.semper.org/info/index.html. Technical report, SEMPER, 1996.
29. R. Rivest and B. Lampson. SDSI – A simple distributed security infrastructure, http://theory.lcs.mit.edu/~cis/sdsi.html. Presented at CRYPTO'96 Rumpsession, April 1996.
30. R. Yaholem, B. Klein, and T. Beth. Trust relationships in secure systems - a distributed authentication perspective. In *Proceedings of the IEEE Conference on Research in Security and Privacy*, pages 150–164, 1993.
31. M. Blaze, J. Feigenbaum, and M. Strauss. Compliance checking in the policymaker trust management system. In R. Hirschfeld, editor, *Financial Cryptography*, volume 1465 of *Lecture Notes in Computer Science*, pages 254–274. Springer Verlag, Berlin, 1998.
32. I. I. S. 9594-8. Information technology, open systems interconnection, the directory, part 8: Authentication framework, 1990.

Online Certificate Status Checking in Financial Transactions: The Case for Re-issuance

Barbara Fox* and Brian LaMacchia

Microsoft Corporation
One Microsoft Way
Redmond, WA 98052 USA
{bfox,bal}@microsoft.com

Abstract. High-value financial transactions underwrite the need for a relying party to check the status of a digital certificate in real time. In this paper, we propose a simple mechanism for online certificate status checking that is particularly well suited to the closed public key infrastructures that characterize financial networks. We further demonstrate how persistent evidence of this status checking request/response becomes a valuable by-product. In financial systems, "transaction receipts" naturally accumulate and by doing so, they encapsulate the entire lifecycle of a single transaction.

Keywords: public key infrastructure, online certificate status checking, certificate re-issuance, high-value financial transactions, risk management

1 Introduction

The financial community has identified the need for a relying party to "real-time" check the validity of evidence supporting a high-value transaction. For example, merchants routinely "authorize" credit cards as a part of a transaction. As these transactions increasingly take place on-line over the Internet, however, and become entirely dependent on digital signatures and supporting evidence in the form of PKI elements, the mechanics of authorization must change.

The first attempt at defining an electronic authorization scheme suitable for Web-based credit card transactions was the Visa/MasterCard Secure Electronic Transactions ("SET" [12]) suite of protocols. The SET model was limited to a Web-based front-end to legacy authorization systems. On the back-end, a SET transaction is virtually indistinguishable from one that originates as face-to-face or via a telephone order.

The next step towards creating a completely web-based analog for authorizations is currently under development by the PKIX working group in the IETF. The X.509 and PKIX standards provide suitable mechanisms for off-line

* The opinions expressed in this paper are those of the authors and are not necessarily those of Microsoft Corporation.

M. Franklin (Ed.): FC'99, LNCS 1648, pp. 104–117, 1999.

or cached authorization operations and certificate revocation lists (CRLs). However, because CRLs are created with specific lifetimes (possibly unbounded) they are not suitable for real-time status checks. For a particular high-value[1] transaction, the relying party's policy concerning that transaction is likely to require a near-instantaneous statement of the validity of the public key/certificate in question; a CRL issued two weeks prior is effectively worthless as evidence of the key's current status. Thus, additional mechanisms are needed within the public key infrastructure (PKI) to provide real-time information.

The most prominent technology proposed for this type of verification within the PKIX infrastructure is the "Online Certificate Status Checking Protocol" [8], and it is on track to become an Internet standard. OCSP has two important characteristics: first, OCSP depends upon the emergence of its own three-tier (Client - Certificate Authority - Designated Responder) infrastructure, and second, OCSP defines a new set of message formats extending beyond those contained in the base PKIX standard (PKIX Part 1).

In this paper, we propose a simple alternative to OCSP for online certificate status checking. Moreover, we argue that requirements for authorizing digitally-signed transactions should be *independent of the underlying form of public key infrastructure* in which they occur[2]. These requirements must minimally include "freshness" check on the evidence submitted in support of the transaction (which could be a digital certificate). As a by-product of doing the check itself, persistent evidence that the check was made must also be created.

It should be understood that OCSP is used merely as an example of current practice in the field of real-time status checking for digital evidence. Nevertheless, OCSP provides an important yardstick for comparing and contrasting and new mechanisms. The chief *infrastructure* difference between this proposal and OCSP is that our approach is targeted to serving the functional and policy requirements of *closed PKIs*, which we believe will host the majority of high-value financial transactions. "Closed" in our context means only that the parties' rights and obligations are defined by mutual agreement or contract. For example, the Automotive Network Exchange (ANX), is a closed PKI comprised of more than 1,200 trading partners.

2 Motivation

Figure 1 below depicts a typical high-value electronic financial transaction using public key credentials. There are three parties of interest: the "end entity"

[1] Throughout this document we use the term "high-value" to denote transactions that, as a matter of relying party policy, require real-time confirmation of the PKI components of the transaction. That is, any transaction in which there is sufficient capital at risk that cached information is insufficient can be thought of as "high-value."

[2] We anticipate that the new joint IETF-W3C work on signed XML [6] will progress quickly to defining new public key infrastructures not based on X.509/ASN.1. Further, we must assume that a single transaction could include some hybrid of these technologies.

(seller of the financial transaction), the "relying party" (the buyer of the financial transaction) and a "certification authority" ("CA"). The role of the CA is to attest to the binding between the end entity and some public/private key pair. Initially, before any particular transaction can occur, the end entity needs to obtain proof of ownership of a public/private key pair that he will use electronically to sign the transaction. The end entity generates a public/private key pair (or uses one previously generated) and submits a certification request to the CA (step 1). The CA processes the request and, if the request satisfies the CA's certificate issuance policy, the CA responds by issuing a certificate to the end entity (step 2). Now, for a particular transaction the seller sends the transaction

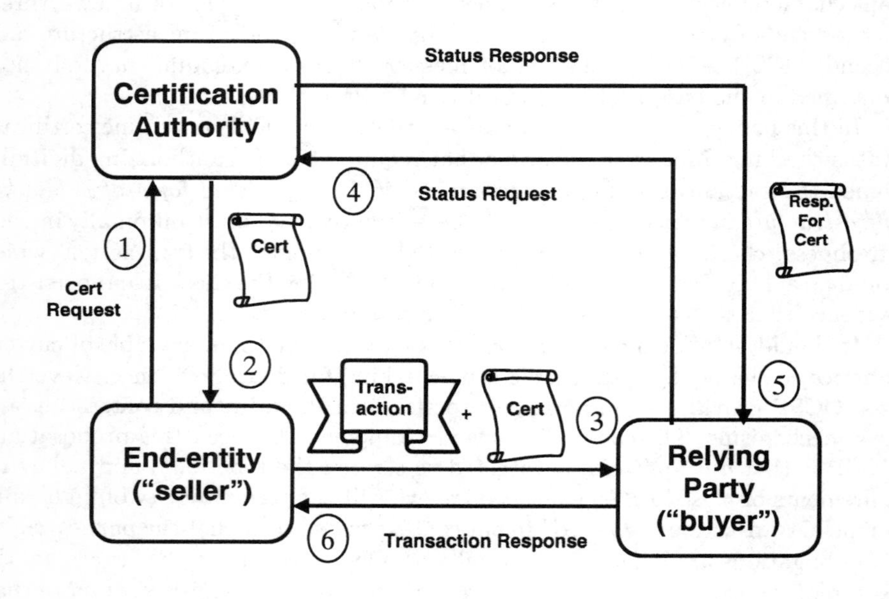

Fig. 1. A typical financial transaction using public-key credentials

to the potential buyer along with some evidence (step 3). The evidence will be used by the buyer to determine (a) whether the seller is who he claims to be, and possibly (b) that the seller has the right to participate in the transaction (e.g. current ownership of the transaction). The certificate previously obtained may be sufficient evidence on its own; it is more likely, though, that certificate will be used in conjunction with other signed statements contained within the transaction itself. Having received the transaction and supporting evidence, the relying party not must make a policy decision and determine whether the submitted evidence satisfies *his own acceptance policy* for the transaction.

As part of this evaluation of evidence, the relying party requires a real-time status check on the certificate issued by the CA-that is, is the binding in the certificate still valid? The buyer thus makes a real-time status request of the issuing CA[3] for confirmation of the validity of the certificate (step 4). The CA issues its status response (step 5) attesting to the current validity of the subject certificate. The status information is then combined with the transaction, the certificate and other submitted evidence by the relying party to make his policy determination. The result of that decision (i.e. whether the transaction will be bought and any receipts if it is) is returned to the seller in step 6.

Our concerns in this paper are with the protocols and signed statements used to form the status request in step 4, the status response in step 5, and the transaction response in step 6. The chief *technical* difference between OCSP and our proposal is that we issue a new X.509 certificate in step 5 as the response to a status inquiry. While it may seem obvious to simply issue a new certificate, OCSP goes out of its way to avoid doing so. In fact, OCSP crafts a response that looks not surprisingly like a CRL. Here is the structure of a single OCSP status response:

```
SingleResponse ::= SEQUENCE {
  certID                      CertID,
  certStatus                  CertStatus,
  thisUpdate                  GeneralizedTime,
  nextUpdate            [0]   EXPLICIT GeneralizedTime OPTIONAL,
  singleExtensions      [1]   EXPLICIT Extensions OPTIONAL
}

CertStatus ::= CHOICE {
  good                  [0]   IMPLICIT NULL,
  revoked               [1]   IMPLICIT RevokedInfo,
  unknown               [2]   IMPLICIT UnknownInfo
}
```

Within a SingleResponse, the certID identifies a particular certificate and the certStatus is the returned assertion about that certificate - one of “good,” “revoked,” or “unknown.” This assertion is then signed by the responder, creating a digitally-signed statement about the referenced certificate. (OCSP, unlike our proposal, does not explicitly permit status requests concerning only a public/private key pair.) As such, the OCSP response itself is semantically equivalent to a certificate[4], but is written in a new format. The only explanation for this

[3] In OCSP terms, this is an OCSP request message. Note that although we have depicted the status request being sent directly to the issuing CA, in practice the request may be directed to a third party authorized to emit status information on behalf of the issuing CA.

[4] To be precise, a certificate is a digitally-signed statement about a public/private key pair. An OCSP response is a digitally-signed statement about a certificate, so it may be thought of as a “certificate for a certificate.” As we show below, certificates can easily be made to make statements about other certificates, thus eliminating any need for new syntax.

distinction is that the OCSP authors could attach one value to a certificate and another value to its real-time status. This is economics, not technology.

What is unavoidable, though, is that the digitally-signed statement containing status information is itself an *independent* assertion and, as such, carries liability for its signer. In typical financial applications, other new criteria, such as current credit-worthiness, are brought into the transaction as a result of a status check and the role of the signer is unambiguous: the signer owns the risk.

"Ownership" as the result of issuing a status response becomes literally correct when we replace the word *risk* with *transaction.* Transactions are the commodity that is bought and sold in every financial market. In the credit card case, for example, the card merely bootstraps a transaction. When the merchant authorizes a sale, he sells the transaction to his bank at a discount. If the bank is also the card issuer, then it does not need to re-sell the transaction; it may settle directly with the merchant and cardholder. If the bank is not the issuer of the presented card, then it sells the transaction to a settlement agent at another discount. In each case, a sale represents a shift of risk from the seller to the buyer *for which the buyer creates a receipt.* During the life of a transaction, what matters is the issuer's signature on an assertion that turns it into a receipt, not the signature on the card.

Figure 2 below overlays Figure 1 with the flow of policy evaluation, confirmation, and the generation of receipts. Again, there are three parties of interest: the "end entity" (seller of the financial transaction), the "relying party" (the buyer of the financial transaction) and a "certification authority" ("CA"). Steps 1 through 3 are essentially the same: (1) The end entity generates a public/private key pair and submits a certification request to the CA (2) The CA processes the request and, if the request satisfies the CA's certificate issuance policy, the CA responds by issuing a certificate to the end entity and (3) In the context of a particular transaction the seller sends the transaction to the potential buyer along with some evidence. The important distinction here is that the action of the relying party breaks down into two policy-driven steps.

In step 3, the relying party's external interface receives the transaction and supporting evidence and uses it to formulate a trust management question (step 4), "Is my policy satisfied?" Policy evaluation may include a number of real-time queries:

(a) a real-time status check on the submitted certificate (step 5),
(b) an application-specific real-time check, such as communication with a bank to determine current credit-worthiness, and
(c) a evaluation of locally-held policy-related information, such as the buyer's prior transaction history with this particular seller.

The relying party's policy evaluation engine combines externally gathered status information with local policy and generates an acceptance or denial result. In either case, a statement of the decision is returned to the seller (step 7).

There is a second important concept at work here that is often overlooked: *receipts outlive transactions.* Long after a transaction has run to completion and terminated, the receipts involved in that transaction are still "live" because they

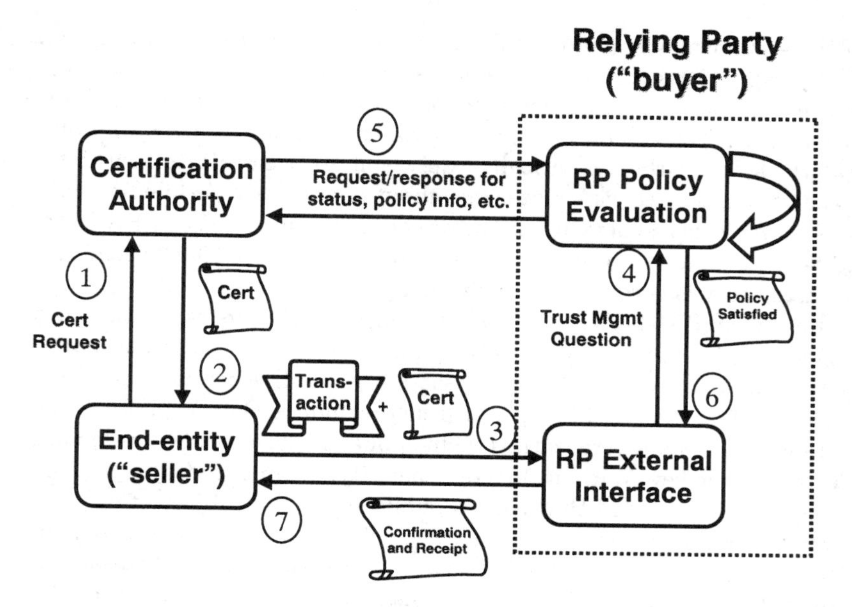

Fig. 2. Policy evaluation, confirmation and receipts

provide evidence of what took place. Should the transaction be repudiated at a later date, for example, it is the signed receipts that will be required to prove or refute the claim. By having buyers issue certificates as receipts for transactions, we replicate this financial model in the PKI domain. Furthermore, because the infrastructure for issuing certificates already exists, it is not only feasible but also simple to leverage existing software to create, forward, evaluate and store them.

3 Mechanisms

For lack of a better term, we call our proposed on-line status mechanism "certificate re-issuance." The idea behind certificate re-issuance is deceptively simple:

> Any useful response to a real-time query concerning the status of a public key is necessarily a (digitally-signed) statement about that public key. Similarly, the response to a query concerning the status of a certificate for a public key is necessarily a (digitally-signed) statement concerning that certificate, which is itself a (digitally-signed) statement about a public key. In both cases, the response can be expressed completely as yet another (digitally-signed) statement about a public key. *That is, the response to a real-time query is just another certificate.*

In an X.509v3/PKIX-based PKI, we make statements about a public key by issuing certificates that contain both the subject public key and the semantic content of the statement we wish to make about it. In a real-time status query, our goal is typically to ask one of two questions: (a) has some particular subject public key been compromised, or (b) is some particular statement about a public key no longer valid? The response to (a) is a statement about the validity of a public key, which is clearly semantically equivalent to a certificate issued for that key. The response to (b) is a statement about a certificate. While we could choose to use some other syntax to embody such a statement (e.g. a PKCS#7 [9] or CMS [4] signed message), it is possible to use standard X.509v3 certificate syntax and doing so yields some nice additional properties.

Consider a typical PKI-based scenario involving a high-value transaction. Let Alice and Bob be respectively the requesting and relying party in a two-party, high-value transaction. As part of the transaction request, Alice presents a set of credentials (evidence) that she hopes will help convince Bob to perform the requested transaction. These credentials include one or more certificates c_i that relate to Alice's public key. Without loss of generality, assume that $c_0, c_1, \ldots, c_n$ is a single certificate chain and that Alice's public key is the subject of c_n.

Bob's policy for the requested transaction will accept the certificate chain $c_0, \ldots, c_n$ as proof that Alice's public key is authorized to make the transaction request. However, due to the specifics of the transaction Bob's policy additionally requires real-time proof that Alice's key has not been compromised in order for the transaction to be processed. So, Bob asks Irwin, the issuer of certificate c_n, whether the binding attested to within c_n is still valid. (Note that it was Irwin who validated the name-key binding between Alice and her public key in the first place.)

In response to this request, Irwin issues a second certificate, c'_n, which restates the binding between Alice's name (or other identifying information) and her public key but with semantics that reflect the binding's state at the current time. For example, c'_n might have a very short validity period covering only the duration of Bob's real-time request, where cn may be valid for a year or more. Assuming that c'_n was signed by Irwin with the same public key as was used to sign c_n, Bob may validate c'_n using the same certificate chain that validates c_n. That is, if $c_0, c_1, \ldots, c_{n-1}, c_n$ is a cryptographically-valid certificate chain, then so is $c_0, c_1, \ldots, c_{n-1}, c'_n$. The evidence gathered in $c_0, \ldots, c_{n-1}$ that validates Irwin's public key with respect to c_n also validates that key with respect to c'_n.

The two certificates c_n and c'_n do have different semantics, so we need to distinguish them in some fashion. This may be easily achieved through the use of standards X.509v3 certificate extensions. For the inbound request for real-time status information there are a few standards-based syntax options, all of which are approximately equal in function and expressive capabilities.

3.1 The Response

We first detail the *response* to a real-time status check rather than the *request* itself because in our particular case the response is the more interesting of the two messages. By viewing a real-time status request as a certificate request, we accomplish two significant tasks missing from other proposed standards such as

OCSP. First, we leverage existing syntax, message formats and infrastructure as opposed to creating new messages out of whole cloth. Second, we keep our risk-related semantics consistent; responding to a real-time status check is yet another risk transference, just like certificate issuance.

There are compelling practical and technical reasons to avoid creating new syntax for real-time status requests and responses, the most important one being that "we have too many different messages types already." In order to construct PKI message components you need two things: a standard format for making digitally-signed statements and some agreements on semantic meaning for some forms of statements. We have a standard format for making digitally-signed statements: the PKCS#7/CMS family of message types [4,9]. Anyone who has labored in the X.509v3/PKIX realm knows that as these two message types are arbitrarily extensible they are more than sufficient for expressing any desired semantics concerning signed statements. This includes certificates and certificate requests, of course. Had PKCS#7 come first we might have avoided X.509v3 entirely and simply made certificates be a special type of PKCS#7 message. (Similarly, PKCS#10 certificate requests could easily have been based on PKCS#7 too.)

However, since X.509v3 did come first we have lots of infrastructure for dealing with both certificates and PKCS#7 messages, with instances of the former normally thought of as providing the evidence for accepting instances of the latter. This distinction is not really important however, since X.509v3 certificates are themselves extensible and fully capable of making statements about keys and other certificates. Thus X.509v3 is a perfectly reasonable and practical standard for on-line status responses; we need only define the semantics of an extension or two to provide the new functionality.

Assume that an on-line status responder receives a request to provide current information on the key contained with certificate c_n. (We view requests for status information concerning c_n itself versus the public key contained within c_n identically as the only difference in the two responses will be a minor semantic distinction indicated in one extension.) Section 3.2 proposes some mechanisms for delivering the actual request to the responder; for our immediate purposes the particular mechanism is not important, only that the responder receives the request and accurately identifies it as a "freshness check" on c_n. If the responder can confirm that the subject certificate has not been revoked and/or wishes to apply new policy, he then issues c'_n, a new certificate, which differs from c_n as follows:

1. The validity period of c'_n is narrowed to the window in which this freshness certificate is valid. (This period is likely to be significantly shorter than the validity period of c_n itself, and in practical terms is probably less than one day in duration.)
2. The responder adds to c_n a new extension indicating that it is a freshness assertion about a public key or another certificate. The presence of the extension itself (which is identified by its own OID) can server as notice that the certificate is a response to a status check. The data contained in the

extension, which we call the *ResponseSubject*, must necessarily reference the object for which status was requested: a public key or a certificate. The easiest way to do that is to use a modified form of the AuthorityKeyIdentifier data type defined in PKIX Part 1, Section 4.2.1.1:

```
ResponseSubject ::= SEQUENCE {
  keyIdentifier        [0] KeyIdentifier               OPTIONAL,
  certIdentifier       [1] CertIdentifier              OPTIONAL,
  certIssuer           [2] GeneralNames                OPTIONAL,
  certSerialNumber     [3] CertificateSerialNumber OPTIONAL,
}

KeyIdentifier ::= OCTET STRING

CertIdentifier ::= SEQUENCE {
  hashAlgorithm              AlgorithmIdentifier,
  certHash                   CertHash
}

CertHash ::= OCTET STRING
```

A ResponseSubject may be one of three types: a reference to a particular public key, a reference to a particular certificate via hash, or a reference to an issuer/serial-number pair (which should only correspond to a single certificate). (We expect that these three options will be used exclusively: a ResponseSubject is likely to contain exactly one of keyIdentifier, certIdentifier and the pair (certIssuer, certSerialNumber).) Note that since the keyIdenfier is presumed to correspond to a SubjectKeyIdentifier contained within certificate c_n there is no need to identify a hash algorithm for it. For the CertIdentifier structure we need a certificate hash (algorithm and hash function output) to uniquely identifier the certificate that is the subject of the response.

3. Additionally, the responder may choose to add other extensions to further qualify the status statement being made in the certificate.

In the failure case the responder has a couple of options. First, the responder could simply fail to return a response, although this is not particularly useful to the requesting party. More likely, the responder will return some other signed statement including information concerning why the status check failed. A third possibility is to require that certificates issued in response to an on-line status check contain two extensions; one containing the ResponseSubject information described above, and a second (call it ResponseStatus for lack of a better term) that explicitly contains success/failure information. A requesting party's policy could easily check such explicit information as part of its evaluation of c'_n.

3.2 The Request

Having defined the response message in our real-time status protocol, we now turn to the syntax for requesting a real-time status certificate. The request message is not as interesting technically as its sole purpose is to convey, from requestor to responder, the key or certificate for which status information is desired. Even restricting our set of available protocols to those defined by the IETF PKIX and S/MIME working groups, there are still a number of possible methods to perform this task. We outline three of these below; any of them would suffice.

The first possibility for delivering the request message is to view the request as a variant of the enrollment process for a new key pair, since the outcome of both processes is the issuance of a certificate. The *de facto* industry standard for requesting a certificate for a public/private key pair is defined by the PKCS#10 protocol [10]; however, PKCS#10 messages are self-signed to provide proof-of-possession of the corresponding private key. Since we assume that in the case of real-time status checking the requesting party is not normally the same entity as that possessing the key pair in question, a standard PKCS#10 message is not sufficient.

The second standards-based possibility for real-time status checking is to model the request as a variant of the certificate renewal enrollment process. The difference between certificate renewal and enrollment for a new key pair is that in renewal one or more certificates have already been issued against the key pair in question. These certificates may be submitted to the issuing authority as evidence that a new certificate should be issued. In our case, if the requestor wants status information concerning a particular certificate c, the message delivered to the responder may be exactly that particular certificate. If the requestor wants status information concerning a particular public/private key pair, a certificate containing the public component may again be used as the message to the responder. Note that in the latter case some additional information must be sent in addition to indicate that a response about the *key* is desired and not a response about the *certificate* carrying the key.

A third possibility for the request message format, and perhaps the most satisfying of the trio, is simply to leverage the existing extensibility in the proposed CMS-based certificate enrollment protocol [3]. In CMC, the Full Enrollment Request message is a signed CMS with a payload of zero or more commands and enrollment requests. We can use the ResponseSubject structure defined above as the value in an OID-value pair, and include any referenced certificates in the CertificateSet portion of a SignedData CMS content payload. That is, the body of the CMS SignedData message becomes simply a data structure of the form:

```
SEQUENCE OF
  SEQUENCE {
    id-realtime-status-request  // an OBJECT IDENTIFIER
    requestSubject                         // a ResponseSubject
  }
}
```

where ResponseSubject is as defined above and provides a reference either to a particular public/private key pair (by referencing the key identifier of a public key), or to a particular certificate (either by hash or by an (*issuer name*, *serial number*) pair). The type of request being made (key versus certificate) is implicit in the choice of identifier[5].

In summary, both the request and response messages in our proposed real-time status protocol easily fit within the bounds of current PKI infrastructures. The request message can be built on top of the PKCS#10, X.509v3 or CMS standards (CMS being the most convenient and straightforward of the three). The response message is an X.509v3 certificate. Obviously, there is a clear advantage to extending current standards as opposed to inventing new message types as existing PKI clients and certificate servers will require minimal modifications to take advantage of our proposed protocol.

4 Economics

Our proposal differs from the OCSP model in one more significant way: the pricing model for digitally-signed statements. OCSP pre-supposes a particular pricing model that attaches high cost (and high liability) to the issuance of every certificate. At the same time, OCSP also presumes that there exists a relatively small community of qualified certificate issuers and designated status responders. We believe this is a narrow view; there is no *a priori* reason to so restrict the universe of possible issuers of signed statements. Ultimately risk lies not with the issuer of a "global certificate" that provides some particular long-term binding (such as an "identity certificate" binding some name-related information to a key pair), but rather with the numerous parties that issue receipts.

The premise that individual certificates are relatively scarce and relatively expensive also pre-supposes that acceptance policy is dictated to third parties by the certificate issuer. That is certainly not the case in financial transactions; acceptance policy is strictly a policy of the party buying the risk. This is simply an extension of the principles of decentralized trust management [1,2] to the financial realm. In this model, when a transaction is purchased and the buyer issues a certificate as a receipt, the receipt simultaneously represents two distinct assertions. First, of course, the receipt denotes the transfer of ownership. Second, and more subtlety, the receipt represents proof that the seller submitted sufficient evidence to the buyer to *satisfy the buyer's policy.* The receipt, therefore, is proof of a two-way commitment between seller and buyer.

Finally, notice what happens when the buyer of a transaction, after issuing a receipt, turns around and re-sells it. Buyer becomes seller, and the receipt issued previously is now a piece of evidence submitted to the new buyer proving that

[5] As CMC allows multiple message bodies to be encapsulated in a single CMC payload, we also get the ability to request status on an arbitrary number of keys and certificates simultaneously. Each request will generate a response certificate from the responder; all of these certificates may be returned to the requestor in a single CMC Full PKI Response message.

the old buyer applied his own policy at the time he purchased the transaction. In fact, the set of receipts generated by every transfer of the transaction forms a digitally-signed chain of evidence binding not only every step of the transaction but also every policy application that happened along the way. In practice these policy assertions are explicitly detailed in the contractual relationships between parties that govern rights of repudiation[6] around transactions, but they are not explicitly bound into the transactions themselves.

Figure 3 illustrates how accumulated signed receipts, generated as part of the process of selling and re-selling a single transaction, encapsulate the transaction's history. Initially, party A holds transaction T and receipt Cert_A (the receipt describes how A came to hold the transaction in the first place). He proposes to sell the transaction to party B (step 1) and sends B the transaction along with his certificate and other supporting evidence. B evaluates the evidence to see that it satisfies his policy and issues a receipt–Cert_B-as proof that his policy was satisfied (step 2). The new receipt is returned to party A in step 3 and the transaction between A and B concludes. B now holds transaction T, certificate Cert_A (which references T) and certificate Cert_B (which references both T and Cert_A).

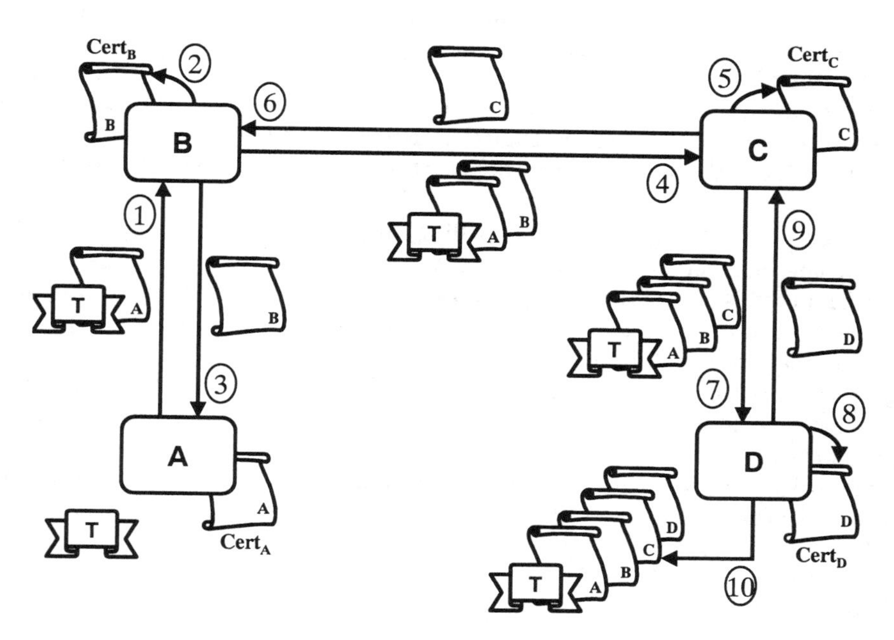

Fig. 3. Accumulated receipts encapsulate transaction history

[6] In the credit card world, for example, it is the "operating regulations" that encapsulate such policies.

Now B decides to re-sell the transaction to party C. As above, B first sends the transaction to the proposed buyer along with his supporting evidence (step 4). Notice that the evidence submitted by B includes both the evidence submitted by A to B when B bought the transaction in the first place as well as the receipt B issued showing that B's acceptance policy was satisfied. Party C performs his own acceptance policy evaluation in step 5 and issues certificate Cert_C as proof of acceptance of the transaction. This new receipt, which references T, Cert_A and Cert_B, is returned to B (step 6) to complete the resale of the transaction. A further resale of the transaction from C to D is shown in steps 7-9, resulting in D issuing receipt Cert_D.

At the conclusion of the three sales of transaction T (step 10), party D holds the transaction and four receipts–Cert_A, Cert_B, Cert_C and Cert_D. Together, these receipts detail exactly how transaction T moved among the four parties, what policy decisions were made along the way, and the commitments made by each party in the process. Even after the transaction terminates and no longer exists, the receipts persist and continue to provide evidence.

5 Conclusions

The need for real-time status information in closed PKIs for financial transactions is clear; what is dubious is the need for new infrastructure to convey such information. We have shown above that is not only possible but preferable, from technical and economic perspectives, to use reuse the existing certificate issuance mechanisms and infrastructure. Digitally-signed status information about a certificate is itself the semantic equivalent of a certificate; we should treat it as such.

There is one final (yet quite compelling) argument to leverage certificate (in lieu of new non-certificate-based) infrastructures for real-time status information, and that is the infant (but growing) body of international law surrounding digital signatures and certificates. Only now are we beginning the process of creating the legislative underpinnings for certificates to have legal effect, and legal effect is an absolute requirement for the application of digital signatures and certificates to financial transactions. It is not at all clear that a new message type, with new syntax and semantics, would automatically fall within the legal frameworks currently being constructed. Why, absent a solid technical reason to do so, take that chance?

References

1. M. Blaze, J. Feigenbaum, and J. Lacy, “Decentralized Trust Management,” in *Proceedings of the 1996 IEEE Symposium on Security and Privacy*, pp. 164-173.
2. Yang-Hua Chu, Joan Feigenbaum, Brian LaMacchia, Paul Resnick and Martin Strauss, “REFEREE: Trust Management for Web Applications,” *Proceedings of the Sixth International World Wide Web Conference*, Santa Clara, CA, April 1997.

3. PKIX Working Group, Internet Engineering Task Force, "Certificate Management Messages over CMS," M. Myers, X. Liu, B. Fox, J. Weinstein, eds., work in progress. (Draft as of March 1999 available from http://www.ietf.org/internet-drafts/draft-ietf-pkix-cmc-03.txt.)
4. S/MIME Working Group, Internet Engineering Task Force, "Cryptographic Message Syntax," R. Housley, ed., work in progress. (Draft as of April 1999 available from http://www.ietf.org/internet-drafts/draft-ietf-smime-cms-13.txt.)
5. RFC 2511, PKIX Working Group, Internet Engineering Task Force, "Certificate Request Message Format," M. Myers, C. Adams, D. Solo, D. Kemp, eds., March 1999. (Available from http://info.internet.isi.edu/in-notes/rfc/files/rfc2511.txt.)
6. World Wide Web Consortium Digital Signature Initiative. (Information available from http://www.w3.org/DSig/Overview.html.)
7. Barbara Fox and Brian LaMacchia, "Certificate Revocation: Mechanics and Meaning," in Proceedings of Financial Cryptography '98, *Lecture Notes in Computer Science* **1465**, New York: Springer-Verlag, 1998.
8. PKIX Working Group, Internet Engineering Task Force, "Online Certificate Status Protocol - OCSP," M. Myers, R. Ankney, A. Malpani, S. Galperin, C. Adams, eds., work in progress. (Draft as of March 1999 available from http://www.ietf.org/internet-drafts/draft-ietf-pkix-ocsp-08.txt.)
9. RFC 2315, Network Working Group, Internet Engineering Task Force, "PKCS #7: Cryptographic Message Syntax v1.5," B. Kaliski, ed., March 1998. (Available from http://info.internet.isi.edu/in-notes/rfc/files/rfc2315.txt.)
10. RFC 2314, Network Working Group, Internet Engineering Task Force, "PKCS #10: Certification Request Syntax v1.5," B. Kaliski, ed., March 1998. (Available from http://info.internet.isi.edu/in-notes/rfc/files/rfc2314.txt.)
11. RFC 2459, PKIX Working Group, Internet Engineering Task Force. "Internet X.509 Public Key Infrastructure: Certificate and CRL Profile," R. Housley, W. Ford, W. Polk, D. Solo, eds., January 1999. (Available from http://info.internet.isi.edu/in-notes/rfc/files/rfc2459.txt).
12. Secure Electronic Transaction protocol. (Available from http://www.setco.org/.)
13. ISO/IEC JTC1/SC 21, Draft Amendments DAM 4 to ISO/IEC 9594-2, DAM 2 to ISO/IEC 9594-6, DAM 1 to ISO/IEC 9594-7, and DAM 1 to ISO/IEC 9594-8 on Certificate Extensions, 1 December, 1996.

Playing 'Hide and Seek' with Stored Keys

Adi Shamir[1] and Nicko van Someren[2]

[1] Applied Math Dept., The Weizmann Institute of Science,
Rehovot 76100, Israel,
shamir@wisdom.weizmann.ac.il,
[2] nCipher Corporation Limited,
Cambridge, England,
nicko@ncipher.com.

Abstract. In this paper we consider the problem of efficiently locating cryptographic keys hidden in gigabytes of data, such as the complete file system of a typical PC. We describe efficient algebraic attacks which can locate secret RSA keys in long bit strings, and more general statistical attacks which can find arbitrary cryptographic keys embedded in large programs. These techniques can be used to apply "lunchtime attacks" on signature keys used by financial institutes, or to defeat "authenticode" type mechanisms in software packages.

Keywords: Cryptanalysis, lunchtime attacks, RSA, authenticode, key hiding.

1 Introduction

In this paper we consider the problem of efficiently locating cryptographic keys in large amounts of data. As a motivating example, consider a financial institute which uses the manager's PC to digitally sign wire transfers. In our "lunchtime attack" scenario, the attacker (who can be a secretary, technician, customer, etc.) can sneak into the manager's office for a few minutes while he or she is away for lunch. We assume that the PC is off line, and cannot be directly used to sign unauthorized wire transfers. The goal of the attacker is to quickly scan the gigabytes of data on the hard disk in order to find the secret signature key. This key may be kept as a separate data file on the PC (due to overconfidence), or permanently embedded in the cryptographic application itself (due to poor design). Even worse, the key may be stored on the PC unintentionally and without the knowledge of its security conscious user. For example, the key may appear in a Windows swap file which contains the intermediate state of a previous signing session, or it may appear in a backup file created automatically by the operating system at fixed intervals, or it may appear on the disk in a damaged sector which is not considered part of the file system. We assume that the attacker can use a diskette to bring in a short program and to bring out the discovered key, but he does not have enough storage to copy the whole contents of the hard disk, and does not have enough time to try each subsequence of bits from the hard disk as a possible signature generation key.

M. Franklin (Ed.): FC99, LNCS 1648, pp. 118–124, 1999.

Another example in which an attacker may wish to locate cryptographic keys in large files is in "authenticode" type applications. In many systems a software producer wishes to exercise some control over what code is run on a user's computer. There are many reasons for wanting to do this. A vendor might want to ensure that files have not been corrupted when being used in a mission critical system or that vendor might want to limit third party add-ons to ones it has authorised. If the application is a security sensitive one then it might be necessary to ensure that none of the security features have been subverted. If the application allows cryptographic extensions to be added, a government might insist that any extensions are authorised before they can be used. Clearly there are a number of reasons, both good and bad, for wanting code authentication.

As well as reasons for authenticating code there are also reasons, both good and bad, for wanting to bypass the authentication. A third party software producer might want to try to break the monopoly of the original author by providing add-ons that have not been authorised, or they may want to develop cryptographic extensions for use when they might not otherwise be available. A hacker might maliciously want to subvert the security of a secure system or damage the code in a safety critical system.

2 Finding Secret RSA Keys

In this section we assume that the attacker knows the public key n and e of an RSA[2] scheme used by his victim, and has temporary access to a long string of u bits (representing the full contents of the hard disk) which is known to contain the corresponding secret key d as a contiguous substring of v bits. A typical value of u can be 10^{10}, while a typical value of v can be 10^3.

The simplest solution to the problem (which is applicable to any cryptosystem) is to obtain a cleartext/ciphertext pair, and then to scan the long bit string and perform trial decryption with each subsequence of length v as a possible key. Rare false alarms can be discarded by trying additional pairs. Ciphertext only attacks are also possible, but typically require more decryptions with each candidate key to identify the expected cleartext statistics. In public key cryptosystems, it suffices to know the victim's public key, since the attacker can generate by himself the required cleartext/ciphertext pairs.

The main problem in applying this technique to the RSA scheme is that each modular exponentiation is very expensive, and its time complexity grows cubically with the size v of the modulus. If we have to try about u possible substrings as candidate values for the decryption exponent d, we get a total complexity of $O(uv^3)$, which is polynomial but impractical (about 10^{19} for the typical parameters mentioned above).

A faster algorithm is based on the observation that consecutive candidates for d have a huge overlap. When we move a window of size v over a string of size u, the contents of two consecutive windows can differ only in their first and last bits, and in the fact that their other bits are shifted by one bit position. When the contents of the two windows are interpreted as binary integers d' and d'', we can relate them via:

$$d'' = 2d' + c_1 - c_2 2^v$$

where c_1 and c_2 are either 0 or 1. Given a value of the form $m^{d'} \pmod{n}$, we can compute the value of $m^{d''} \pmod{n}$ by performing one modular squaring, and 0, 1, or 2 additional modular multiplications with precomputed numbers. Since the complexity of each modular multiplication is $O(v^2)$, the total complexity drops from $O(uv^3)$ to $O(uv^2)$, or about 10^{16} in our typical scenario.

Our next observation is that when the public exponent e is small, this result can be greatly improved. Small e such as 3 and $2^{16}+1$ are very common in software implementations of RSA, since they make the encryption and signature verification operations 2-3 orders of magnitude faster than full size exponents.

Consider the case of $e = 3$. The secret exponent d is known to satisfy $3d = 1(\bmod\ \phi(n))$, where $\phi(n) = (p-1)(q-1) = n - (p+q-1)$. We can thus conclude that $3d = 1 + cn - c(p+q-1)$ where c is either 1 or 2. The value of $(p+q-1)$ is unknown, but it contains only half as many bits as n. We can thus perform approximate division by 3, and get for each one of the two choices of c a candidate value for the top half of d. For the typical parameters, this implies that we can easily compute two candidate values for the top 500 bits of d. Such a large number of random bits makes it extremely unlikely that we will encounter false alarms, and thus we can use a straightforward string matching algorithm to search for the known half of d, and recover the other half from any successful match. The time complexity of such an attack is just $O(u)$, and for all practical purposes it is only limited by the maximal data transfer rate of the hard disk.

This technique can be used for larger values of e, but its efficiency drops rapidly since the number of candidate values for the top half of d grows exponentially in the size of e. We now describe an alternative technique, which remains reasonably efficient for values of e whose binary size is smaller than half the size of n. The basic idea is to compute for each candidate substring d' the value of $d'e-1$. For the correct value d, the result is zero modulo $\phi(n)$. In other words, it is equal to $c.\phi(n)$ in which the multiplier c is smaller than half the size of n. When we reduce $d'e-1$ modulo the known n instead of modulo the unknown $\phi(n)$, we get zero minus an error term which is somewhat smaller than n, i.e., a small negative value.

To use this observation, we consider two windows of length v in the given bit string of length u, which are shifted by a single bit position with respect to each other. Denote their numeric values by d' and d'', which are related by $d'' = 2d' + c_1 - c_2 2^v$. Assume that we have already computed $d'e-1 \pmod{n}$, and would like to compute $d''e-1(\bmod\ n)$. Since c_1 and c_2 are single bit quantities, we need a constant number of additions/subtractions to carry out this computation. The algorithm can thus scan the whole bit string in time $O(vu)$, and announce any location which makes the computed result a small negative number, a candidate value for d. If e is sufficiently small (compared to half the size of n), there are likely to be no false alarms. This technique can be optimized further in a variety of ways, such as updating only the most significant bits of $de-1 (\bmod n)$ during the scan, and recomputing its precise value only infrequently in order to prevent excessive buildup of computational errors.

A completely different approach is to look for the secret primes p and q whose product is the known value of n. The signature generation procedure does not have to know these values in order to compute $m^d (\bmod n)$, but in almost all the practical implementations of the RSA scheme the signature generation process uses these factors to speed up the computation by a factor of 4 by using the Chinese Remainder Theorem.

We make the reasonable assumption that p and q occur next to each other on the long bit string, and thus the distance between their least significant bits is about $v/2$. We can thus try to multiply any pair of substrings of length $v/2$ in which the second substring is shifted with respect to the first by $v/2+i$ bits for $i = 0, 32, 64$, and compare the result to n. The total complexity of this approach is $O(uv^2)$. However, it can be reduced to just $O(u)$ by performing the test modulo 2^{32}, i.e., by multiplying the least significant words of p and q, and comparing the bottom half of the result to the least significant word of n. Since multiplication of 32 bit numbers on a PC is a very fast basic operation, and the probability of false alarm is sufficiently small, the algorithm is quite practical.

3 Finding Public Keys

In the previous section we looked at finding the secret keys in the context of some sort of "lunchtime attack". In this section we look at finding public keys (usually signature verification keys) with a view to subverting a public key infrastructure.

Consider the case of an "authenticode" system. While it is usually possible to completely disable all signature checking on code, it is rarely desirable to do so. If all checking is removed it may leave a system wide open to naïve attacks. A better method of bypassing code signature checking is to replace the signature verification key with a key of your own choosing. Of course if you can do this, someone else can too, but it can protect against a less able attacker.

The usual process for locating anything is to try to identify some characteristic of what is being located and then to look for that characteristic. One characteristic of cryptographic keys is that they are usually chosen at random. Most code and data is not chosen at random and it turns out that this differentiation is significant. When data is random it has higher entropy than patterned information that is not random. This means that we should be able to locate cryptographic keys among other data by locating sections with unusually high entropy.

During our work we considered one particular system which we knew to contain an RSA signature verification key. The system is a modular cryptographic application programming interface produced by a major software vendor and it is widely used in commercial applications. The file we suspected of holding the key was approximately 300 kilobytes and we had no information as to where the key might be.

3.1 Visual identification of high entropy regions

The human eye and human brain between them are very good at picking up on patterns. Since the majority of the data in programs have some structure, while we expect to see very little structure in key data we can pick out the location of the keys simply by *looking* at the data in some suitable representation. Figure 1 is a one bit per pixel image from part of the program data in the code authentication system. The middle section of the image contains the signature verification key and it is visibly more noisy than the surrounding data.

Fig. 1. Key information (in the middle of the figure) looks more noisy than the rest of the data

While visual inspection of the program data allows us to locate the keys in a body of data, it is rather slow and labour intensive. We can achieve the same result by more mechanical means.

3.2 Identifying keys by measuring entropy

Since we know that key data has more entropy than non-key data, one way to locate a key is to divide the data into small sections, measure the entropy of each section and display the locations where there is particularly high entropy.

While getting a true measure of entropy is a complex task, in practice the entropy of most program code is so low that a true measure is not needed. In our experiments we found that examining a sliding window of 64 bytes of data and counting how many unique byte values were used gave a good enough measure of entropy. Throughout the first body of code we worked on the average window of data contained just under 30 unique values (with a standard deviation of close to 10). The windows which covered the key data averaged 60 unique byte values; a full 3 deviations from the mean. In a body of 300 kilobytes of data only 23 windows had a 'score' greater than 50 and of these 20 were consecutive and corresponded to the location of the key data.

In the general case, where we are faced with locating a key of length v bits in a body of code made up of u bits we can find the areas of highest entropy with a complexity of order u, since our method does not depend on the key and can be performed using only linear passes of the data. Clearly the success of this statistical method depends on the nature of the program concerned.

4 Better Methods of Hiding Keys

In the specific case of hiding RSA private keys, there are many countermeasures which can be used to make the described attacks less likely to succeed. The most obvious technique is to keep all the cryptographic keys on a detachable device such as a smart card, or to keep them encrypted under a strong memorized password on the hard disk. However, such a key must be used by the application in decrypted form during the signature generation process, and thus may be left in such a state somewhere in the PC's file system, as described in the introduction.

A simple example of one such countermeasure when e is small is to replace the standard decryption exponent d by an equivalent exponent of the form $d' = d + c\phi(n)$ for a moderately large c with several dozen bits. The user can directly use d' instead of d in his modular exponentiation operations, and its complexity grows by a negligible amount. The advantage of such a d' is that the attacker can no longer predict some of the bits of the decryption exponent just from the fact that the encryption exponent is small. However, it does not prevent the other attacks described in this paper.

Entropy based attacks to find key data can be resisted by matching the levels of entropy in non-key and key data. In practice we are concerned with the entropy density, not the total entropy; we must have the same amount of information over all but having the large concentration of entropy in the key data makes it easy to spot. We can achieve this either by trying to lower the entropy density of the key data or by raising the entropy of the other data.

We can lower the entropy density of the key by spreading the key out over more of the program. There are various options here. One way we could do this is to construct a set of values, each with relatively few bit value changes and thus with lower entropy, such that some simple combination of these values results in the key value we require. This works well in spreading the information but it incurs a computation overhead to set the key up. Another way would be to generate some code which when run results in the key value being placed into a buffer. Again, this requires some computational overhead but with luck this can be small compared to the computation to use the key.

There is another option for hiding the key, which can potentially not only do away with the computation overhead but also be more robust than other options. Consider that the key must be known at the time that the program is built. Given suitable tools we can present the key as a constant in the computation which is carried out using that key and then we can *optimise* the code given that constant. This will cause the key to be intimately intertwined with the code which uses it. Not only will the resulting code look very much like normal code (making the key hard to find), but it may also make the computation run faster than if the key were placed in a separate memory buffer. Furthermore if the optimisation process is thorough it will likely be extremely hard to change the key without replacing the entire section of code which uses that key.

The other class of solutions for hiding the key is to make the entropy of the rest of the data appear higher. One way to do this is to encrypt the program so that it decrypts itself before it runs. Work has been carried out in this field by

Intel Corporation[1] and others and it can lead to systems which are very hard to subvert but it does so at a cost. There will always be a computation overhead involved in decrypting the code and data before it is used and this will slow the system down.

5 Conclusions

The problem of efficient identification of stored secret keys in lunchtime attacks (as opposed to efficient computation of unknown secret keys by cryptanalysis) had received almost no attention in the literature so far, even though we believe that it poses a great threat to many enterprises with commercial grade physical security (such as banks, brokers, lawyers, travel agencies, etc.). Such attacks are particularly effective when a company sends its computers to a repair shop or sells them as junk, since it leaves no traces and there is no risk of detection (compared to attacks based on sneaking into the manager's room or installing a virus in his computer).

Our techniques seem to be applicable to a wide variety of other public key schemes, in addition to the RSA scheme. For example, in the Fiat-Shamir signature scheme, the secret key s is the square root of the public key a modulo n. A simple scan of the long bit string which checks for each candidate substring s' whether $s'^2 = a(\text{mod } n)$ has time complexity $O(uv^2)$. By using the algebraic relationship between any two consecutive candidates s' and $s"$, we can update the value of $s'^2(\text{mod } n)$ into $s"^2(\text{mod } n)$ in a constant number of addition/subtraction operations, and thus the total time complexity can be reduced to $O(uv)$. We are now in the process of developing similar attacks on other public key cryptosystems.

The problem of keeping a "public" key secret has also received little attention even though a great many public key infrastructures place huge value on a small number of root public keys. If computer programs must be operated in an hostile environment they need to have some form of protection. While it is relatively easy to build tamper resistant hardware it is much harder to protect computer software. It should be observed that re-keying a code authentication scheme is an attack on the Public Key Infrastructure rather than an attack on the cryptosystem. Over the years we have seen that attacking the PKI is often by far the most efficient way to break public key cryptosystems and this is no exception.

References

1. Aucsmith, D.: Tamper resistant software. Lecture Notes in Computer Science: Information Hiding **1174** (1996) 317–333
2. Rivest, R., Shamir, A., Adleman, L.: Cryptographic communications system and method. U.S. Patent no. 4,405,829 (1983).

On Channel Capacity and Modulation of Watermarks in Digital Still Images

Markus Breitbach and Hideki Imai

Third Department, Institute of Industrial Science, University of Tokyo
7–22–1 Roppongi, Minato–ku, Tokyo 106–8558, Japan

Abstract. An adversary who knows a watermarking scheme can extract the watermarked coefficients and attack them directly. This situation can be understood in a similar way to jamming as known from military communications and system performance can be described in terms of channel capacity and distortion. Using a gradient method, the attack is optimized from the adversary's viewpoint by minimizing channel capacity. It turns out that then for the same level of distortion and equiprobable modulation symbols binary modulation can achieve a higher channel capacity than modulation alphabets of larger size.
Keywords. Copyright protection, Watermarking, Fingerprinting, Jamming, Channel Capacity, Modulation

1 Introduction

A significant advantage of the digital recording of sound and image signals in comparison to their analog representation is their higher play back quality. This higher quality is preserved when the data are copied or transmitted: The copy of a digital media cannot be distinguished from the original, and received digital data are identical to the transmitted data unless they are subject to severe noise or interference.

In the past few years, these advantages lead to an explosive growth in the use of digital media. Since digital recording devices and data networks are becoming increasingly widespread, the advantage of lossless copying and transmission has turned more and more into a drawback: Creators and distributors of digital data are hesitant to provide access to their intellectual property.

As means to enforce copyright protection, the technologies of digital watermarking and fingerprinting have been proposed. Both are based on the idea to embed a watermark into the digital data in such a way that it can neither be perceived nor detected by statistical means. However by showing its existence within the data, the copyright holder can prove that this data is his intellectual property. In fingerprinting, the watermark is designed to characterize the user of digital data so that a dishonest user who illegally distributes copies of the media can be identified.

Unfortunately software programs to circumvent such copyright protection schemes spread on the internet at least as rapidly as the data to be protected

M. Franklin (Ed.): FC'99, LNCS 1648, pp. 125–139, 1999.

itselves. Besides of legal methods of signal processing and source compression there are mainly three attacks directed precisely against watermarks, namely watermark forgery, jamming, and collusion. Therefore copyright owners legitimately ask for the security of the available protection mechanisms. Up to now, mostly simulations have been used to demonstrate their performance. Simulations, however, cannot give a satisfactory answer on this question. They are always spot checks, limited to a certain set of test data as well as to certain attacks; but an owner is interested in the level of security provided to his particular work. Furthermore the rapid increase in computational power raises the doubt that in the near future attacks on the watermarking scheme might be possible that cannot be simulated on currently available computers.

The goal of this contribution is a fundamental investigation of the potential of watermarks. A jamming attack is studied to determine their performance limits. Jamming is known from military communications, where data transmission has to be unnoticeable and an attacker tries to destroy the data by superimposing another signal of limited power. In [1] communication in the presence of jamming is described as game between transmitter and receiver on one side and the attacker on the other. Transmitter and receiver determine modulation and demodulation scheme trying to maximize channel capacity while the jammer chooses a probability distribution of the jamming signal minimizing capacity.

As usual, the use of theory in place of simulations requires a simplification of the investigated system. The watermarking scheme considered here is intended for digital still images. The watermark is embedded by shifting the magnitude of mutually independent coefficients generated from the image. In many cases, dependencies between watermark coefficients can be represented by encoding, e. g. watermarks based on spread spectrum techniques [2,3] can be understood as a simple repetition code. However these dependencies must be hidden by encryption to avoid that an adversary exploits them for his attack. Another assumption, well–known from cryptography, is that the watermarking scheme is known in public. This permits an adversary to add his jamming signal directly onto the watermark. Unlike common image signal processing methods, against which the robustness of watermarking schemes is tested usually, the damage inflicted to the watermark by this jamming attack is not only a side effect, but its sole purpose. Therefore in the authors' opinion it is a more severe threat to watermarking schemes than other signal processing methods.

Based on this simple, but nevertheless fairly general watermarking scheme, a framework is presented how the effect of this jamming attack can be analyzed in terms of channel capacity and distortion. Distortion is a measure for the extent in which the embedding of the watermark respectively the attack cause perceptible damage to the image, while channel capacity measures the amount of data that can be transmitted from the watermark embeddor to the extractor to characterize the proprietor (in watermarking) or a certain customer (in fingerprinting). The concept of channel capacity implies as preliminary a reliable, i. e. a, by appropriate encoding, asymptotically error–free data transmission and thus maximum possible robustness of the watermark. The proposed analysis method essentially aims at optimizing the attack from the adversary's viewpoint. By means of a gradient method it determines the probability distribution of the jamming signal such that capacity becomes minimum. In this way a watermarking scheme can be evaluated without restriction to certain test images and without simulations. This method has been used to investigate the influence of the size of the modulation symbol alphabet, and it has turned out that for a given distortion smaller alphabets of equiprobable symbols achieve a higher capacity.

The remaining part of this paper is organized as follows: The next section presents a watermarking scheme to provide a basis for the subsequent investigations. In section 3, an adversary's possibilities to attack this system are studied and an attack is proposed. Section 4 describes a method to analyze this attack numerically with respect to the remaining data transmission capacity of the watermarking channel on one hand and to the amount of visual damage that must be accepted by the adversary on the other. Results and suggestions for the choice of the modulation alphabet will be given in section 5.

2 System model

The three main evaluation criteria for watermarking systems are their robustness, the amount of data carried by the watermark and the perceptibility of the image modifications caused by embedding the watermark respectively by an attack.

In this contribution, the tradeoff between channel capacity and perceptibility of an attack is investigated. The notion of channel capacity implies asymptotically error–free transmission, i. e. maximum possible robustness. To maximize the data rate, coherent watermark extraction, i. e. with access to the original unwatermarked image, is assumed. In incoherent extraction, the original image acts as a kind of noise signal being superimposed to the watermark. Since the original image's signal is much stronger than the watermark signal the SNR is very low; so, powerful error–correcting codes must be applied and the amount of data carried by the watermark is small. It is up to the copyright holder to trade off the higher watermark performance against the drawbacks of keeping the original of his work and providing it in the extracting process. The analysis below, however, cannot be based on such personal preferences, of course. Therefore only the coherent system is considered as it gives an upper bound on the performance of both coherent and incoherent watermarking schemes.

2.1 Watermarking scheme

In the sequel a fairly general watermarking scheme is presented, which comprises many of the schemes presently known in literature. Fig. 1 depicts the transmitter side of this scheme.

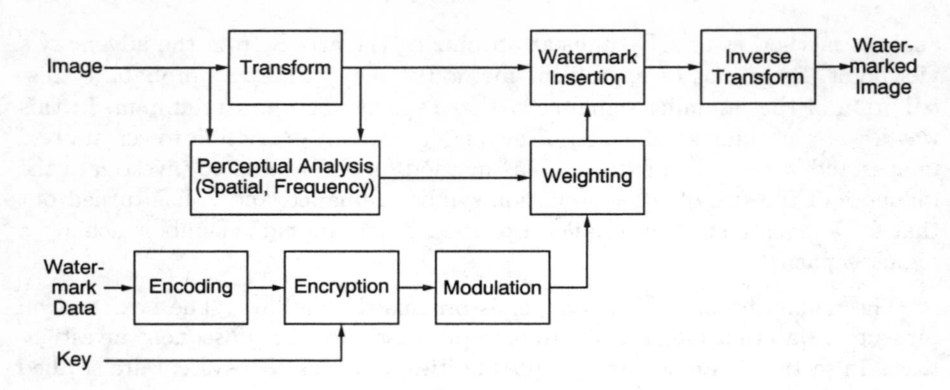

Fig. 1. Watermark embedding

At first, the original image is transformed before the watermark signal is embedded in the transform domain. Common transforms are the Discrete Cosine Transform (DCT) as well as wavelet transforms; other possibilities are the Fourier and the Walsh transform or even the null–transform, i. e. watermark embedding in the spatial domain. For the watermarking scheme under investigation here, the DCT of blocks of 8×8 pixels is assumed. This is the same transform as in the JPEG image compression standard (see e. g. [13]) in order to achieve a high degree of robustness with respect to this presently most important lossy image compression scheme.

The watermark is generated as follows: The data that will be carried by the watermark are first encoded by some error–correcting code to make them robust against modifications on the channel. Then the codewords are encrypted. This has two reasons: First it shall hinder an adversary to understand the contents of the watermark in the case that he succeeded in extracting it. Second it complicates a potential attack by hiding the original image as well as the structure of the error correcting code. The latter is why encryption must follow encoding, and as consequence of this order, encryption must be done using a stream cipher, e. g. by adding a pseudo–random sequence from a keyed random generator. After encryption follows modulation, i. e. the mapping of the watermark's representation over a (usually) finite field onto a real–valued signal. Denoting the ith coefficient in a DCT block before and after watermarking by c_i and $\tilde{c}_i$, respectively, amplitude modulation can be described as

$$\tilde{c}_i c_i + x_i \tag{1}$$

where the watermark x_i is from the set $\mathcal{X}_i \{X_{i,0}, \ldots, X_{i,q-1}\}$ of transmission symbols

$$X_{i,j} \alpha c_i \cdot \left(-1 + 2\frac{j}{q-1}\right), \quad j \ldots q-1, \tag{2}$$

defined by q–ary amplitude shift keying (ASK) modulation; herein α is a positive real–valued constant. For binary modulation, this simplifies to

$$\mathcal{X}_i \begin{Bmatrix} X_{i,0} \\ X_{i,1} \end{Bmatrix} \begin{Bmatrix} -c_i\alpha \text{ to embed a "0"} \\ +c_i\alpha \text{ to embed a "1"} \end{Bmatrix}.$$

Many other modulation schemes can be understood as a combination of this ASK with some specific encoding, e. g. spread spectrum as the combination of ASK with a repetition code. This does not hold for the flipping of the least significant bit, which maybe was the first modulation scheme used in watermarking. However, it turned out in the meantime to be not robust enough and does not need to be considered any further.

The factor α in eq. (2) serves to weight the watermark to adapt it to the original image and thus make it imperceptible. It is well–known that in human vision masking effects occur. Weighting the watermark signal exploits these effects to hide the watermark imperceptibly in the original image. The weighting of course depends on the original image, which therefore before must be analyzed in the spatial domain as well as in the transform domain. The weighting method used here will be explained in more detail in the next section.

The inverse of watermark embedding is watermark extraction shown in fig. 2. The first step of extraction is a kind of "channel estimation": The suspicious

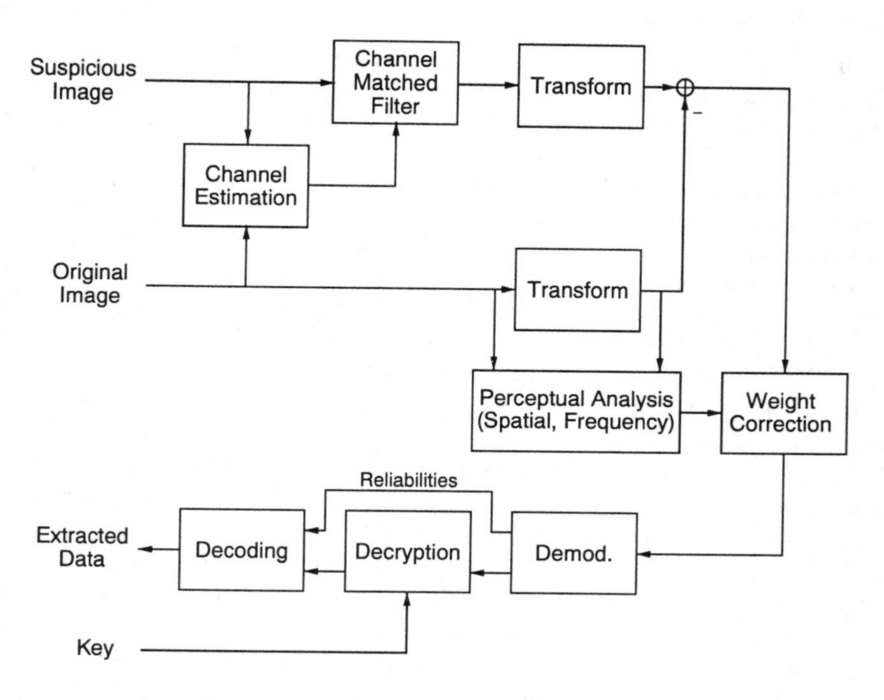

Fig. 2. Coherent watermark extraction

image is compared to the original, which serves so to say as "pilot signal". This permits to detect, and in the subsequent "channel matched filter", to remove some typical modifications of the channel, like some linear filtering operations or geometrical distortions (affine transforms) [3]. E. g. two–dimensional affine transforms, attacks that destroy the synchronization necessary for the 8×8 DCT transform, can be undone after determining the offset of four points between the suspective and the original image.

Afterwards, both the original as well as the suspective image are transformed in the same manner as on the transmitting side. Subtracting the transform of the original image from that of the suspicious image yields a probably modified version of the watermark. To permit a proper demodulation, the weighting for perceptual masking must be inverted. Clearly, this requires beforehand the same analysis of the original image in spatial and transform domain as on the transmitting side. Afterwards, demodulation, decryption and decoding follow. If possible, soft reliability information should be passed from the demodulator to the decoder to improve its performance.

2.2 Model for human vision

A key issue in watermarking is the model for the human visual system (HVS). It provides the basis for the perceptual analysis and via the weighting and the selection of the coefficients to be watermarked, it influences the modulation scheme. Furthermore it can be used to assess the distortion caused by an attack.

One of the most important image compression techniques presently is the JPEG standard. It performs lossy compression, i. e. it separates visually important from invisible and therefore unimportant information and encodes only the important part. For this purpose, it applies the DCT: The DCT concentrates most of the image's signal energy in the low–frequency coefficients, particularly in the DC–coefficient. Due to their lower magnitudes, the high–frequency coefficients are visually less important and JPEG quantizes them more coarsely.

To survive JPEG as well as other lossy image processing techniques, a watermark must be placed within the visible information part, but nevertheless has to be imperceptible. This can be achieved by a combined analysis of the image in the DCT domain and in the spatial domain.

In the DCT domain, the N AC–coefficients with greatest magnitude are selected to incorporate the watermark. Typically, N is in the range from 8 to 12. This avoids embedding the watermark in the perceptually unimportant and thus error–prone high–frequency coefficients as well as in the DC–coefficients. Changes in DC–coefficients likely result in visible damage.

In the spatial domain, the factor α in eq. (2) is selected dynamically for each DCT block based on an analysis by the regional classification algorithm proposed in [4]. This algorithm assigns each block to one of the following six classes: 1. Blocks containing an edge; 2. blocks with uniform structure and moderate intensity; 3. blocks with uniform structure with either low or high intensity; 4.–6. moderately to highly textured blocks. According to their decreasing sensitivity to image modifications, blocks in these classes are assigned the values $\alpha 0.1$, 0.12, 0.15, 0.2, 0.25, or 0.3, respectively.

Defining modulation and watermark embedding according to eq. (2) with α chosen properly by regional classification follows the presumption in [3] according to which a coefficient can be modified without perceptible distortion to the image as long as the watermarked coefficient $\tilde{c}_i$ is in the range

$$c_i\,(1-\alpha) \;\leq\; \tilde{c}_i \;\leq\; c_i\,(1+\alpha). \tag{3}$$

In reality of course, distortion will not change abruptly from being imperceptible to being a severe damage just in the moment when exceeding the borders of the range given above. Rather it will become more and more noticeable the more it exceeds the borders. Therefore in the sequel, distortion is measured by the signal power of the signal outside this range:

$$S_D \min\left\{[c_i' - c_i(1 \pm \alpha)]^2\right\} \tag{4a}$$

if the distorted coefficient c_i' does not fulfill ineq. (3) and

$$S_D 0 \tag{4b}$$

otherwise.

Obviously, the above descriptions characterize a particular system in order to permit simulations. The essential preliminary, however, for the theoretical analysis presented in the following two sections is given in eq. (3): The existence of a range within which modifications of the DCT coefficients are considered to result only in imperceptible changes of the image. Insofar the analysis below is not constrained to the DCT and the regional classification algorithm as proposed for the particular system above but can easily be extended to incorporate other concepts like e. g. that of the "Just Noticeable Difference (JND)" used in [5] or the visual model described in [6].

3 Jamming attack

3.1 Preliminaries

The goal of an adversary is to make the watermark unreadable or even to remove it while preserving the image quality. For this purpose he can apply common signal processing methods, like affine geometric transforms [7], various filters, contrast enhancement techniques and many others. Of course a watermark has to be resistent against these methods; nevertheless, the damage to a watermark caused by these operations is only a side effect which cannot be directed precisely against the watermark.

More efficient attacks from the adversary's viewpoint are possible when, as usually in cryptography, the algorithms for watermark embedding and extraction are known in public. Then he can add a jamming signal directly onto the watermark and thereby avoid to damage any unwatermarked part of the image. Below, focus is on this jamming attack. Other attacks precisely aimed at watermarks are collusion attacks and watermark forgery.

Here, however, it is assumed that an adversary has only one watermarked copy of the image at his disposal, what excludes collusion attacks like the simple averaging over multiple copies as well as the more complicated comparison between copies as basis for an intelligent attack. This assumption holds in the case of watermarking applications and it is also realistic regarding non–professional adversaries in fingerprinting schemes that are not willing to pay for sufficiently many copies, e. g. when private individuals distribute copyright protected media among friends. Protection against collusion attacks by professional pirates is a difficult research problem [8,9,10] which possibly can be solved using coding theoretic methods. This, however, is beyond the scope of this contribution.

Watermark forgery means that the adversary embeds his own watermark additionally. If it comes to a trial in court, both the legal proprietor and the adversary will claim that their watermark proves their ownership, resulting in a deadlock situation. An efficient solution of this problem is to determine the key for encryption resp. decryption from the original image by applying a one–way function [11].

3.2 Description

Since an adversary knows that the watermark has been embedded in the DCT domain, he can transform the watermarked image, too, and thereby separate the watermarked from the unwatermarked coefficients. He can also apply the regional classification algorithm to the watermarked image. The weighting factors α he obtains will be almost completely identical to those used in watermark embedding since the difference between the watermarked and the original image has to be imperceptible. Consider now a watermarked coefficient $\tilde{c}_i$ and assume that α has been determined correctly. According to eq. (2) the modulation alphabet $\mathcal{X}_i$ is scaled by the coefficient's original value c_i. To destroy the watermark, the adversary can add a random jamming signal n_i. Then the attacked coefficient $\hat{c}_i$ and the extracted watermark signal y_i yield

$$\hat{c}_i \tilde{c}_i + n_i \quad \text{and} \quad y_i x_i + n_i, \tag{5}$$

respectively. He must scale his jamming signal appropriately before adding it to the watermarked image to avoid unnecessary distortions. However because of encryption, he cannot tell which $x_i \in \mathcal{X}_i$ has been embedded and thus to him the original coefficient $c_i \tilde{c}_i - x_i$ remains secret.

So all he can do is to scale the jamming signal n_i by $\tilde{c}_i$:

$$n_i \tilde{c}_i \alpha \beta \tag{6}$$

where β is a real–valued number from $[\beta_{min}, \beta_{max}]$ with probability distribution function $\Pr(\beta)$.

A reasonable definition for β_{min} and β_{max} is the following: The distortion is defined in eq. (4) by the distance of the actual coefficient from the range in which modifications of the coefficient are considered as imperceptible or — indirectly — from the original coefficient c_i. In particular, this definition is symmetric. Thus it is near at hand to demand that $c_{i,min} \leq \hat{c}_i \leq c_{i,max}$ where $c_{i,max} - \hat{c}_i, \hat{c}_i - c_{i,min} \leq D$. Then $c_{i,max}$ is taken when the maximum watermark $x_i \alpha c_i$ is embedded and the adversary selects β_{max}, i. e. $c_{i,max}\tilde{c}_i(1+\alpha\beta)c_i(1+\alpha)(1+\alpha\beta_{max}) \leq D + c_i$. Thus

$$\beta_{max}\frac{1}{\alpha}\left[\frac{\frac{D}{c_i}+1}{1+\alpha}-1\right].$$

Similarly c_i becomes minimum for $x_i - \alpha c_i$ and selection of β_{min}, what yields $c_{i,min}\tilde{c}_i(1+\alpha\beta)c_i(1-\alpha)(1+\alpha\beta_{min}) \geq -D + c_i$ and

$$\beta_{min}\frac{1}{\alpha}\left[\frac{-\frac{D}{c_i}+1}{1+\alpha}-1\right].$$

The possible outcomes of modulation and attack can easily be shown graphically for binary modulation as in the following two examples:

Example 1: Assume that the extracted watermark will be demodulated by a threshold decision with threshold y_i. Knowing this, the adversary can choose $\beta \in \{(1+\epsilon)/(1-\alpha), -(1+\epsilon)/(1+\alpha)\}$ with a small positive constant ϵ. The resulting situation is shown in fig. 3. Obviously in each decision region the probability is 1/2 that either "0" or "1" has been embedded. This is the behavior of a binary symmetric channel (BSC) with cross–over probability 1/2, and it is well–known that the capacity of such a channel is zero. In other words, it is impossible in this manner to transmit any data within the watermark from the embedding to the extracting party. Also depicted in fig. 3 are the borders of the range of imperceptible modifications to c_i resp. x_i according to eq. (3). Obviously a wrong choice of the adversary always leads to that y_i leaves this range. Consequently this attack inherently bears a certain risk to perceptually damage the image.

Example 2: Clearly the extracting party cannot be satisfied with a zero–capacity of the watermark channel. It is near at hand to improve demodulation by taking into account the magnitudes of the extracted coefficients. The simplest way to do so is to define a region, e. g. $[-\frac{1}{2}c_i\alpha, \frac{1}{2}c_i\alpha]$, within which an extracted coefficient is regarded as erasure. Again assuming that this is known in public, the adversary can choose $\beta \in \frac{1}{2}\{(1+\epsilon)/(1-\alpha), -(1+\epsilon)/(1+\alpha)\}$ as shown in fig. 4. The channel capacity now evaluates to $C/2$ bit per coefficient. So, this attack does not reduce channel capacity as drastically as in the previous example. On the other hand, the extracted watermark exceeds the range of imperceptible modifications by a smaller amount, and the adversary has a smaller risk of damaging the image by his attack.

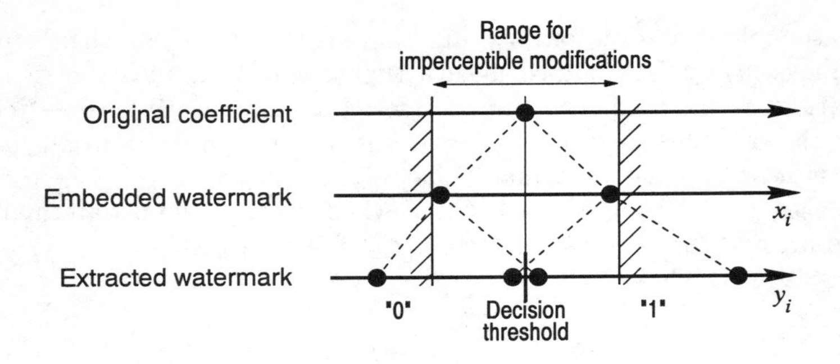

Fig. 3. Signaling in the case of binary threshold demodulation

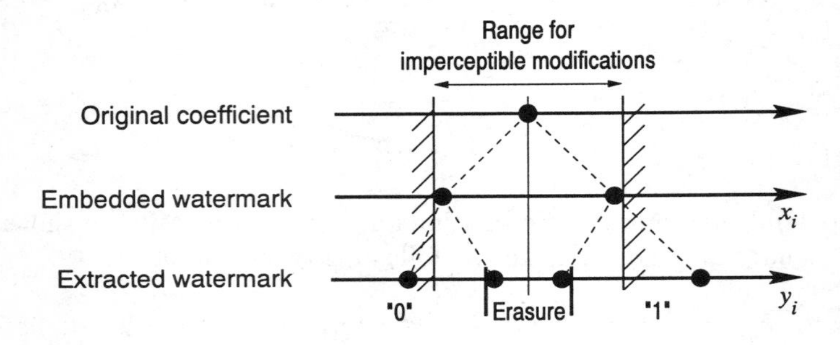

Fig. 4. Signaling in the case of erasure demodulation

Both examples show that the adversary's choice of the jamming signal n_i and the demodulation scheme strongly depend on each other. Two questions are coming up in this situation.

From the adversary's viewpoint:

i) Given the maximum allowed difference D between the actual and the original image coefficient and knowing the demodulation rule, which probability distribution should the jamming signal follow in order to minimize the data transmission capacity of the watermark?

From the copyright holder's viewpoint:

ii) How should the size q of the modulation alphabet $\mathcal{X}_i$ be chosen to maximize transmission capacity?

4 Numerical analysis

The key problem in answering these questions is to determine the particular probability distribution function for β that permits an adversary to minimize the data transmission capacity. In this section it will be shown how this can be accomplished numerically by means of a gradient method. Before this method itself can be described, calculation of the channel capacity and of its gradient need to explained.

Due to encryption, all possible transmission symbols $X_{i,k}$ are equally likely, thus $P(X_{i,k})q^{-1}$ for all $X_{i,k} \in \mathcal{X}_i$. For numerical analysis, assume that the received watermark signal y_i is sufficiently fine quantized by rounding to the nearest quantizer level in the set $\mathcal{Y}_i\{Y_{i,0}, \ldots, Y_{i,l_{max}-1}\}$. Then the channel capacity C is given [12] by

$$C \sum_{k}^{q-1} \sum_{l}^{l_{max}-1} P(X_{i,k}) P_{Ch}(Y_{i,l}|X_{i,k}) \log_2 \frac{P_{Ch}(Y_{i,l}|X_{i,k})}{P(Y_{i,l})}. \tag{7}$$

Herein $P_{Ch}(Y_{i,l}|X_{i,k})$ is the channel transition probability for the case that symbol $Y_{i,l} \in \mathcal{Y}_i$ is received after $X_{i,k} \in \mathcal{X}_i$ has been transmitted. $P(Y_{i,l})$ is the probability that $Y_{i,l}$ is received regardless of which symbol $X_{i,k}$ has been transmitted; therefore $P(Y_{i,l}) \sum_{k}^{q-1} P_{Ch}(Y_{i,l}|X_{i,k})\, P(X_{i,k})$. To calculate the $P_{Ch}(Y_{i,l}|X_{i,k})$ numerically, replace the continuous probability density function $\Pr(\beta)$ by a discrete probability function at the positions $\underline{\beta}(\beta_0, \ldots, \beta_{j_{max}-1})$: $\underline{Q} \Pr(\underline{\beta})(\Pr(\beta_0), \ldots, \Pr(\beta_{j_{max}-1}))$.

Now successively for each transmission symbol $X_{i,k}$, the probabilities of the n_i can be calculated according to eq. (6) and those of the corresponding y_i by eq. (5). Finally taking into account the quantization, the $P_{Ch}(Y_{i,l}|X_{i,k})$ are obtained.

The goal of the gradient method is to vary the probability function $\underline{Q}$ iteratively such that in each iteration the channel capacity $C(\underline{Q})$ is reduced until the minimum of $C(\underline{Q})$ is reached. For this the partial derivatives of $C(\underline{Q})$ with respect to each component of $\underline{Q}$ are needed. They are also approximated numerically:

To obtain the partial derivative with respect to the jth component of $\underline{Q}$, $j \ldots j_{max} - 1$, a test vector $\underline{Q}_{Tj}(1-\varepsilon)\underline{Q} + \varepsilon(\delta_{j,0}, \ldots, \delta_{j,j}, \ldots, \delta_{j,j_{max}-1})$ is constructed where $\delta_{j,i}1$ if j and 0 otherwise and where ε is a very small constant, typically $\varepsilon 10^{-3}$. This construction rule takes into account that since $\underline{Q}$ as well as $\underline{Q}_{Tj}$ are probability functions the sum of all their components must equal 1. Using $\underline{Q}$ and $\underline{Q}_{Tj}$ as probability functions for β, the respective channel capacities are evaluated. Their difference yields

$$\Delta C_j C(\underline{Q}) - C(\underline{Q}_{Tj}) \tag{8}$$

and $\Delta \underline{C}(\Delta C_0, \ldots, \Delta C_{j_{max}-1})$.

With these preliminaries, the gradient method itself can be explained. In the sequel, the index $^{(\nu)}$ marks the νth iteration.

As initial value, let all $\beta_0 \ldots \beta_{j_{max}-1}$ be equally likely, i. e. $P^{(1)}(\beta_j) j_{max}^{-1}$ and $\underline{Q}^{(1)} 20(j_{max}^{-1}, \ldots, j_{max}^{-1})$.

Then in the νth iteration

1. calculate $C(\underline{Q}^{(\nu)})$ according to eq. (7) and
2. calculate $\Delta\underline{C}^{(\nu)}$.
3. Let $\underline{Q}^{(\nu+1)}\underline{Q}^{(\nu)} + \gamma\Delta\underline{C}^{(\nu)}$. If any of the components should become negative, set it to 0. Afterwards normalize $\underline{Q}^{(\nu+1)}$ such that the sum of all its components equals 1.

This iteration is repeated until the improvement $C(\underline{Q}^{(\nu)}) - C(\underline{Q}^{(\nu+1)})$ in minimizing C falls below a fixed threshold, e. g. 10^{-9}.

5 Results

Channel capacity and distortion in the presence of an optimized attack have been evaluated for various alphabet sizes q^i, $i \ldots 5$. D has also been varied what lead to attacks with different distortions. The obtained results are depicted in fig. 5.

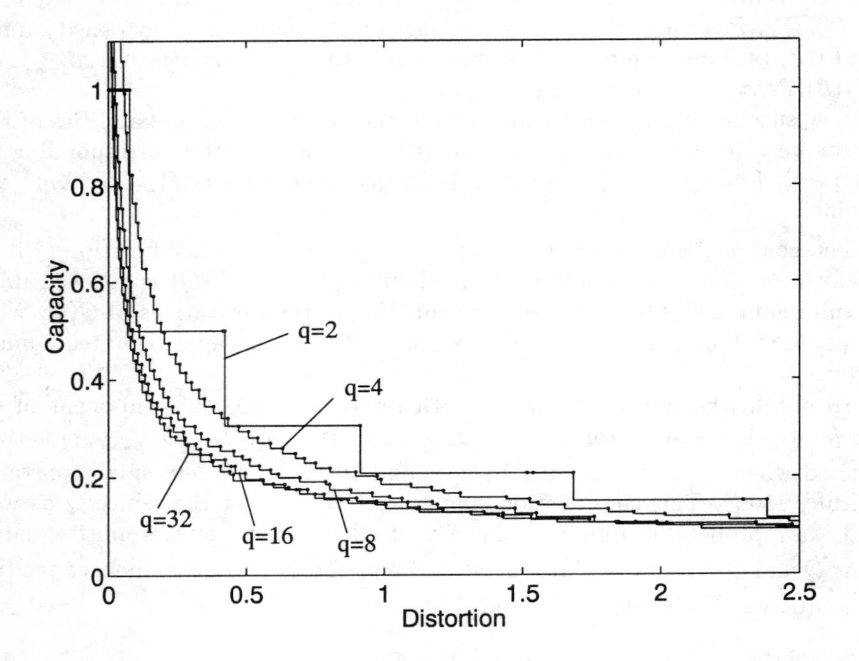

Fig. 5. Channel capacity C vs. distortion S_D for various q (distortion normalized to $c_i\alpha$; $\alpha.2$)

Clearly for the same level of distortion that an adversary might be willing to accept a small modulation alphabet achieves a higher channel capacity than a large alphabet.

Two reasons for this can be mentioned. First, with increasing q the Euclidean distance $X_{i,j+1} - X_{i,j}\alpha c_i/(q-1)$ between two neighboring modulation signals decreases. Then already a small amplitude of the jamming signal is sufficient to introduce errors and decrease capacity. Hence, distortion is smaller for large q. For the second reason note that in the case of binary signaling as shown in figures 3 and 4 half of the attacked coefficients will leave their range of imperceptible modifications and that then the jamming signal completely contributes to distortion. For large modulation alphabets, however, the symbols are equally spaced within the whole range. So for the symbols in the center it is not unlikely that an attacked coefficient stays within the range, so that no distortion occurs at all. And if it should leave the range, only a part of the jamming signal contributes to distortion.

To get an idea of what level of distortion might be acceptable to an adversary, the watermarking scheme as described in section 2 has been implemented with binary signaling and simulated under the optimum attack as found above. Fig. 6 shows the test image "Girl" (a) before and (b) after watermarking and (c) – (f) after attacks with $D = 0.39, 0.54, 0.67$, and 0.77, respectively. In fig. 6(d) some small damages become noticeable. The corresponding level of distortion is $S_D.912 \cdot (c_i\alpha)^2$, the channel capacity $C.306$ bit per coefficient.

6 Conclusion

In this paper, watermarking has been studied in the presence of an intelligent adversary who exploits his knowledge on the watermarking scheme by adding a noise signal directly targeted onto the watermarked coefficients. This situation has been identified as being closely related to jamming in military communications. Here the probability density function of the jamming signal has been optimized for various levels of distortion and for different sizes of the modulation alphabets. It has turned out that binary signaling provides the highest data transmission capacity at a given level of distortion.

Up to here, all coefficients were treated and attacked separately. It is an open problem of image processing how the correlations between coefficients from neighboring DCT blocks can be taken into account. This might further improve the described attack and again decrease channel capacity.

References

1. M. Hegde, W. W. Stark, D. Teneketzis: On the Capacity of Channels with Unknown Interference. *IEEE Trans. Inform. Theory,* vol. 35, no. 4, July 1989, pp. 770–782
2. J. J. K. Ó Ruanaidh, W. J. Dowling, F. M. Boland: Watermarking Digital Images for Copyright Protection. *IEE Proceedings on Vision, Signal and Image Processing,* vol. 143, no. 4, Aug. 1996, pp. 250–256
3. I. J. Cox, J. Kilian, T. Leighton, T. Shamoon: Secure Spread Spectrum Watermarking for Multimedia. *IEEE Trans. on Image Processing,* vol. 6, no. 12, 1997, pp. 1673–1687

4. B. Tao, B. Dickinson: Adaptive Watermarking in the DCT Domain. *Proc. Int. Conf. Accoustics, Speech, Signal Processing,* 1997
5. C. I. Podilchuk, W. Zeng: Perceptual Watermarking of Still Images. *Proc. First IEEE Signal Processing Society Workshop on Multimedia Signal Processing,* June 1997, Princeton, New Jersey
6. B. Girod: The Information Theoretical Significance of Spatial and Temporal Masking in Video Signals. *Proceedings of the SPIE, Human Vision, Visual Processing, and Digital Display,* vol. 1077, pp. 178–187, 1989
7. F. A. P. Petitcolas, R. J. Anderson, M. G. Kuhn: Attacks on Copyright Marking Schemes. *Proc. 2nd Workshop on Information Hiding, Portland / Oregon, April 1998;* Springer Verlag, Lecture Notes in Computer Science, vol. 1525, pp. 219–239
8. D. Boneh, J. Shaw: Collusion–Secure Fingerprinting for Digital Data. *IEEE Trans. Inform. Theory,* vol. 44, no. 5, 1998, pp. 1897–1905
9. J. Löfvenberg, N. Wiberg: Random Codes for Digital Fingerprinting. *Proc. ISIT '98,* Cambridge, MA, USA, Aug. 16-21, 1998, p. 80
10. J. Kilian, F. T. Leighton, L. R. Matheson, T. G. Shamoon, R. E. Tarjan, F. Zane: Resistance of Digital Watermarks to Collusive Attacks. *Proc. ISIT '98,* Cambridge, MA, USA, Aug. 16-21, 1998, p. 271
11. M. D. Swanson, M. Kobayashi, A. H. Tewfik: Multimedia Data–Embedding and Watermarking Techniques. *Proceedings of the IEEE,* vol. 86, no. 6, June 1998, pp. 1064–1087
12. J. G. Proakis: *Digital Communications.* Third edition, McGraw–Hill, 1995
13. W. B. Pennebaker, J. L. Mitchell: *JPEG Still Image Data Compression Standard.* Chapman & Hall, New York, 1993

(a) Original image

(b) Watermarked image

(c) $D0.39$

(d) $D0.54$

(e) $D0.67$

(f) $D0.77$

Fig. 6. Test image "Girl"

Towards Making Broadcast Encryption Practical

Michel Abdalla[1*], Yuval Shavitt[2], and Avishai Wool[3]

[1] Dept. of Computer Science & Engineering, University of California at San Diego, 9500 Gilman Drive, La Jolla, CA 92093, mabdalla@cs.ucsd.edu.
[2] Bell Laboratories, Lucent Technologies, 101 Crawfords Corner Rd., Holmdel, NJ 07733, shavitt@ieee.org.
[3] Bell Laboratories, Lucent Technologies, 700 Mountain Ave., Murray Hill, NJ 07974, yash@acm.org.

Abstract. The problem we address is how to communicate securely with a set of users (the target set) over an insecure broadcast channel. In order to solve this problem, several broadcast encryption schemes have been proposed. In these systems, the parameters of major concern are the length of transmission and number of keys held by each user's set top terminal (STT). Due to the need to withstand hardware tampering, the amount of secure memory available in the STTs is quite small, severely limiting the number of keys each user holds. In such cases, known theoretical bounds seem to indicate that non-trivial broadcast encryption schemes are only feasible when the number of users is small.
In order to break away from these theoretical bounds, our approach is to allow a controlled number of users outside the target set to occasionally receive the multicast. This relaxation is appropriate for low-cost transmissions such as multicasting electronic coupons. For this purpose, we introduce *f-redundant* establishment key allocations, which guarantee that the total number of recipients is no more than f times the number of intended recipients. We measure the performance of such schemes by the number of transmissions they require, by their redundancy, and by their opportunity, which is the probability of a user outside the target set to be part of the multicast. We first prove a new lower bound and discuss the basic trade-offs associated with this new setting. Then we present several new f-redundant establishment key allocations. We evaluate the schemes' performance under all the relevant measures by extensive simulation. Our results indicate that, unlike previous solutions, it seems possible to design practical schemes in this new setting.

1 Introduction

1.1 The Problem

The domain we consider in this paper is that of broadcast applications where the transmissions need to be encrypted. As a primary example we consider a

* Supported in part by CAPES under Grant BEX3019/95-2. Work done while author was visiting Bell Laboratories.

M. Franklin (Ed.): FC'99, LNCS 1648, pp. 140–157, 1999.

broadband digital TV network, broadcasting either via satellite or via cable [MQ95], but other applications such as Internet multicasts are similar.

In this context, the *head-end* occasionally needs to multicast an encrypted message to some subset of users (called the target set) using the broadcast channel. Each network user has a *set-top terminal* (STT) which receives the encrypted broadcast and decrypts the message, if the user is entitled to it. For this purpose the STT securely stores the user's secret keys, which we refer to as establishment keys. Because of extensive piracy [McC96], the STTs need to contain a secure chip which includes secure memory for key storage. This memory should be non-volatile, and tamper-resistant, so the pirates will find it difficult to read its contents. As a result of these requirements, STTs have severely limited secure memory, typically in the range of a few Kilobytes [Gem98].

Earlier work on broadcast encryption (cf. [FN94]) was motivated by the need to transmit the key for the next billing period or the key for the next pay-per-view event, in-band with the broadcast, since STTs only had uni-directional communications capabilities. The implicit assumption was that users sign up for various services using a separate channel, such as by calling the service provider over the phone. In such applications it is reasonable to assume that the target set is almost all the population, and there are only small number of excluded users. Moreover, it is crucial that users outside the target set are not able to decrypt the message since it has a high monetary value, e.g., the cost of a month's subscription.

However, current STTs typically follow designs such as [CEFH95] which allow bi-directional communication, where the uplink uses an internal modem and a phone line, or a cable modem. These new STTs upload the users' requests and download next month's keys via a callback mechanism, and not through the broadcast channel. This technological trend would seem to invalidate the necessity for broadcast encryption schemes completely. We argue that this is not the case—there are other applications where broadcast encryption is necessary, such as multicasting electronic coupons, promotional material, and low-cost pay-per-view events. Such applications need to multicast short-lived, low value messages that are not worth the overhead of communicating with each user individually. In such applications, though, the requirements from the solution are slightly different. On one hand, it is no longer crucial that only users in the target set receive the message, as long as the number of free-riders is controlled. On the other hand, it is no longer reasonable to assume anything about the size of the target set.

1.2 Related Work

Fiat and Naor [FN94] were first to introduce broadcast encryption. They suggested methods of securely broadcasting key information such that only a selected set of users can decrypt this information while coalitions of up to k other users can learn nothing, either in the information-theoretic sense, or under a computational security model. Their schemes, though, required impractical numbers of keys to be stored in the STTs. Extensions to this basic work can be found in [BC94,BFS98,SvT98].

Recently Luby and Staddon [LS98] studied the trade-off between the transmission length and the number of keys stored in the STTs. They assumed a security model in which encryptions cannot be broken, i.e., only users that have a correct key can decrypt the message. We adopt the same security model. Their work still addressed fixed-size target sets, which are assumed to be either very large or very small, and no user outside the target set is allowed to be able to decrypt the message. A main part of their work is a disillusioning lower bound, showing that either the transmission will be very long or a prohibitive number of keys need to be stored in the STTs.

A related line of work goes under the title of "tracing traitors" [CFN94,NP98]. The goal is to identify some of the users that leak their keys, once a cloned STT is found. This is achieved by controlling which keys are stored in each STT, in a way that the combination of keys in a cloned STT would necessarily point to at least one traitor.

Key management schemes for encrypted broadcast networks, which give the vendor the flexibility to offer program packages of various sizes to the users, can be found in [Woo98]. The problem of tracking the location of STTs in order to prevent customers from moving an STT from, e.g., a home to a bar, is addressed in [GW98].

1.3 Contributions

Our starting point is the observation that the requirement "no users outside the target set can decrypt the message" is too strict for some applications. For instance, for the purposes of multicasting electronic coupons, it may be enough to guarantee that the recipient set contains the target set, and that the total number of recipients is no more than f times the size of the target set. Service providers can afford a small potential increase in the number of redeemed coupons, as long as this simplifies their operations and lowers their cost. We call establishment key allocation schemes that provide such guarantees "f-redundant broadcast encryption schemes". Relaxing the requirements in this way allows us to depart from the lower bounds of [LS98].

On the other hand, we have a more ambitious goal when it comes to possible target sets. Unlike earlier work, we require our schemes to be able to multicast to *any* target set, not just those target sets of very small or very large cardinality.

We concentrate on schemes which store only very few keys in each STT. As we mentioned before, STTs typically have only a few Kilobytes of key storage. With a key length of 128 bits this translates to around 100 keys. Thus, for systems with several million users, it is reasonable to require the maximum number of keys per user's STT to be $O(\log n)$, where n is the total number of users, or at most $O(n^\epsilon)$, where, say, $\epsilon \leq 1/4$.

Subject to these constraints, we are interested in several measures of the quality of an establishment key allocation. The first is the number of transmissions t: we can always attain our requirements trivially if we assign each STT a unique key, but then we suffer a very high number of transmissions. The second parameter, which we call *opportunity*, is the proportion of free riders in the population outside the target set. The opportunity measures the incentive a customer has to avoid paying (in cheap pay-per-view type services). If the opportunity is very high, close to 1, there is no incentive for customers to pay, as they can almost surely get a free ride.

After discussing the basic trade-offs associated with the problem, we present some simple examples, that show the problem difficulty. We then prove a new lower bound on the tradeoff between transmission length and number of keys stored per STT, that incorporates the f-redundancy of our establishment key allocations. We show that the f-redundancy gives us a substantial gain: for the same number of transmissions t we can hope for only $\exp(\Omega(n/tf))$ keys per STT, whereas the bound of [LS98] is $\exp(\Omega(n/t))$.

We then present several establishment key allocation constructions, and an approximation algorithm that finds a key cover with minimal number of transmissions, for any given target set of users. Since this problem is similar to the minimum set cover problem that is known to be NP-hard, we cannot expect to find an optimal solution efficiently. Instead we use a greedy approximation algorithm to find good key covers. We conducted an extensive simulation study of the problem, from which we present only the interesting results.

Organization: In the next section we formally define the problem and the various parameters we are interested in. In Section 3 we show some simple solutions. In Section 4 we prove our new lower bound on the trade-off between the number of keys per user, the redundancy factor, and the transmission length. In Section 5 we discuss how to find which keys to use given an establishment key allocation. In Section 6 we show our schemes and the results of their performance evaluation. We conclude in Section 7.

2 Definitions and Model

Let $\mathcal{U}$ be the set of all customers (STTs) connected to a head-end, with $|\mathcal{U}| = n$. We use K to denote the *target set*, i.e., the set of paying customers, and denote its size by $|K| = k$.

We describe the allocation of the establishment keys by a collection $\mathcal{S} = \{S_1, S_2, \ldots\}$ of *key sets* such that $\cup S_i = \mathcal{U}$. We associate a unique establishment key e_i with each set $S_i \in \mathcal{S}$. A key e_i is stored in the secure memory of every STT $u \in S_i$. Hence the number of keys an STT $u \in \mathcal{U}$ stores is equal to the number of sets $S_i \in \mathcal{S}$ it belongs to. Formally,

Definition 1. *Let $\mathcal{S}$ be an establishment key allocation. The* degree *of an STT u is $deg(u) = |\{i : S_i \ni u\}|$. The degree of a collection $\mathcal{S}$ is $deg(\mathcal{S}) = \max_{u \in \mathcal{U}} deg(u)$.*

Definition 2. *Given a target set K, a* key cover *of K is a collection of sets $S_i \in \mathcal{S}$ whose union contains K:*

$$\mathcal{C}(K) \subseteq \mathcal{S} \text{ such that } K \subseteq \cup_{S_i \in \mathcal{C}(K)} S_i .$$

The minimal key cover *is $\mathcal{C}_{\min}(K) = \mathcal{C}(K)$ for which $|\mathcal{C}(K)|$ is minimal.*

Suppose the head-end needs to send a message μ to all the members of a target set K. Given any key cover $\mathcal{C}(K)$, the head end encrypts μ using the establishment keys e_i corresponding to the sets $S_i \in \mathcal{C}(K)$, and broadcasts each encryption separately.[1].

Definition 3. *We denote the best possible number of transmissions that the head-end can use for a target set K by $t_K = |\mathcal{C}_{\min}(K)|$. Thus the worst case number of transmissions is $t_{\max}(\mathcal{S}) = \max_K t_K$.*

In order to define the redundancy and opportunity measures we need the following technical definition.

Definition 4. *We denote the set of recipients of a given key cover $\mathcal{C}(K)$ by $R_{\mathcal{C}}(K) = \cup\{S_i \in \mathcal{C}(K)\}$ and the total number of recipients by $r_{\mathcal{C}}(K) = |R_{\mathcal{C}}(K)|$.*

By the definition of a key cover $\mathcal{C}(K)$, every member of the target set K has at least one of the keys used to encrypt μ. However, other STTs outside K usually exist, which are also capable of decrypting the message. All our establishment key allocations are constructed with a worst case guarantee that there are never too many of these free riders. Formally,

Definition 5. *An establishment key allocation $\mathcal{S}$ is said to be f-*redundant *if $\frac{r_{\mathcal{C}}(K)}{k} \leq f$ for every $K \subseteq \mathcal{U}$ with $|K| = k$.*

A variant measure of redundancy is the *actual redundancy* f_a, which is the proportion of non-paying customers in the recipient set $R_{\mathcal{C}}(K)$. We are interested in the average case f_a, so we define it as a function of the target set K. Formally,

Definition 6. *For a target set K with $|K| = k$ the* actual redundancy *is $f_a = \frac{r_{\mathcal{C}}(K)-k}{k}$.*

If $\mathcal{S}$ guarantees a worst case redundancy factor f, then $0 \leq f_a \leq f - 1$ for any target set K.

Finally, we define the opportunity, η, as the proportion of non-paying recipients (free riders) in the non-paying population ($0 \leq \eta \leq 1$). The opportunity measures the incentive a customer has to avoid paying (e.g., in cheap pay-per-view type services). Again, this is a function of the target set K.

Definition 7. *For a target set K with $|K| = k$ the* opportunity *is $\eta = \frac{r_{\mathcal{C}}(K)-k}{n-k}$.*

[1] This method was called the OR protocol in [LS98].

3 Simple Examples

To demonstrate our definitions and the trade-offs associated with the problem let us examine some simple solutions for the problem. See Table 1 for a summary of the examples.

$\mathcal{S}$	$deg(\mathcal{S})$	$t_{\max}(\mathcal{S})$	f	η
$\{\mathcal{U}\}$	**1**	**1**	n	1
$\{1,\ 2,\ \ldots,\ n\}$	**1**	n	**1**	**0**
$2^{\mathcal{U}}$	2^{n-1}	**1**	**1**	**0**

Table 1. A summary of some simple examples. Bold numerals indicate an optimal parameter.

Example 1. The "always broadcast" solution: $\mathcal{S} = \{\mathcal{U}\}$.

Both the degree, $deg(\mathcal{S})$, and the number of transmissions, $t_{\max}(\mathcal{S})$, required to distribute the message are optimal and equal to 1 in this case. However, the redundancy is $f = n$ in the worst case and the opportunity, η, is always 1. The last two parameters are very bad since the system gives no incentive for a customer to pay for a program; a single paying customer enables the entire population a free ride.

Example 2. The "key per user" solution: $\mathcal{S} = \{\{1\}, \{2\}, \ldots, \{n\}\}$.

Here the degree $deg(\mathcal{S}) = 1$ is optimal, and so are the redundancy $f = 1$, and the opportunity $\eta = 0$. However, the number of transmissions is a very poor $t_{\max}(\mathcal{S}) = n$.

Example 3. The "all possible sets" solution: $\mathcal{S} = 2^{\mathcal{U}}$.

The degree here is an impractical $deg(\mathcal{S}) = 2^{n-1}$, however, all the other parameters are optimal: $t_{\max}(\mathcal{S}) = 1$, $f = 1$, and $\eta = 0$. This is because every possible target set K has its own designated key.

4 The Lower Bound

4.1 Tools

Before presenting our lower bound on the degree of an f-redundant establishment key allocation, we need to introduce some definitions and results which we use in the proof.

We start with *covering designs*, which are a class of combinatorial block designs. A succinct description of covering designs can be found in [CD96, Ch. IV.8]. A more detailed survey is [MM92].

Definition 8. *A k-(n,d)* covering design *is a collection of d-sets* (blocks) $\mathcal{D} = \{D_1, \ldots, D_\ell\}$ *over a universe of n elements, such that every k-set of elements is contained in at least one block.*

Definition 9. *The* covering number $C(n,d,k)$ *is the minimum number of blocks in any* k-(n,d) *covering design.*

Theorem 1 ((Schönheim bound)). [Sch64] $C(n,d,k) \geq L(n,d,k)$, *where*

$$L(n,d,k) = \left\lceil \frac{n}{d} \left\lceil \frac{n-1}{d-1} \cdots \left\lceil \frac{n-k+1}{d-k+1} \right\rceil \right\rceil \right\rceil \geq \binom{n}{k} \Big/ \binom{d}{k}.$$

We also rely on the following result of Luby and Staddon, which addresses *strict* broadcast encryption protocols.

Definition 10. *An establishment key allocation* $\mathcal{S}$ *is called* strict *for a collection of target sets* $\mathcal{D}$ *if the sets in* $\mathcal{D}$ *can be covered without redundancy. Formally,* $R_{\mathcal{C}}(D) = D$ *for all* $D \in \mathcal{D}$.

Theorem 2. [LS98] *Let* $\mathcal{D} = \{D_1, \ldots, D_\ell\}$ *be a collection of target sets, with* $|D_i| \geq d$ *for all* $D_i \in \mathcal{D}$. *Then any establishment key allocation* $\mathcal{S}$ *which is strict for* $\mathcal{D}$, *and which can transmit to any* $D_i \in \mathcal{D}$ *using at most* t *transmissions, must have*

$$deg(\mathcal{S}) \geq \left(\frac{\ell^{1/t}}{t} - 1 \right) \Big/ (n-d).$$

Remark: The precise statement we use here is a generalization of [LS98, Theorem 12]. In their original formulation the target sets D_i all have a cardinality of exactly d, and the collection $\mathcal{D}$ consists of all $\binom{n}{d}$ possible d-sets. However, their proof can be easily extended to any arbitrary collection of target sets, of cardinality d or larger.

4.2 The Bound

Theorem 3. *Let* $\mathcal{S}$ *be an* f*-redundant establishment key allocation over a universe* $\mathcal{U}$ *of size* n, *for which* $t_{\max}(\mathcal{S}) = t$. *Then*

$$deg(\mathcal{S}) \geq \max_{1 \leq k \leq n/f} \left(\frac{1}{t} \left[\binom{n}{k} \Big/ \binom{kf}{k} \right]^{1/t} - 1 \right) \Big/ (n-k).$$

Proof: For a target set K of size $|K| = k$, let $R(K)$ be the minimal possible recipient set for K (or one such set if many minimal recipient sets exist). Consider the collection of minimal recipient sets, $\mathcal{D} = \{R(K) : |K| = k\}$. Note that covering K f-redundantly, using the $t' \leq t$ key sets that define $R(K)$, is precisely equivalent to covering $R(K)$ *strictly* with (the same) t' key sets. Therefore we see that $\mathcal{S}$ is an establishment key allocation which is strict for $\mathcal{D}$, and can transmit to any $R(K) \in \mathcal{D}$ using at most t transmissions. Note also that, trivially, $|R(K)| \geq k$ for any $|K| = k$. Thus we can apply Theorem 2 to obtain

$$deg(\mathcal{S}) \geq \left(\frac{|\mathcal{D}|^{1/t}}{t} - 1 \right) \Big/ (n-k). \quad (1)$$

By definition $|R(K)| \leq kf$ for all K, however, some sets $R(K) \in \mathcal{D}$ may have fewer than kf elements. Define a modified collection $\mathcal{D}'$ in which each $R(K) \in \mathcal{D}$ is replaced by some superset $\hat{R}(K) \supseteq R(K)$ with $|\hat{R}| = kf$. Note that $|\mathcal{D}'| \leq |\mathcal{D}|$ since $\hat{R}(K_1) = \hat{R}(K_2)$ is possible when $R(K_1) \neq R(K_2)$. But now $\mathcal{D}'$ is a k-(n, kf) covering design. Thus we can lower-bound its size by the Schönheim bound, Theorem 1, to obtain

$$|\mathcal{D}| \geq |\mathcal{D}'| \geq L(n, kf, k) \geq \binom{n}{k} \Big/ \binom{kf}{k}. \tag{2}$$

Plugging (2) into (1) and maximizing the expression over the choice of k yields our result. □

Using standard estimations of binomial coefficients, and maximizing over k, we can obtain the following asymptotic estimate.

Corollary 1. *Let $\mathcal{S}$ be an f-redundant establishment key allocation over a universe $\mathcal{U}$ of size n, for which $t_{\max}(\mathcal{S}) = t$. Then $deg(\mathcal{S}) \geq \exp(\Omega(n/tf))$.* □

We therefore see that the f-redundancy gives us a substantial gain in the degree: the bound of [LS98] for strict establishment key allocations is $deg(\mathcal{S}) = \exp(\Omega(n/t))$. In other words, if we allow a redundancy factor of f we can hope to use only an f'th root of the number of keys required per STT in a strict establishment key allocation for the same number of transmissions.

Theorem 3 and Corollary 1 give a lower bound on the required number of keys an STT needs to store. As we said before, this is typically a small fixed value which we can reasonably model by $\log_2 n$ or n^ϵ. Thus we are more interested in the inverse lower bound, on the number of transmissions t. Asymptotically we can obtain the following bound.

Corollary 2. *Let $\mathcal{S}$ be an f-redundant establishment key allocation over a universe $\mathcal{U}$ of size n. Then*

$$t_{\max}(\mathcal{S}) \geq \begin{cases} \Omega\left(\frac{n}{f \log\log n}\right), & \text{when } deg(\mathcal{S}) = O(\log n), \\ \Omega\left(\frac{n}{f \log n}\right), & \text{when } deg(\mathcal{S}) = O(n^\epsilon). \end{cases}$$

□

The asymptotic bound of Corollary 2 hides the constants, and inverting Theorem 3 gives a rather unwieldy expression for the lower bound on t. Therefore, we choose to invert Theorem 3 numerically and to plot the result, as a function of the target set size k, in Figure 1. As we shall see in the sequel, the highest point on this curve ($t \approx 19$ for $n = 1024$) is significantly lower than that of our best constructions, which suffer from a worst case of $t_{\max}(\mathcal{S}) = 3n/8 = 384$ when $n = 1024$.

5 Finding a Good Key Cover

An f-redundant establishment key allocation guarantees that an f-redundant cover exists for every target set K. In particular, singleton target sets $K = \{u\}$

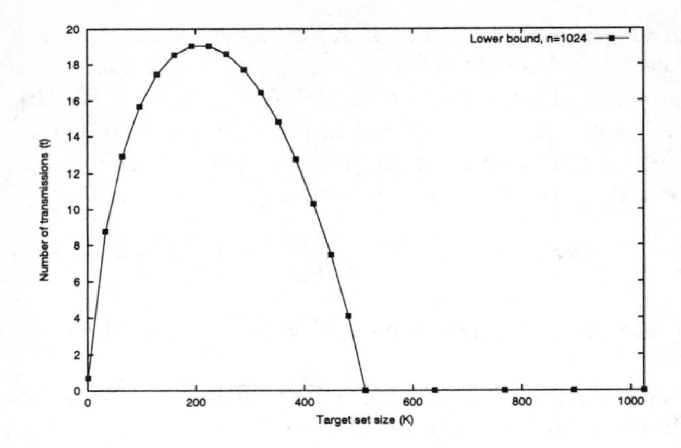

Fig. 1. The lower bound for the number of transmissions (t) as a function of the target set size k, with $n = 1024$, $f = 2$, and $deg(\mathcal{S}) = \log_2 n$.

need to be addressed. Thus, $\mathcal{S}$ must include enough sets S_i with $|S_i| \leq f$ so that every user is contained in one of them. For simplicity, we shall assume that $\mathcal{S}$ contains the singletons themselves as sets, i.e., every STT is assumed to hold one key that is unique to it.

Once we decide upon a particular f-redundant establishment key allocation $\mathcal{S}$, we still need to show an efficient algorithm to find an f-redundant key cover $\mathcal{C}(K)$ for every target set K. Among all possible f-redundant key covers that $\mathcal{S}$ allows, we would like to pick the best one. By "best" we mean here a cover that minimizes the number of transmissions t. Trying to minimize the actual redundancy f_a would lead to trivialities: Since we assumed that $\mathcal{S}$ contains all the singletons we can always achieve the optimal $f_a = 0$. Thus, for every target set K, we obtain the following optimization problem:

Input: A collection of sets $\mathcal{S} = \{S_1, \ldots, S_m\}$ and a target set K.

Output: A sub-collection $\mathcal{C}_{\min}(K) \subseteq \mathcal{S}$ with minimal cardinality $|\mathcal{C}_{\min}(K)|$ such that $K \subseteq \cup\{S_i \in \mathcal{C}_{\min}(K)\}$ and $| \cup \{S_i \in \mathcal{C}_{\min}(K)\}|/|K| \leq f$.

Input: Target set K, establishment key allocation $\mathcal{S} = \{S_1, \ldots, S_m\}$.

0. $R \leftarrow \emptyset$; $\mathcal{C} \leftarrow \emptyset$
1. **Repeat**
2. $\quad \mathcal{A} \leftarrow \{S_i : \frac{|S_i \setminus R|}{|(K \cap S_i) \setminus R|} \leq f\}$. (* Candidate sets *)
3. $\quad A \leftarrow S_i \in \mathcal{A}$ which maximizes $|(K \cap S_i) \setminus R|$.
4. $\quad R \leftarrow R \cup A$; $\mathcal{C} \leftarrow \mathcal{C} \cup \{A\}$.
5. **until** the candidate collection $\mathcal{A}$ is empty.
6. **return** R, $\mathcal{C}$.

Fig. 2. Algorithm f-*Cover*.

This is a variation of the Set Cover problem [GJ79], and thus an NP-hard optimization problem. We omit the formal reduction proving this. Moreover, it is known that no approximation algorithm exists for Set Cover with a worst case approximation ratio[2] better than $\ln n$ (unless NP has slightly super-polynomial time algorithms) [Fei98].

On the positive side, the Set Cover problem admits a greedy algorithm, which achieves the best possible approximation ratio of $\ln n$ [Joh74,Lov75]. Moreover, the greedy algorithm is extremely effective in practice, usually finding covers much closer to the optimum than its approximation ratio guarantees [GW97]. For this reason, our general algorithm *f-Cover* for choosing a key cover is an adaptation of the greedy algorithm. See Figure 2 for the details.

Theorem 4. *If* $\{\{1\},\ldots,\{n\}\} \subseteq \mathcal{S}$ *then algorithm f-Cover returns an f-redundant key cover of* K *for any target set* K.

Proof: Omitted due to space limitations.

It is easy to see that the time complexity of algorithm *f-Cover* is $O(m^2)$ where m is the number of sets in $\mathcal{S}$. In order to make the algorithm even more efficient, we do not use it in its most general form. Instead, we split the establishment key allocation $\mathcal{S}$ into *levels*, each containing sets of the same size. Formally, we break $\mathcal{S}$ into $\mathcal{S} = \mathcal{S}^1 \cup \mathcal{S}^2 \cup \cdots$, such that $|S_i^\ell| = k_\ell$ for some k_ℓ and for all $S_i^\ell \in \mathcal{S}^\ell$. The algorithm is performed in phases, where only sets belonging to level $\mathcal{S}^\ell$ are considered in the candidate set $\mathcal{A}$ during in phase ℓ. The algorithm starts at the highest level, the one containing of the largest sets in $\mathcal{S}$. When $\mathcal{A}$ is empty at a certain level, the cover so far, R, and the covering sets, $\mathcal{C}$, are fed to the execution phase of the algorithm in the next (lower) level.

6 Practical Solutions

6.1 Overview

Our basic goal is to construct an f-redundant establishment key allocation, namely to construct an $\mathcal{S}$ that will satisfy the following requirements: (i) the number of establishment keys per user (degree) is low; and (ii) $|R_{\mathcal{C}}(K)|/|K| \leq f$ for every target set $K \subseteq U$. Given such an establishment key allocation, we evaluate its performance with respect to the number of transmissions t, the actual redundancy f_a, and the opportunity η, using computer simulations.

We are interested in "average" performance, although we do not want to assume any particular probability distribution over the choice of target sets. To avoid this contradiction to some extent, we evaluate the performance measures separately for each target set size k, and show the results as functions of k. Thus, if something is known about target set size (e.g., that sets of size $> n/4$ never occur in some application), only portions of the graphs need to be consulted.

[2] [Hoc95] contains a good discussion of approximation algorithms and in particular a chapter on Set Cover.

Each data point for a target set size k in the graphs represents the mean of the relevant measure, averaged over r samples of k-sets chosen uniformly at random. We show the 95% confidence intervals (see [Jai91] for definition) for each data point, unless the graphical height of the confidence intervals is very close to the size of the symbols depicted on the curves. We typically use $r = 25$ samples per data point.

Unless stated otherwise, we assume that the redundancy is $f = 2$. We also conducted experiments with other values of f but they showed qualitatively similar results.

6.2 The Tree Scheme

The Scheme's Description. A simple multi-level establishment key allocation is a balanced tree, that is built by recursively partitioning the sets of a high level into equally-sized, disjoint sets in the next level. Sets that form a partition of a single set, one level above them, are considered children of this set in the tree. The number of keys each STT holds in this scheme is only $1 + \log_a n$, where a is the arity of the tree. In the sequel we always assume a binary tree ($a = 2$).

An important advantage of a tree scheme (besides its simplicity) is that the greedy algorithm of Figure 2 can easily be made to run in time linear in the size of the cover set, rather than in the total number of sets in the collection. The idea is to start at the root of the tree (the set $\mathcal{U}$) and then traverse it either in a DFS or in a BFS order. Whenever an f-redundant set is found, select it and ignore the subtree under it.

The problem with the tree scheme is its worst case behavior. Consider the case where $f = 2$ and the collection is a full binary tree. If the target set comprises $k = n/4$ users such that no two of them belong to a common set of size 4 or less, then we are forced to use $t = n/4$ transmissions. It is easy to see that this is the worst possible configuration.

The average behavior of the basic tree is substantially better than the worst case. Figure 3 shows the average number of transmissions on several variants of a tree for a population of $n = 1024$ users. We see from the "threshold at sets of size 2" curve in the figure that the peak of the average t is 164, which is 36% less than the worst case of 256. We explain this threshold and discuss the different variants of the tree in the sequel.

We conducted the same tests for larger populations and noticed that the qualitative behavior does not change significantly, so we omit the details. Here we focus on simulations of small populations for another reason. We shall see in Section 6.4 that we can capitalize on the detailed understanding of small populations when we discuss partitioning large populations. Our results show that breaking a large population into small subgroups and solving the problem independently for each subgroup results in a good performance trade-off.

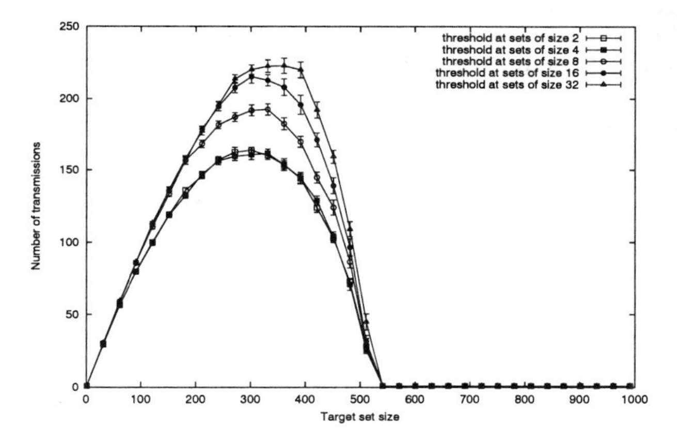

Fig. 3. The effect of the "$\leq$" threshold T on the number of transmissions (t), for a tree with $n = 1024$.

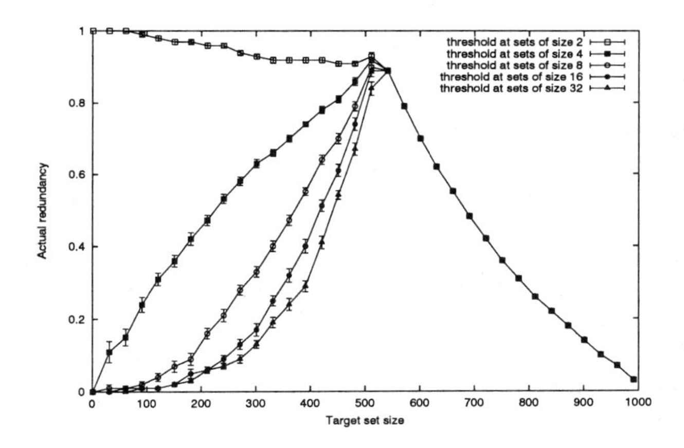

Fig. 4. The effect of the "$\leq$" threshold T on the Actual redundancy (f_a) for a tree with $n = 1024$.

"$<$" or "$\leq$"? A subtle issue in the execution of algorithm *f-Cover* is whether the inequality in step 2 is strict ($<$) or not ($\leq$). Assume that $f = 2$ and that the collection $\mathcal{S}$ is a full binary tree. If a set of size S_i with $|S_i| = 2$ is tested using non-strict inequality, and only one member of S_i is in the target set K, then S_i is selected as a candidate and may be part of the cover. However, using a strict inequality gives a better choice, which is to select the singleton containing that user, thereby reducing the actual redundancy without increasing the number of transmissions. On the other hand, using strict inequality for larger set sizes tends to increase the number of transmissions. So, intuitively, we would like to use "$<$" in the lowest levels of the tree, and use "$\leq$" for sets of size T or larger, for an appropriate threshold T. Figures 3, 4, and 5 compare the performance of a tree scheme when the threshold is varied. Note that the $T = 2$ curve, which we commented on before, represents using "$\leq$" everywhere.

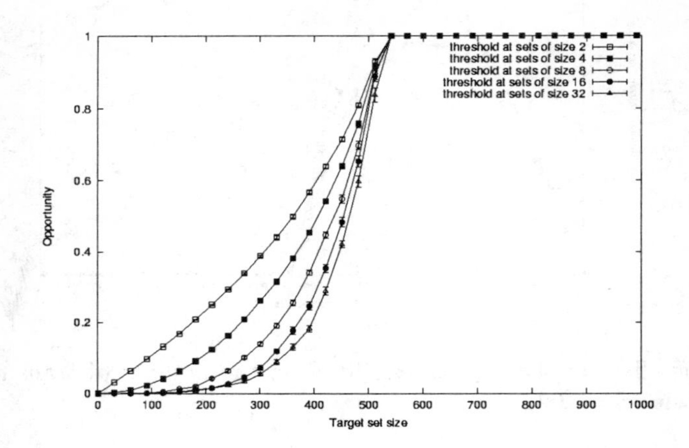

Fig. 5. The effect of the "$\leq$" threshold T on the Opportunity (η), for a tree with $n = 1024$.

The most striking graph is that of the actual redundancy (Figure 4). We see that when we use strict inequality in the level of the tree corresponding to sets of size 2 (i.e., the "$\leq$" threshold is $T = 4$) the actual redundancy, f_a, drops dramatically for target set sizes below $n/2$. At the same time, the number of transmissions, t, remains unchanged. There is also an improvement in the opportunity, η. Moving the threshold further up improves f_a and η at the cost of increasing t. We found out that, in most cases, and especially when extra keys are added (see below), it pays to set the threshold at $T = 8$ since the increase in t is very small while the gain in f_a and η is substantial. Thus, in all the following simulations we only use strict inequality for sets of size 4 and below.

Note that choosing $T = 8$ has an effect on the worst case performance since now $k = 3n/8$ users can be selected such that no four of them belong to a common set of size 8 and no three of them belong to a common set of size 4. As a result, we would be forced to use $t = 3n/8$ transmissions, all at the level corresponding to singleton sets.

When $T = 8$, the peak number of transmissions t is $193 \approx n/5$ (see Figure 3), which means a 50% improvement over the worst case performance of 384, and achieves actual redundancy that is always lower than 0.9. However, in most of the range the results are much better. In particular, if the interesting target set size range is below $k = n/5$, we get $t < n/6$, $f_a < 0.16$, and $\eta < 0.04$.

6.3 Where Extra Keys Are Effective

The basic tree scheme requires only $\log_2 n$ keys to be stored in each STT. Therefore it is reasonable to consider schemes with slightly more keys: For populations

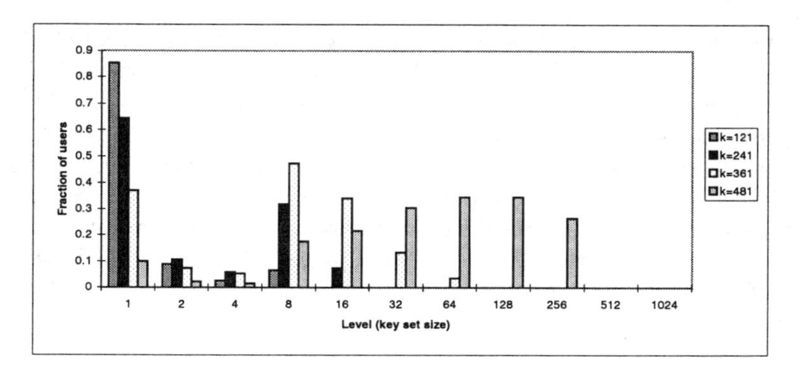

Fig. 6. A histogram of the key sizes used for several target set sizes k, for $n = 1024$.

of several millions, we can afford to keep twice or four times as many keys in an STT.

In this section, we study schemes in which a tree is augmented by additional sets. The motivation for doing so is clear: by increasing the number of sets (and thereby keys), the probability of finding a smaller cover increases. We are interested in locating the levels where it best pays to add sets, subject to the constraints on the number of keys per STT.

In order to generate the extra key sets, we start with a "level-degree" profile, which specifies how many keys each user should hold at each level. For a level with set size k, a degree of d implies that each user should belong to $d-1$ extra sets, in addition to the one basic tree set it belongs to at this level. Thus we need to be able to generate nd/k sets of size k, such that each user belongs to exactly d of them. We achieve this by randomly permuting the n users $d-1$ times, and for each random permutation we add the users in positions $(i-1)k+1, \ldots, ik$ as a set, for $i = 1, \ldots, n/k$.

A vivid explanation for the preferred placement of the extra keys can be found in the histogram in Figure 6. The histogram depicts the fraction of users covered by keys from each level of sets, for target sets of four sizes. We used a population of $n = 1024$ users and a basic tree scheme with 11 levels. The histogram clearly shows that the small sets are the ones used most often. As the target set size grows, some larger key sets are also used. However, even when the target sets are $k = 241$ and $k = 361$, i.e., target sets requiring the highest number of transmissions, relatively few keys are used for sets of size 32 and up. Therefore it seems that adding key sets at the low levels of the tree is the right approach.

Figure 7 depicts the performance of an 11-level tree ($n = 1024$) augmented with 9 extra keys. This choice allows us to double the number of keys per level in all the intermediate levels ($1 < |S_i| < n$). Following the conclusions we draw from the key usage histogram in Figure 6, these extra keys are distributed as uniformly as possible among the levels from the bottom (couples) level up to some level ℓ. We varied ℓ in order to find the most effective distribution.

We first note that regardless of how the extra keys are distributed, the peak number of transmissions drops by at least 23% (from 193 down to 147 for the "up to sets of size 2" distribution) in comparison to a non-augmented tree.

Figure 7 shows that the best t is achieved by distributing the extra keys at the three lowest levels, i.e., adding couples, quadruplets, and octets. Adding sets of size 16 as well resulted in an almost identical performance. However, adding even larger sets gave significantly inferior performance. This improvement comes at the expense of an increase in f_a for small target set sizes, although the actual redundancy is still well below the guaranteed worst case of $f_a \leq f - 1$ (= 1 when $f = 2$).

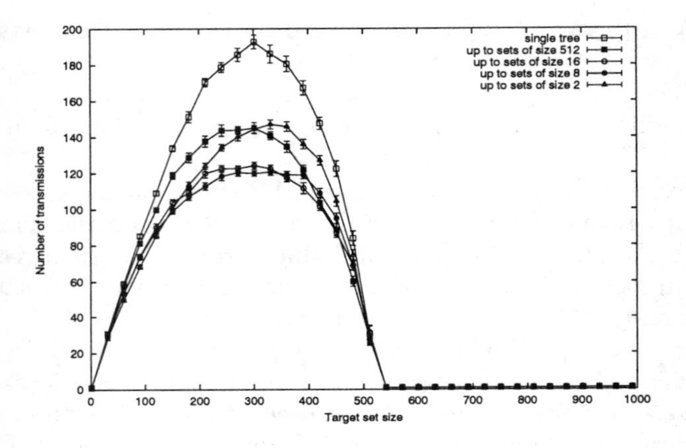

Fig. 7. Number of transmissions (t) as a function of the target set size k, with $n = 1024$, $f = 2$, 11 levels, and 9 extra keys.

In a similar experiment with 38 extra keys ($= 11 + 3 \times 9$), the best t was achieved by spreading the keys among the lowest 4 levels (up to sets of size 16); the peak t for this experiment was about 94 transmissions, for target sets of size 271 ($= n/3.8$), which is 22% lower than the 121 achieved in Figure 7 by the "up to sets of size 8" distribution. We also ran the same experiments for larger and smaller values of n, with similar results. We omit the details.

Our conclusions from this set of experiments are that (a) adding a few extra keys substantially reduces the number of transmissions t, and (b) it pays to add these extra keys at the lower levels of the tree rather than to distribute them at higher levels as well.

6.4 Partitioning

The results in the previous sections suggest that keys are more "valuable" at the lower levels of the tree than at the higher levels. Thus, it seems reasonable to discard the keys of the largest sets (highest levels) altogether, and to use the additional key space for more lower level keys. We achieve this by partitioning the population, n, into ν disjoint partitions of size n/ν. The space occupied by the $\log_2 \nu$ deleted keys per user is then used to increase the number of low level sets in each partition.

In this section we concentrate on larger, more realistic user population sizes. However, since each individual partition is small, we can apply the insight we have gained from our earlier small-population experiments.

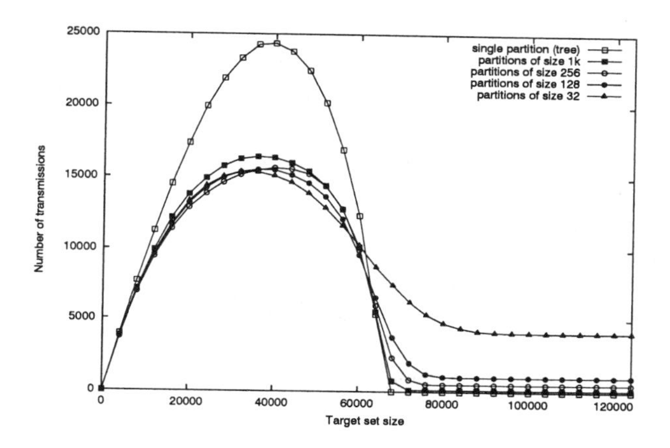

Fig. 8. Number of transmissions (t) as a function of the target set size k, with $n = 128K$, $f = 2$, and 18 keys in total.

Figure 8 compares the performance of the a single tree scheme for a population of 128K customers with the performance of schemes that employ the same number of keys (18) but with ν partitions. Within each partition we distribute the $\log \nu$ extra keys to achieve the lowest peak t; as we have seen before, this means that the extra keys are distributed among the lowest levels in the tree, thus adding key sets of sizes between 2 and 32. For each value of ν we ran the equivalent of the experiment we discussed in Section 6.3. We report only the results of the best (lowest peak t) extra-key distribution for each value of ν.

Figure 8 shows that the decrease in t is dramatic for a large range of target set sizes. In particular, the peak t drops by about 36%, from 24337 for a single partition to 15526 for $\nu = 1024$ partitions of size 128 each. Increasing the ν further reduces t for some values of k. However, for large target set sizes, and especially those with $k > n/2$, we pay a penalty in the number of transmissions. For such large target sets we have to use $t = \nu$ transmissions instead of one. We argue that as long as ν is substantially smaller than the peak t, the savings in t for smaller target sets far outweighs the penalty incurred for large target sets. Moreover, dealing with targets with $k > n/2$ can be done by maintaining a single additional broadcast key together with the partitions' keys.

We have found that partitioning the users increases f_a for target sets with $k < n/2$. However, the peak f_a actually drops since we no longer use the very large key sets, e.g., those with size $n/2$ or $n/4$. Partitioning also improves the opportunity for $k \sim n/2$ (graphs omitted).

We conclude that partitioning the users is an effective method for designing establishment key allocations. It is better to discard the large high-level key sets in favor of extra sets at the low levels. As a rule of thumb we suggest to use at least $\nu \approx \sqrt{n}$ partitions, and possibly more for larger values of n.

7 Conclusions and Future Work

We have demonstrated that by allowing a controlled number of free-riders we are able to design establishment key allocations that meet the hard limitations placed on secure key storage by current technology. We do this while addressing the ambitious goal of allowing *every* possible subset of users to be a target set (rather than only sets of a small fixed cardinality). We showed that despite these constraints, our schemes use substantially fewer transmissions than the naive designs. Moreover, although our schemes guarantee that the ratio between the numbers of free riders and intended receivers is at most $f - 1$, the achieved redundancy ratio f_a is typically much better than the guarantee. We conclude that our schemes are quite practical for applications where some free riders may be tolerated.

We have also identified some general design principles for such systems. We found that adding extra establishment key sets helps, provided that they are added at the low levels. We also found that partitioning the population into many small partitions is more effective than handling the whole population at once, since by eliminating the very large key sets we can add extra keys in each partition without exceeding the key storage limitations.

We believe that more can be done in this area. Our best constructions use five or ten times more transmissions than our lower bound suggests. Although this may seem like a small gap asymptotically, it is important in realistic scenarios. Therefore finding either better schemes or better lower bounds is still interesting.

References

BC94. C. Blundo and A. Cresti. Space requirements for broadcast encryption. In A. De Santis, editor, *Advances in Cryptology – EUROCRYPT'94, LNCS 950*, pages 287–298. Springer-Verlag, 1994.

BFS98. C. Blundo, L. A. Frota Mattos, and D. R. Stinson. Generalized Beimel-Chor schemes for broadcast encryption and interactive key distribution. *Theoretical Computer Science*, 200(1–2):313–334, 1998.

CD96. C. J. Colbourn and J. H. Dinitz. *The CRC Handbook of Combinatorial Designs.* CRC Press, Boca Raton, 1996.

CEFH95. J. L. Cohen, M. H. Etzel, D. W. Faucher, and D. N. Heer. Security for broadband digital networks. *Communications Technology*, pages 58–69, August 1995.

CFN94. B. Chor, A. Fiat, and M. Naor. Tracing traitors. In Yvo G. Desmedt, editor, *Advances in Cryptology – CRYPTO'94, LNCS 839*, pages 257–270. Springer-Verlag, 1994.

Fei98. U. Feige. A threshold of $\ln n$ for approximating set cover. *J. ACM*, 45(4):634–652, July 1998.

FN94. A. Fiat and M. Naor. Broadcast encryption. In *Advances in Cryptology – CRYPTO'93, LNCS 773*, pages 480–491. Springer-Verlag, 1994.

Gem98. Gemplus: Catalog of products and services. `http://www.gemplus.com/global_offer/index.htm`, 1998.

GJ79. M. R. Garey and D. S. Johnson. *Computers and Intractability: A Guide to the Theory of NP-Completeness.* Freeman, San Francisco, 1979.

GW97. T. Grossman and A. Wool. Computational experience with approximation algorithms for the set covering problem. *Euro. J. Operational Research*, 101(1):81–92, August 1997.

GW98. E. Gabber and A. Wool. How to prove where you are: Tracking the location of customer equipment. In *Proc. 5th ACM Conf. Computer and Communications Security (CCS)*, pages 142–149, San Francisco, November 1998.

Hoc95. D. S. Hochbaum. (ed.) *Approximation Algorithms for NP-Hard Problems.* PWS Publishing Company, Boston, MA, 1995.

Jai91. R. Jain. *The Art of Computer Systems Performance Analysis.* John Wiley & Sons, 1991.

Joh74. D. S. Johnson. Approximation algorithms for combinatorial problems. *J. Computer System Sci.*, 9:256–278, 1974.

Lov75. L. Lovász. On the ratio of optimal integral and fractional covers. *Disc. Math.*, 13:383–390, 1975.

LS98. M. Luby and J. Staddon. Combinatorial bounds for broadcast encryption. In K. Nyberg, editor, *Advances in Cryptology – EUROCRYPT'98, LNCS 1403*, pages 512–526, Espoo, Finland, 1998. Springer-Verlag.

McC96. J. McCormac. *European Scrambling Systems 5.* Waterford University Press, Waterford, Ireland, 1996.

MM92. W. H. Mills and R. C. Mullin. Coverings and packings. In J. H. Dinitz and D. R. Stinson, editors, *Contemporary Design Theory: A Collection of Surveys*, pages 317–399. John Wiley & Sons, 1992.

MQ95. B. M. Macq and J.-J. Quisquater. Cryptology for digital TV broadcasting. *Proceedings of the IEEE*, 83(6):944–957, 1995.

NP98. M. Naor and B. Pinkas. Threshold traitor tracing. In *Advances in Cryptology – CRYPTO'98, LNCS 1462.* Springer-Verlag, 1998.

Sch64. J. Schönheim. On coverings. *Pacific J. Math.*, 14:1405–1411, 1964.

SvT98. D. R. Stinson and T. van Trung. Some new results on key distribution patterns and broadcast encryption. *Designs, Codes and Cryptography*, 14(3):261–279, 1998.

Woo98. A. Wool. Key management for encrypted broadcast. In *Proc. 5th ACM Conf. Computer and Communications Security (CCS)*, pages 7–16, San Francisco, November 1998.

Conditional Access Concepts and Principles

David W. Kravitz and David M. Goldschlag

Divx,
570 Herndon Parkway, Herndon, VA 20170, USA
+1 703-708-4000 (voice),
+1 703-708-4088 (fax)
{david.kravitz, david.goldschlag}@divx.com

Abstract: This paper describes concepts and principles for infrastructures that manage chargeable content, more commonly known as conditional access (CA) systems. We present a functional overview of CA systems and the security components and design principles that enable the solutions. We then present concepts that may be used to quantify the risk associated with the delivery of particular valued content in a particular way. Finally, we describe how the threat model changes as the networking bandwidth available to pirates and their customers increases, and propose a possible long-term solution.

Keywords: Auditability, authentication, conditional access, copyright protection, smart cards, trust management.

1. Introduction

We are concerned with infrastructures for managing chargeable content, more commonly known as conditional access (CA) systems. CA systems are attempting to solve an inherent paradox: How is access to content enabled yet still controlled? CA systems also have a particularly severe threat environment: Neither the honest consumer nor the pirate wants to pay for security, so the consumer devices must be very low cost. Furthermore, every consumer is a potential adversary, and none can be audited, so tamper detection is irrelevant. From a cryptographic perspective, efficient broadcasting requires universal shared secrets, since typically a single data stream is broadcast for any content. Protecting universal keys, yet still make them usable by legitimate consumers, is very difficult. The threat model also must bound the scope of conditional access systems: Is local copying a concern? Is content redistribution a threat?

CA systems protect content delivered in a variety of ways: At one extreme on the risk spectrum are satellite systems with a large footprint. The content (e.g., a movie) received by one subscriber to the service is available to many other

M. Franklin (Ed.): FC'99, LNCS 1648, pp.158 -172, 1999.

subscribers and non-subscribers. So the keys used to protect the broadcast are valuable to the pirate because they can be used cheaply by many people. In a similar fashion, content distributed by a fixed media like DVD (high density optical discs) is logically broadcast, since low cost disc pressing mechanisms require that all discs corresponding to a single title contain the same bits. Although one needs the disc to play the content, the pirate can redistribute the same key to every disc holder. At the other extreme are cable or even point-to-point distribution schemes, where the community of recipients is isolated to a neighborhood or even to a single home. The extremes also correspond to the editing of content for a particular recipient—highly specific and timely information (a snapshot of an individual's stock portfolio), while valuable, is not a good candidate for large-scale piracy.

The pirate may take advantage of the broadcast footprint when building his infrastructure: at one extreme the pirate redistributes the content directly; this requires building a significant distribution infrastructure, the development and maintenance of which may be far more expensive than obtaining the pirated content to be redistributed. In a less complicated attack, the pirate leverages off of the legitimate infrastructure for content distribution, but redistributes the minimum secrets needed to decrypt the content—like the content, this material is untraceable (since the secrets are used globally). At the other extreme, the pirate attempts to leverage off of the legitimate infrastructure for key distribution also—clones of one compromised CA module (CAM) interoperate with the legitimate infrastructure.

This paper is organized in the following way: Section 2 describes an overview of CA systems. Section 3 presents the security building blocks that enable solutions. Section 4 presents concepts that may be used to quantify the risk associated with the delivery of particular valued content in a particular way. Section 5 describes how the CA threat model changes as networking bandwidth increases, and proposes a possible solution. Section 6 presents some concluding remarks.

2. CA Overview

Conditional access (CA) systems control access to chargeable content. This content includes both data and entertainment products such as movies or music. The content may be delivered in many ways, including broadcast from satellite or a local broadcaster, transmitted over cable or the Internet, or delivered by fixed media, such as a DVD. Billing policies also vary greatly: content may be sold as part of a subscription such as premium movie channels, by the unit like pay-per-view movies, or incrementally as in a stock ticker that is charged by access time.

2.1 The CA Infrastructure

The primary function of a CA system is to report content access to a billing system, and to prevent unreported access to content. To force content to be accessed through the CA system, content may be encrypted using cryptographic keys known only by the CA system. In this model, encrypted content is broadcast by a headend system and accessed through a CAM on the user's set-top-box (STB, e.g., a TV or cable tuner). Accesses are reported to a backend billing system. The distribution of content keys is managed by a key management system (KMS) that lets CAMs learn the keys needed to decrypt content. This model is illustrated in Figure 1. Notice that content keys need not be delivered with the content, although they may be, and that the backend billing system may be independent of the headend too.

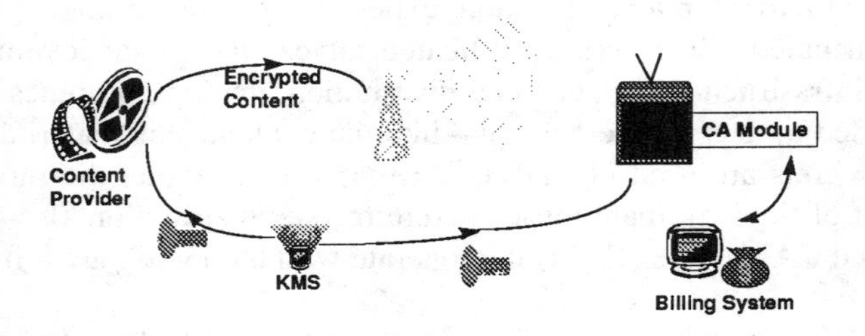

Figure 1: Model of CA Infrastructure

The CAM, which is present in every user's house, must protect cryptographic keys that are universally useful. That is, the keys that a CAM uses to decrypt content are equally useful to other recipients of the broadcast. If those keys are compromised and distributed, other recipients of the broadcast may use the keys to access content for free. In particular, since there is more content than keys (e.g., content takes up more bandwidth than keys), a pirate can leverage off of the original broadcast, only redistribute keys, and make money at the broadcaster's expense.

This suggests that the security concept behind the CAM is to force the pirate to redistribute content instead of keys. Because of economies of scale, the legitimate broadcaster may be able to distribute content much more cheaply than the pirate can. (This is, at present, true for video, but may not be true for audio.) So the CAM may be viewed as a device that converts a broadcast transmission (that is available to everyone) into a point-to-point transmission that makes content (but not universal keys) available to an individual user.

The CAM is a hardware device that protects keys. The security of this hardware decreases over time, because its design flaws become known, and physical attacks against it become cheaper. Furthermore, the pirate may be able to amortize the cost of attacking a single module over the sale of many counterfeit modules. This suggests that the CAM be renewable, so the security of the CA infrastructure may evolve over time. The challenge is to design an infrastructure that admits increasing security at low cost over a long lifetime.

2.2 Copy Protection

Protecting the content against redistribition is a difficult problem, but may not be a significant threat at the present time. Until section 5, we assume that we are protecting high density content like video, that requires significant transmission bandwidth. So we will assume that local piracy, where individuals make copies for themselves, is possible, but cannot be efficiently leveraged into wide-scale distribution. On the other hand, key distribution, because of its low bandwidth requirements, is a threat. In general, we are concerned about attacks that are profit-motivated, and that significantly reduce the legitimate service provider's revenue.

3. CA Building Blocks

This section first describes the building blocks in a conditional access system and then presents several security design principles.

3.1 Content Authoring

Before content can be distributed to customers, it must be prepared for distribution. This involves formatting the data stream for the particular transmission mechanism, and encrypting it under one or more cryptographic keys. These keys are used as the primary mechanism for distinguishing one piece of content from another—that is, if the CAM uses a particular key to decrypt content, the customer can be charged for accessing the content that key is intended to decrypt. So keys are bound to billing units, and the same key must not be used to encrypt different billing units. Furthermore, keys must be named in some way, so the CAM can be instructed to use a particular key when it is given particular content. The integrity of the binding of a key to its identifier must be maintained throughout the system.

It is possible to consider using time to distinguish one piece of billable content from another. But in a satellite pay-per-view system, many movies may be broadcast simultaneously, and the CAM cannot trust the channel information that it may receive from the receiver. In contrast, if the CAM is instructed to use the wrong key, the plaintext will not be reconstructed properly. Using keys in this way serves to implicitly authenticate the content.

3.2 Key Management System

The content authoring system must coordinate with the key management system, the billing system, and the content distribution system. The key management system delivers content keys and their identities to customers' CAMs. These keys may be multicast, broadcast to individual CAMs, or delivered over secure point-to-point sessions. Depending on the system architecture and billing policy, the key management system may send to a customer's CA module only the keys to which he is entitled. Or, the key management system may send all keys, and depend on the CAM to report back use of those keys to the billing system. The former is an appropriate strategy for subscription services like HBO, and serves as a form of mandatory access control. The latter is appropriate for impulse-pay-per-view services, where it is impossible (or inconvenient) to identify the customers for a particular piece of content in advance. In practice, some combination of mandatory and report-back strategies are often used.

3.3 Billing System

The billing system has two security roles: one is to instruct the key management system which keys should be sent to individual CAMs, and the other is to upload logs of key use from CAMs. These two functions correspond to advance billing for subscription services, and credit-type billing for pay-per-view services (i.e., where services are used before they are paid for).

3.4 Renewable Security Modules

In order to constrain the design of the CAM as little as possible, we should define the interface between it and the STB. This has two advantages: It allows innovative CA approaches as pirates become more sophisticated, and it allows for STBs to be built without considering the details of the CA infrastructure. The simplest interface between an STB and the CAM relays the encrypted broadcast received by the STB to the CAM, where it is decrypted and returned to the STB [3]. The STB then plays the decrypted broadcast. This is illustrated in Figure 2:

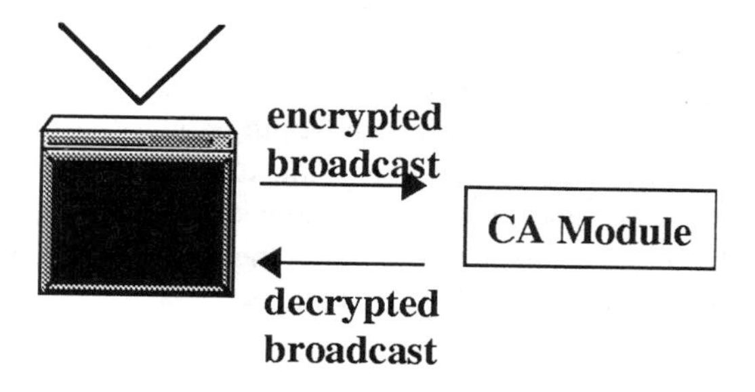

Figure 2: The External Security Architecture

It is interesting to contrast this architecture with the smartcard [5] approach to security (Figure 3). In that architecture, instead of sending the smartcard the encrypted broadcast, the STB extracts encrypted keys (called ECMs) from the broadcast and sends them to the smartcard. The smartcard decrypts those encrypted keys and returns the plaintext keys (called CWs) to the STB, which uses the plaintext keys to decrypt the encrypted broadcast. The smartcard approach has two architectural flaws:

1. The architecture overly constrains the security architecture. In particular, the STB needs to know how to extract encrypted keys from the broadcast and how to decrypt the encrypted broadcast using the plaintext keys.

2. The plaintext keys, which are universally useful, are available to anyone watching the smartcard interface.

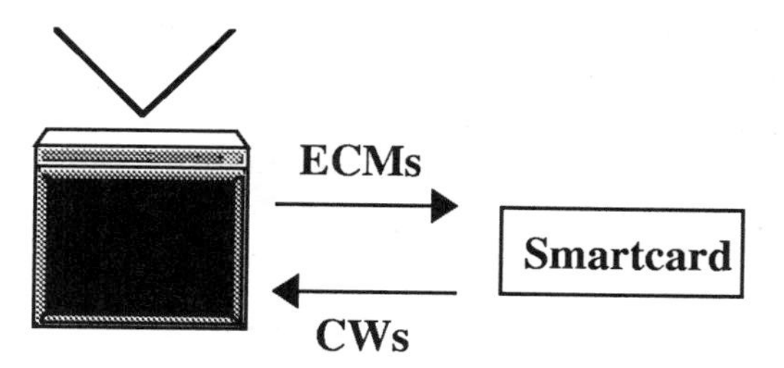

Figure 3: A Flawed Architecture

The second point is the most important: The pirate, instead of being forced to compromise the smartcard, can obtain plaintext keys by watching the output of the smartcard. (This attack works even if the keys are re-encrypted for the STB; in that case the non-renewable STB must be compromised instead of the renewable CAM). This attack was first described in 1992 by John McCormac and named the *Jugular Attack*. In this attack, the pirate redistributes those keys in near real-time to his customers, allowing them to decrypt the broadcast for free. The Jugular Attack allows the pirate to provide continuous access to keys, independent of the security of the smartcard. The smartcard architecture turns security upside-down, by depending upon the difficulty of redistributing and using the pirated keys within the non-renewable infrastructure, instead of depending upon the renewable CAMs to protect those keys in the first place. At some point, the security of the smartcard becomes essentially irrelevant, since the easiest attack concentrates on the non-renewable host instead. Although this attack requires the pirate's ongoing distribution of keys (which may attract the attention of law enforcement), it is not as difficult as redistributing content.

Smartcards are less expensive than CAMs supporting the external security architecture. However, ASIC functionality increases while costs come down, and packaging technologies (e.g., NRSS Parts A & B [6], the former being a thick smartcard, the latter similar to a PCMCIA card) supporting renewable modules with high speed I/O are becoming available.

In the external security architecture, the effectiveness of the hardware security relies in part on cryptographic strength, in part on the difficulty of reverse engineering, and in part on the obscurity of the design.

The pirate can attack the CAM for two purposes: to compromise the universal content keys, or to enable access without logging or charging for access. We are concerned about attacks where the pirate can build a business out of his effort. In the absence of an exploitable flaw in the logging/charging system, the pirate will attempt to learn content keys, or the mechanisms for learning content keys. This sort of attack enables the pirate to spend significant resources on compromising a single CAM (for attacks, see [1]), since he can amortize the cost of his attack. This suggests that if a particular CA market is large enough, the pirate's payoff increases, and system-wide risk increases too. So, in addition to periodic renewal of the security module, it is prudent to make it difficult for the pirate to be able to leverage off of the compromise of a single CAM. One such technique, pirate card rejection, is described in section 3.6.

3.5 Interface/Copy Protection

The external security architecture decrypts broadcast content, and sends the plaintext to the STB. This places the plaintext content over the user accessible interface between the CAM and the STB. Notice that universal keys are not exposed, and the pirate is forced to redistribute content. If even local re-use (local piracy) of the content is undesirable, the CAM may re-encrypt the content under a locally negotiated session key before forwarding it to the STB. Since the STB is not renewable, that session key is not well protected. However, the key is not very valuable anyway, and requiring the customer to compromise his STB to get free local re-use may be a sufficiently high obstacle for the benefit gained.

3.6 Pirate Card Rejection

Although the primary security in the external security architecture depends upon how well the CAM protects keys, it may be useful to leverage off of the legitimate infrastructure to enhance this security. That is, the legitimate infrastructure can reduce piracy by increasing the cost of piracy. For example, an STB may discourage piracy by implementing a pirate card rejection mechanism. If STBs in the legitimate infrastructure make it more difficult for customers to use pirated CAMs, the pirate may be obliged to sell pirated STBs in addition to pirated CAMs. This will complicate his business considerably. One such mechanism enables legitimate STBs to reject pirated CAMs.

In order to reject pirated modules, the STB must identify pirated modules. Unfortunately, this is hard to do, because a pirated module may masquerade as a legitimate module. So the best one can do is to count on STBs to reject modules they are not authorized to communicate with. A STB may be authorized to communicate with only a small set of modules (e.g., the single module the user was given). If a different module is inserted, the STB can reject it. This effectiveness of this approach depends on two assumptions:

1. The pirate can compromise a small number of CAMs, and cost-effectively distribute pirated modules based on the ones he compromised.

2. The pirate cannot cost-effectively produce pirated modules based on each individual customer's legitimate module.

That is, we assume that is it is much cheaper for the CA provider to create each individualized CAM than it is for the pirate to compromise any single module.

There are many protocols for pirate card rejection (also called *verifier functions* [4]). We now summarize a protocol [7] that has several valuable characteristics:

1. Pirate card rejection is separated from interface protection (copy protection). In particular authentication of movie content is separated from its encryption. This orthogonality is important since strong pirate card rejection may be realized, even if only weak interface protection is possible for cost or export reasons.

2. Pirate card rejection is separated from billing policies, so the frequency of the module's authentication is unrelated to the granularity of billing (e.g., the mechanism is indifferent to whether pay TV is billed by the movie, or by the seconds of video decrypted).

3. Pirate card rejection is controlled locally by the STB, and not by the broadcaster. This has several advantages: Poorly implemented STBs do not

compromise the entire system; the broadcaster is not burdened with issuing the authentication challenges associated with pirate card rejection; and the pirate gains no advantage by inspecting the broadcast before it is received by the STB.

4. The running of the protocol is efficient, in part due to the fact that the authentication proofs occur only sporadically, even though they effectively cover all movie content.

5. The protocol can be implemented at low cost and mostly in software, in both the STB and in the CAM.

The protocol is briefly summarized as follows:

(1) STB -> CAM: Negotiate session key
(2) CAM -> STB: ***Challenge***$_{A,E}$, ***Status***$_{A}$
(3) STB -> CAM:

— Return to (1) if out of session-key sync, or

— ***Request Packet Resync***$_{A}$ and return to (2), or

— ***Response***$_{A}$ and return to (2)

The subscript notation denotes that **A**=authentication; **E**=encryption. The challenge refers to ciphertext and plaintext from the data stream.

The effect of pirate card rejection is to shift the burden from relying entirely on securing each card to also leveraging off the fixed infrastructure which includes the high-price consumer electronics (CE) units themselves, namely the STBs. These units typically do not have a substantial profit margin even when produced by experienced CE manufacturers. Furthermore, they may have parts that can wear out, which may make a customer think twice before acquiring such a unit from a pirate rather than an established CE company which provides warranties on its boxes provided they are not mishandled. Opening up the unit to attempt to make modifications would, in particular, qualify as mishandling. Circumvention by a pirate of an effective implementation of pirate card rejection may be too costly: It requires breaking individual customers' CAMs, or either tampering with individual customers' STBs or having customers use pirated STBs.

If the STB is programmable, then pirate card rejection may not be effective. For example, pirate card rejection could be skipped, or the component that validates which CAM the STB is authorized to communicate with could be corrupted. A PC may be an inexpensive, yet programmable "soft" STB, since the customer may already own a PC. One possible solution is to control licensing so enabling components that are not software (e.g., the proprietary TV tuner or disc reader) cannot be part of such programmable architectures.

3.7 CA Design Principles

The pirate may have lower operating costs than the legitimate service provider, since he does not have to pay the content owner for content. So the CA system must attempt to complicate the pirate's business. The design principles attempt to make it difficult for the pirate to learn content keys and distribute them to his customers, and to make it difficult for his customers to use those keys.

Protect keys and not content: Since dense content is expensive to redistribute, and content needs to be made available eventually to non-renewable devices (like a TV), the focus should be on protecting keys.

Protect universal keys: Universal keys should never leave the security perimeter of the renewable device.

Protect universal keys better than local keys: Local session keys which may be used by the CAM to communicate with the non-renewable STB need not be as well protected as universal keys, since the STB makes them vulnerable anyway.

Prevent the pirate from leveraging off of the legitimate distribution system: While this may be impossible with respect to content in certain distribution systems, it is possible with respect to content keys. Instead of broadcasting content keys, which makes passive eavesdropping by counterfeit CAMs an effective means to learn new keys, distribute keys over a different channel than the content, over secure point-to-point connections (e.g., a phone line).

Maintain a tether between the backend systems and the customers: Requiring CAMs to maintain periodic contact with the backend systems, provides indirect audits of CAMs. A tether can be enforced in two ways: By a negative system where the CAM stops working unless it contacts the backend periodically; or, by a positive system, where the CAM needs to contact the backend to learn new keys. The latter approach forces the pirate to maintain contact with his customers also, since he cannot supply them with all future content keys when he sells them the initial device. Forcing a pirate and his customers to maintain a relationship significantly increases the cost and risk associated with an illegal operation.

Harden the legitimate infrastructure to make it difficult to use keys obtained from a pirate. Pirate card rejection is an example of this hardening.

4. Quantifying Risk

Consider the following "threat metrics" in an attempt to quantify risks associated with profit-driven piracy.

Time-sensitivity of content:

- when made available
- when play window begins
- perishability

Cost of legitimate content distribution:

- broadcast footprint
- cost to customer
- return policy
- playback equipment requirements (cost, input/output ports)

Key use costs:

- complexity
- out-of-band vs. direct delivery

Media cost issues:

- packaging
- physical marking for watermarking
- durability
- raw cost of media
- pressing/copy production equipment cost (use/own/modify)

4.1 Examples of Risk Quantification

We now expound upon the threat metrics and, where appropriate, refer to specific types of content distribution mechanisms, such as satellite pay-per-view, media sale with limited license, media rental, cable pay-per-view, and point-to-point video-on-demand via phone. By media sale with limited license, we mean a scheme whereby the customer owns the media, but may pay for access to the content. In particular, media sale allows for rental pricing without media return.

Regarding key use costs, e.g., how much complexity is involved in using the purchased pirated key: In the case of content distribution through remote sources (such as via satellite or cable), TV/VCR equipment which can tune in broadcasts (if built with output ports) may provide the pirate with a cheaper and less obtrusive means of circumventing pirate card rejection techniques, where the pirate device would go between the tuning TV/VCR and the TV monitor. In the media sale model, the content must be obtained locally from the media.

With respect to legitimate content distribution: Satellite pay-per-view has a very large broadcast footprint, while cable pay-per-view has a substantially smaller footprint. Media sale, rental, and point-to-point have none.

Time-sensitivity of content is an issue in that some service providers may lag behind others in terms of movie availability, so that for a certain time window these early-delivery channels are providing content of higher value. If the piracy threat is content redistribution (e.g., via sale of pirated media) then a live pay-per-view boxing match which is of much lower value once the outcome is known, may pose a more difficult target for profitable piracy than, say, media sold under limited license. The fact that media rentals must be returned promptly in order to avoid additional fees means that a certain percentage of customers routinely make a single copy so that they can time-shift their viewing of the movie. This copy is usually made for personal use, and may be of reduced quality in part due to analog copy-protection techniques. With respect to durability of rental media, the rental media itself may already be of diminished quality due to heavy use by non-owners (i.e., less concerned users). In the case of media sold under limited license, the customer retains a copy which would be worthwhile accessing without paying additional (legitimate) charges, if a pirate can provide a convenient lower cost alternative and if enough such titles are deemed worthy of paying for the pirate's service.

As a title's sale price drops to say $5-10, piracy becomes less of an issue, because of the high fixed cost of the raw media.

As it becomes more trivial for pirates to package media so that it is (virtually) indistinguishable from authorized copies, the value of such copies increases. Of course, the pirate does not need to pay for licensed distribution of the content.

Turning again to key use costs, for satellite and cable (unlike distribution channels which rely on certain types of physical media) it is cost effective for the legitimate service to change the content encryption key with each transmission of the movie (while in the case of point-to-point it may not currently be necessary to encrypt at all). If a content distribution system is instantiated so that it does not use point-to-point (e.g., modem) instead of broadcast for delivery of the content decryption keys, but rather relies wholly on the user device to track use of keys, it may be cheaper for a pirate to proliferate devices which directly receive decryption keys (from the broadcast) while circumventing the bill-for-use policy. In the case of a (legitimate) point-to-point key distribution mechanism, the backend of the system may be able to determine if a CAM with a particular ID repeatedly requests the same keys. Even if point-to-point is used for legitimate key distribution, the system may not charge for key delivery if such delivery is not tied closely enough to key use. In particular, a given key may never be used if no movie associated with that key is ever viewed.

If, in order to avoid charges associated with use of keys delivered directly to the legitimate CAM, a customer is dependent upon the pirate for out-of-band delivery of content encryption keys, this provides a pirate with a continuous source of revenue, but requires the customer to enter into a more long-term relationship with the inherently untrusted pirate. If the pirate is to get paid for each instance of such out-of-band delivery of keys, he cannot simply set up an anonymous Website for key delivery. Establishing a means for payment may reveal his identity.

The fact that a particular system must be equipped to handle free content may make it easier for a pirate device to avoid billing or other penalties such as non-availability of service. For example, consumer electronics equipment may be designed to handle multi-sourced content, and, in particular, a VCR needs to be able to play user-generated content such as camcorder output, which can complicate processes such as playback detection/verification of embedded watermarks/digital signatures.

Content distributed on physical media may make use of "physical marks." For example, in [8], there is discussion of a physical mark P, and watermark W, created from a seed U during mastering, such that P=F(U) and W=F(F(U)). According to [8], one realization of such a physical mark is the "wobble groove" in optical discs. For professional publishing, the function F and P are specified such that P contains an ID for the publisher or a serial number of the mastering machine, where a pirate publisher must either know U which is not derivable from the store-bought copyright disc or tamper with his media press. If the pirate is not very large-scale, he may not own the media press he is using, and thus may be barred from modifying it. Each content provider keeps his own secret seed U, but not the means to derive U from arbitrary P, so that the system does not require dissemination of a universal secret.

5. Content Redistribution

If content redistribution is easy, there is no real point in protecting content up front, by encryption, for example. Imagine that bandwidth was very cheap: HBO may have a single customer, a pirate, who redistributes content to everyone else. Service providers cannot sustain businesses in such an environment. In this section, we describe a possible direction for protecting content in such a threat environment.

Notice that securing the input ports in the STB is not an adequate solution, since customers must always be able to play home generated content (like output from a camcorder) and the pirate could redistribute content as if it was generated by a camcorder. We must prevent chargeable content from masquerading as free content.

Key insight: Just like in pirate card rejection we give up on making CAMs impossible to compromise, and instead shift the burden to building individualized pirated CAMs or pirated infrastructures, here we focus on preventing use of the pirated content rather than on preventing acquisition of the pirated content in the first place.

Assume that the content itself can be watermarked in some robust way at authoring time, so legitimate playback devices will detect the watermark. Assume furthermore that the pirate cannot remove this watermark. Watermark removal is usually done by corrupting the content, or by comparing two instances of the content with different watermarks. This latter attack need not be enabled in this approach, since all instances of the content will have the same watermark (i.e., watermarking is done here for playback control purposes, and not for tracing the source of unauthorized distribution). In this approach the content is watermarked at authoring time.

To play watermarked content, each legitimate playback device (i.e., TV monitor) requires authorization from the CAM with which it is allowed to communicate. So instead of decrypting content for the TV monitor, the CAM becomes an authorized licensing device. The legitimate playback device inspects content to see if a playback license is required, and refuses to play marked content if no license is presented.

Compromise of this system requires the pirate to corrupt the watermark while still maintaining product quality, or produce playback devices that ignore the watermark, or compromise individual customers' CAMs. The latter two are akin to the threats we resist in pirate card rejection.

6. Conclusion

This paper presented a functional overview of CA systems, and described the building blocks and principles that may be used in building secure CA systems. Cost-effective security depends upon a careful identification of the significant threats to the legitimate provider's business, renewability of certain security components, and dependence upon the fixed infrastructure. Legal protection is also important, as this may serve to offset the pirate's lower costs of content acquisition.

References

1. R. Anderson and M. Kuhn, "Low Cost Attacks on Tamper Resistant Devices," 5th Security Protocols Workshop, Lecture Notes in Computer Sciences 1361, Springer-Verlag, 1997, pages 125-136.

2. International Business Machine. 1997. Cryptolope containers: A white paper.

3. J. L. Cohen, M. H. Etzel, D. W. Faucher, and D. N. Heer, "Security for Broadband Digital Networks," Communications Technology, August 1995, pages 58-69.

4. 'Open Verifier' Functionality in Consumer Electronics Devices, GD-T204, Release B, News Data Systems, Ltd.

5. ISO 7816 Identification Cards, Integrated Circuit Cards with Contact, 1987.

6. EIA-679, National Renewable Security Standard (NRSS) Parts A and B, March 1998.

7. D.M. Goldschlag and D.W. Kravitz, "Pirate Card Rejection," Cardis 98, Louvain-la-Nueve, Belgium, September 14-16, 1998.

8. J.P.M.G. Linnartz, "The 'Ticket" Concept for Copy Control Based on Embedded Signalling," ESORICS 98, Louvain-la-Nueve, Belgium, September 16-18, 1998.

Fair Use, Intellectual Property, and the Information Economy
(Panel Session Summary)

Jon Callas[1]*, Joan Feigenbaum[2], David Goldschlag[3], and Erin Sawyer[4]

[1] Network Associates, Inc.
3965 Freedom Circle, Santa Clara, CA 95054 USA
jon@callas.org

[2] AT&T Labs – Research
180 Park Avenue, Rm. C203, Florham Park, NJ 07932 USA
jf@research.att.com

[3] Divx
570 Herndon Parkway, Herndon, VA 20170, USA
David.Goldschlag@divx.com

[4] Cooley Godward LLP
One Maritime Plaza, 20th Floor, San Francisco, CA 94111 USA
jdsafari@earthlink.net

1 Introduction

Because the growing use of cryptography and other security technology by the entertainment industry is an important fact of life in our field, the Financial Crypto '99 Program Committee decided to hold a one-hour panel discussion on *Fair Use, Intellectual Property, and the Information Economy.* Roughly the first half of the session was devoted to the moderator's introduction and five-minute talks by each of the panelists. Approximately 10 days before the conference, the moderator distributed her list of questions (Section 2 below) to the panelists and told them to prepare to speak for five minutes on one of them or on a similar question about the interplay of technological and non-technological aspects of Intellectual Property (IP) management. The rest of the session consisted of a lively audience-driven discussion.

In Sections 3, 4, and 5 below, three of the panelists summarize their own remarks and some of the audience reaction to those remarks.

We are very grateful to the rest of the panel and to the audience for making the session a success. We look forward to more sessions on technical, legal, and economic aspects of IP management at future Financial Crypto conferences.

* Current address: Kroll-O'Gara Information Security Group, 3600 West Bayshore Blvd., Suite 200, Palo Alto, CA 94303.

M. Franklin (Ed.): FC'99, LNCS 1648, pp. 173–183, 1999.

2 Questions for Panelists (Joan Feigenbaum)

1. Widespread use of the Internet and personal computers presents an opportunity for fast, cheap, and flexible creation and distribution of digital works. It also threatens to make copying and modification of these works much less controllable than it is in more traditional media. This threat has frightened enough powerful constituencies to give rise to UCC2B (Uniform Commercial Code, Article 2B), DMCA (Digital Millenium Copyright Act), US participation in the WIPO (World Intellectual Property Organization) treaty, *etc.* Are these constituencies over-reacting? Fears that VCRs would destroy the movie business or that copiable floppy disks would destroy the software business proved unwarranted. Do creators and distributors really need as much control over copying and modification as they think they do, or can they make money without it?
2. The traditional strengths of the cryptology and security R & D community position us perfectly to respond to creators' and distributors' fears by inventing and improving techniques to control copying and modification. Could we be just as good at (and have more fun) inventing and improving techniques for alternative forms of IP management? Do our types of ideas and technology suggest some alternative business models that are not centered on copy-control?
3. In another effort to control copying and modification, "content distributors" have pushed for "anti-circumvention legislation."

   (a) Does this mean that they do not believe that the cryptology and security R & D community can produce a "technological protection measure" (TPM) that actually works?
   (b) There is some recognition, *e.g.*, in the DMCA, that experimental circumvention is an integral part of the security R & D process. The DMCA approach is to make circumvention illegal except when it's done for certain purposes, one of which is "encryption research." Is this a viable approach, and, if so, what are the shortcomings of its implementation in the DMCA? What are alternative approaches?

4. While "anti-circumvention legislation" may be viewed as an expression of pessimism about our community's technical competence, certain aspects of the proposed UCC2B may be viewed as an expression of extreme optimism about both our technical competence and our ethics. What are the pros and cons of using technical mechanisms as substitutes for social and legal mechanisms?
5. Is contract law a more useful framework for digital IP-management than traditional copyright law? If so, what technological challenges are presented by this use of contracts?

More information about UCC2B, DMCA, and WIPO can be found at the following web sites:

`http://www.2BGuide.com/index.html`

`http://sims.berkeley.edu/BCLT/events/ucc2b/`

`http://www.hrrc.org/DMCA-leg-hist.html`

`http://www.wipo.org`

3 The Digital Millenium Copyright Act (Jon Callas)

The DMCA has in it a number of provisions that are of concern to people who work in cryptography and information security. The DMCA is the US Congress's law that implements the WIPO treaty on protecting information property world-wide.

The goals of the treaty are laudable, even if there are a number of issues about copyright and electronic media that we might disagree on. For example, I could make a reasonable argument that, because I can clip an article from a newspaper and send it to my mother without violating copyright law, I ought to be able to do the same from the web with email. Some disagree with this. However, I think very few people would be sympathetic to a site in the country of Elbonia that mirrored that newspaper's content and put up its own ads. Similarly, few people are sympathetic to those who copy and distribute unauthorized movies, music recordings, and software packages. It is these things that the WIPO treaty and the DMCA are trying to address.

The problem with the DMCA is its implementation of the law to serve these goals and the effect it could have on research and on the high-tech industry. The most glaring problem is the so-called anti-circumvention provision. This provision in the DMCA makes it a felony to circumvent any (TPM) that "effectively controls access to a work protected" by the DMCA. There are a number of unresolved issues with this provision, as well as unsettling questions.

First, there is no definition of the term "technological protection measure," nor is there a clear statement of what it means for such a measure to be "effective." It may help to stand back for a moment before I pick nits to look at the goal again. The goal is to make it a more serious crime to infringe a work that the owner actively tried to protect than to infringe one that the owner merely stated ownership of. If we go back to my example of the newspaper article on a web site, that article has no TPM, as opposed to a copy-protected motion picture, which does, and most likely an effective one.

The problem exists on both sides of this question. It is easy to get into a gray area of what an effective TPM is, particularly in computers. Years ago, a certain computer's file system had a "don't copy" flag that one could set on a file. This computer's "copy" command would not copy files with this flag set, but backup utilities would copy the file, and it was certainly trivial to write a program that opened the file, read its contents, and wrote them back to another file. Was this TPM effective? Arguably yes, arguably no. This gray area causes a small concern to toolmakers who might accidentally circumvent a TPM (does the backup utility circumvent the no-copy flag?). It is only a small concern, because there are parts of the provision that ban only those tools that have "only limited commercially significant purpose or use other than to circumvent." However, if you are in favor of this provision, the gray area opens up the possibility of the provision's being struck down by a court on vagueness grounds. (It is my opinion that the provision should be struck down on vagueness. There are many exceptions and descriptions of what might be banned that laudably get rid of almost all overt absurdities like banning backup utilities, but we are finally left with a vague definition. In my experience, it is ironically harder for technical people to tell what is acceptable than non-technical people; the toolmakers don't even know what's unacceptable when they see it.)

The next problem with the anti-circumvention provision is that it does not tie circumvention to infringement. Circumvention outside of infringement is still a felony punishable by five years imprisonment. The DMCA is thus not merely a copyright law; it also creates the new crime of circumvention. This crime is also separate and distinct from violating someone's copyright. It is a crime to use intellectual property that you have the right to use but that someone else has protected.

A potential serious problem for the high-tech industry is where circumvention collides with fair use. Most people think of fair use as simply the right to quote in a review, but it extends past that. Every high-tech researcher or worker should know that it is fair use to reverse engineer something for the purpose of making compatible equipment. At FC99, the discussion came up as to whether fair use is a right or merely a defense in the United States. In some cases, particularly this one, it is undeniably a right, and one of the most strongly upheld rights there is. (Another is the right to fair use for the purpose of constructing a parody.) Ever since the Supreme Court ruled against IBM – who claimed that their copyrights on the "channel" prevented anyone from making compatible computer peripherals – this has been a fundamental right that has fueled the high-tech explosion. Invention is now not only making a better mousetrap, but making a compatible one that is cheaper. I think there is no question that someone will try to use the circumvention provision to squash competition. We can only hope that they fail in court.

Somewhat related to this is the fact that the DMCA goes far beyond what the WIPO treaty requires. Like all international treaties, the requirements of WIPO are minimal and come nowhere close to requiring that circumvention be addressed at all. The copyright holders may in fact merely stifle innovation by their countrymen, while teaching other countries how to break the protections that are slowly built.

Finally, there is the burden placed upon cryptographic researchers. Among the many compromises and exceptions in the DMCA are those relating to research. The copyright holders understandably do not want to catch someone with a warehouse full of bootleg videotapes and have them offer in their defense, "but I was only doing research." The researchers, on the other hand, do not want to show that a security system is worthless, only to be rewarded for their good deed with a felony charge. This is further compounded by the fact that, in the last few years, unknowns have done the most compelling work.

There are a number of compromises and exceptions have been put into the DMCA for researchers. The most important is a defense added for researchers who ask permission of a copyright holder to break the protection and then inform the holder of the result. (Note that it is not necessary to receive permission, merely to ask). Like all compromises, this makes all sides unhappy. Researchers don't like having to ask permission and worry that this could chill research. Ironically, any chill on research directly hurts the copyright holders, because they are the consumers of protection technologies.

In summary, changes to copyright law in the DMCA provide a number of difficulties to information security researchers and workers. None of them is a disaster, but they are annoyances. The law itself may be subject to challenges, because of its mix of vague terms and a patchwork of exceptions, exemptions, and wordings. The law also goes far beyond what is required by the WIPO treaty. During hearings, Congress itself was concerned that portions of the law will not solve the problems the copyright holders want solved and may be overturned in the courts. Only time will tell here.

4 Content Protection in a World where Everyone Can Be a (re-)Distributor (David M. Goldschlag)

The social/legal/technical focus of content protection should not be on the threat of local copying but rather on the use of redistributed pirated content, because redistribution is the main threat to revenue. In a world of cheap bandwidth, significant piracy can occur through a web of piracy, and such limited local redistribution is difficult to counter.

4.1 Overview

Some bits are more valuable than others, and the creator of bits must have some way to control their use, to justify and profit from his investment. Titanic's production budget could never have been recouped if each theater could show the movie for the cost of the film media. Ticket-based revenue sharing is one way to price bits to limit both studios' and theaters' financial risk.

In a world of cheap bandwidth, everyone can be a distributor, and every purchaser of bits can redistribute them. In the absence of social, legal, and technical controls over the use of bits, expensive bits will not be produced. Even giving away bits for free and paying for them by advertising does not solve the problem if the advertisements can be filtered out.

Producers of both video and music have focused on legal and technical mechanisms limiting the consumer's ability to copy content that he has purchased. Such copy-control constraints have been justified as protection against both local copying and large scale piracy. With respect to local copying, the constraints have to be sufficiently high to enable the legitimate distributor to price his product differently for different usage by typical consumers: A movie videotape may be rented for two days for $3 or sold for unlimited non-commercial use for $20; if copying were trivial, then few consumers would buy the movie outright.

But to claim that copy-control mechanisms protect against large scale piracy ignores the real threat to revenue: None of these mechanisms can prevent the serious pirate from obtaining his own clean digital copy of the bits and redistributing them to others to play on their own equipment as if they were free bits. The pirate can afford to surmount the copy protection hurdles because they are his only production cost. In a world of cheap bandwidth, he can then compete, unfairly, in direct commercial competition with the content owner's proprietary distribution channels.

The cryptographic community has benefited from the focus on copy control and has delivered to the entertainment industry sophisticated and complex solutions depending on public and symmetric key cryptography, certificates, certifying authorities, and certificate revocation. But these solutions are a dead end, because their robustness is limited by their implementation in highly price sensitive, long lived, and insecure consumer electronics equipment, and they do not address the real threat of large scale piracy anyway.

4.2 The Threat is Redistribution

Piracy can be cast as an economic question, whether the pirate is able to underprice the legitimate distributor. Since the pirate has no significant production costs, his main costs are distribution, the risk of legal prosecution, and consumer resistance to piracy. Depending upon the product, these costs may be high enough to allow the legitimate distributor to compete (and make a profit). In the electronic world, where distribution may be free, and avoiding prosecution (by identity hiding) may be easier, the pirate may gain an advantage.

It is helpful to consider analogies from today's world, while predicting how piracy will work when bandwidth is cheap. For example, when VCRs were first introduced, studios worried that their business would be hurt by the easy copying of movies. But the VCR enabled home video rental, which is now the studios' largest single revenue source. It turned out that the threat of local copying was not high, because a limited viewing license is appropriate for most movies for most consumers. Furthermore, mass redistribution by the consumer is not easy. Even if the consumer wanted to copy the movie for redistribution, his costs include the cost of the blank videotape, a second VCR, making the copy, and giving the copy to a friend. It is probably cheaper and easier for the friend to rent the movie. In a similar way, video rental stores can operate more efficiently than a pirate selling video tapes on a street corner, especially since those pirates cannot make much profit selling at rental prices (and pirates cannot rent their product).

Music is different from movies, because consumers may not want a limited license. But music cannot be legally rented in the US, because music has an exception to the first sale doctrine. However, music rental in Japan is legal, and the rental store is used (in effect) as the re-distribution mechanism. Not surprisingly, the sale price of music in Japan is about 80% higher than in the US (about $22 per CD, compared with $12). This allows the studio to shift its expected revenue from unit sales to consumers to lower unit sales to rental stores. Even with this premium, studios are attempting to prevent the rental of new releases in Japan.

In the US, studios often use the same model with movies. Either movies are rented with revenue shared between the rental store and the studio (RentTrak), or movies are sold to rental stores for a high up-front cost.

As redistribution becomes easier (*i.e.*, bandwidth becomes cheaper), piracy become more significant. Consider digital music, whose bandwidth requirements are less dense than video. A customer can purchase a CD, convert it to MP3 on his PC, and send it by e-mail to his friends. One purchased album may end up in many households.

The threat of piracy depends upon the price of legitimately purchased content, the license that is appropriate for that content, the ease of redistribution, and who the redistributor is. Content unsuitable for limited license that is easy to redistribute anonymously is hard to protect.

4.3 Conclusion

Local copying must not be trivial, and cryptography and legislation (*e.g.*, anti-circumvention) have a role in copy-control mechanisms. But these mechanisms do not prevent the use of pirated content.

It is entirely possible that new business models will emerge that enable the production and distribution of expensive bits without concern about piracy. The VCR is an example of a technology that undid content providers' concerns. However, cheap bandwidth and the digitization of expensive bits makes everyone a distributor. And this enables the emergence of a web of piracy: A significant piracy threat without any one person doing much more than limited redistribution. If one person surmounts the local copying hurdle, converts protected bits to free ones, and redistributes them (by e-mail) to just a few friends, soon everyone would have those bits. The threat of prosecution also disappears, because no one is stealing very much, and no one is advertising his role in piracy.

5 Article 2B of the UCC (Erin Sawyer)

With the speed of technological development overwhelming even the most vigilant observers, many wonder what should be the role of law in shaping and directing the new digital economy. Law is generally not the trend-setter, preferring to script a careful and detailed history after a critical mass of information has been accumulated through court cases and business transactions. Law does not play the soothsayer or the prognosticator; it codifies and formalizes the wealth and knowledge of past experience. Until now. Article 2B of the Uniform Commercial Code takes an entirely different approach. Article 2B is being drafted by the National Conference of Commissioners on Uniform State Laws and the American Law Institute, voluntary associations of practitioners, professors and judges. Once the draft is complete (sometime in the next few months), Article 2B would go to the legislatures of each state for approval.

Article 2B is designed to be a default rule for contracting across a wide range of "electronic commerce" areas. Through drafting sessions, studies of industries and existing laws, and consideration of a wide range of political, business and social interests, the drafters hope to craft a law that would govern the universe of contractual arrangements surrounding computer software and other information that can be digitally transmitted. This universe of contracts includes arrangements for development, licensing, distribution, sale and post-sale support, as well as rules concerning relative fault of contracting parties, the scope of liability, and the remedies available to those parties.

In many ways, the entire project of drafting a revision to the UCC that would be attentive to special issues of contracting in a digital economy represents a certain optimism on the part of the legal community – an optimism that law can be a guiding force in this confusing time of rapid technological development. Historically, contract law has relied on custom and usage of trade as an important evaluation mechanism for all stages of the contracting process from the earliest negotiations to offer and acceptance, performance, breach, and available remedies. The digital economy presents a problem in this respect, because there is no clear custom and usage of trade. Industries that come under the rubric "technology" are diverse and varied, each with different needs and demands, each with a potentially different way of doing business. To attempt to write a law of default contract principles that prospectively addresses the needs of all technologies and all business models is a daunting and, some would argue, impossible task. A task that could do far more harm than good if Article 2B moves past the drafting stage and becomes actual law.

So what are some concrete problems apart from the difficulty of predicting the evolution of an industry that has so far exceeded expectations and defied conventional wisdom? One key area of concern relates to licensing in general and to mass-market licenses in particular. Remember that Article 2B strives to be a default rule; thus, it would not apply to negotiated licenses between parties of equivalent bargaining power. As the draft currently reads, vendors have a great deal of power over consumers. They can require buyers to commit to an order before the buyers are able to review the terms of the license. These shrink-wrap and "click-wrap" licenses would be enforceable, even though there would be no real offer and acceptance process, a hallmark of traditional contract law. Additionally, vendors can prohibit the transfer or assignment of a license without permission, and they would have the power to shut down a buyer's system on little more than the belief that the buyer has breached the contract! Not only do these abilities place the vendor in an advantaged position in a business sense, they also make the vendor judge and jury regarding breach of contract and appropriate remedy.

A second area of conflict and concern is the interaction of Article 2B with existing laws regarding digital signatures at the state level. State legislatures have had varied responses to digital signatures. While some have enacted complex laws focusing on digital signatures as a source of consumer protection and a guarantor of contractual integrity, others have done nothing at all. A uniform national law regarding digital signatures may be desirable from a number of perspectives, both legal and commercial. However, there is not enough transactional experience to determine, with the level of certainty required, how the law should treat the use of digital signatures. For states that already have digital signature laws in place, the question would be how to mesh the new law with the old, whether to apply a grandfather rule, and to what set of transactions or to what time period. For states with no digital signature laws, Article 2B might still present conflicts with existing consumer-protection laws. Issues of federal preemption and the right of states to propagate their own laws is outside the scope of my comments, but it is a tangled issue that the drafters of Article 2B have not thoroughly or consistently addressed, opting instead for the optimistic vision of national uniformity under a law that accurately captures the business and technical landscape of electronic contracting. While it is true that digital signatures could theoretically protect consumers from many possible frauds, the technology behind digital signatures is in such ferment and active development that it is unwise to eliminate standard consumer protections in the hope that technology will come up with failsafe protections of its own.

Connected to the debate on the interaction between Article 2B and existing digital signature laws is the issue of liability. The liability regime of Article 2B casts a very wide net. Basically, if a person uses a digital signature or other secure authentication technology and then loses control of that authentication procedure in a negligent manner, that person would be liable for all losses related to that negligent act. In other words, if a transaction is visualized as series of events with multiple tangents, the negligent act would create liability for all subsequent losses along any of those tangents, as long as the losses were caused by the negligent act and the person sustaining the loss relied on the authentication procedure. Obviously, the speed at which transactions take place in the digital context as well as the potential for a very high number of transactions through any given conduit makes the scope of liability theoretically endless.

This way of understanding the scope of liability represents a significant departure from the way liability is conceptualized in traditional contract law, bringing us back to the original point that there is not enough transactional experience for the law to codify liability and damages regimes. Without comprehensive (or at least extensive) custom and usage of trade, with attention to the varying needs of different technology industries and different digital transactions, there is no way the law can predict how parties will interact, how technology will be able to facilitate or harm that interaction and what different industries will require as their position in the digital economy evolves.

The efforts of the Article 2B drafters are admirable in the sense that they are trying to take stock of a developing industry and predict the problems early. As more and more people do business on the web and over email, it is useful for the law to consider how the problems they face differ from those in more traditional contracting settings. In addition, evaluating the legal landscape at this stage is a valuable recognition that technology has legal, social, and political consequences that are just as important as the technical specifications.

But whether such discourse and analysis should lead to codified law is another matter. Although the law has come under attack as being slow-moving, risk-averse, and unresponsive to changes brought about by doing business in the digital economy, it is important to remember that it has never been the role of law to predict trends or to set the rules of business before business has had a chance to try out different ways of transacting and explore the consequences of those methods in a less restrictive environment than the one provided by a codified legal regime. The implementation of Article 2B across states with divergent existing legal regimes is bound to create confusion rather than uniformity and to hinder rather than encourage efficient business transactions.

6 Participants' Biographies

Jon Amster (panelist) is a lawyer at InterTrust Technologies. InterTrust provides a unique interoperable, trusted, and secure foundation for electronic commerce. Its software products and services enable the efficient sale, fulfillment and protection of digital content over any digital media, including the Internet, DVD, and future commerce appliances.

Dan Boneh (panelist) is an Assistant Professor at the Department of Computer Science at Stanford University. His research focuses on cryptography, specifically the security of cryptographic primitives and their application in real world systems. He is the author of numerous technical papers in the field as well as several patents. At Stanford he is leading a number of systems security projects on topics such as intrusion tolerance, security applications for handheld devices, and intellectual property protection.

Jon Callas (panelist) is Chief Technology Officer for the Total Network Security division of Network Associates, Inc. He was Chief Scientist at PGP, Inc. before its acquisition. He has worked in computer security for over ten years, ranging from operating system security to network security to cryptography. He is the inventor of a language-independent password generator and a design system for cryptographic random number generators. In 1998, he testified to the United States Congress on behalf of the Electronics and Software industry for the Digitial Millenium Copyright Act. Before working for Network Associates/PGP, he worked for a number of companies, including Apple Computer as a Senior Scientist. He was founder of his own company, World Benders, which developed collaboration tools for the Internet. He also worked for DEC for many years on the VMS operating system.

Joan Feigenbaum (moderator) received the BA in Mathematics from Harvard and the PhD in Computer Science from Stanford. She has been with AT&T

since receiving her PhD in 1986 and currently heads the Algorithms and Distributed Data Department at AT&T's Shannon Laboratory in Florham Park, NJ. Her research interests are in security and cryptology, computational complexity theory, and algorithmic techniques for massive data sets. Security and cryptology research areas that she has contributed to include trust management, instance-hiding, remotely keyed encryption, and complexity theoretic foundations. Her current and recent professional service activities include Editor-in-Chief of the Journal of Cryptology, editorial-board member for the SIAM Journal on Computing, and National Research Council panel member for Intellectual Property Rights in the Emerging Information Infrastructure.

David Goldschlag (panelist) is manager of the Security Systems group at Divx, which is responsible for the design, implementation, and evolution of Divx's conditional access infrastructure. He has published numerous research papers in cryptography, security, and formal methods and is a co-inventor of Onion Routing, a system for private and anonymous communication over the Internet. Prior to Divx, he worked at the U.S. Naval Research Laboratory and the National Security Agency. He holds a Ph.D. in Computer Science from the University of Texas at Austin.

Brian A. LaMacchia (panelist) received the S.B., S.M., and Ph.D. degrees from the Massachusetts Institute of Technology in 1990, 1991, and 1996, respectively. He is currently the Program Manager for Core Cryptography at Microsoft Corporation in Redmond, WA. Currently he is working on the the design and implementation of trust-management services as part of the Windows^{TM} platform. Prior to joining Microsoft, Brian was a member of the Public Policy Research Department at AT&T Labs – Research in Florham Park, NJ. His homepage may be found at `http://www.farcaster.com/bal/`.

Erin Sawyer (panelist) is an associate in the San Francisco office of Cooley Godward, LLP and focuses on the representation of emerging growth companies. Her current research and practice interests include the taxation and regulation of electronic commmerce as well as corporate governance and financing of startup companies. Erin received her J.D. with distinction from Stanford Law School, where she was elected to the Order of the Coif. While at Stanford, Erin received a John M. Olin fellowship in Law and Economics and co-authored a publication with Professor Margaret Jane Radin entitled, "Intellectual Property and Intellectual Capital: The Role of Nonproprietary Technologies," in *Capital for Our Time: The Economic, Legal, and Management Challenges of Intellectual Capital*, Nicholas Imparato, ed. (Hoover Institution press, 1998). Erin was also the Features Editor for the Stanford Law and Policy Review and an active member of the Stanford Law and Technology Association. Erin received her A.M. from Stanford University in 1995 in philosophy and religion and her B.A. from Swarthmore College in 1993.

Anonymous Authentication of Membership in Dynamic Groups

Stuart Schechter[1], Todd Parnell[2], and Alexander Hartemink[2]

[1] Harvard University
stuart@post.harvard.edu
[2] Massachusetts Institute of Technology
{tparnell,amink}@mit.edu

Abstract. We present a series of protocols for authenticating an individual's membership in a group without revealing that individual's identity and without restricting how the membership of the group may be changed. In systems using these protocols a single message to the authenticator may be used by an individual to replace her lost key or by a trusted third party to add and remove members of the group. Applications in electronic commerce and communication can thus use these protocols to provide anonymous authentication while accommodating frequent changes in membership. We build these protocols on top of a new primitive: the *verifiably common secret encoding.* We show a construction for this primitive, the security of which is based on the existence of public-key cryptosystems capable of securely encoding multiple messages containing the same plaintext. Because the size of our construct grows linearly with the number of members in the group, we describe techniques for partitioning groups to improve performance.

Keywords: anonymity, authentication, key replacement, identification, verifiably common secret encoding

1 Introduction

We present a protocol for authenticating an individual's membership in a group without revealing that individual's identity and without restricting the frequency with which the membership of the group may be changed.

Authenticating membership in a group is a common task because privileges, such as the right to read a document, are often assigned to many individuals. While permission to exercise a privilege requires that members of the group be distinguished from non-members, members need not be distinguished from one another. Indeed, privacy concerns may dictate that authentication be conducted anonymously.

For instance, subscription services such as *The Wall Street Journal Interactive Edition* [19] require subscribers to identify themselves in order to limit service to those who pay, but many subscribers would prefer to keep their reading habits to themselves. Employee feedback programs, which require authentication

M. Franklin (Ed.): FC'99, LNCS 1648, pp. 184–195, 1999.

to ensure that employees can report only on their satisfaction with their own supervisor, also stand to benefit from enhanced privacy. Adding anonymity protects those employees who return negative feedback from being singled out for retaliation.

Most existing systems that authenticate membership in a group do so by identifying an individual, then verifying that the individual is a member. The requirement that an individual must identify herself to authenticate her membership can be eliminated by distributing a single group identity key to be used by all group members. However, this approach makes supporting dynamic groups unwieldy: whenever an individual is removed from the group, a new group identity key must be distributed to all remaining members. Not until every member receives this key can authentication be performed anonymously.

We achieve anonymous authentication using *verifiably common secret encodings*. The current construct of this primitive allows us to reduce its security properties to those of a restricted set of public-key cryptosystems. Using this new primitive, we show how to build anonymous authentication systems for dynamic groups in which a trusted party may add and remove members of the group in a single message to the authenticator. We also show how group members may replace their authentication keys if these keys should become compromised. Our protocols ensure that even if a key does become compromised, all previous and future transactions remain anonymous and unlinkable. We call this property *perfect forward anonymity.*

Section 2 of this paper introduces some notation and conventions. Section 3 presents a set of requirements for anonymous authentication protocols. In Section 4, we define a verifiably common secret encoding and list the operations supported by this primitive. We use these encodings in Section 5 to create an elementary anonymous authentication protocol. In Section 6, we extend this elementary system to provide key replacement. In Section 7, we give a trusted third party the ability to add and remove group members by communicating only with the authenticator. In Section 8, we show how to encode, decode, and verify VCS vectors, an implementation of verifiably common secret encodings. Section 9 describes how to scale anonymous authentication for very large groups. We provide a context for our research by discussing related work in Section 10 and then conclude in Section 11.

2 Conventions

Throughout this paper, we refer to any individual requesting authentication as *Alice*. The authentication process exists to prove to the authenticator, *Bob*, that *Alice* is a member of a group, without revealing *Alice's* name or any other aspect of her identity. When a trusted third party is needed, we call him *Trent*.

All parties are assumed to have a public-key pair used for identification. We represent public keys using the letter $\mathbf{p}$ and secret (or private) keys using the letter $\mathbf{s}$. For any message m and key $\mathbf{p}$, we define $\{m\}_{\mathbf{p}}$ to represent public-key encryption or the opening of a signature. For any message m and key $\mathbf{s}$, we define $\{m\}_{\mathbf{s}}$ to represent public-key decryption or signing. Symmetric encryption of message m with key k is represented as $E_k[m]$. When necessary, messages to be signed are appended with a known string to differentiate them from random strings. Messages sent by either *Bob* or *Trent* are also assumed to include a timestamp.

The set $\mathbf{P}$ is a set of public keys associated with a group. An individual whose public key is in $\mathbf{P}$ is called a *member* of $\mathbf{P}$. More precisely, a member of $\mathbf{P}$ is an individual possessing a secret key $\mathbf{s}$ corresponding to a public key $\mathbf{p} \in \mathbf{P}$, such that for the set M of messages that may be encoded using $\mathbf{p}$, $\forall m \in M, m = \{\{m\}_{\mathbf{p}}\}_{\mathbf{s}}$. To be authenticated anonymously is to reveal only that one is a member of $\mathbf{P}$. This definition of *anonymity* provides privacy only if there are other members of $\mathbf{P}$. We thus assume that the set $\mathbf{P}$ is public knowledge and that one can verify that the public keys in $\mathbf{P}$ are associated with real individuals.

Finally, we assume that all communication takes place over an anonymous communication channel [4,1,16,17]. This prevents an individual's anonymity from being compromised by the channel itself.

3 Requirements for Anonymous Authentication Protocols

The following three requirements are essential to anonymously authenticate membership in $\mathbf{P}$.

> SECURITY: *Only members of* $\mathbf{P}$ *can be authenticated.*
> ANONYMITY: *If an individual is authenticated, she reveals only that she is a member of* $\mathbf{P}$*. If she is not authenticated, she reveals nothing.*
> UNLINKABILITY: *Separate authentication transactions cannot be shown to have been made by a single individual.*

Note that the above definition of *anonymity* is the broadest possible, since *security* requires that only members of $\mathbf{P}$ can be authenticated.

The authenticator may choose to compromise *security* by authenticating an individual who is not a member of $\mathbf{P}$. Similarly, an individual may choose to forfeit her *anonymity* by revealing her identity. Therefore, we must assume that authenticators act to maintain security and that individuals act to preserve their own anonymity.

The above requirements do not account for the fact that membership in $\mathbf{P}$ is likely to change. Moreover, people are prone to lose their keys or fail to keep them secret. For a system to be able to address these concerns, we add to the list of requirements the following:

> KEY REPLACEMENT: *A member of* $\mathbf{P}$ *may replace her authentication key with a new one and need only confer with the authenticator to do so.*
> DYNAMIC GROUP MEMBERSHIP: *A trusted third party may add and remove members of* $\mathbf{P}$ *and need only confer with the authenticator do so.*

To make membership in $\mathbf{P}$ dynamic, a third party is trusted to add and remove members. If this third party is not trustworthy, he can manipulate the set $\mathbf{P}$ to reduce *anonymity*. For instance, if he shrinks $\mathbf{P}$ so that the group contains only one member, that member's identity will be revealed during her next authentication transaction.[1]

4 Verifiably Common Secret Encodings

We begin with a set of public keys, $\mathbf{P}$. Recall that we defined a *member* of $\mathbf{P}$ to be an individual possessing a secret key $\mathbf{s}$ corresponding to a public key $\mathbf{p} \in \mathbf{P}$. A *verifiably common secret encoding* e, of a value x, has the following properties:

SECRECY: *Only members of* $\mathbf{P}$ *can decode* e *to learn* x.
COMMONALITY: *Any member of* $\mathbf{P}$ *can decode* e *and will learn the same value* x *that any other member of* $\mathbf{P}$ *would learn by decoding* e.
VERIFIABILITY: *Any member of* $\mathbf{P}$ *can determine whether commonality holds for a given value* e, *regardless of whether* e *is properly constructed.*

We manipulate this primitive using the following three operations:

$$e \leftarrow \text{ENCODE}(x, \mathbf{P})$$

$$x \leftarrow \text{DECODE}(e, \mathbf{s}, \mathbf{P})$$

$$isCommon \leftarrow \text{VERIFY}(e, \mathbf{s}, \mathbf{P})$$

In the next three sections, we use these three functions to build anonymous authentication protocols. In Section 8, we provide a concrete algorithmic implementation for these functions.

5 Anonymous Authentication

We start by presenting a simple anonymous authentication protocol that satisfies the requirements of *security*, *anonymity*, and *unlinkability*. It establishes a session key y between *Alice* and *Bob* if and only if *Alice* is a member of $\mathbf{P}$. The protocol will serve as a foundation for more powerful systems providing *key replacement* and *dynamic group membership* to be described in Sections 6 and 7.

This protocol requires that *Bob* be a member of $\mathbf{P}$. If he is not, both *Alice* and *Bob* add $\mathbf{p}_{bob}$ to $\mathbf{P}$ for the duration of the authentication transaction.

5.1 The Authentication Protocol

Before the authentication transaction in Figure 1 commences, *Alice* randomly selects a session key y. She then encrypts y with *Bob's* public key to form

[1] In the case that a trusted third party cannot be agreed upon, *anonymity* can still be protected by imposing rules governing the ways in which $\mathbf{P}$ can be modified. These rules should be designed to prevent any excessive modification of $\mathbf{P}$ that might compromise *anonymity*. Violations of the rules must be immediately detectable by an individual when she receives changes to the membership of $\mathbf{P}$ during authentication.

message (1). This message, which represents a request for authentication, may also be augmented to specify the group in which *Alice's* membership is to be authenticated.

In response, *Bob* randomly picks x. He creates a message containing a verifiably common secret encoding of x, signs it, and then encrypts with the session key y. He sends this to *Alice* as message (2).

Alice decrypts the message and verifies *Bob's* signature to reveal a value e. If $\text{VERIFY}(e, \mathbf{s}_{alice}, \mathbf{P})$ returns true, *Alice* is assured that e is an encoding that satisfies *commonality*. Only then does she use $\text{DECODE}(e, \mathbf{s}_{alice}, \mathbf{P})$ to learn x. If $\text{VERIFY}(e, \mathbf{s}_{alice}, \mathbf{P})$ returns false, *Alice* cannot be assured that e satisfies *commonality* and halts the transaction.

In message (3), *Alice* proves her membership in $\mathbf{P}$ by encrypting x with the session key y. Upon decrypting message (3) to reveal x, *Bob* concludes that *Alice* is a member of $\mathbf{P}$. Authenticated communication between *Alice* and *Bob* may now begin.

Alice may later wish to prove that it was she who was authenticated in this transaction. We show in Appendix A how *Alice* may request a receipt for this transaction. With such a receipt in hand, *Alice* may, at any point in the future, prove the transaction was hers.

5.2 Satisfying the Requirements

Secrecy ensures that only members of $\mathbf{P}$ can decode e to learn x. *Security* is therefore maintained because an individual is authenticated only when she can prove knowledge of x. By requiring that *Bob* be a member of $\mathbf{P}$ we prevent *Bob* from staging a man in the middle attack in which he uses *Alice* to decode a verifiably common secret encoding that he would not otherwise be able to decode.

Commonality guarantees that any member of $\mathbf{P}$ can decode e and will learn the same value x that any other member would learn by decoding e. If *Alice* is certain that e exhibits *commonality*, it follows that by using x to authenticate her membership, she reveals nothing more than that she is a member of $\mathbf{P}$.

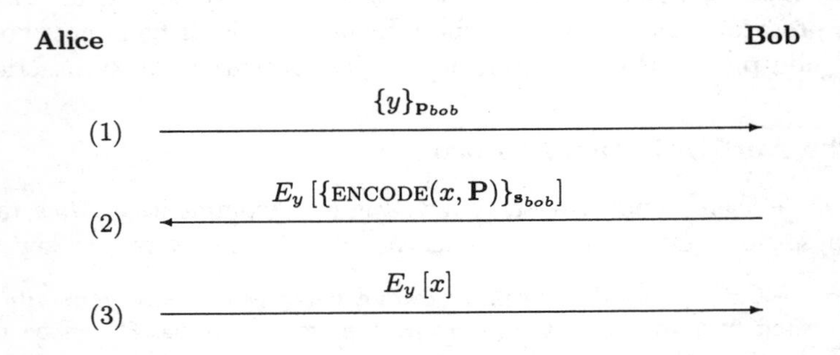

Fig. 1. An Elementary Anonymous Authentication Transaction

Verifiability is required so that *Alice* may prove for herself that the encoding e exhibits *commonality*, even though she did not create this encoding. Thus, by sending message (3) only when VERIFY() returns true, *Alice* ensures that her authentication will be both anonymous and unlinkable. If *Bob* should be malicious and attempt to construct e in a way that would allow him to discover *Alice's* identity from her decoding of e, verification will fail. *Alice* will halt the transaction before she decodes e. Since message (2) must be signed by *Bob*, *Alice* can use the signed invalid encoding as proof of *Bob's* failure to follow the protocol.

The authentication transaction appears the same regardless of which member of $\mathbf{P}$ was authenticated. As a result, even an otherwise omniscient adversary cannot learn which member of $\mathbf{P}$ was authenticated by inspecting the transaction. Thus, even if *Alice's* key is compromised before authentication, the transaction remains anonymous and unlinkable. We call this property *perfect forward anonymity.*

6 Key Replacement

In the protocol above, *Alice* uses a single key pair $(\mathbf{p}, \mathbf{s})$ to represent both her identity and her membership in the group. Because she uses the same key pair for both functions, an adversary who compromises her secret key $\mathbf{s}$ can not only authenticate himself as a member of $\mathbf{P}$, but can also pose as *Alice* in any other protocol that uses $\mathbf{s}$. Ideally, compromising the key used in the authentication process should not compromise *Alice's* identity. By using two key pairs, one to represent her identity and one for authentication, *Alice* significantly reduces the potential for damage should she lose her authentication key. Using two key pairs for the two separate functions also enables *Alice* to replace a lost authentication key.

We continue to use the pair $(\mathbf{p}, \mathbf{s})$ to identify an individual. Each member of $\mathbf{P}$ now generates an authentication key pair $(\mathbf{p}', \mathbf{s}')$ for each group in which she is a member. Because of the severe consequences of losing $\mathbf{s}$, we assume that $\mathbf{s}$ is kept well guarded. Because only $\mathbf{s}'$ will be needed during the authentication transaction, we only consider the case where an authentication key $\mathbf{s}'$, not an identity key $\mathbf{s}$, is lost or compromised. When $\mathbf{s}'$ is lost or compromised, the individual can disable the key and obtain a replacement by conferring only with the authenticator.

In order to validate her public authentication key $\mathbf{p}'$, each member uses her secret identity key $\mathbf{s}$ to sign a certificate $c = \{\mathbf{p}'\}_{\mathbf{s}}$. This certificate can be opened to reveal the public authentication key as follows: $\{c\}_{\mathbf{p}} = \{\{\mathbf{p}'\}_{\mathbf{s}}\}_{\mathbf{p}} = \mathbf{p}'$.

To initialize the system, all members of $\mathbf{P}$ send their certificates to *Bob*. *Bob* collects all the certificates to form the set $\mathbf{C}$. The set of public authentication keys, $\mathbf{P}'$, can then be generated by opening each certificate in $\mathbf{C}$: $\mathbf{P}' = \{\{c_i\}_{\mathbf{p}_i} : c_i \in \mathbf{C}\}$.

6.1 Modifications to the Authentication Protocol

The only modification to the authentication protocol is to require *Bob* to add the set of certificates **C** to message (2). The augmented message will be labeled (2a):

Alice **Bob**

$$\text{(2a)} \quad \xleftarrow{E_y\,[\{\mathbf{C}, \text{ENCODE}(x, \mathbf{P}')\}_{\mathbf{s}_{bob}}]}$$

¿From the set of certificates **C** and public identity keys **P**, *Alice* computes **P′** using the technique shown above. She then verifies e using $\text{VERIFY}(e, \mathbf{s}'_{alice}, \mathbf{P}')$. If the encoding exhibits *commonality*, *Alice* learns x from $\text{DECODE}(e, \mathbf{s}'_{alice}, \mathbf{P}')$.

6.2 The Key Replacement Transaction

If *Alice* believes her secret authentication key has been compromised, she simply generates a new authentication key pair, creates a certificate for the new public authentication key, and sends that certificate to *Bob*. *Bob* returns a signed receipt to *Alice* acknowledging the new certificate. Since we assume that *Bob* acts to maintain security, we expect him to use *Alice's* new certificate and authentication key.[2]

7 Dynamic Group Membership

We now describe how a trusted third party, *Trent*, may be given sole responsibility for maintaining the set of certificates **C**. To this end, *Alice* requires that any **C** used by *Bob* be signed by *Trent*. During the authentication transaction, message (2a) is replaced by message (2b):

Alice **Bob**

$$\text{(2b)} \quad \xleftarrow{E_y\,[\{\{\mathbf{C}\}_{\mathbf{s}_{trent}}, \text{ENCODE}(x, \mathbf{P}')\}_{\mathbf{s}_{bob}}]}$$

If *Alice* is to be granted membership in **P**, she generates an authentication key pair, creates the certificate c_{alice}, and sends it to *Trent* who updates **C** and distributes a signed copy to *Bob*. To remove *Alice* from **P**, and thereby prevent her from being authenticated, *Trent* simply removes *Alice's* certificate c_{alice} from **C** and dist ributes a signed copy to *Bob*. In both cases, *Bob* and other members of **P** can compute the new **P′** using **P** and the new set of certificates **C**.

[2] Even if *Bob* fails to use the new certificate, *Alice* can either proceed using her old key (in the case that it was compromised and not lost) or can use the signed message (2a) as proof of *Bob's* failure to use the new certificate.

8 Constructing Verifiably Common Secret Encodings

We use public-key cryptography to construct verifiably common secret encodings that we call VCS vectors. Assuming that M_i represents the set of messages that can be encrypted by a public key $\mathbf{p}_i \in \mathbf{P}$, the set of messages that can be encoded as a VCS vector for group $\mathbf{P}$ is $\mathbf{M} = \bigcap M_i$.

A *VCS vector* encodes a value x as follows:

$$\boldsymbol{e} \leftarrow [\{x\}_{\mathbf{p}_1}, \{x\}_{\mathbf{p}_2}, \cdots, \{x\}_{\mathbf{p}_n}] \text{ where } n = |\mathbf{P}|$$

Encoding, decoding, and verifying VCS vectors can be performed by the following three functions:

$$\text{ENCODE}(x, \mathbf{P}): \qquad \boldsymbol{e} \leftarrow \begin{cases} [\{x\}_{\mathbf{p}_1}, \{x\}_{\mathbf{p}_2}, \cdots, \{x\}_{\mathbf{p}_n}] & x \in \mathbf{M} \\ [] & x \notin \mathbf{M} \end{cases}$$

$$\text{DECODE}(\boldsymbol{e}, \mathbf{s}_i, \mathbf{P}): \qquad x \leftarrow \{\boldsymbol{e}[i]\}_{\mathbf{s}_i}$$

$$\text{VERIFY}(\boldsymbol{e}, \mathbf{s}_i, \mathbf{P}): \qquad \textit{isCommon} \leftarrow \boldsymbol{e} = \text{ENCODE}(\text{DECODE}(\boldsymbol{e}, \mathbf{s}_i, \mathbf{P}), \mathbf{P})$$

When using VCS vectors, *secrecy* holds only if x is not revealed when encrypted multiple times with different public keys. This is not true of RSA with small exponents or Rabin [13,14,8]. For this reason, caution must be exercised when selecting a public-key encryption technique.

Commonality holds because any secret key corresponding to a key in $\mathbf{P}$ can be used to decode $\boldsymbol{e}$ to learn x. Decrypting $\boldsymbol{e}[i]$ with $\mathbf{s}_i$ yields the same secret x for all i.

Any member of $\mathbf{P}$ can use DECODE() to learn x from $\boldsymbol{e}$ and then re-encode x using ENCODE() to obtain a valid encoding of x. Because ENCODE() generates a valid encoding, *commonality* will hold for this re-encoded vector. If the re-encoded vector equals the original vector $\boldsymbol{e}$, then $\boldsymbol{e}$ must also satisfy *commonality*. Hence, as long as ENCODE() is deterministic,[3] we can verify the commonality of any encoding $\boldsymbol{e}$. Consequently, *verifiability* is satisfied.

That the VERIFY() operation can be expressed as a simple composition of the ENCODE() and DECODE() operations is a general statement, independent of how we construct our verifiably common secret encodings. For this reason, if we can construct ENCODE() and DECODE() operations for which *commonality* holds, *verifiability* becomes automatic. Thus, we can replace our implementation-specific definition of VERIFY() with a general definition:

$$\text{VERIFY}(e, \mathbf{s}, \mathbf{P}): \qquad \textit{isCommon} \leftarrow e = \text{ENCODE}(\text{DECODE}(e, \mathbf{s}, \mathbf{P}), \mathbf{P})$$

[3] Probabilistic encryption [12,2] may still be used under the random oracle model. We simply make the ENCODE() function deterministic by using its first input parameter, the secret x, to seed the pseudo-random number generator with $\mathcal{O}(x)$.

9 Making Anonymous Authentication Scalable

The number of entries in a VCS vector grows linearly with the number of members of **P**, as does the time required to generate, transmit, and verify the entries. This growth could make anonymous authentication impractical for very large dynamic groups.

We can address this issue by authenticating using subsets of **P**. Individuals will now remain anonymous and unlinkable only among the members of their subset rather than among all members of **P**. Because membership in a subset of **P** implies membership in **P**, *security* is not affected. We propose two ways of assigning subsets: random generation of single-use subsets during each authentication transaction and the use of a static assignment algorithm.

9.1 Single-Use Subsets

During each authentication transaction, *Alice* selects a subset of **P** at random. To ensure her membership, *Alice* augments the subset to include herself. She sends this subset to *Bob* when requesting authentication. *Alice* and *Bob* then use this subset in place of **P** for the remainder of the protocol.

Alice picks her subset of **P** at the time she initiates the authentication transaction. If she has limited long-term storage, she can select the subset by picking keys in **P** by their indices. She then requests keys in **P** from *Bob* by index at the start of the authentication transaction. To prevent *Bob* from sending fraudulent identity keys, *Alice* maintains a hash tree of the keys or their fingerprints.

Alice must be cautious when using single-use subsets. If external circumstances link two or more transactions, *Alice* is anonymous only among the intersection of the subsets used for authentication.

9.2 Statically Assigned Subsets

Subsets may also be assigned by a static algorithm such that each member of **P** is always assigned to the same subset $\mathbf{P}_i \subseteq \mathbf{P}$ where $\bigcup \mathbf{P}_i = \mathbf{P}$. These subsets may change only when members are added or removed from **P**. As above, *Alice* uses $\mathbf{P}_i$ wherever she previously would have used **P**.

Even if *Trent* picks the subsets, he may do so in a way that unwittingly weakens anonymity or unlinkability. Using a one-way hash function, preferably generated randomly before the membership is known, ensures that no party can manipulate the assignment of individuals to subsets.

10 Related Work

Chaum assumes that institutions collect information about individuals who use those institutions' systems [5]. He therefore proposes that individuals use different pseudonyms when conducting transactions with different institutions to prevent those institutions from sharing information and linking user profiles together. This fails to protect those whose right to use a system comes from a pre-existing relationship in which their identity is already known. Moreover, Chaum's approach does not provide unlinkability, leaving open the possibility an individual might reveal her identity through behaviors that can be profiled.

Group signatures schemes [3,7] give an individual the ability to anonymously sign messages on behalf of a group. Kilian and Petrank [15] exploit these signatures to create a scheme for identity escrow. Identity escrow provides anonymous authentication, though an individual's anonymity can be revoked by a trusted third party. While individuals may be added to the signature groups, no provision is made for removing members from these groups. Thus, group signatures in their current form are not a sufficient primitive for anonymously authenticating membership in dynamic groups.

Anonymous identification was first addressed as an application of witness hiding in zero knowledge proof systems [11,9]. The most efficient such scheme, recently presented by De Santis *et al.* [10] in their paper on anonymous group identification, relies on the assumption that factoring Blum integers is hard. While the extension of the protocol into a full system that supports key replacement and dynamic groups is not explicitely addressed by the authors, such an extension is trivial.

For a group of n individuals and an m bit Blum integer, an instance of the De Santis *et al.* proof requires communication complexity $(2m + n)$, and rejects a non-member with probability $\frac{1}{2}$. Thus, to authenticate an individual's membership with certainty $1 - \left(\frac{1}{2}\right)^d$, $(2m + n) \cdot d$ bits of communication are required. This would appear to approach a lower bound for such a zero knowledge proof system.

When implementing our current protocol using VCS vectors with k bit encryptions, identification requires $n \cdot m$ bits of communication. The security of the protocol relies on the existence of a public-key function that may securely encode the same plaintext in multiple messages with distinct keys. If the group size n exceeds $\frac{2md}{m-d}$, then the proof system of De Santis *et al.* requires less communication.

It is not clear that VCS vectors approach the lower bound for the size of a verifiably common secret encoding. A better encoding would require a change in cryptographic assumptions, but would have the potential of improving the efficiency of anonymous authentication protocols beyond that which is possible using zero knowledge proof systems.

Syverson *et al.* [18] introduce a protocol for unlinkable serial transactions using Chaum's notion of blinding [6]. The protocol is designed for commercial pay-per-use services and relies upon the possibility that any particular service request may be forcibly audited. An audit requires the individual to reveal her identity or risk losing future service. After passing an audit, the individual must make another request before receiving the service originally requested. If requests are infrequent, she may have to wait a significant amount of time before making the second request lest the two requests become linked. This system does not provide adequate anonymity if the timing of any request indicates its nature, as audits can be made at any time. The system also cannot guarantee that a revoked individual does not receive service, as that individual may still make a request that is not audited.

11 Conclusion

Anonymous authentication is an essential ingredient in a new domain of services in the field of electronic commerce and communication. Real world systems require dynamic group membership and key replacement.

In this paper we have shown how verifiably common secret encodings may be used to anonymously authenticate membership in dynamic groups. We have also shown how to replace keys in these authentication systems. We presented VCS vectors as an example of how verifiably common secret encodings can be constructed. Because the size of of our construct grows linearly with the size of the group $\mathbf{P}$, we described how to authenticate membership using subsets of $\mathbf{P}$.

12 Acknowledgements

We would first like to thank Matt Franklin and the anonymous reviewers who provided invaluable suggestions and references. We are also indebted to Michael Bender, Yanzong Ding, Nailah Robinson, Jenn Vinson, and especially David Savitt for feedback on earlier drafts of this paper. Michael D. Smith also helped review drafts of both the paper and conference presentation. Michael Rabin's lively discussions served as excellent sanity checks. Classes and discussions with Ron Rivest, Silvio Micali, and David Gifford provided inspiration for our work.

References

1. Anonymizer, Inc., *http://www.anonymizer.com.*
2. M. Blum and S. Goldwasser, "An Efficient Probabilistic Public-Key Encryption Scheme which Hides All Partial Information," *Advances of Cryptology — CRYPTO '84 Proceedings*, Springer-Verlag, pp. 289–299.
3. J. Camenisch and M. Stadler, "Efficient Group Signature Schemes for Large Groups," *Advances in Cryptology — CRYPTO '97 Proceedings*, Springer-Verlag, v. 1294, pp. 410-424
4. D. Chaum, "Untraceable Electronic Mail, Return Addresses, and Digital Pseudonyms," *Communications of the ACM*, v. 24, n. 2, Feb 1981, pp. 84–88.
5. D. Chaum, "Security without Identification: Card Computers to make Big Brother Obsolete," *Communications of the ACM*, v. 28, n. 10, Oct 1985, pp. 1030–1044.
6. D. Chaum, A. Fiat, and M. Naor, "Untraceable Electronic Cash," *Advances in Cryptology — CRYPTO '88 Proceedings*, Springer-Verlag, pp. 319–327.
7. D. Chaum and E. van Heyst, "Group signatures," *Advances in Cryptology — EUROCRYPT '91 Proceedings*, Springer-Verlag, pp. 257-265.
8. D. Coppersmith, "Small Solutions to Polynomial Equations, and Low Exponent RSA Vulnerabilities," *Journal of Cryptography*, v. 10 n. 4, Autumn 1997, pp. 233-260.

9. R. Cramer, I. Damgard, B. Schoenmakers, "Proofs of partial knowledge and simplified design of witness hiding protocols," *Advances in Cryptology — CRYPTO '94 Proceedings*, pp. 174–187.
10. A. De Santis, G. Di Crescenzo, G. Persiano, "Communication-efficient anonymous group identification," *5th ACM Conference on Computer and Communications Security*, November 1998, pp. 73–82.
11. A. De Santis, G. Di Crescenzo, G. Persiano, M. Yung, "On monotone formula closure of SZK," *FOCS '94*.
12. S. Goldwasser and S. Micali, "Probabilistic Encryption," *Journal of Computer and Systems Sciences*, v. 28 n. 2, Apr 1984, pp. 270–299.
13. J. Hastad and A. Shamir, "On Using RSA with Low Exponent in a Public Key Network," *Advances in Cryptology — CRYPTO '85 Proceedings*, Springer-Verlag, pp. 403–408.
14. J. Hastad, "Solving Simultaneous Modular Equations of Low Degree," *SIAM Journal on Computing,* v. 17 no. 2, Apr 1988, pp. 336–341.
15. J. Kilian and E. Petrank, "Identity Escrow," *Advances in Cryptology — CRYPTO '98 Proceedings*, Springer-Verlag, pp. 167–185.
16. M. Reed, P. Syverson, and D. Goldschlag, "Anonymous Connections and Onion Routing," *IEEE Journal on Selected Areas in Communication Special Issue on Copyright and Privacy Protection*, 1998.
17. M. Reiter and A. Rubin, "Crowds: Anonymity for Web Transactions" *DIMACS Technical Report 97-15*, Apr 1997.
18. P. Syverson, S. Stubblebine, and D. Goldschlag. "Unlinkable Serial Transactions," *Financial Cryptography '97*, Feb 1997.
19. The Wall Street Journal Online, *http://www.wsj.com.*

A Obtaining Proof of Authentication

Alice may obtain a receipt from *Bob* proving that she was authenticated at time t. To obtain such a receipt, *Alice* chooses a random z and uses a one-way hash function h to generate $Q \leftarrow h(\{z\}_{\mathbf{s}_{alice}})$ and $R \leftarrow h(z)$. *Alice* includes Q and R in message (3a):

Alice **Bob**

(3a) $\xrightarrow{E_y[x, Q, R]}$

Bob can issue a receipt when he authenticates *Alice*. The receipt he sends is:

$$\{\text{"}Q \text{ and } R \text{ reveal whom I authenticated at time } t\text{"}\}_{\mathbf{s}_{bob}}$$

If she chooses, *Alice* can at any later time prove she was authenticated by *Bob* by revealing the receipt and the value $\{z\}_{\mathbf{s}_{alice}}$. Anyone can verify the receipt by checking that $Q = h(\{z\}_{\mathbf{s}_{alice}})$ and $R = h(\{\{z\}_{\mathbf{s}_{alice}}\}_{\mathbf{p}_{alice}})$.

Some Open Issues and New Directions in Group Signatures

Giuseppe Ateniese and Gene Tsudik

USC Information Sciences Institute,
4676 Admiralty Way, Marina Del Rey, CA 90292, USA

Abstract. Group signatures allow any member of a potentially large group to sign on behalf of the group. Group signatures are anonymous and unlinkable for everyone with the exception of a designated group manager who can co-relate signatures and reveal the identity of the actual signer. At the same time, no one (including a group manager) can misattribute a valid group signature. Group signatures are claimed to have many practical applications in e-commerce as well as in military and legal fields.
Despite some interesting and eclectic results, group signatures remain confined to academic literature. The focus of this paper is two-fold. First, it discusses certain issues that stand in the way of practical applications of group signatures and uses the example of on recent group signature scheme to illustrate certain problems. Second, this paper (informally) introduces some practical security services that can be constructed using any group signature scheme. Sample realizations of these services are provided.

Keywords: Public-key Cryptography, Digital Signatures, Group Signatures, Multi-Group Signatures, Sub-Group Signatures, Coalition Attacks, Revocation.

1 Introduction

Digital signatures are rapidly becoming ubiquitous in many aspects of *electronic* life. They are used to obtain security services such as authentication, data integrity and non-repudiation. **Group** digital signatures are a relatively new concept introduced by Chaum and Van Heyst in 1991 [6]. A group signature – similar to its traditional counterpart – allows a signer to demonstrate knowledge of a secret with respect to a specific document. It is also publicly verifiable: anyone in possession of a group public key can validate a group signature. However, group signatures are anonymous in that, no one, with the sole exception of a designated group manager, can discover the identity of the signer. Furthermore, group signatures are unlinkable which makes it computationally hard to establish whether or not multiple signatures are produced by the same group member. In exceptional cases (such as a legal dispute) any group signature can be "opened" by the group manager to reveal unambiguously the identity of the actual signer.

M. Franklin (Ed.): FC'99, LNCS 1648, pp. 196–211, 1999.

At the same time, no one (including the group manager) can misattribute a valid group signature.

The salient features of group signatures make them attractive for many specialized applications such as voting and bidding. More generally, group signatures can be used to conceal organizational structures, e.g,, when a company or a government agency issues a signed statement. They can also be integrated with electronic currency mechanisms (as blind group signatures) [8] to provide both anonymity and untraceability of currency issuers.

Despite appealing features and interesting research papers, group signatures remain in the domain of theoretical results. To this end, the purpose of this paper is twofold. First, we briefly review the state of the field and try to examine certain issues that hinder wider acceptance and use of group signatures. Second, we discuss and demonstrate some practical services that can be built on top of group signature schemes.

The paper is organized as follows. Next two sections summarize basic properties and features of group signatures and provide a brief overview of previous work. Then, Section 4 discusses some open issues and, to illustrate the point, Section 6 presents a weakness in a recently proposed scheme. Sections 7-9 introduce two new services built upon secure group signatures and sketch out example schemes.

2 Preliminaries

We begin with a definition of group signatures.

Definition 1. *A* `group signature scheme` *is a digital signature scheme comprised of the following procedures:*

- `SETUP` *an algorithm for generating the initial group public key* $\mathcal{Y}$ *and a group secret key* $\mathcal{S}$*.*
- `JOIN` *a protocol between the group manager and a user that results in the user becoming a new group member.*
- `SIGN` *a protocol between a group member and a user whereby a group signature on a user-supplied message is computed by the group member.*
- `VERIFY` *an algorithm for establishing the validity of a group signature given a group public key and a signed message.*
- `OPEN` *an algorithm that, given a signed message and a group secret key, determines the identity of the signer.*

A group signature scheme must satisfy the following **security properties**:

- **Unforgeability.** Only group members are able to sign messages on behalf of the group.
- **Anonymity.** Given a signature, identifying the actual signer is computationally hard for everyone but the group manager.
- **Unlinkability.** Deciding whether two different signatures were computed by the same group member is computationally hard.

- **Exculpability.** Neither a group member nor the group manager can sign on behalf of other group members.[1]
- **Traceability.** The group manager is able to open a signature and identify the actual signer; moreover, a signer cannot prevent the opening of a valid signature.
- **Coalition-Resistance.** A colluding subset of group members cannot generate valid group signatures that cannot be traced.

The **efficiency** of a group signature scheme is typically based on the following parameters:

- The size of the group public key $\mathcal{Y}$.
- The size of a group signature.
- The efficiency of `SIGN` and `VERIFY`.
- The efficiency of `SETUP`, `OPEN` and `JOIN`.

3 Previous Work

The concept of group signatures was introduced and realized by Chaum and Van Heist in 1991 [6]. They proposed four schemes of which three provide computational anonymity whereas the fourth provides information-theoretic anonymity. Some of schemes do not allow a group manager to add group members after the initial setup. Others require the group manager to contact each member in order to open a signature, i.e., to reveal the identity of the signer.

A number of improvements and enhancements followed the initial work. Some notable results are due to Chen/Pedersen [7], Camenisch [3], Petersen [9] and Camenisch/Stadler [4]. In [7], two schemes were proposed providing information theoretic and computational anonymity, respectively. Unfortunately, the proposed scheme allows the group manager to misattribute a signature, i.e., falsely accuse a group member of having signed a message.

In [3] an efficient group signature scheme was presented, providing computational anonymity, ability to add (or remove) group members after the initial setup, and the possibility of being generalized by allowing authorized set of group members to sign collectively (appearing to verifiers as a single signer) on behalf of the group. This scheme can be extended to allow the functionality of the group manager to be shared among several entities. The drawbacks include the size of the public key and the signature size (both proportional to group size).

As also noted in [4], most previous results exhibit some or all of the following shortcomings:

1. The size of the group public key depends on the size of the group.
2. The length of a group signature depends on the size of the group.

[1] Note that the above does not preclude the group manager from creating fraudulent signers (i.e., nonexistent group members) and then producing group signatures.

3. New member addition requires restarting the entire system or involves re-issuing all members' keys and changing the group public key.
4. Exclusion/revocation of group members requires re-issuing all members' keys and changing the group public key.

The state-of-the-art in the field is exemplified by the recent result of Camenisch and Stadler [4]. It addresses the first three of the above issues; albeit, at significant cost. The basic scheme (referred hereafter as CS97), while quite elegant, involves costly computation and reliance on new problems conjectured to be computationally difficult to solve. (One such problem is the difficulty of computing double discrete logarithms in finite groups. Another – the difficulty of computing roots of discrete logarithms.) Nonetheless, CS97 is, in principle, simple and appealing in that the group public key and the group signature are both of constant size. The computational complexity of SIGN and VERIFY are also independent of group size.

4 What Stands in the Way?

Schemes such as CS97 make group signatures more attractive and bring the entire concept closer to practice. While there is still no single *killer app*, a number of applications can be envisaged for group signatures. Examples include:

- Government, military and commercial press releases
- Email messages in anonymous support groups
- Electronic cash (with banks forming a cash-issuing group)
- Issuance of stock, bond and other financial reports
- Voting applications
- Document signing by certified (but anonymous) professionals, e.g., lawyers, notaries public, auditors, etc.

There remain, however, some bothersome issues that stand in the way of real-world applications and deployments of group signatures. In this paper we concentrate on two that we believe to be the most important:

- Security against coalitions
- Member deletion (revocation) complexity

The first problem is straight-forward. If a scheme is vulnerable to coalition attacks, its utility is limited to environments where member collusion is not a threat. Although such environments might exist[2], in general, coalition resistance must be **provable**. This is, unfortunately, not achieved by any existing scheme. In order to better illustrate this point, in Section 6 we present a coalition-related weakness in a recently proposed group signature scheme.

The second problem is more subtle. It is related to the notoriously difficult task of credential revocation in regular (non-group) public key signature schemes. However, as discussed below, revocation in the context of group signatures is a more complicated problem.

[2] For instance, electronic lotteries.

5 Member Deletion

One intuitive and seemingly effective way to delete group members is via Certificate Revocation Lists (CRLs). A group manager periodically issues a new CRL wherein each entry identifies a group member (or a specific group certificate) whose membership has been revoked. There are many ways to generate and distribute CRLs. Unfortunately, the CRL approach is unsuitable for group signatures for the following reasons:

- Since group signatures are anonymous and unlinkable, how can the group manager "identify" a deleted member?
- If the group manager reveals certain (hereto secret) values corresponding to a deleted member, can the anonymity and unlinkability of **past signatures** of the said member be preserved?

The last item is probably the most important issue in member deletion. The preservation of security of past signatures after deletion is reminiscent of Perfect Forward Secrecy (PFS), a property often sought in key distribution protocols. If a member leaves the group voluntarily or a member is excluded for some administrative reason (such as a job promotion) there is nothing to gain (and much to loose) in sacrificing the security of past signatures.

However, in some cases, PFS is not desirable. For instance, suppose that a malicious member of a stock brokerage firm has been detected. It is surely beneficial – in the process of deletion – to inform all potential verifiers (clients) who might hold old signatures by the crooked broker.

A more interesting scenario is the compromise of a member's secrets. Suppose that a member's group certificate and/or group private key are inadvertently divulged. The group manager faces a real problem: to reveal this member's secrets means that all of its past signatures can be linked! Since there is no reason to doubt the validity of past signatures (the deleted member was not malicious) sacrificing unlinkability is clearly undesirable.

Another member deletion tactic is to change the group public key. After generating the new group public key, the group manager simply issues a new set of membership certificates to all remaining members while the rest are automatically excluded. This is an acceptable solution for small and stable groups. In large groups (e.g., lawyers in the state of California) this approach is unworkable due to frequent membership changes (e.g., lawyers being disbar-ed), the computational expense of re-issuing membership certificates and change notifications for all remaining members. Also, we assumed thus far that a member's new certificate can be issued unilaterally (off-line) by the group manager. However, some schemes may require interaction as part of repeated certificate issuance. (Initial certificate issuance always requires interaction). This complicates member deletion even further.

In summary, we have only *scratched the surface* of the member deletion problem. Since it appears that no proposed group signature scheme adequately addresses it, efficient and secure member deletion remains a pressing and interesting open problem.

6 Coalition Resistance: Quasi-Attacks on CS97

Many ground-breaking cryptographic protocols are based on new number theoretic assumptions. There are two ways to invalidate these assumptions. One is by proving that they are false, the other – by proving that they are unsuitable for a specific protocol. The latter is the case with one of the assumptions underlying the Camenisch and Stadler's CS97 group signature scheme [4]. We briefly present some attacks on CS97 and then propose some simple ways of preventing them.

Remark 1. The following text describes two attack scenarios. It is necessary to stress that these are not all-out attacks that really *break* the scheme. Instead, we refer to them as *quasi-attacks* (for lack of better term) that exploit or break only one specific assumption.

A *coalition* attack occurs when a subset of group members pool together their secrets and generate perfectly valid group signatures. Such signatures have the property that even the group manager is unable to open them. The coalition resistance of Camenisch-Stadler protocol [4] is based on the following number-theoretic assumption:

> Let n and e be RSA-like parameters and $a \in \mathbb{Z}_n^*$ an element of large multiplicative order both the factors of n such that computing the discrete logarithms to the base a is infeasible. It is hard to compute a pair (x, v) of integers such that
>
> $$v^e \equiv 1 + a^x \bmod n$$
>
> holds, if factorization of n is unknown. Furthermore, this is true even when other pairs (x', v'), satisfying the above equation, are known.

Loosely speaking, given one or more group certificate of the form $(a^x + 1)^d$, where $d \cdot e \equiv 1 \bmod \phi(n)$, it should be hard to generate a new valid group certificate without the aid of the group manager.

However, consider the following special cases. Let $(a^x + 1)^d$ be a valid group certificate. It can be re-written as $(a^x + 1)^d = a^{xd}(1 + a^{-x})^d$. Now, suppose that $x = ke$ for some integer k, so that $a^{xd}(1 + a^{-x})^d = a^k(1 + a^{-x})^d$. Obviously, multiplying it by the inverse of a^k mod n we get the new certificate $(1 + a^{-x})^d$. This attack allows a *single* group member to produce a valid and untraceable signature.

This attack can be trivially prevented, for example, by requiring the group member to prove that x is relatively prime with e (i.e. gcd(x,e)=1) without revealing x itself. However, as we now demonstrate, it is possible to generate a valid group certificate even when x is a generic value, e.g., if gcd(x,e)=1.

1. The first member registers and obtains a certificate $A=(a^x + 1)^d = a^{xd}(1 + a^{-x})^d$.
2. The second member then registers a^{-x} and obtains $B = (a^{-x} + 1)^d$ as its certificate.
3. They compute the inverse of B modulo n (using Euler's algorithm) and multiply it by A. The end-result is that two colluding members obtain the value $a^{xd} = A \cdot B^{-1} = a^{xd}(1 + a^{-x})^d \cdot (1 + a^{-x})^{-d} \bmod n$.

   Remark 2. Possession of this value is dangerous: colluding members can take different strategies to generate a new group certificate. For instance, the value a^{xd} can be exponentiated with a random c, obtaining a^{cxd} and its inverse $a^{-cxd} \bmod n$.

4. Then, a third group member registers a^{cx} and obtains $(a^{cx} + 1)^d$ as its certificate. Multiplying $(a^{cx} + 1)^d$ by a^{-cxd} yields a new and untraceable certificate $(a^{-cx} + 1)^d$ (in fact, $(a^{cx} + 1)^d \cdot a^{-cxd} = (a^{cx-cx} + a^{-cx})^d$). It is also possible to generalize this strategy.

A simple way to prevent this kind of attack is to substitute 1 in the certificate structure $(a^x + 1)^d$ with a random value t resulting in $(a^x + t)^d$ as the new certificate form.[3] The scheme must be modified slightly in order to work with this new certificate form but the extra cost is a single exponentiation. Another simple fix, not mutually exclusive with the above, is to randomize (or "salt") the new member's membership key (and certificate) as part of JOIN.

However, we cannot prove that the proposed fixes result in a secure form of membership certificates, i.e., that coalition attacks are, in fact, infeasible. We only showed that 1, as a redundancy factor, is a wrong choice for the CS97 scheme. However, we would like to propose a new challenge with this new certificate's form, i.e. $(a^x + t)^d$ where t is a random value and x is the group member's secret exponent randomized by the group manager. In the rest of the paper we will make use of this modified CS97 scheme.

7 Multi-group Signatures

Thus far, we discussed some outstanding issues that block wider acceptance and use of group signatures. Lest the overall theme of this paper appear downbeat, we now switch gears and turn to "new and exciting" uses and extensions of group signatures.

One novel and practical service that can be built using group signatures as a primitive is **multi-group signatures**. (Not to be confused with so-called multi-signatures [1].)

Informally, we define a multi-group signature (MGS) as a set of regular group signatures generated by the same entity (signer) who is a member of multiple groups. For example, a user belonging to two groups A and B may have a reason

[3] This has been also suggested by J. Camenisch (via private communication).

to sign something as a member of both groups. The need for such signatures may arise in real-life situations as illustrated in the following (admittedly somewhat contrived) examples:

1. A financial (e.g., loan) contract may need to be signed by an authorized loan officer of a bank and by a notary public. If the same person is a member of both groups (loan officers and notaries public) s/he can sign the document with a multi-group signature.
2. A republican senator (anonymously) releasing a statement to the media needs to assure the public that s/he is, in fact, a member of the senate and a republican party member. This can be achieved with a double-group signature.
3. An expert witness testifying in court (or in congress) who is afraid of retribution may need, nonetheless, to convince the public that s/he is, say, a medical doctor and an officer (of a certain rank) in the armed forces. Once again, a double-group signature is appropriate.
4. A person submitting a formal peer complaint to a state judicial review panel might have to sign the complaint text simultaneously as a: i) US citizen, ii) resident of that state and, iii) member of the bar. This requires a triple-group signature.

An interesting property required of MGS is the ability to **link** the individual group signatures comprising an MGS. In other words, it must be evident that the same signer produced each single-group signature which is part of an MGS.

At first, this might seem both counter-intuitive and counter-productive. Recall that one of the basic tenets of group signatures is **unlinkability**, i.e., the computational difficulty of establishing whether two distinct group signatures were produced by the same group member. However, we observe that the property we seek is **linkability** of group signatures **across different groups** rather than linkability of different signatures within a group. Thus, the desired property is not inherently in conflict with traditional group signatures.

We note that, in all other respects, an MGS scheme must have the same properties as a regular group signature scheme.

Now, whether an MGS scheme can be built out of existing group signature schemes is an entirely separate issue. We have considered several group signature schemes from the literature. Some are not easily converted, e.g., [3]. However, at least one scheme, CS97 [4], can be used as building block for a secure MGS scheme.

8 MGS Example

We begin with a short overview of the CS97 basic scheme, modified as shown in section 6.

The scheme is premised on two important building blocks: proofs (signatures) of knowledge of double discrete logarithms (SKLOGLOG) and signatures of knowledge of roots of discrete logarithms (SKROOTLOG). SKLOGLOG entails, given d, demonstrating knowledge of $log_b(log_a\ d)$. SKROOTLOG entails, given c, and e demonstrating knowledge of $(log_a c)^{1/e}$ where $(e, d = 1/e)$ is an RSA key-pair.

As part of setup, *GRMGR* selects the following values:

- an RSA public-key parameter $n = pq$ for two large primes p, q and an RSA key-pair (e, d) $e \cdot d \equiv 1 \bmod n$.
- a cyclic group $G = < g >$ of order n where computing discrete logarithms is infeasible.
- an element $a \in \mathbb{Z}_n^*$ of large multiplicative order modulo both p and q.
- some other parameters not relevant to the ensuing discussion.

A prospective group member can join the group by selecting a random value x_1 randomized by *GRMGR* resulting in the secret x (known only by the group member), computing $y = a^x \bmod n$ and $z = g^y$. Upon sending y to *GRMGR* and proving knowledge of x, the member is issued a certificate: $(y + t)^d$.

A group signature over a message m is defined in CS97 as a tuple $< m, \bar{g}, \bar{z}, V_1, V_2 >$ where:

- m is the message to be signed
- $\bar{g} := g^r$ for $r \in_R \mathbb{Z}_n^*$
- $\bar{z} := \bar{g}^y$
- $V_1 :=$ SKLOGLOG$[x\ :\ \bar{z} = \bar{g}^{a^x}](m)$
- $V_2 :=$ SKROOTLOG$[v\ :\ \bar{z}\bar{g}^t = \bar{g}^{v^e}](m)$ for $v = (y + t)^d$

To verify a group signature, it is sufficient to check V_1 and V_2. We do not elaborate on other details/features of the scheme (such as the OPEN procedure) or its security properties as they are not germane to our discussion.

To further illustrate the MGS concept, we consider the specific case of double-group signatures; the technique can be trivially extended to n-group signatures. Suppose that the same group manager is used for both groups G_1 and G_2. (This is not an inherent requirement but it simplifies the example.) The setup procedure is almost the same as in CS97, i.e., *GRMGR* picks n, $G = < g >$, a and other parameters as above. These values are common for both groups. However, *GRMGR* selects different public key-pairs: (e_1, e_1^{-1}) and (e_2, e_2^{-1}) for G_1 and G_2, respectively.

The JOIN procedure is largely the same as in CS97 except that a member who joins both groups (and is interested in computing MGSs) must use the same secret value x in both registrations[4]: $y_1 = y_2 = a^x \bmod n$. The two respective membership certificates are: $v_1 = (y + t)^{e_1^{-1}}$ and $v_2 = (y + t)^{e_2^{-1}}$.

To produce an MGS (a double-group signature, in this case) a member of both groups constructs a tuple $< m, SIG_1, SIG_2, V_3 >$ where:

- m is the message being signed.
- $SIG_1 = < \bar{g_1}, \bar{z_1}, V_{1,1}, V_{2,1} >$ is a single-group signature of message m where:
- $SIG_2 = < \bar{g_2}, \bar{z_2}, V_{1,2}, V_{2,2} >$ is also a single-group signature of m where:

[4] There does not appear to be any security risk in doing this.

- $V_3 = \text{SKEQLOG}(\bar{z_1}, \bar{g_1}, \bar{z_2}, \bar{g_2})$ is a signature of knowledge of equality of two discrete logarithms (of $\bar{z_1}$ and $\bar{z_2}$) with two different bases $\bar{g_1}$ and $\bar{g_2}$. More generally, SKEQLOG denotes a non-interactive proof of $log_{\bar{g_1}} \bar{z_1} = log_{\bar{g_2}} \bar{z_2}$. One efficient technique for constructing SKEQLOG is due to Chaum and Pedersen [5][5].

As in CS97, $V_{1,1}$ and $V_{1,2}$ each demonstrate knowledge of the secret x, i.e., double-discrete logarithm of $\bar{z_1}$ and $\bar{z_2}$, respectively (which is x in both cases). $V_{2,1}$ and $V_{2,2}$ demonstrate knowledge of e_1-th (and e_2-th) roots of discrete logarithm of b_1 (and b_2), i.e., possession of membership certificates of groups G_1 and G_2. Finally, V_3 demonstrates equality of two discrete logarithms (z_1 and z_2) with two different bases (g_1 and g_2). The last step is crucial to "linking" the two signatures since it asserts that the same y is used in both signatures. Consequently, the same secret x is used in both signatures (since $y = a^x$.)

It appears that no reduction in security is incurred by using this MGS construct. (Assuming, of course, that the underlying CS97 basic scheme is itself secure.) In particular, the OPEN procedure remains the same and MGSs remain unlinkable much like their single-group counterparts.

A potential concern with the above extension is its relative inefficiency. since a generalized i-group MGS involves computing i regular single-group signatures and $(i - 1)$ SKEQLOG-s. However, most expensive constructs are SKROOT-LOGs and SKLOGLOGS required by CS97.

To conclude the MGS discussion, we need to point out that there is no compulsion to use the same group manager for MGS. In the CS97-based example above, the group public key is:

$$\mathcal{Y} = [n, < g >, a, e, \text{other parameters}]$$

If two groups are managed separately, the two managers can independently compute their respective group public and private keys. A member registers with the same secret x in both groups and obtains two corresponding certificates. However, the problem arises when the member tries to prove that s/he uses the same x in generating SIG_1 and SIG_2. Since each group has a distinct base a, the member has to prove **equality of two double discrete logarithms**.

9 Sub-group Signatures

Another interesting outgrowth of conventional group signatures is the notion of **sub-group signatures**. Informally, we define a sub-group signature (SGS) as a function of a member group $GR = \{M_1, ..., M_t\}$, a subset $S \subset GR$ and a message m as:

$$\mathcal{T} = \{SIG_j(m) | M_j \in S\} \quad \#\mathcal{T} = i$$

[5] More formally, a pair (c, s) satisfying $c = H(m||y_1||y_2||a||b||a^s y_1^c||b^s y_2^c)$ is a Schnorr signature of the discrete logarithm of both $y_1 = a^x$ w.r.t. the base a and $y_2 = b^x$ w.r.t. the base b, on the message m. Only the party in possession of the secret x is able to compute the signature, if $x = \log_a(y_1) = \log_b(y_2)$, by choosing a random t and then computing c and s as $c = H(m||y_1||y_2||a||b||a^t||b^t)$, $s = t - cx$ (in $\mathbb{Z}$).

Each $SIG_j(m)$ is a normal group signature by a group member M_j; for a given M_j, at most one SIG_j is in $\mathcal{T}$.

We should stress that the notion of SGS is very different from that of coalition group signatures as defined by Camenisch in [3]. Coalition group signatures are indistinguishable from single-member group signatures by verifiers. Only the group manager can (via OPEN) determine the coalition size and structure. In contrast, in SGS the size of the signing sub-group (or coalition) must be explicit and verifiable by anyone.

(As a sidenote, the scheme in [3] includes a method for obtaining coalition signatures; however, the coalition structures are fixed a priori by the group manager. This limits the utility of the whole concept.)

Consider the following example applications of SGS:

- A petition is circulated among members of a certain group. A number of members (i) sign the petition and then publicly announce that i members stand behind it. Any insider or outsider is able to verify that i distinct (and anonymous) members have indeed signed the petition.
- A military order must be signed by a least t ranked officers. Without exposing any internal command structure, t officers sign the order thus allowing anyone to verify its validity.
- A prospective club member must be vouched for by at least n existing members. These members must be distinct and, while n might be pre-set, there is no upper limit on the number of vouching members. The more members vouch, the faster the new member is admitted.
- A vote on a proposition is conducted by members of the board. Each member is given a single vote and vote tallies must be publicly verifiable.

It is also important to point out the differences between SGS and threshold schemes. Threshold schemes aim to partition a secret (e.g., a signature key) in a way that allows at least a pre-determined number (threshold) of shareholders to re-create a secret. In contrast, SGS does not involve a pre-determined threshold; any number of group members may sign a given message. The central goal of SGS is to demonstrate that a subset of a certain (unknown a priori) size has signed a given message.

In addition to the security properties of regular group signatures, a SGS scheme must feature:

- Compositional integrity: assure the verifier that all signatures comprising a SGS have been generated by distinct signers (group members).
- SGS unlinkability: multiple SGS-s generated by the same sub-group must be unlinkable. We note that this property does not necessarily follow from the unlinkability of the underlying group signature scheme (the latter only assures unlinkability of single-member signatures.)

SGS unlinkability is a natural property. Clearly, if single-member signatures are unlinkable, so should SGS-s. Compositional integrity, on the other hand, seems to contradict the unlinkability of regular group signatures. Recall that in

Section 2 we defined **unlinkability** (in the context of regular group signatures) as the difficulty of deciding whether two distinct signatures were generated by the same group member. Indeed, we may need to weaken the unlinkability property in order to achieve compositional integrity. However, we emphasize that this should be done **only** for SGS; i.e., the structure of other types of group signatures (regular, multi-group) must remain unchanged.

The feasibility of SGS schemes is illustrated by a concrete example in the next section. Once again, we use the CS97 [4] group signature scheme as our main building block.

10 SGS Example

The actual SGS extension is quite trivial. The SETUP, JOIN and OPEN procedures are the same as in CS97. Only SIGN and VERIFY are modified slightly.

The modified SIGN procedure involves a new initial stage whereby the i multiple signers (sub-group members) agree on a common random, one-time base:

$$\bar{g} := g^r \text{ for } r \in_R \mathbb{Z}_n^*$$

In CS97, r (and, hence, $\bar{g}$) is generated at random by one signer. In our case, r needs to be generated collectively by the sub-group of signers. There are many methods for doing this; one possibility is to run a group Diffie-Hellman key agreement protocol (e.g., [2] or [10]) and, as a result, generate a common:

$$\bar{g} := g^r \quad \text{where} \quad r = a^{r_1 \cdots r_i} (modn)$$

and i is the size of the sub-group and each r_j is generated at random by the j-th signer.

Having agreed on a one-time base $\bar{g}$, each signer (M_j) computes a regular CS97 group signature: $SIG_j(m) =< m, \bar{g}, \bar{z}, V_{1,j}, V_{2,j} >$. Pooled together, the signatures form an SGS, $\mathcal{T} = \{SIG_j | 0 < j \leq i\}$. Of course, redundant m and $\bar{g}$ fields can be eliminated from $\mathcal{T}$.

The VERIFY procedure is also modified in accordance to the parameter i, the size of the (claimed) sub-group. The same $\bar{g}$ must be used as a base in verifying every signature in $\mathcal{T}$. In addition, for each $SIG_j(m)$ the verifier must check the uniqueness of $\bar{z}$ contained therein. (An occurrence of a duplicate $\bar{z}$ within a $\mathcal{T}$ indicates a redundant signature by a given signer.)

As a more concrete example, consider a SGS with a sub-group of size two:

$$< m, \ \bar{g}, \ SIG_1, \ SIG_2 \ > \ \text{where:}$$

$$SIG_i =< \bar{z_i}, V_{1,i}, V_{2,i} > \ \text{ and } \bar{z_i} \neq \ \bar{z_j} \text{ for } 0 < i \neq \ j \leq \ 2$$

10.1 Security Considerations

Assuming, once again, that the underlying CS97 scheme is secure, we claim the following:

Lemma 1. *If $\mathcal{T}$ is a valid SGS by sub-group $S = \{M_1, ..., M_i\}$ on message m, then $\mathcal{T}$ has compositional integrity, i.e., anyone can verify that $\mathcal{T}$ is composed of i group signatures (of message m) each generated by a distinct group member.*

Proof outline: Since $\mathcal{T}$ is a valid SGS, for each constituent SIG_j, $\bar{z_j}$ is unique and all SKROOTLOG-s and SKLOGOLOG-s hold with a common base, $\bar{g}$. Suppose, by contradiction, that there exist two signatures $SIG_u, SIG_w \in \mathcal{T}$ that are actually generated by the same group (and also sub-group) member, M_k. Each group member has only one certificate of the form $(a^x + t)^d$.

For SIG_u, $V_{1,u}$ demonstrates knowledge of x_u where $\bar{z_u} = \bar{g}^{a^{x_u}}$ and $V_{2,u}$ demonstrates knowledge of the corresponding certificate $(a^{x_u} + t)^d$. However, SIG_w is also a valid group signature and $V_{1,w}$, $V_{1,w}$ demonstrate knowledge of x_w ($\bar{z_w} = \bar{g}^{a^{x_w}}$) and $(a^{x_w} + t)^d$, respectively. As M_k only has one certificate, $(a^{x_w} + t)^d = (a^{x_u} + t)^d$ and $x_w = x_u$. This means:
$\bar{g}^{a^{x_w}} = \bar{z_w} = \bar{g}^{a^{x_u}} = \bar{z_u}$ which contradicts our assumption. □

Lemma 2. *It is computationally difficult to decide i) whether two different and valid SGS-s $\mathcal{T}_\infty, \mathcal{T}_\in$ are generated by the same sub-group or ii) whether sub-groups that produced $\mathcal{T}_\infty, \mathcal{T}_\in$ have any members in common.*

Proof sketch: Unlinkability of SGS-s, follows directly from the security of CS97. Although the same random base $\bar{g}$ is used in the generation of all single-member group signatures that form an SGS, each signer M_j uses a distinct membership key a^{x_j} in computing its $\bar{z_j} = \bar{g}^{a^{x_j}}$. The sequence:

$$\bar{g} = g^r,\ \bar{z_1} = g^{r \cdot\ a^{x_1}}, \ldots, \bar{z_i} = g^{r \cdot\ a^{x_i}}$$

can be viewed as a sequence of ElGamal encryptions of a fixed message "1" where:

- (r, g^r) represent the one-time private and public keys of the signing sub-group
- every $g^{a^{x_j}}$ $(0 < j \leq i)$ is the "public key" of a given signer, M_j and a^{x_j} is the corresponding "private key".
- $\bar{z_j} = g^{r \cdot\ a^{x_j}}$ is the actual *encryption.*

Since r is unique and random for every SGS, unlinkability is achieved, however, only **outside the sub-group** as discussed in the next section.

10.2 Unlinkability Reconsidered

Having established SGS as a practical construct, we now observe that unlinkability, in the context of SGS, has acquired a new dimension:

> Unlinkability outside the signers' sub-group as opposed to universal unlinkability

The former refers to unlinkability of multiple signatures by **outsiders**, i.e., non-members of the signing sub-group. Whereas, the latter means that SGS-s are unlinkable by anyone with the sole exception of the group manager. To be more specific, consider the following two scenarios:

1. A sub-group $\mathcal{M}$ of like-minded group members (fully aware of each other's identities) decide to sign two documents. No one outside the sub-group (whether group member or not) can link the two SGS-s. However, since members of $\mathcal{M}$ "know" each other, they can implicitly link multiple SGS-s that they produce.
2. All members of a large group vote on two different issues. We consider only the YES votes. The YES-voters on the first issue, form a *de facto* sub-group $\mathcal{M}_1$ and produce SGS_1. Likewise, YES-voters on the second issue, form $\mathcal{M}_2$ and produce SGS_2. Since each member votes independently, the composition of $\mathcal{M}_1$ (and $\mathcal{M}_2$) must be secret even to its own members. A member of $\mathcal{M}_1$ ($\mathcal{M}_2$) needs to know only that s/he signed and the total number of signers.
   Furthermore, if we let $\mathcal{M}_3 = \mathcal{M}_1 \cap \mathcal{M}_2$, then, clearly it is evident that $0 \leq \#\mathcal{M}_3 \leq min(\#\mathcal{M}_1, \#\mathcal{M}_2)$. However, a group member $M_j \notin \mathcal{M}_1 \cup \mathcal{M}_2$ cannot narrow $\#\mathcal{M}_3$ any further. Also, a group member $M_j \in \mathcal{M}_1 \cup \mathcal{M}_2$ can at most narrow $\#\mathcal{M}_3$ to:
   $$1 \leq \#\mathcal{M}_3 \leq min(\#\mathcal{M}_1, \#\mathcal{M}_2)$$
   Put another way, **a signer cannot be linked across multiple SGS-s even by fellow co-signers.**

It is notable that the sample SGS construct of the previous section only provides unlikability of the first kind, i.e., multiple SGS-s can be linked but only by common co-signers. Recall that in the initial stage of our SGS scheme, signers agree on a common r (generated perhaps as a result of a Diffie-Hellman key exchange). Because r is known to all signers, given:

$$z_j = \bar{g}^{a^{x_j}} = (g^r)^{a^{x_j}}$$

produced by some signer M_j, any other signer M_i can compute: $(z_j)^{r^{-1}} = (g)^{a^{x_j}}$. The latter is constant for a given M_j and can thus be linked with other SGS-s where both M_i and M_j are co-signers.

The above may not be a problem in some practical settings since co-signers might choose to identify themselves to one another prior to signing (for other reasons). On the other hand, it turns out to be easy to change our example SGS scheme to provide universal SGS unlinkability.

We first note that there is no requirement in CS97 for a signer to know r used to compute the one-time random base $\bar{g} = g^r$. This allows us to amend the initial stage of SGS generation so that signers compute a common:

$$\bar{g} = g^r \text{ where } r = r_1 \cdots r_i \text{ and } r_j \in_R \mathbb{Z}_n^* \text{ by } M_j$$

The differences with respect to the first SGS scheme are superficial. The same group Difie-Hellman key agreement can be used, except that, instead of computing a common r, the signers compute a common g^r. (And, r itself is unknown.) However, in the resulting scheme, SGS-s are unlinkable even by common so-signers.

10.3 Synchronous *vs* Asynchronous Operation

Our sample CS97-based SGS scheme assumes synchronous or on-line operation. This is due to the nature of the initial stage: members of the signing sub-group (co-signers) agree on a secret r which is contributed to by each co-signer. Consequently, the scheme fails to address certain SGS scenarios, such as:

> Suppose, once again, that members of a large and distributed group are asked to vote. Instead of voting on-line, they are given a time window (say, a week) to cast their votes.

In this case it is clearly impractical to conduct the initial stage as described above. Ideally, each signer should be able to sign asynchronously, at its own leisure. At the same time, the crucial properties of SGS must be maintained; especially, compositional integrity.

One possible solution is to ask a trusted entity to generate a common random base $\bar{g} = g^r$ for all members who choose to sign a given message. This entity can be the group manager who is already trusted with issuing membership certificates and generating group public and group private keys. As noted in the previous section, signers do not need to know r; they must be assured that it is random and fresh. It seems reasonable to trust the group manager with this task.

More concretely, the group manager generates a one-time random base $\bar{g}$ and commits to it by signing (it) with its own private key which is unrelated to the group private key. Furthermore, the signed $\bar{g}$ must be associated with the specific message to be signed. In the voting example, the group manager would generate two signed statements (where SK_{gm} is the group manager's private key):

1. { YES, m=[text], $\bar{g_1}$, GROUP-ID } SK_{gm}
2. { NO, m=[text], $\bar{g_2}$, GROUP-ID } SK_{gm}

The advantage of this approach is the apparent lack of additional overhead imposed by SGS: the total cost is exactly that of computing multiple CS97 group signatures. The main drawback is, of course, the involvement of a trusted third party; whether the group manager or another trusted entity.

11 Summary

In conclusion, this paper identified some open issues in group signatures. In particular, we concentrated on two issues that, in our opinion, prevent the reduction of group signatures to practice: lack of solid foundation (and proofs) for coalition-resistance and the difficulty of deleting group members and, consequently, the difficulty of re-issuing group and individual member's keys.

In the second part of the paper we presented two new and practical services that can be easily built on top of any group signature scheme: multi-group signatures (MGS) and sub-group signatures (SGS). After analyzing their respective security requirements, we presented sample constructs for both MGS and SGS.

Acknowledgements

The authors would like to thank Jan Camenisch as well as the anonymous and unlinkable referees for their helpful comments.

References

1. C. Boyd. Digital Multi-signatures. Cryptography and Coding (H.J.Beker and F.C.Piper Eds.), Oxford University Press, 1989, pp 241-246..
2. M. Burmester and Y. Desmedt. A secure and efficient conference key distribution system. In *Advances in Cryptology – EUROCRYPT*, 1994.
3. J. Camenisch. Efficient and generalized group signatures. In *Advances in Cryptology – EUROCRYPT*, 1997.
4. J. Camenisch and M. Stadler. Efficient group signature schemes for large groups. In *Advances in Cryptology – CRYPTO*, 1997.
5. D. Chaum and T. Pedersen. Wallet databases with observers. In *Advances in Cryptology – CRYPTO*, 1992.
6. D. Chaum and E. van Heyst. Group signatures. In *Advances in Cryptology – EUROCRYPT*, 1991.
7. L. Chen and T. Pedersen. On the efficiency of group signatures providing information-theoretic anonymity. In *Advances in Cryptology – EUROCRYPT*, 1995.
8. A. Lysyanskaya and Z. Ramzan. Group blind digital signatures. In *Financial Cryptography Conference*, 1998.
9. H. Petersen. How to convert any digital signature scheme into a group signature scheme. In *Security Protocols Workshop*, 1997.
10. M. Steiner, G. Tsudik, and M. Waidner. Diffie-hellman key distribution extended to groups. In *ACM Conference on Computer and Communication Security*, pages 31–37, March 1996.

Anonymous Investing:
Hiding the Identities of Stockholders

Philip MacKenzie[1] and Jeffrey Sorensen[2]

[1] Information Sciences Research Center, Bell Laboratories,
Murray Hill, NJ 07974,
philmac@research.bell-labs.com
[2] T. J. Watson Research Center, IBM Corporation,
Yorktown Heights, NY 10598,
sorenj@us.ibm.com

Abstract. This paper introduces the concept of an *eshare*, or digital stockholder certificate, which allows investors in companies to buy and trade shares without revealing their identity or the size of their investment. In addition, the eshare protocols presented allow for publicly verifiable elections to be held with each share assigned one vote. Dividend payments to investors are also supported, again without revealing shareholder identities, even if a government taxation agency requires verifiable documentation of shareholder earnings. The protocols presented are based on *certified anonymous public keys* with *trustee-revocable anonymity*, which may be of independent interest.

1 Introduction

In the field of cryptography there has been a continued focus on the concept of digital currency. This has yielded numerous algorithmic techniques (most notably [8,1], but see [32] for an extensive list) that allow the creation of a digital equivalent of paper currency, or ecash. In addition, there have been many proposals for protocols that allow secure voting for elections (see, for example, [32]). This paper introduces an application encompassing both digital currency and electronic voting (among other properties), namely digital stock certificates.[1]

A digital stock certificate, or *eshare*, can be thought of as the digital equivalent of a paper stock certificate. As with stock certificates, one should be able to buy, sell, or trade eshares. Moreover, as with ecash systems, an eshare system may also insure a measure of anonymity for both the purchaser and the seller during trading. However, unlike ecash, eshare ownership should entitle the holder to vote in corporate elections (one vote per share) and to receive dividends, while assuring that the identity of the shareholder is not revealed.

There are many potential reasons why investors may wish to remain anonymous. With the increased use of digital information systems, investment histories

[1] Although Rivest [31] proposes that voting systems and payment systems are "close," it seems that implementing digital stock certificates directly using standard anonymous ecash systems does not seem appropriate (see Section 1.1).

M. Franklin (Ed.): FC'99, LNCS 1648, pp. 212–229, 1999.

will be more easily available and investors may find themselves increasingly targeted based on their past investment choices. However, anonymous investing has the potential to exacerbate problems such as insider trading, extortion, and money laundering. This is interesting from both technical and social perspectives. Following along the lines of recent ecash schemes [2,34], our system addresses these potential problems with the introduction of mechanisms to conditionally revoke anonymity.

Currently, investors often enjoy practical anonymity through the use of intermediaries. For instance non-public companies sometimes have *silent partners* who depend upon their associates not to reveal their identities. For public companies, assuming that brokerage services and mutual funds do not disclose their clients' personal financial information, companies often only see aggregate information about their current owners. Also, investment vehicles such as *trusts* and *holding companies* can act as third-parties that anonymize the money held for their investors. However, this paper is concerned with protocols that allow for a stronger form of anonymity, one that preserves the important aspects of corporate stock ownership, but also insures that the identities of the shareholders are *cryptographically hidden.*

1.1 Comparison to Ecash

Eshares, although similar to ecash on the surface, are used for much more than simply holding value. Eshares must provide the ability to receive dividends from the corporation and vote in corporate elections. In addition, these abilities must be provided in a way that does not compromise the identity of the shareholder.

Typical anonymous ecash, based upon a bank's blind signature on data bits, does not seem to provide these abilities, at least not easily. One problem is how to obtain dividends without actually having an identity. Generally, withdrawal of ecash from a bank requires knowledge of a user's identity, even though after the withdrawal the information about the identity in the coin is information-theoretically hidden. This problem is further complicated by our additional requirement that eshares provide trustee-revocable anonymity, thus each coin would need some (certified) relation to a true identity. Another significant problem with using conventional ecash as stock shares is enabling trading. Without identities, at least pseudonymous identities, and thus, without authentication of messages, it seems difficult, if not impossible, to determine who is willing to trade shares, and at what price.

1.2 Comparison to Electronic Voting

The eshare voting scheme we present seems to be a novel problem in secure electronic voting. Not only do we wish to not reveal the votes of the individual participants, but *we need to hide the identities of the participants themselves.* We provide a very efficient solution to this problem, which provides secure, anonymous, and authenticated voting.

1.3 New Techniques

Because of the differences between eshares and the related concepts of ecash and evoting, we have had to develop some new techniques. The primary enabling technique we use is *certified anonymous public keys* (CAPKs), that is, public keys that are certified as being valid, but not (publicly) linked with any particular individual [26]. Used as pseudonyms [9,7], the anonymous public keys are, during certification, combined with the holder's true identity to provide an off-line mechanism allowing for the revocability of anonymity by a trustee. Pseudonyms have been used in previous systems but generally could be linked to users by the certification authority [26,28], the certification authority could only register a limited number of them [25], or they were of a restricted form [30]. (Other systems that used similar ideas to certified anonymous public keys were [2,34,19,20,21,18,24].) In our scheme, a user may receive many pseudonyms, and only trustees (who remain totally off-line) may revoke their anonymity. Since the pseudonyms we use are actually public keys, and their anonymity is revocable, they can be used in all the same ways as true public keys/identities are used. In particular, they can be used in standard systems for communication, electronic voting, and ecash, yet also provide anonymity.

Note that CAPKs can be considered a tool for granting anonymous *power*. In some sense, standard ecash is a similar form of anonymous power. However, it is *one-time* anonymous power (at least if double-spending can be detected) and it has a rigid structure. One of the novel ways in which we use an ecash system is to use the one-time anonymous power of ecash and bootstrap this to create CAPK pairs, which can be used repeatedly like normal public keys.

Another novel use of anonymous ecash is to provide the ability for fair anonymous taxation. In particular, our protocol is designed so that a government tax agency (like the IRS) can be sure that every anonymous investor in an corporation is correctly declaring all dividends received from their investments. However, the tax agency gains no information about which shares are owned by which investors, even if it colludes with companies or banks. Our solution involves the tax agency creating anonymous *dividend tax scrip* that can be balanced against investment earnings.

2 Model

2.1 Communication Model

For a formal model we use a model of anonymous communication [9] abstracted as an *Anonymous Bulletin Board* (ABB). An ABB has the following properties:

open any person can read the contents of the bulletin board;
public any person may add to the contents of the bulletin board;
secure no person may delete or alter past posts or block new posts;
timely any new post will be readable by all users within a certain fixed time;
anonymous reading and posting do not require the disclosure of identity.

Although an adversary may not block new posts, we do not discount the possibility of an adversary seeing a user's post and inserting a new post before anyone else sees that user's post. Thus, we do not rely on any strict timing of posts, as in Simon [33], to guarantee security. This requires that all posts be authenticated in some way or another. In our proposed protocols, both encrypted an non-encrypted messages may be posted to the ABB. Similar anonymous channel models have been discussed in [27,5,6,29,23,35,33,4].

For the purposes of this paper, we will assume a network that satisfies all of the above properties. However, it is not unreasonable for this application to consider a relaxed communication model which relies on redundancy rather than security, such as a system built using some combination of Usenet, anonymous web-browsing, and anonymous remailers.

In our descriptions of the protocols, frequent use of broadcast messages are used. The format of a message is denoted as

$$message(x, y)$$

where x and y represent the message parameters. Digital signatures are denoted with $Sig_s(x)$ and digitally signed messages are denoted as

$$message_s(x, y)$$

where s is the private key used to sign the message. A signed message can be considered equivalent to

$$message(x, y, Sig_s(message(x, y)))$$

where all components of the message are, typically hashed, and digitally signed.

A digital certification of a public key by a third party is denoted

$$Cert_{\mathcal{A}}(p, x)$$

where $\mathcal{A}$ asserts that public key p is linked to some sort of identity information x. Certification by an authority $\mathcal{A}$ with a public/secret key pair $(p_{\mathcal{A}}, s_{\mathcal{A}})$ of can be considered

$$Cert_{\mathcal{A}}(p, x) = (p, x, Sig_{s_{\mathcal{A}}}(p, x))$$

where $Sig_{s_{\mathcal{A}}}(p, x)$ represents a digital signature applied to p and x using the secret key $s_{\mathcal{A}}$. The validity of the $\mathcal{A}$'s signature can be verified using

$$Ver_{p_{\mathcal{A}}}\left(Sig_{s_{\mathcal{A}}}(p, x)\right) = (p, x)$$

using the $\mathcal{A}$'s published public key.

2.2 Participants

The participants in an eshare system are given here. Note that there will be several investors and companies.

investor An investor $\mathcal{I}$, is a person with a certified key pair linked to their their identity and, potentially, many associated certified anonymous public key (CAPK) pairs.

company A corporation $\mathcal{C}$ that sells eshares.

bank A bank $\mathcal{B}$ issues ecash and maintains an account for the company to redeem endorsed checks.

tax agency A government branch $\mathcal{G}$ that collects taxes on earnings, such as dividends.

trustee A trusted entity $\mathcal{T}$, trusted not to act to reveal secret information except under certain circumstances agreed upon by all participants, such as evidence of wrongdoing. (The trustee may be distributed [2] but that is beyond the scope of this paper.)

certification authority A trusted authority $\mathcal{A}$ who will certify identities.

2.3 Ecash

We assume the existence of an anonymous ecash scheme with trustee-revocable anonymity, such as [14], which builds on [1,13,11], Camenisch et al. [3], or Solages and Traoré [12].

We define one of these ecash schemes as consisting of a bank $\mathcal{B}$, investors $\{\mathcal{I}_i\}$, companies $\{\mathcal{C}_j\}$, and an offline trustee $\mathcal{T}$, each party having certified identities or certified public keys (with their corresponding secret keys) as necessary for the protocols to function correctly. There are three protocols:

- a protocol $c \leftarrow$ **Ecash-Withdraw**(d) between some $\mathcal{I}_i$ and $\mathcal{B}$ in which $\mathcal{I}_i$ obtains a coin c of value d.
- a protocol $c'_q \leftarrow$ **Ecash-Payment**(c, q) between $\mathcal{I}_i$ and $\mathcal{C}_j$, with c being a coin and q being some *information* about how c is being spent (vendor, item, date/time, etc.)[2] in which a spent coin c'_q is obtained by $\mathcal{C}_j$; and
- a protocol $c''_q \leftarrow$ **Ecash-Deposit**(c'_q) between $\mathcal{C}_j$ and $\mathcal{B}$, with spent coin c'_q, in which $\mathcal{B}$ obtains deposited coin c''_q and credits $\mathcal{C}_j$ amount of d.

Informally, the protocols must satisfy the following security requirements:

untraceability (anonymity) If c was withdrawn by $\mathcal{I}_i$, it is infeasible to link c, along with its corresponding spent and deposited coins c'_q and c''_q, to $\mathcal{I}_i$.

unforgeability It is infeasible for any $\mathcal{I}_i$ to create a coin c without participating in a withdrawal protocol with $\mathcal{B}$.

double-spending detection If c was withdrawn by $\mathcal{I}_i$ and spent twice, resulting in spent coins c'_{q_1} and c'_{q_2}, then the identity of the $\mathcal{I}_i$ can be computed from these spent coins.

trustee traceability If c was withdrawn by $\mathcal{I}_i$ and spent, resulting in spent coin c'_q, then the identity of $\mathcal{I}_i$ can be computed from c'_q by the trustee $\mathcal{T}$.

[2] Note that q provides the ability to direct a payment and is accomplished in schemes based on [1] by hashing q along with other required fields when generating a challenge in the Schnorr proof.

Above we list the more interesting security requirements, as they relate to our system. We refer the reader to [15,11] for more complete and formal security requirements.

3 Requirements

A digital stock certificate (eshare) system should allow buying and selling of eshares; payment and retrieval of dividends, with tax reporting where appropriate; and voting, with one vote per share. Through all these protocols, the following security requirements must be met:

anonymity It should be infeasible for anyone except the trustee to obtain the true identity of a shareholder. (Technically, this is pseudonymity rather than anonymity, since the shareholder has a continuous identity that interacts with the company.)

trustee-tracing The trustee should be able to efficiently revoke anonymity of shareholders, but should only be involved when revocation is required, and remain off-line otherwise.

no impersonation No party should be able to impersonate shareholders.

secure voting Each shareholder should be able to vote once per share held, and the voting should be publicly verifiable.

taxable income verification A government tax agency should be able to verify and tax all investment income received by shareholders.

investor security An investor can detect and prove if a company has behaved dishonestly (such as taken cash, but not issued an eshare).

company security It is infeasible for an investor to frame the company as being dishonest if the company behaves honestly.

certificate unforgeability It is infeasible to forge certificates.

bank and merchant security The bank and merchant security properties provided by anonymous ecash with trustee-revocable anonymity are maintained.

4 Eshare Scheme

First we describe the basic eshare mechanism. Then we describe the different protocols for buying and selling, voting, receiving dividends, etc.

As we have stated in the introduction, our new scheme is based upon the use of *certified anonymous public keys*, or CAPKs. Formally, a CAPK is a public key p and its associated certificate, signed by a certification authority $\mathcal{A}$, that guarantees that:

1. $p_{\mathcal{I}}$ has been registered with $\mathcal{A}$ as the (non-anonymous) public key associated with investor $\mathcal{I}$, and
2. the certificate contains information that could be sent to the trustee $\mathcal{T}$ that would reveal the (non-anonymous) public key of $\mathcal{I}$ and subsequently the true identity of $\mathcal{I}$ according to $\mathcal{A}$'s registry.

In other words, a CAPK is a *certified pseudonym* for $\mathcal{I}$.[3] Note that even the certification authority $\mathcal{A}$ cannot link a CAPK with any particular $\mathcal{I}$.

Pseudonyms are a perfect fit for an eshare scheme, since there is ongoing communication between a company and the holder of an eshare including: voting, dividends, and associated business announcements. Pseudonyms also allow for efficiency for purchasers of multiple shares (by using the same pseudonym). While linkage is often a major concern in both ecash systems and cryptographic voting protocols, there does not seem to be a reason for such concern in the eshare setting. In any case, if potential linkage of the shares is a concern for a particular investor, a pseudonym associated with any share can be changed as desired, and any investor may have an arbitrarily large number of pseudonyms. As with any pseudonymous system, investors will need to be aware of and balance their convenience against the potential for linkage whenever large blocks of shares are held by a single CAPK during voting and trading. Investors will also need to be aware that linkage (of CAPKs) could occur if the votes associated with each CAPK that they own have a similar, detectable voting pattern. From a cryptographic standpoint, such linkage does not compromise the user's identity. However, it may make monitoring of users possible outside the framework of the eshare system.

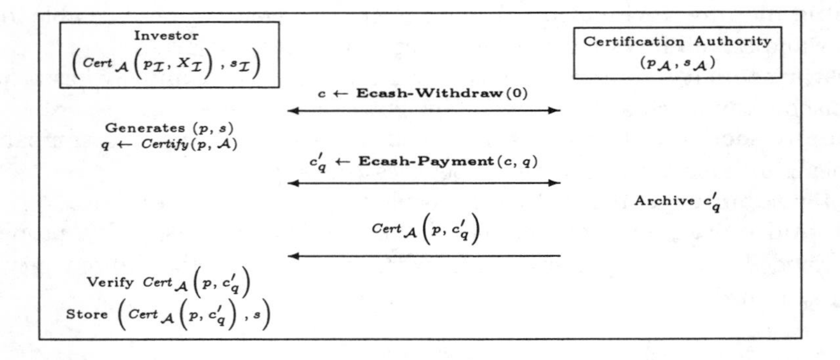

Fig. 1. Obtaining a Certified Anonymous Public Key Pair. The value c'_q contains the trustee tracing information for p.

[3] This may seem like a strange concept, since usually one certifies a public key in order to link it to an identity, and here we attempt to maintain anonymity. However, a CAPK certificate can really be thought of as linking to an "encrypted identity," that is, the link has a level of indirection — the identity information has to be processed by the trustee before it can be used.

4.1 Basic Scheme

A company that sells eshares will have a public database of certified public keys, one per eshare. Each public key will be signed by the company so all can agree on the correct and current public keys in the database. The owner of a eshare x is the investor who knows the private key corresponding to the public key of eshare x in the database.

Anonymity is obtained by allowing CAPKs in the database. Of course, to prevent problems inherent in any type of system with anonymity and money, the certificate does contain extra information that can be used so that a trustee could determine the true owner of the public key.

Some features provided by this scheme include the ability for all investors to verify the number of shares outstanding by consulting this public database, and the ability for shareholders in the company to have private, authenticated communication by means of the CAPKs.

4.2 Obtaining a Certified Anonymous Public Key Pair

A CAPK is a public key and its associated certificate signed by the certification authority. The term CAPK pair refers to the CAPK and its associated private key. Prospective investors, seeking to invest anonymously, can participate in the protocol illustrated in Figure 1 to obtain a CAPK pair. We assume that there is an anonymous ecash scheme (with trustee-revocable anonymity) run by $\mathcal{A}$ in which investors withdraw zero-value "coins" from $\mathcal{A}$ which can only be used to "purchase" certified pseudonyms from $\mathcal{A}$.

Note that the withdrawal should be considered a preprocessing step, and performed well before the remainder of the protocols, so as to prevent linkage of the CAPK to the investor. Also note that the withdrawal requires authenticated messages, which are handled with $\mathcal{I}$'s non-anonymous public key pair.

A description of the protocol follows:

1. $\mathcal{I}$ withdraws a *pseudonym-coin* c from $\mathcal{A}$. This coin will allow an investor to "purchase" a CAPK. (Note that $\mathcal{A}$ might demand payment to mint this coin c, but we have not included that in our protocol.)
2. $\mathcal{I}$ generates a public/secret key pair (p, s), and using c, pays $\mathcal{A}$ to certify p. The payment is directed (as discussed above) to $\mathcal{A}$ for the certification of p. The result is that a spent coin c'_q will be produced which has information that can be used for double-spending detection and trustee-tracing.
3. $\mathcal{A}$ certifies p with c'_q, linking the trustee-traceability information with p.

4.3 Issuance of Eshares

The protocol to purchase a share in a company at price d using a CAPK is given in Figure 2. (We use X to refer to the information with which the trustee could link the anonymous public key p with the investor $\mathcal{I}$.)

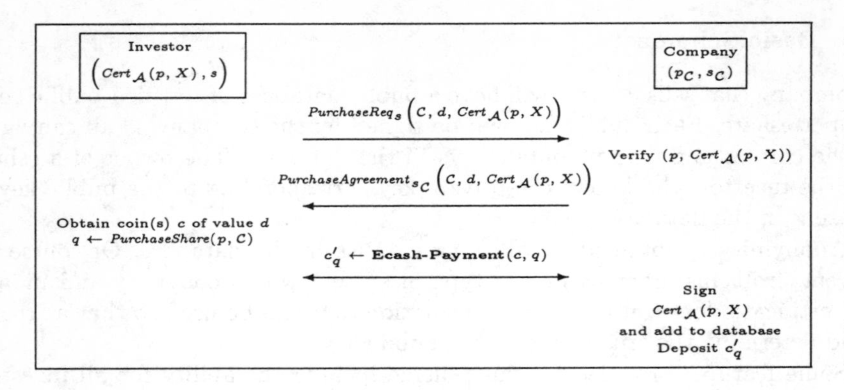

Fig. 2. Obtaining eshares from a company offered at price d

Note that the payment may be performed in the clear since the cash paid is directed to $\mathcal{C}$. The signed message by $\mathcal{C}$, along with the transcript of the ecash payment protocol, prevents any cheating by $\mathcal{C}$.[4]

We stress again that while $\mathcal{C}$'s signature on p indicates assignment of the eshare, it is really the knowledge of the secret key associated with p that determines the owner, since the secret key allows the shareholder to vote, receive dividends, and sell the share. For this reason, it is important that the shareholder carefully guard this secret key.

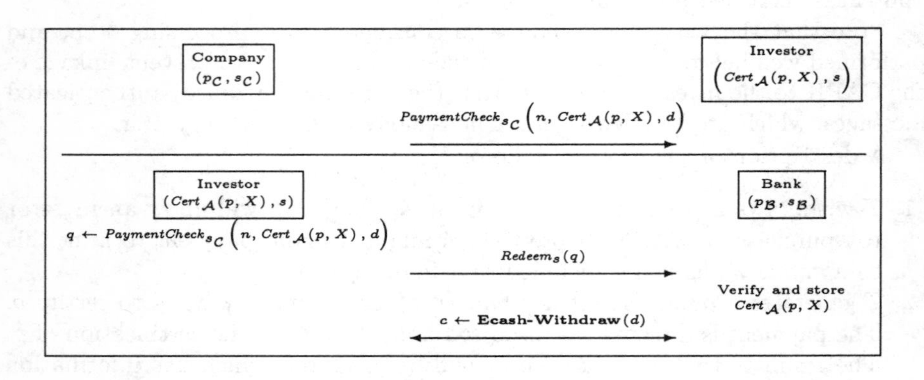

Fig. 3. Payment of d from Company to Shareholder

[4] Note here that the ecash also provides a certification as to the true identity of the shareholder with respect to the bank from which the ecash was issued. With trustee-revocable anonymity, this provides a way for the company to obtain the true identity if necessary. However, it seems safer and more modular to have a separate CA certifying identities.

4.4 Payment from Company to Shareholder

In certain situations, such as quarterly dividends or share transfer, it will be necessary for the company $\mathcal{C}$ to pay shareholder $\mathcal{I}$, while preserving the anonymity of $\mathcal{I}$. This is accomplished quite easily in our system. The protocol is shown in Figure 3.

To pay $\mathcal{I}$ d dollars, $\mathcal{C}$ simply writes an electronic check for d dollars, payable to the shareholder pseudonym $Cert_{\mathcal{A}}(p, X)$. In Figure 3, the check number n is used to prevent replay attacks, and may include other information such as an expiration date. Then $\mathcal{I}$ signs the check with s (thus *endorsing* it), and presents the result to the bank, which then issues ecash using the CAPK as the "identity" in the ecash. The bank uses the endorsed echeck to obtain the money from the company.

Of course, the bank checks $Cert_{\mathcal{A}}(p, X)$ to verify that the owner of p may be identified if necessary, such as if ecash associated with identity p is double-spent. We emphasize that there is a double level of anonymity in the ecash. Peeling off the first level will reveal p. To peel off the second level, one would need to contact the trustee and present $Cert_{\mathcal{A}}(p, X)$.

4.5 Selling/Trading of Eshares

The following protocol is designed to maintain complete anonymity, even between the buyer and seller of the eshare.[5]

1. Say a shareholder $\mathcal{I}_s$ with CAPK pair $(Cert_{\mathcal{A}}(p_s, X_s), s_s)$ wants to sell his share. He can announce this by sending a message
$$ForSale_{s_s}(\mathcal{C}, d, Cert_{\mathcal{A}}(p_s, X_s))$$
indicating that he wants to sell the share associated with $Cert_{\mathcal{A}}(p_s, X_s)$ for d dollars, signing it with his secret key s_s.
2. Investor $\mathcal{I}_b$, the buyer, with CAPK pair $(Cert_{\mathcal{A}}(p_b, X_b), s_b)$ broadcasts
$$OfferPayment_{s_b}(\mathcal{C}, d', Cert_{\mathcal{A}}(p_s, X_s), Cert_{\mathcal{A}}(p_b, X_b))$$
to purchase share $Cert_{\mathcal{A}}(p_s, X_s)$ for d' dollars (which may be different from d), signed with s_b.
3. $\mathcal{I}_s$ can complete the agreement by sending
$$TradeAgreement_{s_s}(\mathcal{C}, d', Cert_{\mathcal{A}}(p_s, X_s), Cert_{\mathcal{A}}(p_b, X_b))$$
4. $\mathcal{C}$ checks $Cert_{\mathcal{A}}(p_b, X_b)$, and if valid, sends a message that it agrees to transfer ownership of the share[6]
$$TransferContract_{s_C}(\mathcal{C}, d', Cert_{\mathcal{A}}(p_s, X_s), Cert_{\mathcal{A}}(p_b, X_b))$$

[5] If less anonymity is required, or there is more trust between the buyer and seller, then simpler protocols could be used.

[6] Some jurisdictions may not allow a company to act as an escrow agent or broker for their own stock. If necessary, a brokerage or other legal entity can be trivially incorporated to perform these operations.

5. $\mathcal{I}_b$ participates in a payment protocol with $\mathcal{C}$, with the ecash c directed to $\mathcal{C}$ for purchase of the share currently assigned to $Cert_{\mathcal{A}}(p_s, X_s)$.
6. $\mathcal{C}$ performs the Payment from Company to Shareholder protocol to pay $\mathcal{I}_s$ d' dollars.
7. $\mathcal{I}_s$ deposits the money received by endorsing the check using the Payment from Company to Shareholder protocol.

The company's signed message and the transcript of $\mathcal{I}_b$'s payment protocol prevent the company from cheating. The signed message of $\mathcal{I}_s$ and the endorsed check prevent $\mathcal{I}_s$ from cheating.

Note that transferral records would have to be kept for a reasonable length of time in order to resolve disputes over eshare ownership.

4.6 Dividends

Any eshare system must have a method for paying dividends. In our system, this is handled simply by using the Payment from Company to Shareholder protocol above. As discussed, there is no loss of anonymity since the dividend check is immediately cashed at a bank, and anonymous ecash is withdrawn in its place.

4.7 Voting

In previously proposed electronic voting protocols, the major issues were to guarantee that each person could only vote once, and that all votes were anonymous. In an eshare scheme, each eshare is entitled to one vote (in proportion to the investment risk) and it is required that not even the identity of who voted should be revealed. Our eshare system is ideally suited to solve this problem.

With CAPKs, the person's identity is decoupled from the eshare, and thus votes can be signed and posted in the clear with no loss of anonymity! Then all shareholders may track and total the votes themselves. Authenticity, and the requirement of one vote per share, are both handled using signatures from the CAPKs. Anonymity follows from the anonymity of the CAPKs.

If a sealed election is required, in which ballots are revealed only after all the votes have been cast, a simple commitment scheme can be used, in which commitments to votes are signed, and the commitments are revealed after the balloting has ended.

Note also that any shareholder may send an announcement or a call-for-vote by posting a message signed by her CAPK pair's private key.

4.8 Withholding of Taxes

A company operating with anonymous shareholders may face substantial legal challenges, as companies have traditionally been required to keep track of their stockholders, mainly for tax purposes. In general, tax cannot simply be withheld by the company, since the amount of tax that actually must be paid could depend on many factors, including the total income of the investor. In any case,

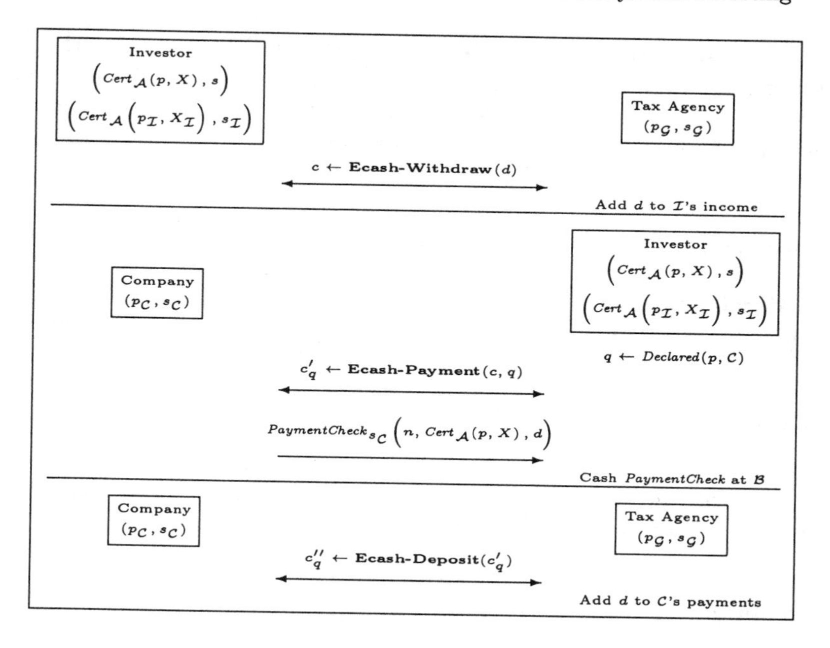

Fig. 4. Payment of d from Company to Shareholder, with tax reporting

our eshare system will support this tax collection problem without revealing the identities of the shareholders.

Basically, our technique is to require shareholders to reveal to the tax agency $\mathcal{G}$ (e.g., the IRS) the extent of their earnings without ever revealing the source of those earnings, while simultaneously requiring companies to prove to $\mathcal{G}$ that all of the money given away in dividends is actually being reported.

In the following, we assume there is an ecash scheme run by $\mathcal{G}$ in which $\mathcal{I}$ withdraws "coins" from $\mathcal{G}$. This corresponds to $\mathcal{I}$ declaring the value of the coins as taxable investment income. We assume this scheme is a fair off-line ecash scheme, i.e. with detection of double-spending and trustee-revocable anonymity. From this point on, we will call the withdrawn coins *dividend tax scrip.*

Say an investor wishes to collect a payment of d dollars from $\mathcal{C}$, in which it owns a share with CAPK pair $(Cert_{\mathcal{A}}(p, X), s)$. The following is added to the Payment from Company to Shareholder protocol.

1. $\mathcal{I}$ withdraws a dividend tax scrip coin(s) c worth d dollars from $\mathcal{G}$. Of course, $\mathcal{G}$ records that $\mathcal{I}$ has declared d dollars of investment income, which will be used when $\mathcal{G}$ computes the tax owed by $\mathcal{I}$.
2. $\mathcal{I}$ anonymously pays $\mathcal{C}$ the dividend tax scrip c directed to $\mathcal{C}$ for payment of a dividend for CAPK p.

3. The company deposits the dividend tax scrip with $\mathcal{G}$ to verify that the income it is paying is actually being reported by its shareholder. Then it sends a payment check to CAPK $Cert_{\mathcal{A}}(p, X)$, which the investor can endorse and cash at a bank, withdrawing anonymous ecash. (Note that we omit the bank withdrawal protocol from Figure 4.7.)

The property of double-spending detection is necessary to prevent shareholders from reusing tax scrip at different companies and cheating $\mathcal{G}$ out of taxes. The anonymity of the dividend tax scrip prevents $\mathcal{G}$ and/or $\mathcal{C}$ from determining which investor is receiving the payment, thus protecting the identity of $\mathcal{I}$.

5 Security

Here we present proofs of security for the protocols above. Recall that all ecash payments in the protocols are directed to a specific payee.

5.1 Anonymity for $\mathcal{I}$

Theorem 1. *It is infeasible to link a CAPK with an investor $\mathcal{I}$.*

Proof. The only linkage between an investor $\mathcal{I}$ and the investor's CAPK is through the pseudonym-coin withdrawn from $\mathcal{A}$ and the dividend tax scrip withdrawn from $\mathcal{G}$. The anonymity then follows from the anonymity of the ecash protocols used by $\mathcal{A}$ and $\mathcal{G}$.

Note that the anonymity proven here inherits the limitations of anonymity in ecash systems. For example, if there is only a single investor with a CAPK, then there is obviously no anonymity. Also, if there are two pseudonymous investors, one who receives a huge dividend check, and one who doesn't, then the real investor who buys a new Mercedes could conceivably be linked to the pseudonymous investor who received the huge dividend check. The problem is exacerbated by tax reporting, since it may be possible to link investors to CAPKs by matching dividends payments to tax script withdrawn by investors. This problem is reduced when there are many investors, each with many CAPKs.

5.2 Security for $\mathcal{A}$

Theorem 2. *It is infeasible to obtain a certificate for a CAPK that is not linked to an investor who has been authorized by $\mathcal{A}$ to receive a CAPK.*

Proof. This follows directly from the existential unforgeability of $\mathcal{A}$'s signatures (i.e. the existential unforgeability of the certificate) and the unforgeability and trustee-tracing properties of the ecash scheme used for the pseudonym-coins.

5.3 Security for $\mathcal{C}$

Theorem 3. *It is infeasible to make a ecash payment to the company that will result in an invalid spent coin, or a dividend tax scrip payment to the company that will result in invalid spent dividend tax scrip, without this behavior being detected.*

Proof. This follows from the security of the ecash schemes used for both normal ecash and dividend tax scrip.

Theorem 4. *It is infeasible to obtain shares or dividends not given by the company, or to frame the company for not providing dividends and/or shares that should be given to an investor.*

Proof. Both follow from the existential unforgeability of a company's signatures.

5.4 Security for $\mathcal{I}$

Theorem 5. *It is infeasible for a company to accept payment for a share and not provide the share to an investor, without this being detected.*

Proof. As in the ecash scheme, the transcript of the payment protocol can be used to verify the share being paid for by the investor.

Theorem 6. *It is infeasible for a company $\mathcal{C}$ or certification authority $\mathcal{A}$ to frame an (anonymous) investor.*

Proof. Framing is prevented by the existential unforgeability of the (anonymous) investor's signature, and the protection against framing provided by the ecash schemes used for regular ecash, pseudonym-coins, or dividend tax scrip.

Theorem 7. *It is infeasible for anyone except the investor $\mathcal{I}$ to obtain dividends paid for shares owned by $\mathcal{I}$.*

Proof. This follows from the payment check being made out to $\mathcal{I}$ and the unforgeability of the company signature.

5.5 Security of Voting

All voting security properties follow directly from the facts that the CAPKs are anonymous, that the CAPKs corresponding to shares are publicly known and signed by the company, and that signatures on votes (using the private keys corresponding to the CAPKs of the shareholders) are existentially unforgeable.

5.6 Traceability

Theorem 8. *All CAPKs are trustee-traceable.*

Proof. This follows from the unforgeability and trustee-traceability of the $\mathcal{A}$'s pseudonym-coins used in obtaining CAPKs, along with existential unforgeability of $\mathcal{A}$'s certificates.

5.7 Security for $\mathcal{B}$ and Other Merchants

The security of the bank $\mathcal{B}$ and other merchants follows directly from the security of the basic ecash system, as long as the CAPKs are trustee-traceable, which is shown above. Obviously, the bank also is protected by the existential unforgeability of a company's signature on checks made out to investors.

5.8 Security for $\mathcal{G}$

Theorem 9. *$\mathcal{G}$ can verify all investment income paid by a company $\mathcal{C}$ is reported by investors, as long as $\mathcal{C}$ is honest.*

Proof. Assuming $\mathcal{C}$ is honest, $\mathcal{C}$ requires $\mathcal{I}$ to pay dividend tax scrip corresponding to all dividend income paid by $\mathcal{C}$ to $\mathcal{I}$. Then $\mathcal{C}$ deposits the dividend tax scrip with $\mathcal{G}$. By the security of ecash, $\mathcal{G}$ is assured that all the dividends given by the company have been reported (i.e., there is no double spending of dividend tax scrip, and no forging of dividend tax scrip). Note that in the case that the payments of dividend tax scrip to the company are performed off-line and double spending is attempted, then when the dividend tax scrip is eventually deposited, the double spending will be detected, and the identity of the investor will be revealed.

Note that we make no claims about security against a company and investor colluding. This cryptographic approach cannot prevent a company from "doctoring its books," and essentially embezzling money. This problem seems outside the reach of a cryptographic solution.

6 Conclusion

We have introduced the problem of anonymous investing, and described a system to support it based on anonymous digital stock certificates. Our system uses new techniques, such as certified anonymous public keys with trustee-revocable anonymity, and novel uses of ecash.

7 Future Work - Anonymous Markets

The protocols presented here are designed for companies that would like to enable anonymous ownership. Capital markets involve many players and due consideration is needed to determine appropriate ways to extend these protocols to incorporate the roles served by market makers and stock exchanges.

One particular challenge for eshares would be handling the reporting of capital gains. Investors are rewarded not only by dividends, but also by the appreciation of a company's share price over time. Further, capital gains taxation is one of the most complicated areas of tax law; capital gains tax rates depend not only on the prices of the assets but also on the total income of the owner and the duration the investment was held. Perhaps ironically, the company is only one party of many involved in setting the share price.

It is not hard to imagine extensions to the transfer protocol that would allow transfer of ownership from one CAPK to another only if the seller can prove that all capital-gains have been duly reported. However, such protocols are an open problem and beyond the scope of this paper.

In addition, the trade protocols presented here are to demonstrate the feasibility of an eshare system. It is unlikely that they would scale effectively. It is certainly undesirable to have the owner of an eshare be required to post a new for-sale message every time the price changes. The more general and interesting problem of enabling anonymous markets, where prices are determined anonymously, is an area of ongoing work.

References

1. S. Brands. Untraceable off-line cash in wallet with observers (extended abstract). In *Advances in Cryptology—CRYPTO '93*, volume 773 of *Lecture Notes in Computer Science*, pages 302–318. Springer-Verlag, 22–26 Aug. 1993.
2. E. Brickell, P. Gemmell, and D. Kravitz. Trustee-based tracing extensions to anonymous cash and the making of anonymous change. In *Proceedings of the Sixth Annual ACM-SIAM Symposium on Discrete Algorithms*, pages 457–466, San Francisco, California, 22–24 Jan. 1995.
3. J. Camenisch, U. Maurer, and M. Stadler. Digital payment systems with passive anonymity-revoking trustees. *Journal of Computer Security*, 5(1):69–89, 1997.
4. J. Camp, M. Harkavy, J. Tygar, and B. Yee. Anonymous atomic transactions. In *Proceedings of the Second Usenix Workshop on Electronic Commerce*, page (n/a), 1996.
5. D. Chaum. Security without identification: Transaction systems to make big brother obsolete. *Communications of the ACM*, 28(10):1030–1044, 1985.
6. D. Chaum. The dining cryptographers problem: Unconditional sender and recipient untraceability. *Journal of Cryptology*, 1(1):65–75, 1988.
7. D. Chaum. Zero-knowledge undeniable signatures (extended abstract). In *Advances in Cryptology—EUROCRYPT 90*, volume 473 of *Lecture Notes in Computer Science*, pages 458–464. Springer-Verlag, 1991, 21–24 May 1990.
8. D. Chaum, A. Fiat, and M. Naor. Untraceable electronic cash (extended abstract). In *Advances in Cryptology—CRYPTO '88*, volume 403 of *Lecture Notes in Computer Science*, pages 319–327. Springer-Verlag, 1990, 21–25 Aug. 1988.

9. D. L. Chaum. Silo watching. In *Advances in Cryptology: A Report on CRYPTO 81*, pages 138–139. Department of Electrical and Computer Engineering, U. C. Santa Barbara, 24–26 Aug. 1981. ECE Report 82-04, 1982.
10. *Advances in Cryptology—CRYPTO '96*, volume 1109 of *Lecture Notes in Computer Science*. Springer-Verlag, 18–22 Aug. 1996.
11. G. Davida, Y. Frankel, Y. Tsiounis, and M. Yung. Anonymity control in e-cash systems. In Hirschfeld [16], pages 1–16.
12. A. de Solages and J. Traoré. An efficient fair off-line electronic cash system with extensions to checks and wallets with observers. In Hirschfeld [17], pages 275–295.
13. Y. Frankel, Y. Tsiounis, and M. Yung. "Indirect discourse proofs": Achieving efficient fair off-line E-cash. In Kim and Matsumoto [22], pages 286–300.
14. Y. Frankel, Y. Tsiounnis, and M. Yung. Fair off-line e-cash made easy. In *Advances in Cryptology—ASIACRYPT '98*, Lecture Notes in Computer Science, page to appear. Springer-Verlag, Nov. 1998.
15. M. Franklin and M. Yung. Secure and efficient off-line digital money. In *Proceedings of the Twentieth International Colloquium on Automata, Languages and Programming*, volume 700 of *Lecture Notes in Computer Science*, pages 265–276, Lund, Sweden, July 1993. Springer-Verlag.
16. R. Hirschfeld, editor. *Financial Cryptography: First International Conference, FC '97*, volume 1318 of *Lecture Notes in Computer Science*, Anguilla, British West Indies, 24–28 Feb. 1997. Springer-Verlag.
17. R. Hirschfeld, editor. *Financial Cryptography: Second International Conference, FC '98*, volume 1465 of *Lecture Notes in Computer Science*, Anguilla, British West Indies, June 1998. Springer-Verlag.
18. M. Jakobsson and J. Müller. Improved magic ink signatures using hints. In *Financial Cryptography: Third International Conference, FC '98*, Anguilla, British West Indies, 1999. Springer-Verlag.
19. M. Jakobsson and M. Yung. Revokable and versatile electronic money. In *Proceedings of the Third ACM Conference on Computer and Communications Security*, pages 76–87, 1996.
20. M. Jakobsson and M. Yung. Applying anti-trust policies to increase trust in a versatile e-money system. In Hirschfeld [16], pages 217–238.
21. M. Jakobsson and M. Yung. Applying anti-trust policies to increase trust in a versatile e-money system. In Hirschfeld [16], pages 217–238.
22. K. Kim and T. Matsumoto, editors. *Advances in Cryptology—ASIACRYPT '96*, volume 1163 of *Lecture Notes in Computer Science*, Kyongju, Korea, 3–7 Nov. 1996. Springer-Verlag.
23. G. Medvinsky and C. B. Neuman. Netcash: a design for practical electonic currency on the internet. In *Proceedings of the First ACM Conference on Computer and Communications Security*, pages 102–106, Fairfax, VA, 1993.
24. D. M'Raïhi. Cost-effective payment schemes with privacy regulation. In Kim and Matsumoto [22], pages 266–275.
25. D. M'Raihi and D. Pointcheval. Distributed trustees and revocability: A framework for internet payment. In Hirschfeld [17], pages 28–42.
26. K. Oishi, M. Mambo, and E. Okamoto. Anonymous public key certificates and the applications. *IEICE Transactions on Fundamentals of Electonics, Communications, and Computer Sciences*, E81-A(1):56–64, Jan. 1998.
27. A. Pfitzmann and M. Waidner. Networks without user observability. *Computers & Security*, 6(2):158–166, 1987.
28. B. Pfitzmann and M. Waidner. Strong loss tolerance of electronic coin systems. *ACM Transactions on Computer Systems*, 15(1):194–213, Feb. 1997.

29. C. Rackoff and D. R. Simon. Cryptographic defense against traffic analysis. In *Proceedings of the Twenty-Fifth Annual ACM Symposium on the Theory of Computing*, pages 672–681, San Diego, California, 16–18 May 1993.
30. C. Radu, R. Govaerts, and J. Vandewalle. Efficient electronic cash with restricted privacy. In Hirschfeld [16], pages 57–69.
31. R. L. Rivest. Perspectives on financial cryptography. In Hirschfeld [16], pages 145–149.
32. B. Schneier. *Applied Cryptography*. John Wiley & Sons, Inc., New York, second edition, 1996.
33. D. R. Simon. Anonymous communication and anonymous cash. In CRYPTO'96 [10], pages 61–73.
34. M. Stadler, J.-M. Piveteau, and J. Camenisch. Fair blind signatures. In *Advances in Cryptology—EUROCRYPT 95*, volume 921 of *Lecture Notes in Computer Science*, pages 209–219. Springer-Verlag, 21–25 May 1995.
35. Y. Yacobi. Efficient electronic money (extended abstract). In J. Pieprzyk and R. Safavi-Naini, editors, *Advances in Cryptology—ASIACRYPT '94*, volume 917 of *Lecture Notes in Computer Science*, pages 153–163, Wollongong, Australia, 28 Nov.–1 Dec. 1994. Springer-Verlag.

Fair On-Line Auctions without Special Trusted Parties

Stuart G. Stubblebine[1] and Paul F. Syverson[2]

[1] CertCo, 55 Broad St. - Suite 22, New York, NY 10004, USA,
stubblebine@{cs.columbia.edu, CertCo.com}*
[2] Center for High Assurance Computer Systems,
Naval Research Laboratory, Washington, DC 20375, USA,
syverson@itd.nrl.navy.mil

Abstract. Traditional face-to-face (English) auctions rely on the auctioneer to fairly interact with bidders to accept the highest bid on behalf of the seller. On-line auctions also require fair negotiation. However, unlike face-to-face auctions, on-line auctions are inherently subject to attacks because the bidders and auctioneer are not copresent. These attacks include selectively blocking bids based on the bidder and amount and selectively closing the auction after a particular bid is received.
In this paper, we present an on-line English auction in which bids are processed fairly and the auction closes fairly without specialized trusted parties. In particular, there is no need to trust the auctioneer to obtain a fair outcome to the auction.

1 Introduction

The number of on-line auctions is rapidly growing. In fact, forecasts indicate that on-line auctions and barter will generally replace conventional purchase of set-price items in the future [4]. Currently, there are nearly one hundred on-line auction houses [21].

A limitation on existing auctions is that bidders must trust the auctioneer concerning a fair outcome. Without detection, the auctioneer may selectively block bids based on the bidder and amount. Also, the bidders must trust that the auctioneer doesn't selectively close the auction after a particular bid is received. An English auction ends when effectively there is a timeout interval following the highest bid. The on-line auctions approximate this property by setting an expiration time and allowing the auction to continue beyond the expiration time as long as higher bids continue to be submitted within a short timeout interval. However, whether they have a fixed expiration time or allow continued bidding, all current on-line auctions still trust the auctioneer to be fair in enforcing this closing time.

There are existing auction designs that provide assurance against repudiation of bids and assurance of fairly closing the bidding, e.g., [5, 8]. However, these

* Work, by this author, was primarily performed at AT&T Research.

M. Franklin (Ed.): FC'99, LNCS 1648, pp. 230-240, 1999.

auctions are sealed-bid, which may not be appropriate to all applications.[1] More importantly, they involve the use of trusted auctioneers. Assurance of auctioneers is increased by employing threshold methods so that a high percentage of compromised trusted auctioneers is necessary to violate the assumed trust. As noted in [7], this approach is not applicable unless the auction is run by a large organization. "In simplistic terms, it is reasonable to expect that, say three out of five employees (servers or server administrators) in a government organization or *xyz_megacorp* will be honest. But it is different to assume that three out of five servers deployed by the relatively small *xyz_little_corp* will not collude." It would therefore be useful to also have assurance in the necessary trust for auctions conducted by small auction houses—or better still to remove the trust entirely.

We present an auction design that provides for the fair close of an auction and makes bid refusal by the auctioneer provable by bidders and others. At the same time, there is no need for the bidders to trust the auctioneer, or vice versa. The only trusted elements employed are ones that are currently available or in development for independent use in the public information infrastructure. These include public-key authorities, public notaries, and certified delivery services.

In Section 2, we present desirable properties and requirements of on-line auctions. In Section 3, we present our basic auction design and some variants. We also informally argue that our design meets the requirements set out in Section 2.

2 Properties and Requirements of Auctions

2.1 Auction Types

In this paper we focus on versions of the English-type auction: bid amounts are revealed during the auction, and bidders attempt to outbid the previous highest bid amount.

Bid Confidentiality.

1. *Open.* The bid amounts are known to all bidders during the auction.
2. *Sealed.* The bid amounts are only known by the bidder until the auction closes.

We will be concerned with open auctions; however, in our auctions bid amounts are not revealed until after they are committed. We will discuss this temporary secrecy of the bids below. Because we are concerned with open-bid auctions, we will not consider subtleties of sealed-bid auctions. (For example, in the auctions of [5, 8] bids are concealed even from the auctioneers until after close. In fact in [8], even after the close of the auction, only the high bids are ever revealed—to anyone.)

[1] The auction in [8] is a Vickrey-type auction, i.e., bids are sealed, and the item goes to the highest bidder—but at the second highest price. This should mean that bid amounts reflect the true valuations people place on the item, despite the auction being sealed-bid. For more, cf. [8].

Bid Cancellation.

1. *Cancellation.* A bidder can cancel a bid.
2. *No Cancellation.* A bidder can *not* cancel a bid.

Auction Closings. The method of closing an auction depends on whether the auction is sealed or open.

1. *Expiration Time (For open or sealed bid auctions).* The auction closes at a predetermined expiration time.
2. *Timeout (For open bid auctions).* The auction closes when no bids higher than the current high bid are made within a predetermined timeout interval.
3. *Combination of Expiration and Timeout (For open bid auctions).* The auction closes when there is a timeout after the expiration time.

Identity confidentiality may also be an issue in certain lotteries. An auction is *conditionally anonymous* if the bidder identity is confidential unless certain parties agree to uncover the identity. An auction is *weakly anonymous* if the bidder identity is anonymous however the identity can be uncovered with time. For example, uncovering occurs when the auctioneer commits to receiving the bid. Finally, an auction is *profile free* if the auctioneer cannot produce profiles of the bidders (even pseudonymous profiles)[15]. Profile freedom may be with respect to different parties such as to the auctioneer versus to other bidders. In this version of the paper, we do not directly address forms of identity confidentiality. We believe orthogonal mechanisms are available to address issues of identity confidentiality.

2.2 Auction Requirements

Integrity.

1. *Bidder Integrity.* Only authorized clients can submit a bid.

The integrity of the auction is compromised if unqualified bidders are able to make bids.

Fairness.

1. *Opportunity to Out-Bid.* Bidders have the opportunity to out-bid the leading bid.
2. *Non-discrimination of Bids.* When committing to bids (and to the bid order), the auctioneer cannot discriminate between bids based on the bidder or bid amount.
3. *Ordering of Bids.* Only bids made within a reasonably small interval of the present time can be reordered.
4. *Timely Bids.*
   Bids can only be committed that are submitted before the prescribed auction closing.

Non-repudiation.

1. *Auctioneer's Remorse.* The auctioneer cannot disavow a committed bid.

Verification.

1. *Timely Verification.* Bidders and sellers can verify the correct operation of the auction in an acceptable amount of time.

3 High Level Auction Design

The basic structure of our design involves a publicly posted database (DB) associated with each auction. The DB should contain a description of the item, and various parameters associated with the auction, e.g., the time bids will begin being taken and conditions for the auction to close. Auction close will be discussed below. There should be an optional minimum bid amount. There should also be a high sales price (effectively a penalty that the auctioneer pays the item owner) that can be invoked if there is evidence that the auctioneer did not perform his duties properly. It should be higher than any reasonable expectation of the maximum bid amount. (The auctioneer and the item owner may want to keep this private between them in case the actual bids are substantially higher than expected.) The DB should also include a history of the bids that have been made so far. This will be used to commit the auctioneer to the status of the auction as it progresses. The commitment takes the form of signatures by a notary on the DB status at regular ***notarization intervals*** and, within those intervals, signatures on the DB status by the auctioneer. Bids are submitted using secret bit commitment (SBC). (A discussion of various approaches to SBC can be found in [14].) This allows that the auctioneer to commit to a bid before he knows who it is from (even pseudonymously) or what the bid amount is. One way to do SBC is for the bidder to submit his bid encrypted with a secret key. After the auctioneer has committed to the bid submission, the bidder can reveal the key.

We will indicate SBC to a given message M using a secret S by $\langle M \rangle_S$. To prevent the auctioneer from identifying the bidder's address prior to release of the SBC secret, bids should be submitted through an anonymizing mechanism, e.g., Mixmaster remailers [3] or onion routing [11].

The owner of an item up for auction has a vested interest in the auctioneer continuing to accept new (potentially higher) bids until the auction is over. In order for him to be able to test that this is happening, we allow him to submit test bids. These can be explicitly indicated as test bids (once the bit commitment is opened). If he detects that his test bids are not being committed during the auction, he should then attempt to send his test bid via a ***certified delivery service***, such as CertMail [1], which is available now, or similar schemes being developed by the US Postal Service. If, within a reasonable period of time, the item owner (or any bidder) can produce evidence that bids were sent without being acknowledged or processed, then the item goes to the highest bidder. But, the sales price is either the high sales amount or the amount of the highest bid, whichever is larger. More specifically, the owner is paid this amount (minus any commission based on the actual highest bid amount). The winning bidder pays only the amount that he bid. The auctioneer is obligated to cover, at his own expense, any difference between this and the amount owed the item owner. Such a circumstance need not imply any wrongdoing on the part of the auctioneer. It may be the result of a technical fault. Of course, an auctioneer clearly has a vested interest in keeping such faults to a minimum.

Note that, while we assume the existence of a certified delivery mechanism, its primary function is not to deliver bids but to act as a deterrent against the auctioneer refusing to commit to received bids. It need only be employed only rarely, when there is indication that the auctioneer might be doing just that. Which of the acceptable certified delivery services are being used should be stipulated with the auction parameters, so that the auctioneer knows where to check periodically for messages whether or not she is notified that a message has arrived for her. Furthermore, the bidder can decide if it trusts the delivery mechanism when deciding on participating in the auction.

3.1 Auction Protocol

Registration Anyone wishing to bid must register with the auction service. We assume that the bidder registers in some standard fashion. For example, he provides the auction service with whatever credentials and evidence of ability to pay are stipulated, e.g., a credit card number, and he receives a public signature key certificate for use in auctions.

In describing our basic design we will not make any provision for anonymity or related privacy protections in the registration of a bidder. Various mechanisms might be incorporated to make this pseudonymous. Alternatively, registration might incorporate an identity escrow mechanism [6] so that the identity of a winning bidder might only be revealed if he failed to pay. In any case, such techniques are orthogonal to our basic design and we will say no more about them.

If signature keys are used in the straightforward way, then bidders must produce one signature per bid. In order to improve performance, we introduce a way that the bidder need only submit one signature per auction, rather than one signature per bid. We will present this in Section 3.1.

Notarizing the Bid History Within intervals published in the auction parameters, the auctioneer must commit to the bids she has received. To do this, she obtains a notarized (timestamped) version of the bid history from an on-line notary. Several of these digital notaries already exist [20, 10, 16], and legislation has been adopted or is being proposed to standardize the industry. The notary's sole action is to issue a certificate that binds its time-stamp to any file sent to it. (To maintain confidentiality, the image of a one-way hash computation of the document to be protected is what is actually sent.) We will use $\prec M, t_N \succ_N$ to indicate the notarization of M by the notary N at time t_N.

Since these notaries exist independently for various purposes, they are no more specific to the auction service than is an issuer of certificates for public signature verification keys or a certified delivery service. The reasons for the notary in our auction are (1) to provide a nonrepudiable record of the auctioneer's claimed auction history at the time of notarization, and (2) to provide a trusted time source on which the auctioneer and bidders must synchronize. (This prevents, e.g., the auctioneer from terminating the auction early by speeding up her own clock.)

The auctioneer should post the notarized bid history at the public site for the auction, e.g., a Web site. If a bidder cannot obtain an appropriately recent bid history, then he may request one by certified delivery. The auctioneer must then respond by making a copy of the history available via the certified delivery service. The auctioneer would no doubt prefer to minimize her sending of certified messages. Thus, she has an interest in making sure that she posts appropriately updated notarized histories. The auctioneer is obligated to maintain a complete collection of the notarized histories for a reasonable period after the sale of the auctioned item is finalized. This must be produced if any disputes arise as to what happened during the auction. As with evidence that the auctioneer has not accepted appropriately submitted bids, evidence that she has not adequately maintained and made available committed bid histories would mean that the auction is subject to the high-sales-price sanction described above.

By using the notary at regular intervals, the auctioneer commits not only to the received bids, but to the order in which they are received. However, this limitation on reordering is only up to the notarization update interval. And, this is likely to be infrequent. Because submitted bids are protected by SBC until they are committed, the auctioneer has no way to distinguish valid bids unless bidders tell her. Thus, it may be of limited concern whether or not she can reorder the bids she cannot distinguish; although she can always list the bids of colluders ahead of those of others in any given interval, even if she cannot determine whether they are higher than the other bids or whose the other bids are.

Bid Submission To submit a bid, a registered bidder downloads the notarized history from the most recent interval (resorting to certified delivery only if necessary). The bidder then submits the bid. The first bid a bidder submits in an auction is different from the later bids. The first bid has the form

$$Bid = AuctionID, \\ \langle Bidder\ ID, \lfloor h(parameters), \prec history_A, t_N \succ_N, bid\ amount \rfloor_{K_{bid}} \rangle_S$$

(Recall our notation: $\langle M \rangle_K$ indicates the SBC to a message M using a secret K.) The bid amount is indicated by the number of elements that are sent from a reverse hash chain. Reverse hash chains are now widely employed for various applications, such as micropayments. A reverse hash chain is formed by repeatedly hashing a random value some large number of times n. The first element of the chain c_0 is then the nth hash of the random value. As each link of the chain is revealed, it is easy to confirm that it is the next link by confirming that its hash is the most recent previously revealed link. So, for the first bid that a bidder submits in an auction

$$\textit{bid amount} = c_0, (i, c_i).$$

The number of chain links revealed reflects the intended amount of the bid. Chain elements have a previously agreed value as part of the auction parameters.

We use $\lfloor M \rfloor_{K_{K_{bid}}}$ to indicate the signature of message M using signing key $K_{K_{bid}}$. The bid key K_{bid} binds the bid back to the bidder, so that the auctioneer can collect on the winning bid. (As noted above this binding may be indirect in various ways so as to protect the privacy of the bidder. The only essential characteristic is that the auctioneer can use this key to collect payment from the bidder, anonymously or otherwise.)

Here, t_N is the time given by the notary in the most recent notarized history submitted by the auctioneer, $history_A, t_N$. The auctioneer must commit to a bid by the end of the notarization interval following the one in which it was received. Of course in the interest of moving the auction along, she will want to commit to it as soon as possible; thus, she will include it in the history submitted for current notarization interval if possible. We will see presently that she can do still more in this respect.

In subsequently sent bids, there is no need for the bidder to sign the bid. Subsequent bids have the form

$$\textit{Bid} = \textit{AuctionID}, \langle \textit{Bidder ID}, \prec \textit{history}_A, t_N \succ_N, \textit{bid amount} \rangle_S$$

In these bids,

$$\textit{bid amount} = (j, c_j).$$

The amount of this bid is indicated by j: the bidder has bid j times the value of a chain link. There is no need to sign this since the auctioneer can always authenticate the bid by binding this back to K_{bid} via the hash chain. The auctioneer can thus show that the bidder has sent whatever total number of chain elements he has sent in that auction. But, the auctioneer cannot frame the bidder for a higher bid since she cannot produce the next unexposed chain element. Nor can she unpack the bid and claim it was for a lower amount since she will have committed to the bid before she knows the amount it contains. This also suffices to bind the bidder to the auction parameters.

The commitment that the auctioneer makes to a bid is contingent on the bidder sending his SBC secret (thus revealing his *Bidder ID* and the *bid amount*). For the bid to be valid, this must be done by the end of the notarization interval following the one in which the auctioneer commits to accepting the bid; although it can be done as soon as the bidder has evidence of the auctioneer's commitment to his bid. To provide this evidence between notarizations, the auctioneer can commit by herself signing (and posting) histories since the last notarization.

Once a bidder has downloaded the auctioneer's signed commitment to a history, he can reveal his secret, even within the same notarization interval.

Just as with bids themselves, if necessary, a bidder should submit his SBC secret through a certified delivery service. The auctioneer should then send a certified response that commits receipt of the SBC secret. The need for certified delivery can be reduced by use of the auctioneer-signed histories just mentioned. To further minimize the need for certified delivery, the bidder should submit his SBC secret early in the interval in which it is due (or sooner if possible) and the auctioneer should sign and post a history including receipt of the SBC secret well before the end of the interval.

In [7] it was noted that since "open cry cyber auctions can take hours or days to conclude, the potential bidders will be hesitant to make such an open ended commitment to buy. Hence the Internet open cry auction mechanisms must give the bidder an opportunity to ask the seller for a commitment or withdraw his bid." In our auction design, bidders cannot withdraw a complete committed bid; nonetheless, a bidder can decide not to reveal his SBC secret, even after the bid is committed by the auctioneer. This amounts to a limited bid-cancellation capability with an added advantage: if the bidder chooses to cancel the bid in this way, then the *Bidder ID* and *bid amount* are never revealed.

Closing the Auction In the published auction parameters there is an auction start time, an expiration time, and a regular timeout interval. The regular timeout interval is an interval during which no new bids that exceed the previous high bid are received. The auction must remain open until at least the expiration time has been passed. This time should be long enough that the item owner, or others, can determine whether the auctioneer is accepting bids and thus can send bids via a certified delivery service if necessary.

If more recently than the timeout interval before the expiration time any new high bids have been received, then a new timeout is set and auction continues until a timeout interval passes without a new high bid. It should be clear that someone waiting until the last moment to submit a bid (or SBC secret) must use a certified delivery service to be sure of receipt (or evidence of availability), even if the auctioneer has not shown any signs of failing to accept bids. The auction parameters should be set so that ordinary bidders paying reasonable attention to the auction should not be forced to resort to such means unless the auctioneer is not committing to bids.

In our auction design, the timeout interval must be at least as long as the notarization interval.

3.2 Auction Design Variants

Eliminating Regular Use of the Notary The above protocol makes only minimal use of (independent) trusted parties: certified delivery is used only when something does not function properly, and notarization is done only periodically. Still, it would be good to further limit the use of trusted parties to just those times when something does not happen as it ordinarily should. We now sketch how to do so.

The reasons for the notary in our auction design are (1) to provide a non-repudiable record of the auctioneer's claimed auction history at the time of notarization, and (2) to provide a trusted time source on which the auctioneer and bidders must synchronize. We can use auctioneer signatures to provide a record of claimed auction history at a time stated by the auctioneer. But, how can we force synchronization of this time without regular use of the notary?

Bidders (and item owners) can use notaries and certified communication (which includes the time-stamp of a trusted authority) to catch the auctioneer in extreme clock skews. In the absence of a notarized history, the auctioneer should post her own time-stamped, signed histories at regular intervals. Bidders or item owners who want to keep the auction honest should now download and keep these so that the auctioneer cannot later produce a conflicting record and deny the previously posted record. (This was not necessary when the notary was used since the auctioneer could not later produce a conflicting *notarized* history.)

As before, if auction participants notice that the auctioneer has not posted an update within the current interval, they can request one by certified delivery. And, the auctioneer should respond with a post via certified delivery. Unlike before, participants must now watch for extreme clock skews on the part of the auctioneer. In this case, they should also download the posted history with the advanced clock and submit it for notarization (or perhaps post it via certified delivery). In this case the difference between the auctioneer's clock and the trusted clock of the notary will show that the auctioneer's clock is skewed beyond acceptable bounds (which should be stipulated in the auction parameters). The auction should then close using the high-sales-price sanction described earlier.

Temporarily Secret *Bid* Commitment Instead of using secret bit commitment in our auction, we could use temporarily secret bit commitment (TSBC) [17]. TSBC is similar to the notion of time-lock puzzles [12]. The basic idea is to commit to a secret that can be uncovered after a predictable amount of time. For example, the secret can be encrypted with a key that is recoverable after an inherently sequential computation of fixed length. Someone receiving such a message would be able to decrypt it after a fixed amount of computation. Nonetheless, the message is not readable until that computation has been performed. Thus, committing to receipt of a TSBC message is committing to the ability to read the message as well (after performing the computation). This removes the contingency of auctioneer commitment to a bid. It is not necessary to reveal any commitment secret.

Nonetheless, it would be good if it were possible to avoid performing that computation once the bid has been committed. If desired, the secret key can be revealed, providing a 'shortcut' access to the TSBC message. We could imagine features of the auction to make it likely that shortcuts to TSBC are revealed. Perhaps client software reveals the bid when proper conditions are met. There could be any number of carrots or sticks to further motivate bidders. A deposit could be collected and returned at the end of the lottery if the client actually reveals all shortcuts. An auctioneer would not likely cheat to keep the deposit at the expense of tarnishing his image with the bidding community. Alternatively, bidders could be given a financial incentive (e.g., they could be entered in a lottery or provided with coupons or rebate offers).

The reason our default design uses SBC rather than TSBC is that, if despite the incentives and/or automation, shortcuts are not revealed for many bids, then a denial-of-service attack on auctioneer performance is possible.

4 Conclusion

We have presented properties of fair English auctions as well as a design for an on-line auction. In current on-line auctions, there are strong trust assumptions about auctioneers. Our auction design uses no specialized trusted parties, it uses only trusted parties that exist independently in the information infrastructure. And, use of those trusted parties is minimized: a notary is used only for periodic updates to insure fair closing conditions, while a certified delivery service is used only when ordinary communication fails or the auctioneer does not perform properly. (And, the auctioneer has disincentives both to not performing properly and to receiving certified deliveries.) In fact, in one of our variants, the notary also is only used when the auctioneer does not operate properly. Despite this minimal use of (only independent) trusted parties, we have been able to give informal arguments that our design meets the properties we set out. In sum, we have presented an auction design that provides for the fair close of an auction and makes bid refusal by the auctioneer provable by bidders and others.

References

1. Certmail: The Certified Electronic Mail System., `www.certmail.com`.
2. D. Chaum. "Untraceable Electronic Mail, Return Addresses, and Digital Pseudonyms", *Communications of the ACM*, v. 24, n. 2, Feb. 1981, pages 84-88.
3. L. Cottrell. "Mixmaster and Remailer Attacks", `http://obscura.obscura.com/~loki/remailer/remailer-essay.html`. Note: Mixmaster remailers are based on the original mix design of Chaum [2].
4. S. Feldman. "Research Directions in Electronic Commerce", Keynote address to the 3rd *USENIX Workshop on Electronic Commerce*, Boston, Mass. September 1998.
5. M. K. Franklin and M. K. Reiter, "The Design and Implementation of a Secure Auction Service", *IEEE Trans. on Software Eng.*, 22(5), May 1996, pp. 302-312.
6. J. Kilian and E. Petrank. "Identity Escrow", in *Advances in Cryptology—CRYPTO '98*, H. Krawczyk (ed.), Springer-Verlag, LNCS vol. 1462, pp. 169–185, 1998.
7. M. Kumar and S. Feldman. "Internet Auctions", 3rd *USENIX Workshop on Electronic Commerce*, Boston, Mass. September 1998, pp. 49-60.

8. M. Harkavy, J.D. Tygar and H. Kikuchi. "Electronic Auctions with Private Bids", 3rd *USENIX Workshop on Electronic Commerce*, Boston, Mass. September 1998, pp. 61–73.
9. R. P. McAfee and J. McMillan, "Auctions and Bidding", *Journal of Economic Literature,* Vol 25, No. 2, June 1987, pp. 699-738.
10. Netdox, Inc., `www.netdox.com`.
11. M. Reed, P. Syverson, and D. Goldschlag. "Anonymous Connections and Onion Routing", *IEEE Journal on Selected Areas in Communications*, vol. 16 no. 4, May 1998, pp. 482–494. (More information and further publications at `www.onion-router.net`)
12. R. Rivest, A. Shamir, and D. Wagner. Time-lock puzzles and timed-release Crypto. Unpublished manuscript, February, 1996.
13. P. Sanders, S. Rhodes, and A. Patel, "Auctioning by Satellite using Trusted Third Party Security Services", 11th *IFIP conference on Information Security*, 1995, pp. 205-219.
14. B. Schneier. *Applied Cryptography, Second Edition: Protocols, Algorithms and Source Code in C*, John Wiley and Sons, 1996.
15. S.G. Stubblebine, P.F. Syverson, and D.M. Goldschlag, "Unlinkable Serial Transactions: Protocols and Applications", forthcoming in *ACM Transactions on Information and System Security*, November 1999. (A preliminary version of this paper appears in [18].)
16. Surety Technologies, Inc., `www.surety.com`.
17. P. Syverson. "Weakly Secret Bit Commitment: Applications to Lotteries and Fair Exchange", *1998 IEEE Computer Security Foundations Workshop (CSFW11)*, Rockport Mass. June 1998, pp. 2–13.
18. P.F. Syverson, S.G. Stubblebine, and D.M. Goldschlag, "Unlinkable Serial Transactions", in *Financial Cryptography: FC '97, Proceedings*, R. Hirschfeld (ed.), Springer-Verlag, LNCS vol. 1318, pp. 39–55, 1998.
19. E. Turban. Auctions and bidding on the internet: An assessment. *International Journal of Electronic Markets*, 7(4), 1997, `www.electronicmarkets.org`.
20. P. Wayner. Digital Timestamps: Punching an Electronic Clock, *The New York Times on the Web: CyberTimes*, Jan. 10, 1999, `www.nytimes.com/library/tech/99/01/cyber/articles/10notary.html`.
21. www.auctioninsider.com/every.html (List of almost a hundred on-line auction houses.)

Cryptosystems Robust against "Dynamic Faults" Meet Enterprise Needs for Organizational "Change Control"

Yair Frankel* and Moti Yung**

Abstract. Business organizations are dynamic, thus they must have sufficient flexibility in expectation of future structural changes (change in personnel, policies, internal reorganizations, external restructuring, etc.). This issue is becoming increasingly important in recent years since nowadays firms operate in a more dynamic and flexible business environment. As automation progresses, it is expected that cryptography will become a major control tool in organizations. Here we discuss what cryptography can provide to enable and manage this business environment of mutating organizations. The main thesis we put forth is the following: "Cryptographic designs traditionally concerned with mechanistic fault tolerance, in which faults are dynamic can, in turn, be the base for a 'flexible design for control functions' in today's business environment."

We show how combining various key management techniques which are robust against "dynamic faults" with proper semantically rich "enterprise view management techniques" – provides a flexible enterprise cryptographic control. Such control can anticipate dynamic changes of the business entity. We demonstrate how to manage group entities which are either visible externally (using modified certification technology) as well as entities whose internal workings are hidden (using certification technology and proactive protocol technology when extended to withstand failing and rejoining elements).

1 Introduction

Cryptographic technology is a basic tool for secure and reliable control of "electronic transactions and processes" within an organization. Control tools in organizations are often required to support multi-entity decision making in remote executions of processes within a commercial and financial body (board decision making, contract signing, memory of understanding signing, buying and selling, hiring, shipping, etc.). However, the inside of an organization (e.g., a commercial and financial body) can be quite complex both legally and technically . An organization can be either a single business entity (a corporation, a partnership, etc.) or a multi-business entity (an inter-banking organization, a consortium, etc.).

* CertCo, N.Y., NY, yfrankel@certco.com, yfrankel@cs.columbia.edu.
** CertCo, N.Y., NY, moti@certco.com, moti@cs.columbia.edu.

M. Franklin (Ed.): FC'99, LNCS 1648, pp. 241–252, 1999.

The notion we deal with in this work is that of "organizational changes" (or "structural changes") inside a commercial or financial entity. This adds a level of complexity in managing the "inside." It is common for commercial and financial bodies to go under organizational changes which may modify the control structure over processes and transactions. These changes generally are not predictable beforehand and therefore there cannot be an a-priori understanding of the security and flexibility implications of these changes. In fact the control structure that are implemented by the security engineers may result in an highly inflexible infrastructure which may be very secure but is also very static. This may be typically attributed to failing to take into consideration the dynamic nature of business. For instance what happens when two banks merge together into a single financial entity? There are new "agents" in the system which will be part of the overall control, there may be new regulations which now apply, and different trading constraints as well as opportunities may develop. How can we assure design of cryptographic control which is flexible enough for the modern global and dynamic market? Namely, how to assure proper "change control?"

We note that this is a very important question with a large financial impact. The smoothness of mergers of organizations and the manner by which they overcome their integration is important to the well being of the new merged organization. Often, integration problems are apparent and they influence the market value of the organization. Moreover, often merging difficulties are attributed to the "information processing infrastructure." Having a "digital strategy" for managing the entity has been advocated recently [DM98].

We deal with the aspect of cryptographic controls within organizations. The position of this paper is the following:

1. Fault tolerant cryptographic designs, in which expected mechanistic faults are dynamic and components may change, give rise to an extended flexible design that enables enhanced functionality of the underlying control. This functionality deals with today's dynamically changing business environment.
2. Flexibility of control is naturally achieved by having a flexible "key management" level which assures that many of the transactions and processes will not be affected by many of the potential "structural changes".
3. We need to enable implicit and explicit change mechanisms for the control functions. The former are invisible externally, whereas the later are noticeable and may need to be registered by the environment. Both require an internal management function, which can be achieved by combining the traditional "key management technology" with dynamic "access control technology". It enables the maintenance of the "semantics" of the organizational structure.

In this work we will first survey (Section 2) some of today's organization dynamics which imply the need for the control of business transactions to be flexible. We then discuss a cryptographic architecture for control of operations within an enterprise (Section 3). Finally, we demonstrate (Section 4) two design paradigms and show how (using the support of the architecture in the previous section), they evolve from being a purely (mechanistic) "fault-tolerance," "reliability" and "recovery" functions to a "flexible control designs." Our examples of mechanistic fault-tolerant technologies are "proactive key management" and "Certification Authority (CA) with CRL Management." The organizational change examples deal with representing group actions within an enterprise, and demonstrate a design of a group action where its structure needs to be externally visible and a group action whose inner workings are hidden.

Remark: We note that there are many possible changes in an organization, thus we do not claim that the above observations will enable flexible design that will automatically overcome any change whatsoever or even any structural change. Such changes may be very specific and may require flexible design outside the cryptographic or security component of the system. For example, changes to names of entities may require management of names as well as maintenance of history, and it should enable aliasing for future reference. New rules and new information technologies may require changes of the logic encoded in the systems and even the information technology of the infrastructure, respectively. Nevertheless, what we claim is that the above observations when incorporated into a system design will ease many of the "structural changes" which business entities are likely to take in the modern business world.

2 Organizational Dynamics

Organization may go through various changes. In today's business environment where technology moves fast and old realities lose their roles yielding to new forces, mutate-ability and flexibility is required from organizations. There are various types of changes:

- **Internal:** Changing of structure like departmental and divisional changes as well as internal personnel changes especially in the world of corporate "reorganization" and "re-engineering". Change of business, for instance, addition or removal of product lines.
- **Environmental:** Change in regulation, law, common practices, underlying technology.
- **External:** Change which is due to interaction with other entities such as merges, acquisitions, adding/removing partners, joining/dismemberment into/from consortia etc. These changes involve previously external parties and may result in an update of what is internal and what is external.
- **Global:** Changing many dependencies, such as changing the entire line of business, etc. while retaining legal connection to the past.

The above are not mutually exclusive. For instance, a merger may bring new officers and directors to a company. Even internal changes have an external affect as would be the case in hiring a new CEO or adding a new commercial/ financial product/ service line.

3 Flexible Control in Enterprise Cryptographic Systems

Next, we concentrate on control in cryptographic systems. We argue that in such systems the "key management" functions include most of the control. Indeed, the group or individual holding a certain key own a cryptographic capability which is typically exclusive and can be employed with confidentiality, authenticity and integrity.

Thus, when we manage the organization we have to manage the **roles** held by individuals and **groupings** of individuals. Business practices typically assign roles to individual, committees, team, or a functional unit in an organization. The role allows the agent to be able to make certain decisions and perform certain tasks. Many tasks need control and recording and in modern organization are computerized and cryptography can be the tool for both. We will suggest a design which is flexible to accommodate dynamically changing enterprises.

Figure 1 schematically demonstrates the dynamic flexible control of cryptographic entities within an enterprise. It distinguishes two layers: the *enterprise description* which manages a dynamic organization and the *operational structure* which is where the entities of the enterprise act.

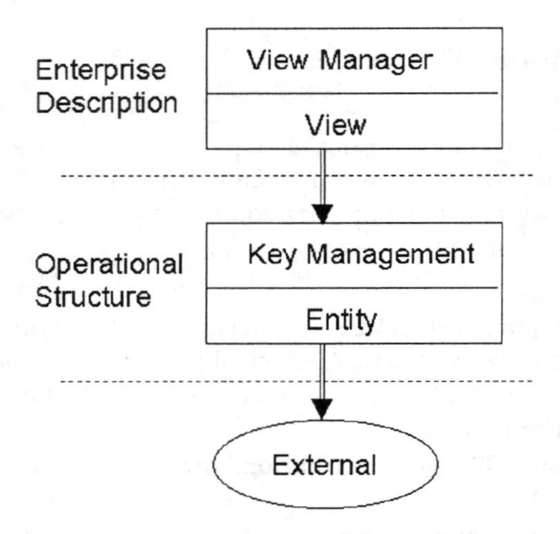

Fig. 1. Enterprise Cryptographic Systems Control

We now explain our design in more details.

In managing the elements holding cryptographic capabilities, we concentrate on representing a group of one or more individuals as an organizational function or a role which we call "an entity". We assume that a quorum of this entity (all members or a majority or some other subset) needs to approve a cryptographic function which represents an "operation". Without loss of generality (an individual role is just a singleton group), we concentrate on managing a group such that a quorum (say majority) of the entity is necessary to perform an entity action. Indeed, many decisions and actions in an organization require a quorum control. Such are decision by the board of directors. Approval of records, minutes etc. as well as management commands such as procurement, selling, contract signing, as well as operational commands in certain organizations such as approving a document and authorizing its publication.

We assume, again without loss of generality, that the cryptographic operation is a digital signature (other cryptographic functions are possible to manage in a similar fashion). A signature is a typical operation and can be used for numerous business processes. The entity may be an internal entity (i.e., known only internally) or an external entity interacting with the environment.

Thus the organization has what we call **Operational Structure**; it has two layers:

1. **Entities:** Which are the operating agents in the enterprise. The entities perform cryptographic actions according to a well-defined set of authorization rules; and
2. **Entity Key Management:** Which provides the cryptographic tools for entities and manages them (for example via an externally visible CA).

The above is a static (instantaneous description) of the enterprise. Next, we have realized that entities and groups (which represent entities) change over the lifetime of the firm. The control of the entities and their roles is a major problem when organizations change. The set of officers, directors, authorized signatories for certain financial transaction change with the organizational change. Also, the authorization rules for applying an "operation" may change and the members of the group have to know about it.

If we want to manage changes we want to control the "key management" layer which assigns cryptographic tools to entity members. We can take the approach that with each key there is a set of "authorization rules" which control its usage and are part of the key, thus authorization changes as well can be managed by controlling key management.

Thus, whereas pure key management (for a static organization) is controlled by a relatively simple semantics (which may include operations such as key-generation, key-validation, key-invalidation, key-expiration, key-replacement, user-elimination, etc.), the key management in a dynamic organization needs richer semantics. This implies the need for a layer of management on top of key management. In fact this layer (See Figure 1) is connected with managing the structure of the enterprise which we call **Enterprise Description** which is similar to the "conceptual schema" of the organization which describes the enterprise. However, security and cryptographic tools are added. It is based on the following two layers:

1. **The View:** The level which defines entities, the groupings which map individuals to "roles" as part of entities, and the "authorization rules" associated with entities. This can be looked as an "access control" of individual

and (sub-)entities to entities. At any point of time, the view's integrity is protected.

2. **View Management:** The management layer which controls the dynamic changes. This is controlled by top management and human resources which act according to restructuring decisions and contracts as the organization change. It is by itself cryptographically controlled (for example by an internal CA).

In Figure 2 the "roles and group database" is represented, each role is associate with a capability which here is represented as a certificate. The association of roles to their capabilities is equivalent to the association of entities to their certificates.

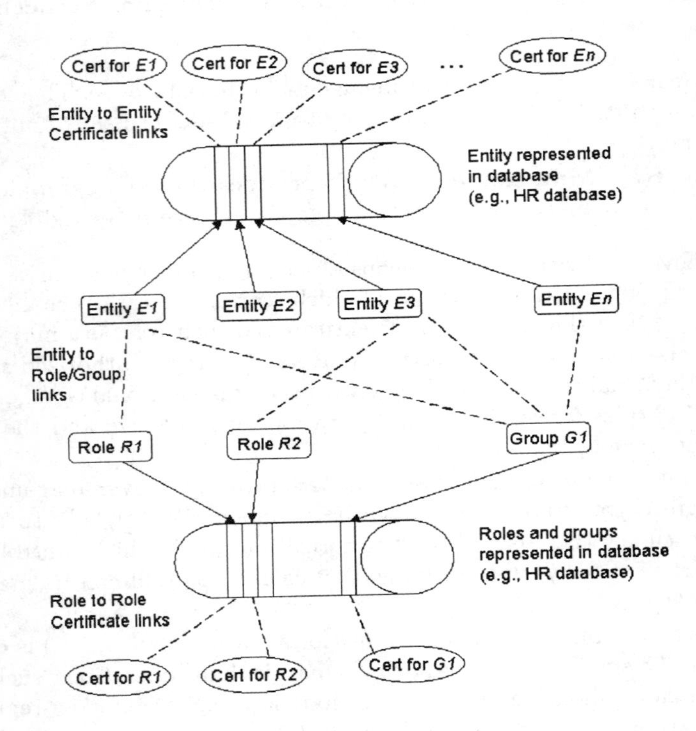

Fig. 2. Entity file, Role File and Their Associations

The association of entities to roles/ groups is also depicted. The view defines the roles and groups, and the view management is the component that deals with the association of entities to roles and groups as well as the management of the roles themselves. Hence, the view management component operates on roles and groups. It is the sub-system which manipulates the Entity to Role/Group links which are the connections between roles and entities. This allows for the dynamic organization.

The view which defines the organization, also define whether an entity's structure and inner workings is "visible" or "invisible" (or "partially visible" which combines the previous two). A visible entity has its structure exposed externally (to the other entity inside or outside the enterprise with whom it interacts), an invisible entity is represented as a "singleton entity" to others. In particular, there may be a need to hide the inner workings of entities which interact with the external world (other enterprises); in order to either hide the structure, or to simplify and abstract the interface to the external world.

4 Implementing Dynamic Enterprise Cryptographic Control

We now describe the basic general designs of the cryptographic control of (group) entities. We show how to manage visible and invisible entities.

4.1 Implementing the Enterprise Description Layer

The "enterprise view" function employs access control technology [L71] (in particular, dynamic access control [HBM98]). It can be used to bridge between "individual based" (Identity based) organization and "role based" organization where functional cryptographic tools are controlled. For large organizations, it can employ CA technology and in particular systems of "trust management" as defined by PolicyMaker suggested by Blaze, Feigenbaum and Lacey [BFL96]; its use here is to define the structure of entities and their group members. Similarly SDSI or SPKI can be used [RL,E98] (and only partial functionality of the above is needed). The layer thus maintains a database of the dependencies and dictates the structure to the entity level.

The view management function is the key management of the enterprise description level. It assures that the organizational changes are performed or authorized by the proper functions within the organization. This assures compliance with restructuring decisions, contracts, policy etc. In a small organization it can be performed by the security officers whereas in larger distributed organizations it will require a quorum management which itself is based on a quorum of security officers and where policy is signed by the enterprise executive management (which makes reorganization, restructuring and personnel assignment decisions, as well as changes required by law and by legal agreements). In case of multi-lateral agreement, the set of security officers act originally in duplication but the result is a "combined enterprise" which can continue to work. Note that the view management layer has to manage itself as well. Namely adding, deleting, merging of officers has to be done at that level itself.

The activation of the control which deals dynamically with an entity, will be done by calling key management functions which involve the agents (individual and sub-entities) comprising the entity itself. The operations which are needed include the following maintenance and management operations:

- **Define Entity:** which assigns a name and characteristics to an entity (in particular it defines the entity's size and the threshold for a quorum (or similar rules) and whether the entity is to be visible or not and similar properties). It also defines an initial set of individuals and other (sub)-entities that define the initial entity.
- **Define Authorization rules:** which defines the operation allowed and the rules for acting.
- **Add member to entity:** which specifies the enrollment of a new member into an entity.
- **Remove member from entity:** which specifies the disenrollment of a member from an entity.
- **Modify rules:** which adds, deletes or change an authorization rule.
- **Change entity characteristics:** which maintains the properties of the entity. (In particular can change its size or size of threshold, change it from being visible to being invisible etc.).
- **Remove/ Refresh/ Suspend Entity:** which discontinues the entity, etc.

4.2 Visible Entity Management Implementation

We need to implement a control of a group of elements which together form an entity with its structure and rules exposed to the outside elements dealing with this entity.

Recall that we focused on the action an entity takes is signing, thus the tool which seems suitable here is the notion of multi signature. This is a static tool which associates a group of users and their individual signature to an entity by requiring everyone (or possibly a subset) to sign with an individual signature. Once a multi signature is given one can verify each individual signature and check that the action is authorized.

However, we need dynamic management and we see that individuals may leave or be added to a group. The technology which deals with creating signature schemes and treating possible faults and failures of such schemes (e.g., compromises, expirations) is a CA (Certification Authority) which works in conjunction with a CRL (Certificate Revocation Lists) publication mechanism. Typically, a certificate is revoked when the key is suspected of being compromised. A certificate is also invalid if expired. A discussion on revocation see [FL98] and the three papers attached to it.

For our dynamic entity management we need the notion of "Entity Certificate" which links to existing individual certificates. We can manage the entities by always changing the entity certificate, revoking the old entity and certifying the new entity. We may want to keep revoked entities and have a history available (a time-stamping technology may help here [HS91]).

Once entity certificate is defined, connections via rules between certificates can be expressed as was defined and also implemented in the work on "certifying trust" by Lehti and Nikander [LN98]. The access control framework of [HBM98] is also applicable.

Let us view how the dynamic management of the enterprise view is performed:

- **Define Entity:** The enterprise (internal or external) CA issues a new certificate to the entity name and assigns characteristics to it. It links the names of the initial set of individuals (point to their key/ certificate) which are members.
- **Define Authorization rules:** The rules are put in the certificate.
- **Any modification:** The old entity certificate is revoked and a new certificate is issued reflecting the change.

We see that we need a basic CA technology and reliable time stamping so that using certification with date and entity management gives us an explicit record. The combination of issuance and revocation which was originally done for security (key renewals) and coping with failures such as key compromises which need revocation, can serve to manage entity dynamically. The Certificate technology can be used to define multi-signature by allowing a certificate which includes pointers to a group of keys (or alternatively aggregate certificates) rather than having its own user key inside the certificate. The user's key may be kept to the internal CA while the group of keys may be visible via the external CA. Such extensions are possible and manageable by the view manager.

In Figure 3 we can observe that the explicit certificate has link or directly includes the certificate for multiple certificates. The certificate also includes a statement defining what is a valid signature with respect to the certificate. That is any two signatures which can be validated from the possible certificate constitute a valid signature. Also depicted in the figure is a message with a multisignature containing signature from entity $E1$ and entity $E3$, this makes a valid signature under the explicit certificate in the figure.

4.3 Invisible Entity Management Implementation

The tool to use in implementing an entity whose internal workings are invisible is naturally that of "function sharing" (threshold cryptosystems). This tool can be used to share a signature key amongst individual such that each one has a shadow key (e.g. [F89,DF91,DDFY,FGMY]). On an input, if any threshold of individuals produces partial signatures (their keys applied to the input), it is easy to combine these to a signature on the input. If less than the threshold collude in arbitrary ways, the signature scheme is secure (in particular the adversary now has to get as many keys as the threshold to break the scheme).

The notion of proactive security, tolerates dynamic adversary [OY91]. When applied to cryptosystems [HJJKY97,FGMY], the notion creates a system which re-randomizes the shares periodically, so its original goal is increased security against mobile adversary (allowing the adversary to control up to the threshold in each period). This technology can however be combined with the "rejoin" failure, originally defined and developed in [GHY87] and allow us (as was done in [FGMY]) to "add" and "remove" individuals and to change the group size

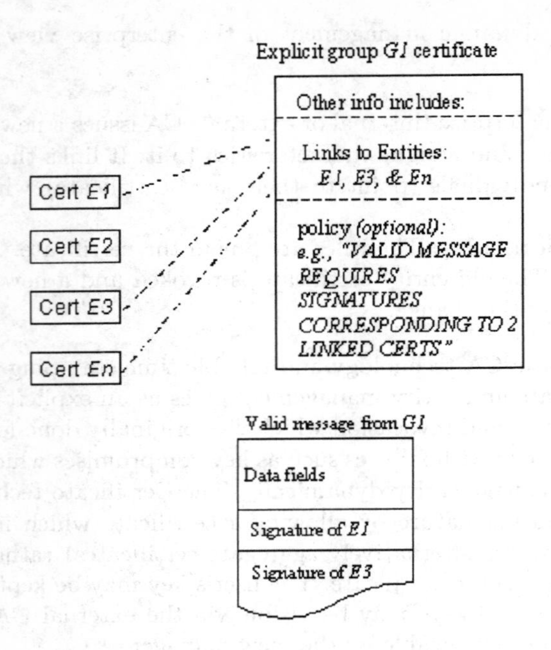

Fig. 3. An explicit group certificate

and threshold size parameters. These are some components of the flexibility we discussed earlier.

Assume now that we have to manage the entity which is the "board of directors" of a company. The board signs records, decisions, and other documents. For instance it signs documents which include decisions regarding the "size and membership" of the board itself. The board is represented by a threshold function and if there is a signature it means that the majority approves. Sometimes, we may want to assure that all have voted so we may have another key representing (unanimous board decision– where the threshold is the size of the board). When the board decides to manage itself, it run some of the proactive maintenance protocols (disenrollment, join, size increase, threshold change).

To manage the operations we still need an internal record, so an "internal CA" manages the view using "entity certificate" as before – pointing to individuals etc. However, in addition, when a change is done the "proactive key management function" of the entity is invoked to perform the maintenance protocol routine. The visible entities is certified by the "external CA" (a few levels of internal/external are also possible). Note that internal CA management is done by the enterprise view level.

Let us see a few examples of maintenance operation of invisible entity:

- **Define Entity:** The entity is created in the internal CA as an entity certificate is issued. In addition a key generation and distribution for the group is executed. The external CA issues an entity certificate for this key.
- **Define Authorization rules:** which defines the operation allowed and the rules for acting and is posed in the internal certificate. The threshold of honest participants in the entity is assumed to enforce the rules.
- **Add member to entity:** which specifies the enrollment of a new member into an entity. This is reflected by a change of the internal entity certificate and in addition a "key re-distribution" amongst the new set of participants is being executed. In [FGMY] a key that was distributed in a t out of n polynomial (polynomial of degree t) will be redistributed into a new t out of $n+1$ polynomial which will be distributed to the old members and the new member.
- **Remove member from entity:** Similar to the above, but the new polynomial will be distributed to $n-1$ members excluding the member that was removed. New shares are held by all old members excluding the removed one.
- **Change entity characteristics:** If we change the threshold size we can re-distribute the secret from a t out of n polynomial to a t' out of n polynomial, which will mean that now t' participants have to act.
- **Remove/ Refresh/ Suspend Entity:** Revoking the external certificate will in effect terminate or suspend the role of the entity, delegation with time-stamp may refresh.

The above demonstrates how a group is managed internally and dynamically by the view manager employing its internal CA and internal protocols, whereas at the same time the external view remains unchanged.

5 Conclusions

We have claimed that dynamic maintenance of enterprises is becoming an important issue. We then claimed that mechanisms that were originally designed to withstand "dynamic faults" are suitable for flexible dynamic maintenance of cryptographic control within an enterprise. It is required that the semantics concerning the dynamics of changes is handled in a view management layer which correctly and securely directs the structure of entities in an enterprise as its structure evolves.

The new enterprise view level manages a secure data base technology, it manages the availability and access to CA's, it manages reliable time-stamping, and it activates the key management function (at the various CA's and by invoking protocols among participants in an entity). It achieves the right level of flexibility that future automated businesses will need once they rely on cryptographic controls.

References

BFL96. M. Blaze, J. Feigenbaum and J. Lacey, *Decentralized Trust Management*, IEEE Security and Privacy, 1996.

DDFY. A. De Santis, Y. Desmedt, Y. Frankel, and M. Yung, *How to Share a Function Securely*, ACM STOC 94, pp. 522-533.

DF91. Y. Desmedt and Y. Frankel, *Shared Generation of Authenticators and Signatures* Crypto 91, pp. 457-469.

DM98. L. Downes and C. Mui, *unleashing the Killer App: digital strategies for market dominance*, Harvard Business School Press, 1998.

E98. C. M. Ellison, SPKI Certificate Document. 1998. (Document available also in URL http://ftp.clark.net/pub/cme/html/spki.html)

FL98. B. Fox and B. LaMacchia, *Certificate Revocation: Mechanisms and Meaning*, Financial Cryptography 98, pp. 158-164.

F89. Y. Frankel, *A practical protocol for large group oriented networks*, In J. J. Quisquater and J. Vandewalle, editor, *Advances in Cryptology, Proc. of Eurocrypt '89*, pp. 56-61.

FGMY. Y. Frankel, P. Gemmel, P. MacKenzie and M. Yung. *Optimal Resilience Proactive Public Key Systems*, FOCS 97.

GHY87. Z. Galil, S. Haber and M. Yung, *Cryptographic Computations: Secure Fault Tolerant Protocols in the Public Key Model*, Crypto 87, pp. 135-155.

HS91. S. Haber and W.S. Stornetta, *How to Time-Stamp a Digital Document*, Journal of Cryptography, v. 3 n. 2, 1991, Springer International, pp. 99-112.

HJJKY97. A. Herzberg, M. Jakobsson, S. Jarecki, H. Krawczyk, M. Yung, *Proactive Public-Key and Signature Schemes*, ACM CCS 97.

HBM98. R.J. Hayton, J.M. Bacon and K. Moody, *Access Control in an Open Distributed Environment*, IEEE Security and Privacy, 98, pp. 3–14.

L71. B. Lampson, *Protection*, 5-th Princeton Symp. on Information Sciences 71, (Published 74 in ACM's Operating Systems Review)

LN98. H. Lehti and P. Nikander, *Certifying Trust*, PKC 98, LNCS Springer 1431, pp. 83–98.

OY91. R. Ostrovsky and M. Yung, *How to withstand mobile virus attacks*, Proc. of the 10th ACM Symposium on the Principles of Distributed Computing, 1991, pp. 51-61.

RL. R. Rivest and B. Lampson, *SDSI– A simple distributed security infrastructure*, (See also, http://theory.lcs.mit.edu/ cis/sdsi.html)

Improved Magic Ink Signatures Using Hints

Markus Jakobsson[1] and Joy Müller[2]

[1] Information Sciences Research Center, Bell Laboratories
Murray Hill, NJ 07974
markusj@research.bell-labs.com

[2] Johannes Gutenberg Universität Mainz, Fachbereich Mathematik
55128 Mainz
joy@dialup.nacamar.de

Abstract. We introduce two improvements to the recently proposed so called *magic ink DSS signatures.* A *first* improvement is that we reduce the overhead for tracing without noticeably increasing any other cost. The tracing cost is linear in the number of generated signatures in the original proposal; our improved version reduces this to a *logarithmic* cost in the common case. A *second* improvement is that we introduce a method for determining whether forged currency is in circulation, without affecting the privacy of honest users.
Our improvements rely on our introducing a so called *hint value.* This is an encryption of the signature transcript received, submitted by the signature receiver. Part of the processing of this hint value is done using a new technique in which the high costs of secret sharing and robust computation on shared data are avoided by manipulation of encrypted data rather than plaintext. (Whereas the idea of computing on encrypted data is not a new notion in itself, it has to the best of our knowledge not previously been employed to limit the use of costly secret sharing based protocols.)

Keywords: efficiently revokable privacy, magic ink DSS, hints, electronic commerce

1 Introduction

Many changes in society are caused by the introduction of vital technology. An example of this is the invention of the printing press in 1457, which by a significant reduction in the costs of printed material caused a drastically increased literacy, and political awareness by allowing inexpensive information dissemination to the masses. Another example of an important step forward is the telephone, invented in 1876. These and innumerable other inventions caused and fueled the industrial revolution, transforming society in an eye-blink of human history. Although hardly anticipated only a few years ago, the Internet now promises to be a similar catalyst of changes to society. An integral part of this new revolution we are facing relates to commerce.

M. Franklin (Ed.): FC99, LNCS 1648, pp. 253–267, 1999.

This new technology, however, promises to be as dangerous as it is useful. On the one hand, we know that given the strikingly low costs of information collection and analysis of the same, payment schemes not offering sufficient privacy may indeed act as an ever-present secret police in the hands of dubious commercial interests. On the other hand, it is also well-known that too *much* privacy may present a threat to society at large, in the form of terrorism, blackmailing, and the undermining of entire economies by corruption of or dissemination of the secret keys of banks (see [33,21]). A recent trend in research in the area of electronic commerce has therefore been to find payment schemes with revokable anonymity (e.g., [5,6,15,18,19,21,22,23,24,26,34,35,36],) allowing a set of trustees to remove the privacy of a given user or payment, but not allowing an attacker to correlate payments to the identities of the payers without corrupting a substantial number of these trustees.

Most signature schemes with revokable anonymity offer two types of tracing, namely: (1) from a given signing session or identity of a receiver to a description of the signature(s) obtained, and the opposite direction: (2) from a given signature to the corresponding signing session or identity of the signature receiver. Magic ink signatures [23] offer a third tracing option, which is to determine if a given signature was obtained in a given session or not. This third type allows a tighter control over tracing by allowing suspicions to be verified, without divulging any more information than whether the signature and the session match or not.

In the magic ink proposal in [23], the first and third tracing options have costs that are independent of the number of signatures that have been generated. The second tracing option, however, has an expected cost which is linear in the number of generated signatures. This is a concern in a practical implementation, especially given that this type of tracing is likely to be the most commonly needed.

A *first result* of this paper is to present a modification of the original magic ink scheme that lowers the cost of this second tracing option to a logarithmic cost [1] in the common case, with a fall-back to a linear cost in a highly unlikely case. This is done without affecting the other tracing costs, and with only a minor increase in storage costs for the signature generating servers.

A second issue we deal with relates to increasing the protection against attacks. One of the main benefits of magic ink signatures compared to other schemes with revokable anonymity is that it allows the signer/bank to distinguish between valid signatures that were produced by the bank servers, and valid signatures that were produced by *another* party holding the signing keys. This is important if there is a suspicion that the signing keys of the banks have been corrupted (corresponding to the so-called *bank robbery attack*). Whereas the availability of this method promises to act as a definitive deterrent against attacks aiming to corrupt the bank keys, the very high cost of the filtering makes

[1] This is using a naive search algorithm. Using a more efficient algorithm in which space is traded off for efficiency, a constant cost can be obtained.

the method impractical unless it is *certain* that the signing keys have been corrupted.

A *second result* of our paper is to answer the important question of how it can be detected at a very early stage that a bank key has been compromised. In previous proposals that are granting privacy to honest users, no such method was available. The crux of the idea is to detect valid bank signatures that have not been produced by the bank without affecting our stringent requirements on the privacy of honest users. This is similar in spirit to the notion of fail-stop signatures [31], which were proposed by Pfitzmann to allow the detection of valid but forged signatures. We propose a method for detecting forged DSA signatures, using the very same constructions introduced to lower the cost of tracing. This allows the above mentioned expensive filtering techniques to be employed only when necessary.

As a result, we obtain a highly efficient and practical signature generation scheme offering the following four important mechanisms: (1) tracing from a given signing session to the corresponding signature (or coin); (2) tracing from a given signature/coin to the corresponding signing session; (3) comparison of sessions and signatures to determine whether such a pair correspond to each other; and (4) detection of signing keys having been compromised. This last feature allows instantaneous installation of new secret and public keys, and an on-line filtering of all deposited coins of the old type to remove forged coins.

Thus, this new scheme, which offers improvements both in terms of efficiency and functionality, would potentially allow a realistic payment scheme that succeeds in balancing the scales of privacy in a way that avoids all known attacks and weaknesses.

Outline

Section 2 presents our general model. In section 3, we define the properties our scheme achieves. In section 4 we explain the tools we utilize to achieve our solution, which is discussed in section 5. This is followed in section 6 by the introduction of the main protocol for improved magic ink signatures and all sub-protocols that are needed. Section 7 presents the second result of our paper, namely a protocol for detecting illicit signatures. In section 8 we enumerate the properties of our scheme; these are proven in the Appendix.

2 Model

We assume that there are three types of (polynomial-time) participants: *signers/tracers* $\mathcal{S}$, *receivers* $\mathcal{R}$, and *verifiers*. A signer/tracer is an entity with two functionalities (as indicated by the name). When acting like a signer, this entity produces signatures on messages provided by the *receiver*; when acting like a tracer, it selectively correlates signatures and sessions that match (this will be elaborated on later.) The *receiver* sends message-signature pairs to a *verifier*, who wants to verify their validity with respect to the public key of the signer.

(Typically, these three entities correspond to banks, payers, and merchants; or, alternatively, to certification agencies, service providers, and users who want to determine whether a given service provider is certified.)

We consider two types of *adversaries.* The first, the so-called *mobile adversary* (introduced in [29]), may control up to a threshold of *signers/tracers*, and any number of *receivers* and *verifiers.* He can adaptively corrupt different signer/tracers for each time period, whose length is a security parameter set by the protocol designers. Our second type of adversary is an adversary of the first type who also has complete read access to the private storage areas of *all* signer/tracer servers. We call this adversary, which was introduced in [23], the *read-all adversary.*

3 Definitions

Terminology: We say that the predicate $match(s_i, \tau_i)$ is true if and only if s_i is the transcript the receiver obtains in the signing session i, and τ_i is the transcript obtained by the signer during the same session i.

Definition 1: Anonymity and Revokable Anonymity

Let $\mathcal{R}$ be a set of honest signature receivers and $\mathcal{S}$ is a set of honest signature servers. Additionally, let $\mathcal{R}'$ be a set of dishonest signature receivers, and $\mathcal{S}'$ a set of dishonest signature servers. We let the receivers in $\mathcal{R} \cup \mathcal{R}'$ interact in the proposed protocols with quorums (i.e., sets of sufficient size to recostruct the related secret) from $\mathcal{S}' \cup \mathcal{S}$ a polynomial number of times n, after which a receiver $R_i \in \mathcal{R}$ obtains a signature s_i on a message m_i of his choice. We assume that S' obtains the *set* of all generated signatures $\{s_i\}$, and a *list* of all signer-side transcripts $(\tau_1, \ldots, \tau_n)$.
We say our protocols implement **anonymity** if it is not possible for $\mathcal{R}' \cup \mathcal{S}'$ to match any signature s_i, obtained by a receiver in $\mathcal{R}$, to its corresponding signer-side transcript τ_i with probability better than what is achieved by making a guess uniformly at random from all transcripts produced during sessions with $\mathcal{R}$.
We say our protocols implement **revokable anonymity** if any quorum of honest servers $\mathcal{S}$ or tracing servers can perform the following three transactions in polynomial time:

1. Given a valid message-signature pair described by s_i and the list of all signer-side transcripts $(\tau_1, \ldots, \tau_n)$, select the value τ_j, such that $match(s_i, \tau_j)$.
2. Given a valid message-signature pair described by s_i and one signer-side transcript τ_j, determine whether $match(s_i, \tau_j)$ holds.
3. Given a signer-side transcript τ_i, compute a value $trace_i$ such that given $trace_i$ and a value s_j, a third party can determine in polynomial time, and without any interaction, whether $match(s_j, \tau_i)$ holds.

Definition 2: Unforgeability

As before, we let $\mathcal{R}$ be the set of honest signature receivers; $\mathcal{R}'$ the set of dishonest signature receivers; $\mathcal{S}$ the set of honest signature servers; and $\mathcal{S}'$ the set of dishonest signature servers. We let the receivers in $\mathcal{R} \cup \mathcal{R}'$ interact with quorums from $\mathcal{S}' \cup \mathcal{S}$ a polynomial number of times. Let σ be the set of valid message-signature pairs obtained by $\mathcal{R}$, and σ' the set of valid message-signature pairs obtained by $\mathcal{R}'$. We say that a signature[2] is *unforgeable* if it is infeasible for the adversary to output a valid message-signature pair that is not in $\sigma \cup \sigma'$.

Definition 3: Illicit Signature Detection

We refer to an *illicit* message-signature pair as any *valid* message-signature pair s for which there is no signer-side transcript τ such that $match(s, \tau)$. (That is, illicit signatures are valid signatures produced by an adversary who has corrupted the secret signing key used, or has broken the computational assumption of the signature scheme.) We call a system *illicit signature detecting* if it allows the signer/tracer to distinguish such an illicit message-signature pair from a message-signature pair that is not illicit, but which is produced by the signer.

4 Building Blocks

Before we introduce the improved version we review some protocols, which will later be used as building blocks.

Notation: Since we use different moduli at different times, we use $[op]_z$ to denote the operation op modulo z where this is not clear from the context.

ElGamal: Our protocol uses ElGamal encryption [16]. To encrypt a value m using the public key y, the person who performs the encryption picks a value $\gamma \in_u Z_q$ uniformly at random, and computes the pair $(a, b) = (my^\gamma, g^\gamma)$. Thus, (a, b) is the encryption of m. In order to decrypt this and obtain m, $m = a/b^x$ is calculated.

Mix-Networks: Consider an input list $(\alpha_1, \ldots, \alpha_n)$. A mix-network produces an output which is a random (and secret) permutation of $({\alpha_1}^x, \ldots {\alpha_n}^x)$, for a given secret key $x \in Z_q$.
We will use a robust (i.e., such that it produces the correct output given an honest quorum of participants) mix-network [10] decryption scheme, such as [1,25,27].

[2] This refers both to the transcript and the method of generating the transcript.

The Digital Signature Standard (DSS): We use the DSS [7] (described herein) as the underlying signature algorithm.

Key Generation. A DSS key is composed of public information p, q, g, a public key y and a secret key x, where:
1. p is a prime number of length l where l is a multiple of 64 and $512 \leq l \leq 1024$.
2. q is a 160-bit prime divisor of $p-1$.
3. g is an element of order q in Z_p^*.
4. x is the secret key of the signer, a random number $1 \leq x < q$.
5. $y = [g^x]_p$ is the public verification key.

Signature Algorithm. Let $m \in Z_q$ be a hash of the message to be signed. The signer picks a random number k such that $1 \leq k < q$, calculates $k^{-1} \bmod q$ (w.l.o.g. k and k^{-1} values compared to DSA description are interchanged), and sets

$$r = [[g^{k^{-1}}]_p]_q$$
$$s = [k(m + xr)]_q$$

The pair (r, s) is a signature of m.

Verification Algorithm. A signature (r, s) of a message m can be publicly verified by checking that $r = [[g^{ms^{-1}} y^{rs^{-1}}]_p]_q$.

Magic Ink Signatures

As the underlying signature algorithm we use the DSS. For simplicity, we only show a single-server method for producing Magic Ink DSS signatures. Since the privacy depends on the distribution of the signer, the latter must be distributed. The real generation and tracing protocols are therefore distributed variants of this protocol, in order to increase the availability and security of the system and to introduce control (see [23]).

1. S generates a random secret session key, $\overline{k} \in_u Z_q$, and computes $\overline{r} = [g^{\overline{k}^{-1}}]_p$.
2. The signature receiver R has a hashed message $m \in Z_q$ that he wants signed. He generates two blinding factors, $\alpha, \beta \in_u Z_q$ and computes $r = [[\overline{r}^{\beta}]_p]_q$, $\mu = [m\alpha]_q$. and $\rho = [r\alpha]_q$.
   R sends (μ, ρ) to the signature generating server S.
3. S produces a tag, which will be a function of the signature transcript, and which uniquely identifies this. (We describe this step in more detail later). This *tag* is used for tracing, in case of anonymity revocation.
   Then, S generates the DSS signature $\sigma = [\overline{k}(\mu + x\rho)]_q$ on the message μ, using the blinded public session key ρ. The server sends σ to R.
4. The signature receiver R unblinds the signature: $s = [\sigma\alpha^{-1}\beta^{-1}]_q$. The triple (m, r, s) is a valid DSS signature on m.

Tracing: There are three types of tracing we can perform:

1. **From known signing session to signed message:** The signature invariant is calculated from the tag of a given session. This signature invariant uniquely identifies the corresponding signature.
2. **From known signed message to signing session:** Given a signature, we wish to find the corresponding signing session. In the first magic ink proposal [21], this was done by computing a trace value that was compared to the tag of each potential signing session. In this paper we suggest a more efficient method for this type of tracing.
3. **By comparison:** The signature invariant of a given signature is compared to the tag of a given session. The output is one bit, whether they correspond to each other or not.

5 Our Solution

Consider the tracing type 2 above, that is, from a given signature to the corresponding signing session. The idea is to introduce values that are voluntarily submitted by the receiver and that can be used to very efficiently trace from a signature to a signing session. The reason we say that these values, which we call *hints*, are *voluntarily submitted* is that due to efficiency requirements, there are no controls on their correctness. It makes little sense for a user to submit an incorrect value, however, since the difference will just be whether the tracing (if needed) will require a low or a medium amount of computational resources. Also, even though an incorrect value will not be detected during the signing (withdrawal) process, it will be detected by the mechanism for illicit signature generation, after which the signature/coin can be traced and revoked, and the user punished. Efficiently, this will make the cost for tracing logarithmic, even though we rely on a fall-back to the linear-time tracing mechanism of the old magic ink solution if the wrong hint value is submitted.

A hint can be thought of as an encryption of the signature the receiver obtains, with the property that it is not possible for an adversary corrupting less than a quorum of signer/tracer servers to compute the hint value corresponding to a signature (and vice versa), while a quorum of signer/tracers can efficiently compute the hint value given a signature. The signing process gives the receiver the signature on a message, and gives the signers, among other things, the hint value, which is stored along with other tracing values and the identity of the receiver.

In order to trace from a signature to a signature session, a quorum of tracing servers compute the hint value from the signature, and select the corresponding record (from a list of sessions that has indices sorted with respect to hint values). If no record is found, we use a fall-back to the linear search method described in [23].

Our signature and hint generation method involves a proof of knowledge by the receiver, to guarantee that the hint value submitted is not a function of hints submitted in previous sessions. (If this were not checked then it would potentially undermine the privacy of other users.) We prove that the addition of the hint value, the process to obtain it, and the other new additions to the scheme do not negatively affect any desired protocol property.

The traditional way to distributively compute and verify the correct form of a value such as the hint value involves sharing of the secret value submitted by the receiver. This is found, however, to drastically increase the costs of the proofs of partial correctness, and we instead take another approach, namely to perform a computation on an encrypted transcript. Although this method is not conceptually novel, it has been used only to a very limited extent, mostly due to the difficulties of computing on encrypted data. We find that the type of computation we need to perform here for the processing of the hint value can be done very efficiently on encrypted data. This method might therefore be of independent interest, and might be applied to similar situations in order to boost the efficiency of other multi-party computations.

Note also that this new method does not affect in any way the resulting signature: the signature obtained by the receiver is still a standard DSS signature (on a message of a particular format.) We believe that this is an important point in order to allow commerial use of the scheme, and to benefit from the careful scrutiny of the DSS that has been performed. The only negative side-effect of our new signature generation scheme, as far as we can see, is the nominal increase in communication and computation of the parties involved, and the small increase in the size of database that is kept by the signer/tracer.

6 Improved Distributed Magic Ink Signatures

Let us now consider a distributed version of the protocols previously presented. Here, let Q be a quorum of t servers in $S_1 \dots S_n$. We assume that the message m to be signed is of the form $m = f^M \, mod\, p$ for a generator f. Commonly, this type of scheme is used to sign a public key, in which m is this public key, and M is its corresponding secret key. (For messages M that can be guessed with a non-negligible probability, an alternative form $m = {f_1}^M {f_2}^R$ for a random R can be employed.)

System initialization: The servers distributively generate a random secret x for signature generation, using a (t_s, n) secret sharing scheme, a random secret x_t for tracing, using a (t_t, n) secret sharing scheme, and a random secret x_h for hint generation, using a (t_h, n) secret sharing scheme. Each server S_i publishes his shares of the public keys $y_i = [g^{x_i}]_p$, $y_{ti} = [g^{x_{ti}}]_p$, and $y_{hi} = [g^{x_{hi}}]_p$, from which $y = [g^x]_p$, $y_t = [g^{x_t}]_p$ and $y_h = [g^{x_h}]_p$ are interpolated (we refer to [30] for a discussion of how this is done.) Each server then proves knowledge of his secret shares x_i, x_{ti} and x_{hi} to the other servers; if some server fails, then he is replaced and the protocol restarts. Finally, the signing public key y is published.

Session initialization: Before starting the signature generation protocol, the receiver R has to send his identity id and a proof of knowledge of the secret key corresponding to *id*. The signers pick a session identification number, $sessionid = id||l$, where l is a number making *sessionid* a unique string.

Signature generation:

1. The servers prepare a temporary key pair:
   (a) The set of servers $S_i | i \in Q$ distributively generate the private session key $\overline{k} \in_u Z_q$.
   (b) Server S_i has a share $\overline{k}_i$ and publishes $[g^{\overline{k}_i}]_p$.
   (c) The servers compute $\overline{r} = [g^{\overline{k}^{-1}}]_p$, using the methods for computing reciprocals in [20].
   (d) $\overline{r}$ is sent to the signature receiver R.
2. The receiver R wants a signature on the message $m = [h^M]_p$.
   (a) He generates two blinding factors, $\alpha, \beta \in_u Z_q$.
   (b) He computes blinded versions of m and $\overline{r}$: $\mu = [m\alpha]_q$, $r = [[\overline{r}^\beta]_p]_q$ and $\rho = [r\alpha]_q$.
   (c) Using a (t_s, n) secret sharing, he computes $(\mu_1, \ldots \mu_n)$ of μ, with public information $(g^{\mu_1} \ldots g^{\mu_n})$ and a (t_s, n) secret sharing $(\rho_1, \ldots \rho_n)$ of ρ, with public information $(y_t^{\rho_1} \ldots y_t^{\rho_n})$.
   (d) He computes an ElGamal encryption of m w.r.t. the public hint key y_h: $(a, b) = (mg^\gamma, y_h^\gamma)$., where $\gamma \in Z_q$.
   (e) He sends (μ_i, ρ_i, a, b) to signature generating server S_i.

3. The tracing values and the signature are generated.
   (a) The servers interpolate the tag, $tag = ([g^\mu]_q, [y_t^\rho]_q)$.
   (b) After they have verified the correctness of the computation of (a, b) (for which we present a robust protocol below), they robustly calculate the hint value $hint = a^{x_h}/b$. If R did not cheat, this value equals m^{x_h}.
   (c) The *hint* is stored in a record along with *tag*, *sessionid* and *id*.
   (d) The set of servers $S_i | i \in Q$ distributively generate the DSS signature σ on the message μ, using the (shared) public session key ρ; σ is calculated as follows: S_i generates $\sigma_i = [\overline{k}_i(\mu_i + x_i\rho_i)]_q$. Then, $\sigma = [\overline{k}(\mu + x\rho)]_q$ is interpolated from the σ_i's using the method for multiplication of secrets in [20].
   (e) The servers send σ to R.

4. The signature receiver R unblinds the signature: $s = [\sigma\alpha^{-1}\beta^{-1}]_q$. The triple (m, r, s) is a valid DSS signature on m.

Hint-generation:

Let x_h be a private key distributively held by the tracing servers; $y_h = [g^{x_h}]_p$ is the corresponding public key.

1. The receiver calculates an ElGamal encryption of m: He chooses a $\gamma \in_u Z_q$ and calculates $(a, b) = (mg^\gamma, y_h^\gamma) = (f^M g^\gamma, y_h^\gamma)$. This pair is sent to the servers.

2. (a) The servers distributively compute $hint_i = a^{x_{hi}}/b$.
   (b) In order to prove that every server has performed the correct exponentiation the servers run a protocol for proving valid exponentiation, e.g., [12,32]. This is a proof that $log_a(hint_i b) = log_g(y_{hi})$ for a given quadruple $(a, g, (hint_i b), y_{hi})$.
   (c) The servers compute *hint* as the Lagrange-weighted product of the shares $hint_i$ of the servers in the quorum. (This value equals $[m^{x_h}]_p$ if R did not cheat.)

We also have to force the receiver to prove that a is computed the right way. This can be done using the method described below:

Avoiding Subliminal Tracing

Attacks are possible if it is possible for an attacker to inject previously seen encryptions, or functions of these, and observe what hint is produced. The potential problem is if an attacker would use the hint-generation protocol as an oracle to compute a hint of a seen signature. For example, assume an attacker could take a value m' of a signature he has seen "on the street", encrypt this (claiming to withdraw a new coin) and send $(a, b) = (m'g^{\gamma}, y_h^{\gamma})$ to the servers. Then one dishonest server would watch to see what value $hint = m'^{x_h}$ is produced: this efficiently traces the value m', because the dishonest participants get to know the corresponding record of the signature. Therefore, the user has to prove that he knows the format of the portion of the encryption that will be raised to the x_h power. If he knows a representation, it cannot be a signature "on the street".

Our solution for the encryption need to satisfy plaintext awareness (The best description of this concept is probably that of Bellare, Desai, Pointcheval and Rogaway [2]). This guarantees that the receiver knows the plaintext, preventing this attack. Note, though that this must be done without revealing any transcript-specific information.

We do it by proving knowledge that $(a, b) = (f^M g^{\gamma}, y_h^{\gamma})$, without leaking any information about the message $m = f^M$. As mentioned above, we are only concerned about the value a; if b isn't of the right form that only would give us a wrong hint-value.

Since the servers have to verify the computation of a in step 3b of the signature generation protocol, the receiver has to prove knowledge during step 2 and step 3a.

1. Each verifier S_i, $i \in Q$ (which in our case corresponds to a participating signing server) selects a value $\epsilon_i \in_u Z_q$. S_i publishes $(\hat{f}_i, \hat{g}_i) = ([f^{\epsilon_i}]_p, [g^{\epsilon_i}]_p)$. The pair $(\hat{f}, \hat{g}) = ([\prod_{i \in Q} \hat{f}_i]_p, [\prod_{i \in Q} \hat{g}_i]_p)$ is sent to the signature receiver.
2. The prover (in our case, the signature receiver) computes $\hat{a} = [\hat{f}^M \hat{g}^{\gamma}]_p$, where M is the preimage of m and γ is the blinding exponent chosen for the ElGamal encryption. The prover sends a commitment $com(\hat{a})$ to the verifiers.

3. Each verifier S_i publishes his value ϵ_i, and $\epsilon = [\sum_{i \in Q} \epsilon_i]_q$ is sent to the prover.
4. The prover verifies that $(\hat{f}, \hat{g}) = ([f^\epsilon]_p, [g^\epsilon]_p)$ and halts if this is not satisfied. Otherwise, he decommits to his commitment of $\hat{a}$ to the verifiers.
5. Each verifier checks that $\hat{a} = [a^\epsilon]_p$, and accept iff this holds.

Tracing

We recall that we have a secret key x for signing, a secret key x_t for tracing, and a secret key x_h for generating the hint. Furthermore we have $tag = ([g^\mu]_q, [y_t^\rho]_q)$. The three types of tracing are performed as follows:

1. **From known signing session to signed message:** *(unchanged)*
   The pair $(trace_a, trace_b) = (tag_a^{x_t}, tag_b)$ is calculated by any size-$(t_t + 1)$ quorum of holders of shares of x_t . This pair is output. A certain signature, described by (m, r, s), corresponds to the given tag if $trace_a^{rm^{-1}} \equiv_p trace_b$.
2. **From known signed message to signing session:**
   Given a description (m, r, s), the tracing servers compute a value $trace_c = [m^{x_h}]_p$. Then they compare $trace_c$ with the stored hints.
   If $trace_c \equiv_p hint$ for a particular record, then the signed message corresponds to the signing session of this record.
   If there is no such *hint* which equals $trace_c$, then the tracing servers have to calculate $(trace_a, trace_b) = ([tag_a^{rm^{-1}}]_p, tag_b)$ for each potential withdrawal session. Using a protocol for verification of undeniable signatures [12], they verify whether $log_g(y_t) = log_{trace_a} trace_b$, which holds if the signature corresponds to the tag.
3. **By comparison:** *(unchanged)*
   Given is a $tag = (g^\mu, y_t^\rho)$ and a signature (m, r, s). The tracing servers calculate $(trace_a, trace_b) = ([tag_a^{rm^{-1}}]_p, tag_b)$. Using the protocol for verification of undeniable signatures, we verify whether $log_g(y_t) = log_{trace_a} trace_b$, which holds if the signature corresponds to the tag.

7 Illicit Signature Detection

This section briefly presents our second result in this paper, which is a method to detect that the secret signing key has been compromised.
We let the signers periodically blind all the hints for valid sessions, and, using a mix-network, blind portions of the recently "deposited" signatures, and then verify that each blinded deposited transcript corresponds to a blinded session transcript. If there is any blinded deposited transcript that has no match, then this is unblinded and traced. If, during tracing, a matching session is not found, then the servers output "signing key compromised" as this signature cannot have been produced by the signature servers. Otherwise, the signature simply had an incorrect hint value submitted, in which case appropriate action is taken to punish the withdrawer.

We will now present the protocol in more detail:

1. As input the mix servers have a list $(hint_1, \ldots, hint_K)$, which have been generated during signature generation protocols. A blinding exponent ζ is distributively chosen so that $\zeta = \prod_{i \in Q} \zeta_i$, where ζ_i is the share held by server S_i. The servers robustly compute $(hint_1^\zeta, \ldots, hint_K^\zeta)$.
2. (a) The servers have a list $(m_1, \ldots, m_k)$ corresponding to the messages of all the recently deposited signatures (i.e., those deposited since the last run of the detection protocol.)
   (b) They robustly blind this list with the same blinding exponent ζ and get $(m_1^\zeta, \ldots, m_k^\zeta)$.
   (c) The mix servers perform a *mix-decryption* on this list, resulting in a permutation of the list $(\hat{hint}_1, \ldots, \hat{hint}_k)$, where $\hat{hint}_i = ({m_i}^\zeta)^{x_h}$.
3. All entries from the second list that exist as entries in the first list are removed. Each remaining item $\hat{hint}_i$ is unblinded by computing $m_i = \hat{hint}_i^{1/(\zeta x_h)}$. Each corresponding signature is traced using standard methods (see section 6). If the trace is successful, the receiver of the signature is punished for having given the incorect hint value; if there is an unsuccessful trace, then the servers output "signing key corrupted".

8 Claims

We claim that our scheme achieves anonymity (Theorem 1), revokable anonymity (Theorem 2), unforgeability (Theorem 3) and illicit signature detection (Theorem 4). The theorems are sketched in the appendix. A full version of the proofs, omitted due to space limitations, is available from the authors upon request, and will be part of the second author's Master's thesis.

Acknowledgements

Many thanks to Ari Juels and Julien Stern for helpful feedback.

References

1. M. Abe, "Universally Verifiable Mix-net with Verification Work Independent of the Number of Mix-servers," Advances in Cryptology - Proceedings of Eurorypt '98, pp. 437–447.
2. M. Bellare, A. Desai, D. Pointcheval, P. Rogaway, "Relations Among Notions of Security for Public-Key Encryption Schemes," Advances in Cryptology - Proceedings of Crypto '98, pp. 26–45.
3. S. Brands, "Untraceable Off-line Cash in Wallets with Observers," Advances in Cryptology - Proceedings of Crypto '93, pp. 302–318.
4. S. Brands, "An Efficient Off-line Electronic Cash Systems Based on the Representation Problem," C.W.I. Technical Report CS-T9323, The Netherlands.

5. E. Brickell, P. Gemmell and D. Kravitz, "Trustee-based Tracing Extensions to Anonymous Cash and the Making of Anonymous Change," Proc. 6th Annual ACM-SIAM Symposium on Discrete Algorithms (SODA), 1995, pp. 457–466.
6. J. Camenisch, U. Maurer and M. Stadler, "Digital Payment Systems with Passive Anonymity-Revoking Trustees," Computer Security - ESORICS 96, volume 1146, pp. 33–43.
7. National Institute for Standards and Technology, "Digital Signature Standard (DSS)," Federal Register Vol 56(169), Aug 30, 1991.
8. J. Camenisch, J-M. Piveteau and M. Stadler, "An Efficient Fair Payment System," Proceedings of the 3rd ACM Conference on Computer and Communications Security, 1996, pp. 88–94.
9. D. Chaum, A. Fiat and M. Naor, "Untraceable Electronic Cash," Advances in Cryptology - Proceedings of Crypto '88, pp. 319–327.
10. D. Chaum, "Untraceable electronic mail, return addresses, and digital pseudonyms," Communications of the ACM, ACM 1981, pp. 84-88.
11. D. Chaum, "Blind Signatures for Untraceable Payments," Advances in Cryptology - Proceedings of Crypto '82, pp. 199-203.
12. D. Chaum,H. Van Antwerpen, "Undeniable Signatures," Advances in Cryptology - Proceedings of Crypto '89, pp. 212-216.
13. D. Chaum, "Achieving Electronic Privacy," Scientific American, August 1992, pp. 96–101.
14. D. Chaum and T. Pedersen, "Wallet databases with observers," Advances in Cryptology - Proceedings of Crypto '92, pp. 89–105.
15. G.I. Davida, Y. Frankel, Y. Tsiounis, and M. Yung, "Anonymity Control in E-Cash Systems," Financial Cryptography 97, pp. 1–16.
16. T. ElGamal, "A Public-Key Crytosystem and a Signature Scheme Based on the Discrete Logarithmus," Advances in Cryptology - Proceedings of Crypto '84, pp. 10-18.
17. N. Ferguson, "Extensions of Single-term Coins," Advances in Cryptology - Proceedings of Crypto '93, pp. 292–301.
18. Y. Frankel, Y. Tsiounis, and M. Yung, "Indirect Discourse Proofs: Achieving Efficient Fair Off-Line E-Cash," Advances in Cryptology - Proceedings of Asiacrypt 96, pp. 286–300.
19. E. Fujisaki, T. Okamoto, "Practical Escrow Cash System", LNCS 1189, Proceedings of 1996 Cambridge Workshop on Security Protocols, Springer Verlag, pp. 33 – 48.
20. R. Gennaro, S. Jarecki, H. Krawczyk, T. Rabin, "Robust Threshold DSS Signatures", Advances in Cryptology - Proceedings of Eurocrypt '96, pp. 354-371.
21. M. Jakobsson and M. Yung, "Revokable and Versatile Electronic Money," 3rd ACM Conference on Computer and Communications Security, 1996, pp. 76–87.
22. M. Jakobsson, "Privacy vs Authenticity," PhD Thesis, University of California, San Diego,1997.
23. M. Jakobsson and M. Yung, "Distributed 'Magic Ink' Signatures," Advances in Cryptology - Proceedings of Eurocrypt '97, pp. 450–464.
24. M. Jakobsson and M. Yung, "Applying Anti-Trust Policies to Increase Trust in a Versatile E-Money System," Advances in Cryptology - Proceedings of Financial Cryptography '97, pp. 217–238.
25. M. Jakobsson, "A Practical Mix," Advances in Cryptology - Proceedings of Eurocrypt '98, pp. 448-461.
26. D. M'Raïhi, "Cost-Effective Payment Schemes with Privacy Regulation," Advances in Cryptology - Proceedings of Asiacrypt '96.

27. W. Ogata, K. Kurosawa, K. Sako, K. Takatani, "Fault Tolerant Anonymous Channel," ICISC '97, pp. 440–444.
28. T. Okamoto, "An Efficient Divisible Electronic Cash Scheme," Advances in Cryptology - Proceedings of Crypto '95, pp. 438–451.
29. R. Ostrovsky and M. Yung,"How to withstand mobile virus attacks," Proc. of the 10th ACM Symposium on the Principles of Distributed Computing, 1991,pp.221-242.
30. T.P. Pedersen, "Distributed Provers with Applications to Undeniable Signatures," Advances in Cryptology - Proceedings of Eurocrypt '91, pp. 221-242.
31. Birgit Pfitzmann, "Digital Signatures Schemes-General Framework and Fail-Stop Signatures," LLNC1100, Springer-Verlag, Berlin 1996
32. C.P. Schnorr, "Efficient Signature Generation for Smart Cards," Advances of Cryptology, Proceedings of Crypto '98, pp.239–252.
33. S. von Solms and D. Naccache, "On Blind Signatures and Perfect Crimes," Computers and Security, 11 (1992) pp. 581–583.
34. M. Stadler, "Cryptographic Protocols for Revokable Privacy," PhD Thesis, ETH No. 11651, Swiss Federal Institute of Technology, Zürich, 1996.
35. M. Stadler, J-M. Piveteau and J. Camenisch, "Fair Blind Signatures," Advances in Cryptology - Proceedings of Eurocrypt '95, pp. 209–219.
36. Y. Tsiounis, "Efficient Electronic Cash: New Notions and Techniques," PhD Thesis, College of Computer Science, Northeastern University, 1997. `http://www.ccs.neu.edu/home/yiannis`
37. B. Witter, "The Dark Side of Digital Cash," Legal Times, January 30, 1995.

9 Appendix

Theorem 1: Let D denote the dishonest signature servers, and H the honest signature servers.
An adversary $\mathcal{A}$, who controls any set of less than or equal to t_t tracing dishonest servers S_j $j \in D$ and dishonest receiver R, cannot break the anonymity of the signature scheme, i.e., he is not able to determine whether $match(s, \tau)$ holds for a particular pair (s, τ) with probability non-negligibly better than a guess.

Outline of Proof of Theorem 1: Employing an oracle for generating valid DSS signatures, we provide a simulator $\mathcal{S}$ for all the protocols. Each simulation generates transcripts that cannot be distinguished from the real protocol transcripts by an adversary $\mathcal{A}$ as above. We then compose the individual simulations to form a simulator for the entire protocol. We show that the adversary $\mathcal{A}$ cannot distinguish the transcripts generated during the simulation from the transcripts generated by a real protocol. ¿From this we can conclude that the adversary cannot break the anonymity of the scheme. This must hold since the adversary can produce the same transcripts himself by the use of the simulator and the simulator does not have access to the secret key for tracing. □

Theorem 2: The system achieves revokable anonymity, i.e., any quorum of honest tracing servers is able to perform the following actions: (a) Given a valid message-signature pair described by s_i and the list of all signer-side transcripts $(\tau_1, \ldots, \tau_n)$, select the value τ_j, such that $match(s_i, \tau_j)$. (b) Given a valid message-signature pair described by s_i and one signer-side transcript τ_j, determine whether $match(s_i, \tau_j)$ holds. (c) Given a signer-side transcript τ_i, compute a value $trace_i$ such that given $trace_i$ and a value s_j, a third party can determine in polynomial time, and without any interaction, whether $match(s_j, \tau_i)$ holds.

We refer to [23] for the proof.

Theorem 3: The system achieves unforgeability, i.e., an adversary $\mathcal{A}$, who controls any set of less than or equal to t_t tracing dishonest servers S_j $j \in D$ and dishonest receiver R', cannot generate a signature that gets accepted as valid.

Outline of Proof of Theorem 3: Assume the contrary. Then it must be possible to construct a valid signature given only the shares of the secret signature generation key x held by the t_t dishonest servers. Since the secret key has been shared with a (t, n) threshold scheme, it is not possible to reconstruct the secret key with less the $t + 1$ shares. Therefore $\mathcal{A}$ only has shares that are statistically uncorrelated to the secret key, this would by a simulation argumentation imply that valid signatures could be generated without any secret knowledge. □

Theorem 4: The system is detecting illicit signatures, i.e., the signer/tracer is able to check whether there exist a signer-side transcript τ such that $match(s, \tau)$ holds.

Outline of Proof of Theorem 4: There are exactly three types of valid signatures: (1) those with *correct* hint values, (2) those with *incorrect* hint values, and (3) those with *no* hint values. For each signature the signature servers generate, a valid or invalid hint is produced (which one depends on whether the receiver is honest or not) and stored in the signer database, to which all writes are detected by the signers, and therefore, to which only the signers can write. When a signature is generated by the adversary, no hint is therefore stored in this database.
Each signature (m, r, s) with a *valid* hint can be matched to its singature session by computing $hint = m^{x_h}$, which can always be done by a quorum of servers. This value identifies the signing session. Each signature with an *invalid* hint can be matched to its signing session by finding a pair (tag_a, tag_b) in the signer database, such that ${tag_a}^{rm^{-1}} = tag_b$. This pair, which again identifies the session, is robustly computed during the signing session, and so, must exist in the database for valid signing sessions. An illicit signature has no session record stored. It is not possible to produce a valid signature (m, r, s) on a known preimage M such that this record matches a recorded hint value or tag value. The former holds since the hint value determines the message m, and therfore also M; the latter holds since a given triple (m, tag_a, tag_b) determines the value r, which would prevent a valid signature to be produced (we refer to a description of DSS for this.) □

Author Index

Lecture Notes in Computer Science

For information about Vols. 1–1574
please contact your bookseller or Springer-Verlag

Vol. 1575: S. Jähnichen (Ed.), Compiler Construction. Proceedings, 1999. X, 301 pages. 1999.

Vol. 1576: S.D. Swierstra (Ed.), Programming Languages and Systems. Proceedings, 1999. X, 307 pages. 1999.

Vol. 1577: J.-P. Finance (Ed.), Fundamental Approaches to Software Engineering. Proceedings, 1999. X, 245 pages. 1999.

Vol. 1578: W. Thomas (Ed.), Foundations of Software Science and Computation Structures. Proceedings, 1999. X, 323 pages. 1999.

Vol. 1579: W.R. Cleaveland (Ed.), Tools and Algorithms for the Construction and Analysis of Systems. Proceedings, 1999. XI, 445 pages. 1999.

Vol. 1580: A. Včkovski, K.E. Brassel, H.-J. Schek (Eds.), Interoperating Geographic Information Systems. Proceedings, 1999. XI, 329 pages. 1999.

Vol. 1581: J.-Y. Girard (Ed.), Typed Lambda Calculi and Applications. Proceedings, 1999. VIII, 397 pages. 1999.

Vol. 1582: A. Lecomte, F. Lamarche, G. Perrier (Eds.), Logical Aspects of Computational Linguistics. Proceedings, 1997. XI, 251 pages. 1999. (Subseries LNAI).

Vol. 1583: D. Scharstein, View Synthesis Using Stereo Vision. XV, 163 pages. 1999.

Vol. 1584: G. Gottlob, E. Grandjean, K. Seyr (Eds.), Computer Science Logic. Proceedings, 1998. X, 431 pages. 1999.

Vol. 1585: B. McKay, X. Yao, C.S. Newton, J.-H. Kim, T. Furuhashi (Eds.), Simulated Evolution and Learning. Proceedings, 1998. XIII, 472 pages. 1999. (Subseries LNAI).

Vol. 1586: J. Rolim et al. (Eds.), Parallel and Distributed Processing. Proceedings, 1999. XVII, 1443 pages. 1999.

Vol. 1587: J. Pieprzyk, R. Safavi-Naini, J. Seberry (Eds.), Information Security and Privacy. Proceedings, 1999. XI, 327 pages. 1999.

Vol. 1589: J.L. Fiadeiro (Ed.), Recent Trends in Algebraic Development Techniques. Proceedings, 1998. X, 341 pages. 1999.

Vol. 1590: P. Atzeni, A. Mendelzon, G. Mecca (Eds.), The World Wide Web and Databases. Proceedings, 1998. VIII, 213 pages. 1999.

Vol. 1592: J. Stern (Ed.), Advances in Cryptology – EUROCRYPT '99. Proceedings, 1999. XII, 475 pages. 1999.

Vol. 1593: P. Sloot, M. Bubak, A. Hoekstra, B. Hertzberger (Eds.), High-Performance Computing and Networking. Proceedings, 1999. XXIII, 1318 pages. 1999.

Vol. 1594: P. Ciancarini, A.L. Wolf (Eds.), Coordination Languages and Models. Proceedings, 1999. IX, 420 pages. 1999.

Vol. 1595: K. Hammond, T. Davie, C. Clack (Eds.), Implementation of Functional Languages. Proceedings, 1998. X, 247 pages. 1999.

Vol. 1596: R. Poli, H.-M. Voigt, S. Cagnoni, D. Corne, G.D. Smith, T.C. Fogarty (Eds.), Evolutionary Image Analysis, Signal Processing and Telecommunications. Proceedings, 1999. X, 225 pages. 1999.

Vol. 1597: H. Zuidweg, M. Campolargo, J. Delgado, A. Mullery (Eds.), Intelligence in Services and Networks. Proceedings, 1999. XII, 552 pages. 1999.

Vol. 1598: R. Poli, P. Nordin, W.B. Langdon, T.C. Fogarty (Eds.), Genetic Programming. Proceedings, 1999. X, 283 pages. 1999.

Vol. 1599: T. Ishida (Ed.), Multiagent Platforms. Proceedings, 1998. VIII, 187 pages. 1999. (Subseries LNAI).

Vol. 1601: J.-P. Katoen (Ed.), Formal Methods for Real-Time and Probabilistic Systems. Proceedings, 1999. X, 355 pages. 1999.

Vol. 1602: A. Sivasubramaniam, M. Lauria (Eds.), Network-Based Parallel Computing. Proceedings, 1999. VIII, 225 pages. 1999.

Vol. 1603: J. Vitek, C.D. Jensen (Eds.), Secure Internet Programming. X, 501 pages. 1999.

Vol. 1604: M. Asada, H. Kitano (Eds.), RoboCup-98: Robot Soccer World Cup II. XI, 509 pages. 1999. (Subseries LNAI).

Vol. 1605: J. Billington, M. Diaz, G. Rozenberg (Eds.), Application of Petri Nets to Communication Networks. IX, 303 pages. 1999.

Vol. 1606: J. Mira, J.V. Sánchez-Andrés (Eds.), Foundations and Tools for Neural Modeling. Proceedings, Vol. I, 1999. XXIII, 865 pages. 1999.

Vol. 1607: J. Mira, J.V. Sánchez-Andrés (Eds.), Engineering Applications of Bio-Inspired Artificial Neural Networks. Proceedings, Vol. II, 1999. XXIII, 907 pages. 1999.

Vol. 1608: S. Doaitse Swierstra, P.R. Henriques, J.N. Oliveira (Eds.), Advanced Functional Programming. Proceedings, 1998. XII, 289 pages. 1999.

Vol. 1609: Z. W. Raś, A. Skowron (Eds.), Foundations of Intelligent Systems. Proceedings, 1999. XII, 676 pages. 1999. (Subseries LNAI).

Vol. 1610: G. Cornuéjols, R.E. Burkard, G.J. Woeginger (Eds.), Integer Programming and Combinatorial Optimization. Proceedings, 1999. IX, 453 pages. 1999.

Vol. 1611: I. Imam, Y. Kodratoff, A. El-Dessouki, M. Ali (Eds.), Multiple Approaches to Intelligent Systems. Proceedings, 1999. XIX, 899 pages. 1999. (Subseries LNAI).

Vol. 1612: R. Bergmann, S. Breen, M. Göker, M. Manago, S. Wess, Developing Industrial Case-Based Reasoning Applications. XX, 188 pages. 1999. (Subseries LNAI).

Vol. 1613: A. Kuba, M. Šámal, A. Todd-Pokropek (Eds.), Information Processing in Medical Imaging. Proceedings, 1999. XVII, 508 pages. 1999.

Vol. 1614: D.P. Huijsmans, A.W.M. Smeulders (Eds.), Visual Information and Information Systems. Proceedings, 1999. XVII, 827 pages. 1999.

Vol. 1615: C. Polychronopoulos, K. Joe, A. Fukuda, S. Tomita (Eds.), High Performance Computing. Proceedings, 1999. XIV, 408 pages. 1999.

Vol. 1616: P. Cointe (Ed.), Meta-Level Architectures and Reflection. Proceedings, 1999. XI, 273 pages. 1999.

Vol. 1617: N.V. Murray (Ed.), Automated Reasoning with Analytic Tableaux and Related Methods. Proceedings, 1999. X, 325 pages. 1999. (Subseries LNAI).

Vol. 1618: J. Bézivin, P.-A. Muller (Eds.), The Unified Modeling Language. Proceedings, 1998. IX, 443 pages. 1999.

Vol. 1619: M.T. Goodrich, C.C. McGeoch (Eds.), Algorithm Engineering and Experimentation. Proceedings, 1999. VIII, 349 pages. 1999.

Vol. 1620: W. Horn, Y. Shahar, G. Lindberg, S. Andreassen, J. Wyatt (Eds.), Artificial Intelligence in Medicine. Proceedings, 1999. XIII, 454 pages. 1999. (Subseries LNAI).

Vol. 1621: D. Fensel, R. Studer (Eds.), Knowledge Acquisition Modeling and Management. Proceedings, 1999. XI, 404 pages. 1999. (Subseries LNAI).

Vol. 1622: M. González Harbour, J.A. de la Puente (Eds.), Reliable Software Technologies – Ada-Europe'99. Proceedings, 1999. XIII, 451 pages. 1999.

Vol. 1625: B. Reusch (Ed.), Computational Intelligence. Proceedings, 1999. XIV, 710 pages. 1999.

Vol. 1626: M. Jarke, A. Oberweis (Eds.), Advanced Information Systems Engineering. Proceedings, 1999. XIV, 478 pages. 1999.

Vol. 1627: T. Asano, H. Imai, D.T. Lee, S.-i. Nakano, T. Tokuyama (Eds.), Computing and Combinatorics. Proceedings, 1999. XIV, 494 pages. 1999.

Col. 1628: R. Guerraoui (Ed.), ECOOP'99 - Object-Oriented Programming. Proceedings, 1999. XIII, 529 pages. 1999.

Vol. 1629: H. Leopold, N. García (Eds.), Multimedia Applications, Services and Techniques - ECMAST'99. Proceedings, 1999. XV, 574 pages. 1999.

Vol. 1631: P. Narendran, M. Rusinowitch (Eds.), Rewriting Techniques and Applications. Proceedings, 1999. XI, 397 pages. 1999.

Vol. 1632: H. Ganzinger (Ed.), Automated Deduction – Cade-16. Proceedings, 1999. XIV, 429 pages. 1999. (Subseries LNAI).

Vol. 1633: N. Halbwachs, D. Peled (Eds.), Computer Aided Verification. Proceedings, 1999. XII, 506 pages. 1999.

Vol. 1634: S. Džeroski, P. Flach (Eds.), Inductive Logic Programming. Proceedings, 1999. VIII, 303 pages. 1999. (Subseries LNAI).

Vol. 1636: L. Knudsen (Ed.), Fast Software Encryption. Proceedings, 1999. VIII, 317 pages. 1999.

Vol. 1637: J.P. Walser, Integer Optimization by Local Search. XIX, 137 pages. 1999. (Subseries LNAI).

Vol. 1638: A. Hunter, S. Parsons (Eds.), Symbolic and Quantitative Approaches to Reasoning and Uncertainty. Proceedings, 1999. IX, 397 pages. 1999. (Subseries LNAI).

Vol. 1639: S. Donatelli, J. Kleijn (Eds.), Application and Theory of Petri Nets 1999. Proceedings, 1999. VIII, 425 pages. 1999.

Vol. 1640: W. Tepfenhart, W. Cyre (Eds.), Conceptual Structures: Standards and Practices. Proceedings, 1999. XII, 515 pages. 1999. (Subseries LNAI).

Vol. 1642: D.J. Hand, J.N. Kok, M.R. Berthold (Eds.), Advances in Intelligent Data Analysis. Proceedings, 1999. XII, 538 pages. 1999.

Vol. 1643: J. Nešetřil (Ed.), Algorithms – ESA '99. Proceedings, 1999. XII, 552 pages. 1999.

Vol. 1644: J. Wiedermann, P. van Emde Boas, M. Nielsen (Eds.), Automata, Languages, and Programming. Proceedings, 1999. XIV, 720 pages. 1999.

Vol. 1645: M. Crochemore, M. Paterson (Eds.), Combinatorial Pattern Matching. Proceedings, 1999. VIII, 295 pages. 1999.

Vol. 1647: F.J. Garijo, M. Boman (Eds.), Multi-Agent System Engineering. Proceedings, 1999. X, 233 pages. 1999. (Subseries LNAI).

Vol. 1648: M. Franklin (Ed.), Financial Cryptography. Proceedings, 1999. VIII, 269 pages. 1999.

Vol. 1649: R.Y. Pinter, S. Tsur (Eds.), Next Generation Information Technologies and Systems. Proceedings, 1999. IX, 327 pages. 1999.

Vol. 1650: K.-D. Althoff, R. Bergmann, L.K. Branting (Eds.), Case-Based Reasoning Research and Development. Proceedings, 1999. XII, 598 pages. 1999. (Subseries LNAI).

Vol. 1651: R.H. Güting, D. Papadias, F. Lochovsky (Eds.), Advances in Spatial Databases. Proceedings, 1999. XI, 371 pages. 1999.

Vol. 1652: M. Klusch, O.M. Shehory, G. Weiss (Eds.), Cooperative Information Agents III. Proceedings, 1999. XI, 404 pages. 1999. (Subseries LNAI).

Vol. 1653: S. Covaci (Ed.), Active Networks. Proceedings, 1999. XIII, 346 pages. 1999.

Vol. 1654: E.R. Hancock, M. Pelillo (Eds.), Energy Minimization Methods in Computer Vision and Pattern Recognition. Proceedings, 1999. IX, 331 pages. 1999.

Vol. 1661: C. Freksa, D.M. Mark (Eds.), Spatial Information Theory. Proceedings, 1999. XIII, 477 pages. 1999.

Vol. 1662: V. Malyshkin (Ed.), Parallel Computing Technologies. Proceedings, 1999. XIX, 510 pages. 1999.

Vol. 1663: F. Dehne, A. Gupta. J.-R. Sack, R. Tamassia (Eds.), Algorithms and Data Structures. Proceedings, 1999. IX, 366 pages. 1999.

Vol. 1666: M. Wiener (Ed.), Advances in Cryptology – CRYPTO '99. Proceedings, 1999. XII, 639 pages. 1999.

Vol. 1671: D. Hochbaum, K. Jansen, J.D.P. Rolim, A. Sinclair (Eds.), Randomization, Approximation, and Combinatorial Optimization. Proceedings, 1999. IX, 289 pages. 1999.